MW01028533

FLAWED PATRIOT

WILLIAM K. HARVEY.
GARSTON WALLACE DRIVER

FLAWED PATRIOT

THE RISE AND FALL OF CIA LEGEND BILL HARVEY

BAYARD STOCKTON

Potomac Books, Inc.
Washington, D.C.

The CIA's Publication Review Board has reviewed the manuscript for this book to assist the author in eliminating classified information. The Board poses no security objection to the book's publication. This review, however, should not be construed as an official release of information, confirmation of its accuracy, or an endorsement of the author's views.

Library of Congress Cataloging-in-Publication Data
Stockton, Bayard.
Flawed patriot : the rise and fall of CIA legend Bill Harvey / Bayard Stockton.—1st ed.
p. cm.
Includes bibliographical references and index.
ISBN 1-57488-990-7 (alk. paper)
1. Harvey, Bill, 1915–1976. 2. United States. Central Intelligence Agency—Biography. 3. Intelligence officers—United States—Biography. 4. Spies—United States—Biography. 5. Cold War. I. Title.
JK468.I6S75 2006
327.12730092—dc22
[B]
2006012651

Printed in the United States of America on acid-free paper that meets the American National Standards Institute Z39-48 Standard.

Potomac Books, Inc.
22841 Quicksilver Drive
Dulles, Virginia 20166

First Edition

10 9 8 7 6 5 4 3 2 1

For the West Berliners during the Coldest War, 1947–1955;

for those who served at BOB under Bill Harvey;

and for Bettina, Jonah, and Cai; Tam and Helene; Annalisa;
and any yet to come.

CONTENTS

PREFACE

Like many men of achievement, William K. Harvey was Winston Churchill's "riddle wrapped in a mystery inside an enigma." Today's term "multifaceted" doesn't begin to describe him because it implies superficiality; Big Bill was anything but superficial. Indeed, the deeper I probed, the more dense yet clear the man's character became. Bill Harvey was a man of the shadows, an obfuscator who was a true-born member of the inner world of espionage.

I saw Bill in several different lights over a decade in mid-twentieth century and was encouraged to delve into his life by his widow several decades later. There came delays, until I finally set out to pull together as many strands of his life as I could gather. I take full responsibility for what appears here and for the conclusions I have drawn, except for those clearly labeled as someone else's thought.

Throughout the text, I quote various sources with whom I spoke or exchanged e-mails in the course of research for the book as if they were still alive. In fact, a number of them died while *Flawed Patriot* was in preparation.

I owe thanks to many people, particularly to Bob Kilroy and Clarence Berry, whose real names I have not used. It would be unjust to single out others. Suffice it to say that all whom I have asked, and all who knew him, responded fully. Many have never before talked for the record.

Those formerly of CIA who talked with me: Jim Critchfield, Dennis Flinn, Warren Frank, Stan and Dottie Gaines, Sam Halpern, Dick Helms, Bill Hood, Adam Horton, George Kirby, Walt Lomac, Alex Macmillan, Dave and Star Murphy, Herb Natzke, Tom Polgar, Anita Adolph Potocki, Neill Prew, Ted and Hazel Shackley, Peter Sichel, Henry Woodburn, and Mark Wyatt. Also, Sam Papich, formerly of the FBI.

By correspondence only: David Chavchavadze, Jack Corris, Ben Cushing, Paul Garbler, Norman and Lois Glasser, Mrs. Vyrl (Ernie) Leichliter, and Richard W. Montague. Also, George Bailey and Peter Lunn, formerly of the British SIS; Gen. Sergei Kondrashev, formerly of the KGB; and an anonymous member of the Dutch Intelligence Service.

Others from a variety of backgrounds with whom I spoke: Jack Anderson, Arthur, Ed Becker, Prof. G. Robert Blakey, Brenda Brady, Michael Dobbs, Doug Fleming, John Foreman, Michael Goldsmith, Dan Hardway, Sen. Gary Hart, Maureen Hughes, Jim Kelly, Jim Lesar, Fred Logevall, Robert Maheu, Scott Malone, Dave Mazzarella, Joe McMoneagle, Jefferson Morley, Andy (Lee) Nelson, Bill Nugent, Connie O'Donnell, Curtis G. (Bill) Pepper, Stephen J. Rivele, Gus Russo, Charles Rappleye, Ann Reynolds, F. A. O. Schwarz Jr., Toni Shimon, David Stafford, Larry Stewart, Anthony Summers, David Suter, Helmut Trotnow, Gore Vidal, Bob Weitershausen, Linda Williams, Robin Winks, and Mick Winter.

Those from Indiana who helped: Tom Cochrun, Dr. Chuck Coffin, Jack Hall, Sally Harvey, Hal Hyde, and David Kahlenberg.

Also, the Association of Former Intelligence Officers (AFIO), the FBI's Freedom of Information Act (FOIA) Section, the CIA's FOIA Section, and the CIA's Publications Review Board (PRB).

AUTHOR'S NOTE: The changes that the CIA's PRB required were primarily semantic in nature: names, cryptonyms, locations, and the like. Some of the deletions insisted on by the CIA were of names, designations, job titles, and locations that have appeared elsewhere in print, in some cases many times over. Thus I am not allowed to use a specific designation for the top CIA man in a specific location, even though, for instance, a book by a former CIA chieftain that appeared in 1976 openly used the term and the same designation appears, as a matter of course, in practically every book about the CIA. Some true names of former colleagues who had granted permission to use their names in the clear, and of officers now dead, were "redacted" by the PRB, in its wisdom. Even some fictitious names that I had dreamed up were blue-penciled by PRB.

When it came to crunch time, the board opted for ludicrous deletion rather than common sense. To back up its edict, the PRB reminded me of my obligations under the secrecy oath I took well over fifty years ago.

The PRB asked for no substantive changes or deletions in material dealing with CIA operations.

INTRODUCTION: BERLIN VIGNETTE

Tuesday, June 16, 1953. Lights blazed in the high-gabled redbrick building rising from a cleft in the wooded Berlin suburb of Dahlem, facing what was now called Clay Allee. The entrance to the building was on an obscure, parallel dead-end street called Foehrenweg. Berlin Operations Base (BOB) was awake but not yet on full alert. That wouldn't come until the next night.

Word was the boss was on his way back in from a meeting outside the compound. Another young man and I slouched on the battered couch facing a desk buried in varicolored paper. Today we would be described as "stressed," enthralled by the drama a few miles away but tense as we reviewed what we would capsule for Bill Harvey, whenever he showed up. It wasn't going to be a crisp, military-style briefing, but it would lack nothing in respect or, we hoped, in accuracy.

Decades later, writers fantasized that Harvey's office at the CIA's main Cold War outpost was an inner redoubt that no hostile could ever penetrate without a furious firefight, in which Harvey himself would go down, twin Magnums blazing. In fact, the room in which we waited contained no gun cabinet, glass-fronted or otherwise, no arsenal of any kind. It was functional, sparsely furnished, even shabby.

The level of tension at BOB was subtle and under control. But, just in case, the administration officer had opened the base's gun cabinet, which played large in imaginations years later. The cabinet was, in fact, a simple plywood cupboard, near the duty officer's niche and the base's vital switchboard. It contained rifles, carbines, grenades, and a couple of World War II submachine guns, nothing more. It was not a full-service arsenal, by the stretch of anyone's standards.

Now, Bill Harvey pushed through the front door, in a rush, as always.

He grunted a couple of brusque-but-friendly words to the armed GI guard who sat behind a counter on a raised dais, rather like the booking sergeant in a police station. It was there, at the building's entrance, that the only shot was ever fired in or near BOB—when a soldier shot himself in the leg while toying with his pistol.

The guard pushed the raucous, klaxon-like buzzer that signaled someone had entered the premises. The duty officer moved Bill's card from the "out" slot to the "in" slot.

Harvey surged down a long, wide hallway, at the end of which was an office with a large bay window. A few other offices sprouted off the main corridor. Two stairwells led to other working areas in a honeycombed basement and an attic. It was a comfortable working space for about forty, maybe fifty, people.

About halfway down the corridor, Bill tacked left, into his secretary's office. To his right was the registry, which contained all the heavy metal safes on the base, and yes, on top of each safe was an incendiary canister. This device was proved later, in Hong Kong, to be less than trustworthy in the destruction of documents. Registry also held an extremely noisy shredder, through which every scrap of waste paper passed before it was burned.

Latter-day writers could not imagine the Russians even considering an invasion of West Berlin. We who were there in the 1950s did not think it a likely possibility, but we were prepared to destroy files—not to protect ourselves but to shield sources, ongoing operations, and information about the inner workings of the CIA.

It was not unusual that Harvey had disappeared that tense evening. We knew he had meetings outside the office, about what and with whom was none of our business. Big Bill was not in the habit of accounting for his movements to anyone.

THE NEW BOYS

On that Tuesday evening, June 16, 1953, Bob Kilroy, my partner, was twenty-five years old. I was a few months short of twenty-three, making me the youngest officer assigned to Berlin. Why on earth would the chief of BOB call on two callow youths to brief him on matters of importance?

Bob and I were the base reports officers who channeled the positive intelligence—"the take" of BOB's espionage operations—back to CIA's German Mission Headquarters in Frankfurt, to Washington, and in some cases, to London. We were the nerve center, the editorial desk.

We had been extremely busy since about noon that day, when we began to get reports, out of the Soviet Zone of Occupation, of protests and uprisings over an impending increase in factory work and production quotas. We followed the day's events with barely stifled excitement, which heightened when workers from the Communists' showcase building project in Stalin Allee marched to the government quarter of East Berlin, three or four miles from where we sat and again when other workers came over to the West to beg for airtime on Radio in the American Sector (RIAS) so they could talk rebellion to their comrades in the Russian zone. After some agonizing, of which we were part, the American government, fearful of what it might spark, turned the workers' request down.

We had reports that the workers were calling for a general strike at dawn on Wednesday. The key question was whether they would try to overthrow the East German government, and, if they did, what the Soviet response would be. The rebellion might not have happened had not the iron-fisted Stalin died in March. It was the first open show of restlessness, of resistance, by any peoples under Communist rule.

At some point during that first twenty-four hours of rebellion, Harvey sent me over to listen to the Army colonel in charge of military intelligence for Berlin Command. The colonel stifled the chagrin he felt when he realized a messenger boy had come to represent the CIA boss; then, almost in tears of frustration, he pleaded for help. "We've lost track of the twenty-two Soviet divisions in the zone, and we need anything you guys can give us." I promised, on Bill's behalf, that we would do our best, and we did.

THE BRIEFING

That night Harvey heaved into his office and swung around the desk. He stood, swaying slightly from fatigue, not, as others would have jumped to conclude, from booze. He stared at us out of his bulbous, bloodshot eyes. "Well?" The voice was rasping, deep, rumbling, well-tilled in the soil of Indiana. "Whatyagot?"

I gulped and started to fill Harvey in on the most recent developments in the streets across the sector border. Kilroy sat on the edge of the couch, ready to note whatever might be required, yet poised to jump in with his contributions.

As I talked, Bill casually reached under his arm, pulled a .38 revolver from his shoulder holster, and dropped it into his right-hand desk drawer. Then, he reached behind, under his gabardine jacket, and pulled out a snub-nosed .32. As he discarded it in the left-hand drawer, he absorbed our bug-eyed glances.

"I was meeting with the Brits. Don't think I trust the bastards, do you, Bob?" At that point, no one else at the base carried a weapon.

There came a moment that has lived with both of us over the years.

Bill sagged into his chair. As I stumbled through my summary of recent events, I watched his eyelids droop. His head began to nod, and he breathed deep, almost rasping. Kilroy and I pantomimed a nudge nudge, wink wink.

Suddenly, Harvey's eyes popped open. His phlegmatic rumble was loud, clear, authoritative yet courteous. "Please continue, Bay!" As I pulled myself together, his eyes closed again, and the chief of base appeared to fall into another snooze. But we were then and ever aware that he absorbed and remembered every detail, every nuance of what we said.

This was vintage Bill Harvey as he approached the peak years of his career. Within a decade, things were sadly different.

1

GROWING UP MIDWESTERN

Bill Harvey was never an open book, even to those he liked, but he was human and caring. Harvey's professional life was secret, interwoven, contorted, and shadowed by alcoholism and his choice of friends. To those he disliked, Harvey was an enigma, often a baleful one.

In his early days in the FBI in Washington, around the time the United States was entering World War II, Bill felt at home among the few he later referred to as *Landsmänner*, that is, his kind of people. The FBI was very much a boys' club; wives stayed at home in the kitchen. When Bill moved to the newly hatched CIA in 1947, he kept up the facade that he'd maintained in the FBI and that stayed with him for the rest of his life. He lowered it only rarely, for the few who proved themselves to him. He was a master at winning trusted henchmen. Friendships with his Landsmänner were based on shared experience and often, too, on an ability to partake liberally of booze. With Harvey, what you saw was what he let you see. One could only speculate what lay behind the facade; Harvey rarely allowed any to glimpse his deeply private side.

Harvey became one of the most outstanding intelligence officers this country has ever produced. He is perhaps the preeminent American master of what decades later came to be called HUMINT (human intelligence). What mattered to Bill was his job, and at it, he worked remorselessly. His drive to succeed in the CIA's stoutly buttressed, exclusive world carried him into Cold War meetings in the White House's Oval Office and bitter confrontations with the U.S. attorney general. It was a long and fraught road that began in Danville, Indiana.

Bill's widow told one of her husband's closest associates that Bill "came from a really wonderful family. When you go all the way back, they are the people who settled Indiana. His ancestors fought in the War

Between the States . . . on both sides. His father, grandfather, his great grandfather, and his great, great grandfather all graduated from Indiana University's Law School. These were the Harvey Men."[1]

FROM THE AMERICAN HEARTLAND

Nearly a century after his birth, Bill's parentage remains as inscrutable as so many aspects of his later years. He may have been illegitimate, born in Cleveland to a woman who was socially and intellectually far in advance of her times. Bill's mother brought him to the family seat in Danville, Indiana, and gave him a proper home and a father who "died of spinal meningitis when Bill was only ten months old."

Among the Harvey family papers is this document:

> Registered No. 14587, birth No. 134, Sept 13, 1915: William Walker born to Sara J. King of Danville Indiana, then aged 25 and Drenan R. Walker of Danville, then aged 27, a lawyer. Signed on Sept. 21, 1915 by attending physician R.H. Boatwright at Maternity Hospital, Cleveland. Mother's usual residences listed as 757 East 90th Street, Cleveland. COPY OF BIRTH CERTIFICATE NO. 8928 ISSUED APRIL 29th, 1959.[2]

The document's date of issue is shortly before Bill Harvey returned from seven years at the key outpost of the Cold War, Berlin. It seems plausible that at that time Sara J. King, who was known as Sara King Harvey, decided it was time to document the true circumstances of Bill's birth, especially since he and his wife, CG, were returning with a newly adopted baby girl.

Bill's remarkable mother was an academic whose field was Elizabethan literature. Indeed, Sara, who did doctoral research at Oxford, must have been one of very few women of her times to have earned a PhD, and she capped that by becoming a full professor at Indiana State University.

The matter of Harvey's birth is significant only because back then, in the first decades of the twentieth century, bastardy carried a stigma. If Harvey knew he was the natural product of a failed romance, his compulsion to best others—especially, as it turned out, those who were to an East Coast manor born—would have been strong.

A SELDOM MOTHER: SARA KING HARVEY

Home for Bill's mother was Danville, which is today a western exurb of Indianapolis. William King, Bill's maternal grandfather, owned the *Danville Gazette*, "the only Democratic newspaper in Hendricks County." One of the CIA women who knew Sara in later years remembers her as "brilliant, brilliant, a kind and gracious lady as well as a distinguished professor of literature."[3]

Sally Harvey, the daughter Bill adopted while in Berlin in 1958, takes up the tale: "My father and grandmother had a very special bond between them. My father rarely addressed her as 'Mother,' always as 'Sally,' her nickname, not 'Sara.' Each thought the sun rose and set on the other.

"Grandmother had a very adventurous side; she loved to travel almost as much as she loved to read. At eighty-five, she went on a safari in Africa! On one excursion her boat capsized in a river, and she had to swim to shore."

Bill's mother was a lady, says Sally. "I never, ever heard her raise her voice or get angry with anyone in my life. Her speech was impeccable, never so much as a hint of nasal 'hoosierese.'

"She spent endless hours reading Shakespeare to me before I even went to kindergarten. She had the perfect tones and inflections to draw listeners in! She even taught me always to wash my hands before I read a book and how to turn the pages properly. . . .

"My grandmother died on June 9, 1975, which was her birthday. My father died on June 9, 1976. I live in my grandmother's house, which has been in the family since it was built."[4]

PRECOCIOUS YOUTH

Bill's youth was Norman Rockwell *Saturday Evening Post* material; then, and later, he was way, way ahead of himself. Bill was Sara's only child, and he did all of the things expected of an achiever: He graduated high school and made Eagle Scout well ahead of schedule. Summers, he worked as an apprentice laborer for the family's Robert King Construction Co.

Bill considered applying for an appointment to West Point but did not pursue the idea. Grandfather King ruled that Bill was too young for university at age fifteen, so Bill went to work at the family's paper "as a reporter and printer" until grandpa felt the young man was ready. At Indiana University, he pledged Sigma Chi and lived at the fraternity house from September 1933 until September 1937.

Bill got some fatherly counsel from a Terre Haute lawyer, B. F. Small, in 1933. Small wrote Bill a letter that is a masterpiece of the kind of advice sanguine elders gave to youth back in those days:

> You have been given by nature what may prove a blessing or a curse to you, depending upon how you handle it . . . a brain far

> above that of the average human being. At twelve and thirteen, you were registering the intelligence of twenty-one and twenty-two. Now, at your present age, you have a brain ability and a comprehension superior to the average man of thirty to forty. . . . When [this] happen[s] to a man in the course of his development, it leaves him pretty much in the situation of a Model T Ford fitted up with a twenty-four cylinder Duisenberg engine. He is overpowered or superpowered. Just as such a powerful engine would tear to pieces a Ford chassis, so will a powerful brain shatter the life career of an individual unless it is throttled down and managed by the sheer will power of the individual.[5]

Small's letter proved a prophetic vision of his godson's life.

2

THE SECRET WORLD: TANGLING WITH BUDDHA

The young Bill Harvey continued to race ahead. He completed enough course work at Indiana University to qualify for fast-track entry into law school after two undergraduate years. He got his LLB with distinction within another two years. Having entered the university in 1933, he passed out as a fully qualified lawyer in 1937.

While at Bloomington in April 1934, only nineteen years old and still an undergraduate, Harvey married a fellow student, Elizabeth Howe McIntire, perhaps to prove his independence from his mother's strong influence. In September 1937 the young couple moved to Maysville, a town on the Ohio River, southeast of Cincinnati, where, at that time, Rosemary Clooney was probably singing in the choir of St. Patrick's Church and where Libby's father was an influential local advocate.

Harvey saw Germany invade Poland in September 1939 from this placid backwater, and he decided to get involved. He applied to the Federal Bureau of Investigation, which quickly launched a preemployment full-field investigation.

"THOROUGHLY AN AMERICAN BOY"

At age twenty-five, Bill carried 195 pounds on his five-foot-eleven-inch frame. He later, under some pressure, went down to a Bureau-acceptable 175; he also grew an inch to make his height a nicely rounded six feet. Sam Papich, the FBI's long-serving liaison officer to the CIA, remembers Bill in the early days as "slim," a description hard for those who knew him later to envision. The FBI found that all of Bill's "systems" were normal, although he had had treatment in 1938 for a goiter that was apparently responsible for the bulging, thyroidic eye condition so many people noted in his later life.[1]

Special agent S. K. Moss nosed around Maysville in mid-October 1940 and found nothing amiss. "Law practice in Maysville grossed $2,215 in 1939. . . . Has been interested in obtaining employment with the Bureau ever since he left Law School. . . . Has indebtedness of $550 which he can clean up. . . . Denies subversive affiliations." Bill said that the minimum salary he would accept was $3,200, which just happened to be FBI's entry-level pay for someone with his qualifications.

Bill had worked in Democratic politics, even organized delegates for a 1936 presidential candidate, should Franklin D. Roosevelt not run. Bill's wife's family was well up in the Maysville pecking order, and the Harveys were highly regarded for their social work as well as for their bridge game. A local judge opined, Bill was "a smart boy, very tactful, and knows his law pretty well. . . . better office lawyer than a trial lawyer . . . always a gentleman." Special Agent Moss continued, Harvey "had expressed his opinion on several occasions against Communism and the Fifth Column activities in this country. . . . Level-headed. . . . Applicant and his wife are very happily married. . . . Neither indulged in intoxicants to excess. . . . Is very much interested in guns and is quite a marksman." And even well before Pearl Harbor, "he spoke of joining the United States Army and becoming an officer, or endeavoring to become a member of the Department of Justice." Chief of Police Harry Stewart summed Bill Harvey up as "one of the most respectable citizens in Maysville . . . thoroughly an American boy."

The background check also covered Bill's childhood in Indiana. At high school in Terre Haute, "a brilliant boy . . . did not participate in athletics, but had a strong and healthy physique . . . a real leader possessed of a healthy confidence and self-assurance . . . not conceited. His mother is a brilliant and cultured woman." His Indiana University record showed As in journalism, Bs in English and psychology, and a C and a D in military science, indicating that Bill might have had some campus ROTC exposure.

Once the background checks were complete, Harvey's ticket out of Maysville came from the FBI in an official telegram:

> VIA WESTERN UNION. NOVEMBER 26, 1940
> YOU ARE OFFERED APPOINTMENT SPECIAL AGENT THIS BUREAU. . . . PROCEED TO WASHINGTON AT YOUR OWN EXPENSE. . . . ARRANGE PERSONAL MATTERS THAT YOU MAY ACCEPT ASSIGNMENT WHERE SERVICES NEEDED. CONSIDER THIS STRICTLY CONFIDENTIAL AND PRESENT WIRE UPON REPORTING. . . .
> J. EDGAR HOOVER DIRECTOR

Harvey replied:

> MAYSVILLE KY NOV 27 758P
> JOHN EDGAR HOOVER
> DIRECTOR FBI JUSTICE DEPT
> I ACCEPT APPOINTMENT SPECIAL AGENT AND . . . WILL REPORT DECEMBER 9, 1940. WILLIAM K HARVEY

IN THE SERVICE OF HIS COUNTRY

Harvey landed in an FBI intake of about fifty new special agents almost precisely a year before Pearl Harbor. His entry medical exam recorded, "Right hand mashed in press 1932; slight injuries in auto wreck [which had brought on the thyroid problem] 1938. . . . Tobacco—Yes; Alcoholics [*sic*]—No. Capable of strenuous physical exertion." At the FBI academy at Quantico, Virginia, Bill qualified on the machine gun with a perfect 100; he scored only an 82 at shooting from the hip.

Bill Harvey's FBI record is catalogued in some three hundred pages of exquisitely stilted gobbledygook. After training, Harvey was sent to the Bureau's glamorous New York field office at the U.S. courthouse and assigned to "custodial detention cases." While working out of Foley Square, Harvey came up with an idea that the special agent in charge forwarded with enthusiasm. The concept was that mail carriers across the country be recruited to provide information "of interest to The Bureau . . . information that can be gathered with comparative ease." Shortly thereafter, Harvey was transferred to the National Defense Squad; he expressed interest in learning about audio surveillance in a future Bureau course on the subject.

OPERATION TRAMP

Part of the Harvey legend is that, while still in his twenties, Bill was the lead case officer on a German counterespionage (CE) case that was the raw material for *The House on 92nd Street*, which won writer Charles G. Booth an Oscar.[2] This exploit is not substantiated in Harvey's personnel dossier, which, an FBI Freedom of Information Act official confirms, was stripped of considerable information before it was made available to inquirers. People who knew Bill in the late 1940s say he was miffed he did not receive the credit due to him for his part in the case.

The case is reported in some detail in Ernest Volkman's *Espionage: The Greatest Spy Operations of the Twentieth Century*.[3] Volkman does not give sources for his account, nor does he name Harvey. He tells the tale of a German émigré named Sebold who returned to his native soil, was recruited by the Abwehr, reported his recruitment to the American consulate in Cologne, and when he later returned to the United States, was run successfully by the FBI. Much of the drama of the case came in the Bureau's ability to deceive the Abwehr in clandestine radio transmissions. Volkman wrote, "A total of 37 agents with varying degrees of access in the American economy came into Sebold's office; in turn Sebold radioed material back to Germany from a wireless station he and the FBI set up at Centerport, Long Island." It was one of the FBI's first counterespionage experiments, and if Volkman can be believed, it was very successful.

Though it seems incredible today, the team that ran Sebold was by February 1941 headed by the new boy, Bill Harvey. (Robert A. Maheu, a Quantico classmate of Harvey and a figure who also appears later in this book, avers that he, too, was involved in the deception, particularly in its Long Island aspects.) Harvey's squad put together skeins of disinformation for Sebold to transmit to the Abwehr from Long Island; to make the transmissions seem more realistic, the FBI peppered the transatlantic signal with static. The Abwehr was nonplussed. Many of their man's reports were gold, but some came through in unusable bursts or were blocked by what seemed to be atmospherics. The Abwehr sent a second wireless telegraphy (W/T) agent to the U.S. station to check out the operation. He and Berlin were puzzled that his signal was too weak to be received at the Abwehr's listening posts and that he ran into a few unexpected technical difficulties. The Abwehr never solved the puzzle.

After Bill's death, his second wife said, "They put [Bill] in charge of the squads that met the German submarines coming in to put saboteurs on shore. We weren't sabotaged once! Bill caught them all. He had some really harrowing stories about his duties then. I thought it was more important than going off to war, but he felt that he had been a slackard [*sic*], staying in the States. He never got over that."[4]

Bill and his counterespionage team spotted and recruited a weak link in the staff of the German consulate in New York. The man was in charge of document destruction, and so, of course, had access to a trove of classified information. The new agent carefully selected the most important dispatches in the waste and stuffed them into a fireproofed pocket of the furnace. He recovered the documents from time to time and turned them over to Harvey. The Bureau shut down the consulate operation in June 1941, with the arrest of the thirty-seven Abwehr agents who had reported to Sebold.

It was a very busy introductory six months for the young special agent in the FBI's Foley Square office, and it was a major shift for the FBI from pure counterintelligence, i.e., arresting and prosecuting, to the more exacting work of counterespionage.

CAREER MAN

Bill's first promotion came in November 1941. In accordance with FBI procedure, at that time, he was also due for rotation out of New York. In a special efficiency report on Harvey written for his six-month review, Percy E. Farnsworth, an assistant director, wrote, "Has taken pains to thoroughly study any matter upon which he is working. . . . A good example has been his work in Italian national defense case [perhaps Harvey's first exposure to the Mafia] . . . in which he has made every endeavor to become expert in Italian matters, especially from the viewpoint of organizations and Italian societies. . . . Initiative . . . originality. . . . Should develop into an above-average Special Agent." Bill was transferred from New York to Pittsburgh.

Dennis Flinn ("the spelling is Protestant Irish") was on the German Desk at FBI headquarters in 1942. As pressures on the desk increased with U.S. involvement in the war, Flinn asked for help. On March 28, 1942, Harvey moved to the National Defense Division, Internal Security Section, German Desk, at "the seat of government," which is how Hoover habitually referred to Washington. For the next few years Harvey continued to work on penetrating German espionage and doubling Nazi agents. He was joined on that desk by Mark Felt, the man who years later became Deep Throat, the main source for Woodward and Bernstein's *Washington Post* articles on the Watergate scandal.[5]

Flinn recalls of Harvey, "We worked across the desk from each other from early 1942 until July 1943," at which time Flinn was reassigned as legal attaché at Lisbon, Portugal. Flinn, Harvey, and Art Thurston formed a close trio.[6]

As early as May 1942, Harvey was feeling restless at the German desk. "Agent advised he was married but that he definitely and conclusively had made up his mind that he was willing to leave the United States without his wife . . . felt it was his patriotic duty. . . . Recommend he be approved" for "special assignment," a euphemism for the FBI's operations in Central and South America. But on June 3, 1942, he was refused because of his "married status; more valuable on National Defense as a Supervisor."

Half a century later CG Harvey, Bill's second wife, made an interesting point: "Bill's . . . aim in life had been to be a Marine general. But the FBI wouldn't let him out. He tried everything."[7] In fact, the FBI file shows that Harvey was repeatedly classified II-A, the draft category for those deemed indispensable to the war effort. October 1943: "Excellent knowledge of the German intelligence picture and organizations, both in this country and in Germany . . . has been of assistance in many of the Bureau's national defense prosecutions." Nothing could have made J. Edgar purr more than a fast-rising junior who helped nail the enemy in court. Further, "Agent has lectured before numerous new Agents and in-Service Schools." This is the first reference to Harvey as a teacher; he later influenced many senior CIA officers in this role.

Another of Harvey's bosses, Hugh H. Clegg, made a significant point: "Agent has no personal problems . . . excellent personality. . . . Particularly well-grounded in the Bureau's espionage cases. . . . Executive ability may be developed at some future date." Supervisor Clegg recommended, though, that after the war, Harvey get some gumshoe experience, "in order to more fully develop him."

All of this praise brought Bill a promotion to CAF-12 at $4,600 in 1944.

HIGH . . . AND LOW

In February 1945, during the last wartime winter, Harvey was recognized for a major, meticulous analysis. He "took it upon himself to review all files in the Bureau on German organizations and prepared a compilation of all available information concerning the activities of the NSDAP [the Nazi Party]. . . . Followed the matter closely and instilled the necessary interest and enthusiasm in the field offices."

World War II ended and Bill was given an automatic in-grade raise in October 1945, but immediately thereafter he overstepped himself, at least in the view of the only person who counted, J. Edgar Hoover.

That month the special agent in charge in New York sent an urgent wire to Washington asking for immediate permission to bug a certain dinner party. Harvey OKed the operation on his own authority. It was the first time—but far from the last—that he acted on what he thought was right, rather than waiting for superiors to give the go-ahead. Soon enough, Bill had to eat very humble pie, though he had, he claimed, only been acting for his boss, who was on leave. "I desire to assure you [Hoover] that there was no intent on my part to by-pass either your approval or that of Mr. Tamm. It is sincerely regretted that this inadvertently occurred." But on November 1, 1945, Buddha frowned on Harvey.

> I feel that you exercised extremely bad judgment in assuming that the matter had previously been considered by higher officials and approved. . . .

> Indiscriminate authorizations of this type cannot be permitted and more sound judgment on your part will be expected in the future.
>
> Very truly yours,
> John Edgar Hoover.

A handwritten note on the carbon copy of the letter says, "Please review. Let me have your complete recommendation re disciplinary action and steps to prevent recurrence."

Harvey had done the right thing at the right time, but he had sinned against the Buddha's doctrine. Regardless, six days after the letter of censure, the Bureau began to take a major Soviet espionage agent seriously and Harvey was back in play.

TAKING ON THE NEW ENEMY

In 1945 Bill was one of three Bureau agents who formed the FBI's—indeed, the United States'—first counterespionage effort targeted against Soviet intelligence activities.[8] The first major case on which Harvey worked—which is, again, not mentioned in his personnel file and for which he is not credited in Curt Gentry's *J. Edgar Hoover: The Man and the Secrets*—was the matter of Elizabeth Bentley.

In November 1945 Elizabeth Bentley made an appointment with the FBI office in New York. Worried that her cover was blown by the recent defections of two KGB agents to the West, she confessed to the FBI that she was a courier for a KGB espionage network.[9] The first defection that caused her concern was that of former Communist Louis Budenz, who went to the New Haven FBI office in August. The defection of Igor Gouzenko, a code clerk at the Soviet embassy in Ottawa, seems to have been what finally made her ready to confess.

FBI men interrogated Bentley, starting on November 7, 1945. She eventually named more than one hundred Soviet agents and contacts. She "had carried secret data to the Russians from U.S. government employees in the OSS, the Air Force, the War Department, the War Production Board, Foreign Economic Administration, and the Departments of Treasury, Agriculture, and Commerce. This was a staggering penetration of the U.S. government by the Soviets. Bentley's initial confession was of such moment that Hoover sent an immediate digest to the White House on November 8, 1945."[10] He followed up with a comprehensive report to President Truman on November 27. Someone put in a huge amount of overtime.

A longtime FBI employee states with certainty that "Harvey was head of Division Five—National Security—when Bentley came in. He was the logical person to handle her." Was it FBI custom that a medium-rank officer whose forte had been desk analysis be assigned to handle a very hot walk-in source? The employee I spoke to indicated that there was nothing out of the ordinary in the assignment at the time.[11]

Bentley's handler was Harvey, and Bentley was Harvey's first major vest-pocket operation. Clarence Berry says that part of the Harvey legend in the late 1940s was that Bill played the Bentley case so close to the vest only top brass knew about it. Knowledge of the case was, in fact, more widespread than that, but the perception fed the legend.

I have seen one undated photograph that shows Bentley appearing before a House of Representatives committee flanked by a man who appears to be Bill Harvey. Alger Hiss is also in the photo. The shot was probably taken at a session of the House Un-American Activities Committee (HUAC) in 1947, shortly before Harvey resigned from the Bureau. It is the only published photograph of Bill, except for copies of mug shots, that I have ever seen.

Robert L. Lamphere, a colleague and contemporary of Harvey, comments sourly in his autobiography, "The 'major case' squad [i.e., Harvey and his people] that had been cleaning up matters relating to wartime German and Japanese espionage was running out of work and the Bentley case was taken away from the experts in Soviet espionage and given to this other squad. My colleagues were disgusted at this bureaucratic move."

By July 1947 Lamphere was in charge of the Gerhard Eisler case, a major Communist prosecution. The trial took place in Washington. "Each day after court, I reported to Bill Harvey who was the headquarters supervisor in charge of the Eisler case. . . . His voice was like that of a bullfrog; once you heard it . . . and the intellect behind it . . . you never forgot it. The resident Bureau expert on counterintelligence, Bill had been so busy handling the Bentley case that I'd been pretty much left alone on Eisler. In our meetings, he'd offer a few suggestions, but little more."

Then, a further interesting note from Lamphere: When the Eisler case ended, "Bill Harvey said to me that new blood was needed on the counter-intelligence desks at Headquarters, and asked if I would informally sound out some of the people on the New York Soviet Espionage squad about coming down to Washington. Harvey's request was an absolute breach of Bureau procedure."[12]

BACK IN GOOD GRACES?

Harvey continued to rack up creditable efficiency ratings. Edward A. Tamm, a senior FBI official, wrote, "I am impressed with the amount of both intelligent research and file review and logical thinking and conclusions . . . a manifestation of real supervision."

The cause for this encomium was a tight, sixteen-page analysis and operational brief cum order dated December 9, 1945—only a few weeks after Bentley started to talk seriously to the FBI—on possible American connections to the famous Rote Kapelle/Rote Drei Soviet GRU (military intelligence) espionage apparatus going back into prewar and, especially, 1941–42 files. Harvey's action dispatch to FBI bureaus said, "Every possible investigative technique should be utilized for the purpose of fully and completely developing the significance of this information and the identities. . . . Of particular importance in this connection is complete coverage of all communications to and from these individuals. . . . The investigation is considered of the utmost importance."

An efficiency report called Bill, four months before his departure from the FBI, "vigorous, forceful and aggressive . . . definitely outstanding as to intelligence, ability and application. . . . One of the best supervisors at the Seat of Government." But shortly after this glowing review, something happened to change Harvey's career and, indeed, American Cold War history. It was an incident that involved booze. It could be interpreted as a precursor of much else in Bill's future.

THE ROCK CREEK PARK INCIDENT

The official version in Harvey's FBI personnel file is an internal memorandum dated July 15, 1947, from Edward A. Tamm to the director.

Just before 10:00 on the morning of July 12, Libby Harvey reported Bill missing in a phone call to Mickey Ladd, head of the FBI's Domestic Security Division. "She stated that Mr. Harvey had recently been despondent and discouraged about his work at the Bureau and had been moody."

On the dark and rainy night of Friday, July 11, 1947, Harvey and a number of other FBI men attended a stag party in Arlington, Virginia, for Harvey's boss. Harvey imbibed "about two cans of beer." Robert Lamphere, in his memoir, comments flatly, "Harvey had drunk too much."

Bill eventually got into his car and led his immediate boss, Patrick Joseph Coyne, across Memorial Bridge back into the District of Columbia. At some point, Coyne found his bearings and peeled off. Bill took the urban highway through Rock Creek Park, on course for 39th Street, in the northwestern reaches of D.C. But he didn't show up at home. Libby kept silent for a number of hours before she called Mickey Ladd. We can't know whether her reticence was a sign there was already coolness in the marriage.

Ladd was about to order agents to check the Metropolitan Police and hospitals when "we were advised that Mr. Harvey had arrived at his residence."

Bill told the office that "he was proceeding towards his residence in a heavy downpour of rain." His car stalled when he drove through a puddle and was heavily splashed by an oncoming vehicle. "He coasted to the curb, but was unable to get his car started again, and accordingly went to sleep . . . until approximately 10.00AM, when he awakened and proceeded to his home." The fix was in: it could not be admitted in official documents, perhaps not even in verbal reports to the director, that Harvey and everyone else at the party had been drunk.

Tamm stuck his neck out for Harvey. "Record during his assignment at the Seat of Government has been a very good one. . . . I personally have seen Harvey at his desk late at night on many occasions. . . . I do not believe in the light of all the circumstances in this case that there is any administrative action which should be taken." Harvey was "very much upset about the matter. . . . [Tamm was] convinced Harvey was telling an accurate story." Up the chain of command, Mickey Ladd took the soft option, saying, "While we had no question as to his sobriety on this occasion, we were concerned about the possibility of his being completely exhausted from overwork or worry . . . [we wondered] whether it would be better for him if he were transferred to another assignment, particularly in light of his wife's statement that he has been despondent and discouraged about his work.

"Mr. Harvey indicated . . . that he did periodically become discouraged about the ineffectiveness of the overall Government program in dealing with the Communists and Communist espionage. . . . [He] prefers his present desk to any assignment. . . . His worry was the natural worry [of] anyone who dealt as intimately with the Communist problem as he had been doing for several years."

For Hoover, Harvey's sin was that he had been unreachable for a number of hours, should the director have suddenly needed him.

One week after the incident report, Hoover wrote a letter to Clyde A. Tolson, whom Gentry calls "the director's inseparable companion."

> July 23, 47
> PERSONNEL CHANGES
> It is recommended that Special Agent Supervisor William K. Harvey of the Security Division be transferred to Indianapolis on general assignment.

J. Edgar ordered a clear humiliation, to emphasize that no one was exempt from Buddha's wrath.

Less than a month after the incident, Harvey put in his resignation from the FBI. "Necessary at this time because of personal and family considerations . . . greatest pride and personal satisfaction . . . extreme reluctance. . . .Very real appreciation [for the] consideration and kindnesses which you have extended to me. . . . I would be grateful for the opportunity of seeing you after your return."

Hoover replied, equally blandly, on August 13, 1947. "Gratifying to know that your association with the Bureau has been a source of pride and personal satisfaction. . . . With kindest regards and best wishes . . . "

Harvey's file details what an intense professional he had become by the time he wrapped up his career in the Bureau. His final FBI fitness report shows that he had accumulated ninety-seven days and five hours of unused leave. "A tremendous amount of voluntary overtime work . . . entitled [Harvey] to the adjective rating of excellent," wrote Joseph P. Coyne, the special agent whom Harvey had led across Memorial Bridge. The final rating was approved by Mickey Ladd, who added a laconic note: "[Harvey] had an excellent knowledge of Russian espionage and Communist activities." The special agent in charge of the Los Angeles FBI office recorded, "His grasp of the details of Russian espionage operations in this country was a revelation. . . . Agents are so enthused. . . . It is hoped that eventually it will be possible to give [the course on Soviet espionage] to every Special Agent who is investigating Communist and Russian matters." Harvey's exit record also shows he had improved as a hip shooter.

Just two months after the car incident and less than three weeks from his effective date of resignation the Central Intelligence Group (soon to become the Agency) officially told the Bureau that it was hiring Harvey. The Bureau tried without success to find out how much Central Intelligence was going to pay its prize new catch and what he would be doing.

When Harvey left the Bureau, he was almost thirty-two years old. He had handled the FBI's hottest espionage cases and was sitting on revelations that would make headlines for years, but Hoover's snap-brim conformity made Harvey's decision to jump from national to international espionage operations easy. Peter M. F. Sichel, one of Harvey's predecessors at the Berlin Operations Base, recalls that Harvey was resentful that the value of his work against the Abwehr's agents in the United States during World War II had never been recognized and indeed that his efforts on the Bentley case had been largely ignored, even within Hoover's Bureau.[13]

THE MAN WHO BARELY WAS

In the interesting mind of J. Edgar Hoover, Bill Harvey became an object of scorn, a traitor to the preened and glistening FBI. Hoover continued a periodic campaign to damn Harvey. A Buddha note, dated March 2, 1949, long after Bill's departure, was part of the continuing, vengeful character assassination campaign. "Why were Supervisors Harvey and [ ] allowed to so mishandle their work? . . . Harvey was a known procrastinator and he permitted items to accumulate on his desk which probably accounted for the large accumulation of reports. . . . Harvey was frequently criticized by Mr. Ladd. . . . In fact, Mr. Ladd advised that he called the attention of the Inspector to this particular type of dereliction on the part of Harvey."

W. R. Glavin to Clyde Tolson, March 21, 1949: "This former Agent bears the brunt of the responsibility for the haphazard assignment of the supervision of the [ ] case. . . . There does not appear to be any excuse for instructions of this [delinquent] kind being issued." Glavin recommended that "this inadequate supervision be borne in mind in the case any inquiries are received concerning Harvey in the future."

From the time of Harvey's resignation until its close, all references in Bill's FBI personnel file are negative.

A VERY PRIVATE PERSON

Throughout his careers in the FBI and the CIA, Harvey never openly showed the slightest doubt in his own abilities. At the FBI, Bill discovered his great analytical capacity, yet he resolved not to spend his career as a desk jockey. He wanted to run and direct field operations overseas. By 1946, while still in the FBI, his country of choice for special assignment had been Germany. He was prepared to leave Libby (at least temporarily) to get there.

At the FBI, Harvey established a work pattern that astonished all around him: he appeared to exist on cigarettes and, latterly, martinis. An eighteen-hour day was usual; later, in Berlin, it routinely became twenty. Harvey's home life took a definite second place. Later, in his second marriage, the equation changed.

It can easily be assumed that Bill confided next to nothing to Libby. Apart from people with whom he associated professionally, Bill was not a social animal, whereas Libby, as many women who came to Washington, wanted to join one of the district's social carousels. Libby pined. Her outlet, increasingly, was the bottle.

CIA TAKES SHAPE

The Office of Strategic Services (OSS), the wartime intelligence-and-executive-action agency, officially shut down in September 1945, when Gen. "Wild Bill" Donovan said farewell to his people in a disused skating rink. An OSS rump survived, concealed as the Strategic Services Unit (SSU), under the umbrella of the War Department. "Allen Dulles was God. Dick Helms was chief of ops. Harry Rositzke and Gordon Stewart had set up a headquarters in Wiesbaden," commented Peter Sichel.[14]

In 1947 Alex MacMillan, who had been in the FBI and then gone to OSS, at Wild Bill Donovan's behest, returned from being OSS/SSU chief of station, Shanghai. "The whole agency in those days was in that red stone building on top of the hill overlooking the brewery, at 2430 E Street, NW. . . . That was the whole show."[15]

Prodded by Harry S. Truman, Congress that year passed legislation establishing the Central Intelligence Agency. The intelligence-gathering wing of CIA's Clandestine Services was called the Office of Special Operations (OSO), and it was staffed by fewer than two hundred officers who ran only seven operating bases, all of which were in areas like Germany, Austria, and Japan under American military occupation. The State Department then, and for several years thereafter, was more than reluctant to provide embassy slots for the guttersnipe of the new intelligence department.

Clarence Berry recalls the physical location of America's intelligence apparatus during the immediate postwar years: "When I arrived in August 1948, pretty much all of CIA was located in a group of old buildings near the old brewery off Rock Creek Parkway, near Foggy Bottom. . . . Around 1951, CIA took over all four of the temporaries along the Reflecting Pool, I, J, K, and L."[16]

In 1949 the CIA launched its first operations to parachute agents into the Soviet Union. Only after the outbreak of the Korean War did OSO's case officers, mainly those in Berlin and Vienna, begin vigorously to probe the far side of the iron curtain. They also quickly learned from their early efforts that the Soviets were pouring agents into the West.

With the founding of CIA, Hoover was forced to yield the FBI's grip on Central and South America, but only with the greatest reluctance. "Under his direct orders . . . [field] agents burned their files and dismissed their informants, rather than turn [anything] over to the new rival." But many of Hoover's cherished Secret Intelligence Service (SIS) agents jumped to the new outfit, gladly. "A number of them, including Eric Timm, Raymond Leddy, Winston MacKinlay Scott, and William King Harvey later occupied key positions in the CIA, while others, such as Robert Maheu, found employment on the covert side."[17]

About fifty special agents left the Bureau for the Agency. Art Thurston, the fellow Hoosier, had switched from the FBI earlier and by 1947 was the CIA's deputy chief of operations. Dennis Flinn, the other old-time FBI hand who was part of the Harvey triumvirate, says flatly that Art "arranged for a job" for Bill because Harvey was "the most highly trained, most professional man available for CI [counterintelligence] work." It was almost as if Harvey had designed the scenario that moved him onto the international stage, into a role that he had yearned for all the way back in Kentucky, that had been denied him by the FBI.

Who actively encouraged Bill to transfer? Alex MacMillan "came back from Shanghai to take over what became our counterintelligence branch. My predecessor was Art Thurston, also a former FBI man, and from Indiana. I heard Bill was coming over. . . .

"There was a lot of whispering . . . but no one knew quite what we were going to do. It was difficult to take men who had been involved in domestic operations and switch them to foreign targets. We weren't thinking about [aggressive] CE [counterespionage] operations against the Sovs abroad then."[18]

Once aboard Harvey did not go about establishing his presence meekly. He probably laughed off his disgrace in Rock Creek Park, but that and earlier scrapes with Hoover foreshadowed later upheavals in Harvey's career, a series of confrontations with authority in which Bill was usually bested because he argued from an operational point of view and too often ignored the practicalities that drove other players in the bureaucratic amphitheater.

IMPOLITIC LIAISON: THE BUREAU AND THE AGENCY

Many CIA people could not stand Hoover's posturing. Coincidentally, or perhaps by design, Harvey got to ruffle the Bureau's feathers right away, as a liaison channel to the FBI for the Agency's counterintelligence desk, Staff C.

> July 10, 1950
> COOPERATION WITH CIA
> (Report of a meeting between Cartha (Deke) De Loach and Admiral Roscoe Hillenkoetter, then Director of Central Intelligence)
> Adm. Hillenkoetter replied that he sincerely regretted allowing the initial letter [about lack of cooperation] . . . to go out of his agency. He stated that the former SA William K. Harvey prepared the letter

> in question and it was now evident to him that Harvey had no proof or background upon which to base his charges. . . . [Hillenkoetter] intended to censure Harvey.
>
> Mr. De Loach advised Admiral Hillenkoetter that we had no interest in his employees being censured, however the FBI would appreciate factual statements, of some background, before 'trumped-up' charges were hurled erroneously. . . . The Admiral requested that Mr. Hoover be advised that he would carefully examine all mail . . . addressed to the FBI.

Ladd's handwritten endorsement: "Place a copy in personnel file of Former Agent Harvey." Hoover appended: "Yes, by all means."

In retrospect, it sounds like a hissy fit. But tensions were high in Washington. American troops were barely hanging on in South Korea. Reinforcements were being rushed to them as quickly as possible. On August 2, 1950, Hillenkoetter caved. Ladd to Hoover:

> [ ] advised . . . that former Special Agent William K. Harvey, now employed by the CIA, was unfriendly and hostile towards the FBI and that we would prefer to have Liaison relations with another individual.
>
> Admiral Hillenkoetter . . . advised that it was unfortunate that Harvey possessed a most ambitious and forceful personality which at times made letters written by Harvey quite pointed and sarcastic. He stated that on occasions he had found it necessary to "tone down" letters that Harvey had written to the Bureau. . . .
>
> Admiral Hillenkoetter advised that he would appoint anyone suggested by the Bureau for liaison. . . . If [the director] wished to take any administrative action against Harvey, he would be glad to do so.

The next day, Harvey crawled, and it must have been painful. "[Harvey] stated that Admiral Hillenkoetter had informed him of the Bureau's displeasure . . . and that he desired to call and rectify what he feels sure is an honest mistake. . . . He has highest regard for the Bureau. . . . He would like to see The Director sometime and express his regrets in this regard. I advised him you were out of the city at the present time. . . .

"The Director indicated that the liaison arrangements with Mr. Harvey could continue for the present to determine whether his attitude was as he has indicated."

At a small working lunch given by Gen. Bedell Smith for J. Edgar Hoover, shortly after Smith took over the Agency in 1951, the general asked the director to explain the animosity between the two agencies. "Well, General, the first thing wrong is all these ex-Bureau people over here sniping and proselytizing, and particularly Bill Harvey."

Then came the Philby affair, dealt with more extensively in the next chapter, which undoubtedly rankled in the Bureau. Hoover's revenge was to heap petulantly furious blame on Harvey, even for years afterward. One example: A memo on December 20, 1951, from the director to the special agent in charge of the Washington field office, ordered agents to keep close tabs on former FBI men, specifically Harvey. This correspondence was followed by an undated memo in Hoover's handwriting, which reads, "It is regretted that not one of these ex-agents with whom we come into contact in our dealings with CIA had a clean record either while in FBI or an attitude of good will toward FBI after leaving it. I cannot help but conclude that much of the difficulty with CIA has been engineered by this group." At the end of September 1952 Harvey's unpopularity down Pennsylvania Avenue was reinforced in a memo written by Mickey Ladd and endorsed by Hoover.

> CIA PROSELYTING OF BUREAU PERSONNEL.
> . . . I have heard that there are two individuals within the CIA who are particularly anxious to recruit key Bureau personnel. One . . . is former Special Agent William K. Harvey. . . . [He] would use any device to proselyte former Bureau personnel and will even go so far as to approach former Bureau personnel presently with CIA to go out and make contact . . . to entice them with offers of higher grades to go to CIA. . . .
> [ ]
> . . . It has also been reported, however, that they have the dream of one day taking over Communist and counter-espionage activities in the United States.

When Bill went to Rome in 1963, the FBI's legal attaché was made fully aware of the derogatory matters in Bill's personnel file. And years later the Bureau made its suspicions of Bill Harvey's association with Johnny Rosselli, the infamous mafioso, very apparent.

Bill had played in Hoover's china shop. In courting Buddha's wrath, Harvey established a pattern of disdain for high bureaucracy that took him to the peaks and plunged him into the valleys of his later career.

3

THE HEARTLANDER: BUILDING THE LEGEND

When Bill Harvey defected from the unbending FBI to the looser CIA, he set about distinguishing himself, a guy from the boondocks, from the run of his new colleagues. He was not Back Bay or Park Avenue or Lake Forest or Marin; he didn't own a trench coat; and he would never have been described as elegant. Where some other transfers from the Bureau melded fairly easily with the Office of Strategic Services (OSS) players who populated the early CIA, Harvey consciously emphasized his rough edges.

Bill wasn't about to let false modesty stand in the way of his ambition. He knew that his perspicacity and his ability to sketch the broad picture set him apart. He linked his future inseparably with the aggressive protection of American security. His horizons were limited not by a lack of daring but by rivalries, the practicalities of government, the lack of trained personnel, and to some extent, the limits of espionage technology.

Weaknesses? Bill is often reputed to have boasted that he had a woman every day of his adult life. Adam Horton, who served briefly and unhappily under Harvey in Berlin, relays a secondhand tale from Washington days: "One evening, well after hours, my friend had just finished the security check for his section and turned out the lights when what should appear across the way, but Bill Harvey having it off on his desk with one of the secretaries.

"My friend rang the number which Bill, never one to miss the call of duty, answered. My friend suggested that Harvey's activity was improper. Bill lost his cool, demanding to know the identity of the caller. My friend, sensing Harvey's rage, decided humor was better than valor. In his most sepulchral voice, he announced himself, 'God calling!' and hung up. He got out of the building undetected before Bill could collect himself."[1]

In the dank halls of L Building, Harvey was looked at askance. He presented a larger-than-life target for those who, for whatever reason, wanted to snipe. In the 1940s, if any of the wellborn got tiddly at a Georgetown soiree, it was funny. If Harvey had a few too many, it was a sign that the midwestern underclass couldn't drink like gentlemen. Besides, Bill Harvey was always flipping the lid of his Zippo lighter, spinning the cylinder of his pistol, and paring his nails with a hunting knife, and he used uncouth language in mixed company.

From the beginning, Harvey, the quintessential red-blooded Eagle Scout American, emphasized his differences, indeed waved them under the Ivy Leaguers' noses.

EARLY DAYS

Allen W. Dulles, the CIA's godfather, has often been quoted as having commented that Bill Harvey was great at what he did, "but the trouble is I don't know if he's more conspiratorial or more cop." The original source and circumstances of the quote are lost in time.

Tom Polgar, a meticulous observer of the CIA scene, who was in at the beginning, knew Bill early in his career. "Harvey came in with high prestige as an expert on Soviet espionage. This was what CIA at that time required. . . . No one cared that Harvey had run afoul of J. Edgar Hoover's chickenshit regulations.

"As chief of Staff C, Harvey outranked Jim Angleton, but the Black Prince had more money and better personal and social connections. Controlling the Israeli account, Angleton was able to charm General Smith and Dulles, and the relative influence of Harvey declined."[2]

Bill Hood is a distinguished writer whose clandestine career goes back to OSS. One afternoon in the late 1940s Hood and Harvey were lunching in Georgetown when they noticed a CIA Ivy Leaguer at a nearby table. Harvey growled, "Fucking namby-pamby. Not worth shit." Hood said: "Listen, Bill, that man was a radio operator who dropped into France with less protection on him than you're wearing right now!"[3]

Once, Frank Wisner, then head of Clandestine Services, was chairing a meeting. Wisner asked a couple of questions that touched off a Harvey monologue, the kind of bureaucratic drone for which Bill became famous. As he listened to Bill, the red crept up the back of Wisner's neck and thence to his ears. "He's standing behind the chair at the end of the table, and all of a sudden, he leans forward, and grabs the top of his chair with both hands, glares at Harvey and explodes: 'Goddammit, Harvey, will you let me finish what I came here to do?!' There was a long, measured beat, then Bill says, 'Sure, Frank.'"[4]

Harvey was a more-than-fair actor. Some called it ego, but his ambition to soar to the top of CIA, which became more evident in later years, was not a quest for power per se; rather it was based on his conviction that he was a better intelligence officer than anyone else he knew.

None of the calumny that was later dumped on Harvey hit the bookstores until after Bill was long dead. Many on the foreign intelligence side of the Agency to this day believe Harvey at his peak—and despite his manifest personal failings—epitomized all that was sound and solid in the intelligence business during the depths of the Cold War. Harvey was a determined, inspired and inspiring, persevering, sleep-deprived taskmaster. There were none like him.

One of the originals, Alex MacMillan recollects, "Bill was much maligned; very intelligent, although he didn't appear to be. That was part of his pattern. . . . He wanted to get up there to the top and fix everybody. I'm sure he had no heroes [in the higher echelons]. I never figured out what he thought about Allen Dulles."[5]

DICK HELMS

If the CIA and Office of Special Operations/Foreign Intelligence (OSO/FI) human intelligence gatherers ever had a saint, it was Richard M. Helms. Helms was an Ivy Leaguer, a cautious career officer who disdained political and psychological warfare and who rose from OSO eventually to be the director of central intelligence (DCI).

Harvey and Helms could hardly have been more disparate. Helms was cool, elegant, suave, socially adept, and quiet, and he kept his relationships with his colleagues purely professional. This was fine by Harvey. To Bill Harvey, Helms was "the Boy Diplomat," and though Helms was the one man senior to him who consistently stood by him and with whom he shared chunks of very touchy knowledge, Harvey consciously irked Helms in later years. By 1968 Helms felt compelled to turn against Harvey.

Years later, in the measured mellowness of retirement, the ever-graceful Helms urged me to embark on this study. He had this to say about the man he came to view with suspicion and whom he forced to retire from the Agency: "Bill was rarely seen without a pistol stuffed in his belt. The professional persona he seemed to favor was that of a senior police officer, a master of the terrain assigned to him, wily, informed, perceptive, and deeply patriotic. He was also deliberately blunt and loudly outspoken. . . . Bill was not, and never pretended to be, a man for all seasons. But what he did best, he did very well."[6] Bill Hood, who coauthored Helms's autobiography, says he never knew Helms to be so outspokenly in favor of a man, "even though they had nothing in common."[7]

INTO OPS

Once in CIA harness, Harvey was logically assigned to head what had been OSS's counterespionage branch, soon to be called "Staff C."

Even then, there were rivalries between CIA's Clandestine Services staffs. Clarence Berry: "When I first entered on duty in August 1948, Staff C was just in its early stages, while Staff D [communications intelligence procurement] seemed to be a more going concern. Even during the short time I was around headquarters . . . there was a bit of antagonism between the two staffs, but even then, staffers almost invariably referred to Harvey as 'Big Bill.'"[8]

Harvey did what he could to launch operations against the Soviet intelligence services. Alex MacMillan: "About all we did was go to cocktail parties and look the Russians over, trying to pick up stuff. I don't think we accomplished a hell of a lot. Bill was at first employed well below his capabilities. He complained about it privately. A bit later, Bill and I worked together planning counterespionage activities. . . . Bill was responsible for most of it. We'd pore over documents late at night, changing words, even single letters in the master plan we were putting together."[9]

It was that kind of cocktail party contact that led Harvey to his next major coup in the world of counterespionage: the unmasking of Kim Philby.

THE PHILBY AFFAIR

The Brits had proven during World War II that they were masters of the double game. OSS learned from them that the true intelligence prize was to know the enemy intimately, perhaps even to lead him astray with disinformation—goals and tactics that were far more valuable than the detention and trial of enemy agents.

From October 1949 on, the British Secret Intelligence Service's (MI-6's) chief representative to the American security and intelligence apparatus in Washington was H. A. R. (Kim) Philby, a Cambridge graduate and wartime boss of British writer Graham Greene. Philby forged firm friendships with some of the men who were integral to the young Central Intelligence Agency, Frank Wisner, Tracy Barnes, and James Jesus Angleton, the former OSS officer who had lived in wartime London and later worked in Italy.

The problem was that Philby, who could drink and party with the best of them, had for years been a deeply covered KGB agent, one of the later-notorious Cambridge Five, a handful of bright young undergraduates who had been recruited in the mid-1930s by an NKVD illegal (Arnold Deutsch) in London. Each of the five rose to appreciable professional standing and provided the Russians with extremely valuable information over a skein of years.

In Washington after the war, Philby set about eliciting information from his new chums, while other Americans were monitoring and deciphering a stream of radio messages from a KGB resident in New York, known as the Venona intercepts. Philby saw some of the intercepts, and so, as has often been noted, he must have become worried that the Bureau would catch on to him.

Then came an incident which practically everyone who has written about the CIA's early days mentions: a dinner party in January 1951 at Kim Philby's house on Nebraska Avenue that went disastrously wrong and had consequences that shook both the British and the American governments. The story made its public debut in David Martin's *Wilderness of Mirrors*, but all versions are substantially the same, even to the one in Norman Mailer's *Harlot's Ghost*.[10] Kim had invited "twenty-five to thirty" of his closest American associates, including Bob Lamphere and his wife, and "Mickey and Catherine Ladd, Emory and Molly Gregg," all of the FBI. The CIA contingent included the top brass from Clandestine Services; Jim Angleton and his wife, Cicely; and the Harveys.[11]

The party was a disaster, far worse than any host's worst nightmare. First, there was the obvious social split between Bureau and Agency people. Harvey was somewhere in the middle: not, socially, CIA, but no longer FBI. Then, into this tense-but-bibulous group of guests waltzed Guy Burgess, a second secretary at the British embassy, who was bunking with Philby. Burgess had already come to the attention of the American civil authorities because of a flagrant traffic incident in Virginia. He had been spared a driving under the influence citation only because of his diplomatic immunity.

Bob Lamphere:

> Libby Harvey joined us [at the party]. She'd already had a lot to drink and wanted to share her disgust at the entire array of dinner guests and the party itself with anyone who'd listen. Somehow she became my dinner partner, and I spent most of the meal attempting to quiet her. She hated the typically British cold roast beef and loudly said, "Isn't this God-awful!" about every detail of

> food and service. The end of the dinner came none too quickly for me, and as soon thereafter as we could politely manage, the Greggs and my wife and I left the party. We should have stayed. . . .
>
> Burgess got into an insulting debate with Mickey Ladd, which Ladd probably enjoyed. . . . But then Burgess turned to Libby Harvey. He said to her, "How extraordinary to see the face I've been doodling all my life!" She invited him to sketch her portrait. Burgess executed a caricature so lewd and savage that Libby demanded to be taken home immediately.[12]

Burgess's sketch was a vividly obscene cartoon of Libby, dress hiked above her waist, crotch bared. Burgess, very drunk, showed the sketch around. Enraged, Harvey swung at Burgess and missed. The party lurched close to mayhem. Winston MacKinlay Scott, former FBI station chief in Mexico City, now CIA, described the dinner to John Barron, the well-known chronicler of the secret world: "Harvey jumped on Burgess and was choking him with both hands. It took Scott and Philby and one other guest to pull him off."[13] Angleton quickly steered Harvey out the door and walked him around the block. Others took care of the now-hysterical Libby.

It was not just that an international soiree got out of hand. The dinner took place at a time when the CIA started putting agents into denied areas to establish contacts with resistance groups. Agents dropped into the Soviet Union were rolled up or never heard from again. Airborne operations out of Germany and Italy into Albania had gone bad. The parachutists involved were summarily arrested and shot, and a counterintelligence-security investigation, albeit mild by today's standards, was already under way. The quiet suspicion began to arise that perhaps the knowledgeable Philby had been the source of a leak to the Soviets who had then jointly rolled the operations up with their Albanian subordinates. Frank Wisner, at the time the Office of Policy Coordination, or black warfare, chief, continued to send people in, and they continued to be apprehended. Wisner was chummy with Philby.

The Venona intercepts had indicated that a very highly placed British source was working for the Soviets. Gradually, it became apparent that the source was Donald MacLean, the third of the Cambridge Five, a comer in the British Foreign Office who had served in Washington and been privy to high-level policy discussions during and after World War II.

Shortly after the disastrous party, Philby sent Burgess back to London to warn MacLean that the Americans strongly suspected him of treachery. Burgess and MacLean took a night ferry across the English Channel on May 25, 1951. Philby and the MI-5 man in Washington briefed the FBI's Lamphere about the defections. Philby immediately buried his KGB espionage equipment in woods along the Potomac River. Burgess and MacLean did not appear again until they surfaced at a Moscow press conference in 1956.

With a head of steam behind him, Harvey made it is his business to go over Philby's files in the CIA with a thoroughness that, to others, was remarkable, but to the workaholic Harvey, was merely good, solid counterintelligence tradecraft. He pulled together details of Philby's career in prewar Franco Spain and in Turkey during World War II. Harvey pinpointed Philby's dual role using the same analytical techniques he had perfected at the FBI, first in analyzing German intelligence operations, later in the Rote Drei/Rote Kapelle study, then in his backstopping work on the Elizabeth Bentley case.

In June 1951, six months after the dinner party, on the specific order of Gen. Walter Bedell Smith, now DCI, Harvey and, a few days later, Jim Angleton submitted memoranda about their knowledge of Kim Philby. Harvey's memorandum became an indictment. He had no proof, aside from a series of suspicious coincidences that Philby had been here or there at times when things just seemed to go in the Soviets' favor to the detriment of British, and Western, intelligence.[14]

General Smith paraphrased Harvey's memo in a formal letter to his opposite number at MI-6 in London, which all but demanded that King George VI's government not return Philby to his liaison post in Washington. Philby was quietly fired from the Secret Intelligence Service (SIS), but he was never arrested. In 1955 Philby's name became public in the consternation over the Burgess-MacLean-and-the-"Third-Man" affair. In January 1963 Philby got a tip and defected to the Soviet Union from his post in Beirut as a correspondent for the *London Observer*. He was accorded high honor in Moscow and died in exile, still advising the Soviet service on its dealings with the West.

PHILBY: OTHER ACCOUNTS

John Barron thinks Harvey got the last bit of information for his memo of accusation in London. If so, it was Bill's first venture overseas and would have required clearance from General Smith. According to Barron, Harvey established a personal relationship with at least one SIS/MI-6 officer. MI-6 did not have or could not present evidence of Philby's treachery in a court of law. Perhaps, by telling Harvey, the Brits reckoned they might be able to flush Philby out and get enough to prosecute.

> Barron:
>
> Bill was drinking with an MI-6 officer in London. The Brit said, "I know what you're after, and I'll tell you now." The British officer gave Harvey "the final bit of evidence he needed." Bill flew back to Washington the next day. On a Sunday morning, he met with General Smith, who sent a cable to the head of MI-6 indicating Philby was no longer welcome in the United States. . . .
>
> The epilogue to that story came a bit later during a party the MI-6 station chief in Berlin gave. Everyone had a lot to drink. The MI-6 man turned to Bill during a speech and said, "I respect you as a professional intelligence officer, but as a man, I hate your guts."
>
> The next day, the Brit called Harvey to apologize. Bill gracefully accepted the apology: "That's quite all right. We both had too much to drink. . . . I stake my reputation on a prophecy that you will come to me one day and say Kim Philby was one of them."[15]

The Brit was Peter Lunn, Harvey's opposite number in Berlin, who worked closely with him on the Berlin Tunnel, as we shall see. Harvey and Lunn became close friends, as later attested by Lunn himself. Barron: "Years later, when Bill was stationed in Rome, he was invited to a Swiss Alpine village ski resort where the Brit's daughter was being married. . . . When Bill alighted from the train, Peter Lunn said to Bill, 'You were right. Philby was one of them.'"

Philby's KGB-authorized book, *My Silent War*, dealt thus with Harvey:

> Apart from Angleton, my chief OSO contact was a man I shall refer to here as William J. Howard. He was a former FBI man whom Hoover had sacked for drunkenness on duty. The first time he dined at my house, he showed that his habits had remained unchanged. He fell asleep over the coffee and sat snoring gently until midnight when his wife took him away, saying: "Come, now, Daddy, it's time you were in bed." I may be accused here of introducing a cheap note. Admitted. But, as will be seen later, Howard was to play a very cheap trick on me, and I do not like letting provocation go unpunished. Having admitted the charge of strong anti-Howard prejudice, it is only fair that I should add that he cooperated well with SIS in the construction of the famous Berlin Tunnel. . . .
>
> I learnt later that the letter [from General Smith, indicating the CIA's suspicions of Philby] had been drafted in great part by

> William J. Howard, whose wife Burgess had bitterly insulted during a convivial party at my house. I had apologized handsomely for [Burgess's] behavior, and the apology had apparently been accepted. It was therefore difficult to understand Howard's retrospective exercise in spite. From Howard, of all people![16]

Philby seems to have still been smarting at having been undone by a flatfoot from the American Midwest. Why he chose to use a thinly veiled pseudonym for Harvey is a riddle, though he may have been worried about a libel suit.

The Philby affair had shattering repercussions within the CIA. It is highly probable that Angleton's overriding future preoccupation with "the Mole" inside CIA—a preoccupation that disrupted the Agency for years and that led to the unconscionable persecution of one officer, S. Peter Karlow,[17] and the horrible, long-term confinement of a KGB defector—stemmed from Angleton's own abiding guilt about the amount of information he had passed to Philby during their frequent drinking sessions.

Adam Horton, who worked under Harvey in Berlin and later served under Angleton for many years, says: "Kim played Jim like an organ. JJA got Philby a pass which meant Philby could move freely through the buildings. JJA gave Philby everything, including the Albanian agents.

"Harvey? He had strong personal feelings about Philby. The dinner was only the tip of the iceberg. Harvey moved heaven and earth to get Philby."[18]

Dennis Flinn also adds some detail: "I had met Philby in London in January 1945, and I had some suspicions as early as 1947. Bill and I had some talk about our 'good friend.' . . . Philby was a troubled personality. It was very difficult to carry on a conversation with him because he stammered so badly. I told Bill at that time that I would be very careful if I were dealing with Philby.

"During that period, after I left the FBI, I used to stop into Mickey Ladd's house. Ladd led a peculiar life: he'd work at the office till 9:00, come home; his wife would give him dinner, then friends would drop by till around 2:00 AM . . . ex-FBI friends, including Bill Harvey. Mickey existed on three, maybe four hours of sleep a night." At these bull sessions, working-level Bureau and Agency officers exchanged information—as well as juicy gossip—informally.

Flinn continues:

> Philby didn't live very far away . . . on Nebraska Avenue . . . and

> sometimes he came and joined in the open discussions. And Harvey was there.
>
> I went to Ladd privately, and said, 'Mickey, it's not right. You're all talking about FBI internal affairs here, with Philby present. I'd like you to consider desisting.' Mickey answered that Philby was 'a friend of ours.' . . . I have some suspicions. Others also raised the issue with Mickey Ladd.
>
> At that time, Burgess and MacLean were in the British embassy in Washington. I had met Burgess in Portugal once, when he was passing through on his way to or from the United States. I didn't think much of him, either.
>
> In 1952, when I was in Washington again, before being transferred to Australia, Bill told me he had been influential in getting Philby kicked out. I didn't ask the details, but I knew he had dealt with Bedell Smith. I guess that Bedell—with whom I also had some dealings, and I knew how he worked—that Bedell took something in writing from Bill, or maybe a personal presentation, and said that Philby had to go.
>
> I always understood Bill Harvey was the first to blow the horn on Philby. It was not part of a broad program of investigation. Bill Harvey, whatever else he may have been. . . . He was the one on Philby.[19]

More than his work on the Bentley case, Bill's dogged sifting of active and dormant files to produce a convincing pattern of betrayal made a considerable impact on his colleagues. The Philby case marked Bill Harvey as a comer, a tough player to be reckoned with in the future, and it gave him ready access to the top level of CIA—then General Smith, soon to be Allen Dulles. Perhaps he also refined his nocturnal habits, his ability to work on limited sleep, from Mickey Ladd's example.

HARVEY AND ANGLETON

When Harvey moved from Staff C to Berlin, he left a vacuum in the counterintelligence element of CIA. Soon after Harvey's departure, Jim Angleton was appointed head of the counterintelligence staff. Angleton wielded far more power than the job called for over many years. According to Sam Papich, the FBI liaison officer, Angleton enjoyed Dick Helms's complete confidence and, as a result, was the one Helms turned to for special assignments.[20] Angleton also held a special, watching brief over Italian operations, and Italy also plays a subsequent role in the Harvey legend.

David Martin in *Wilderness of Mirrors* makes much of the rivalry between Angleton and Harvey and underlines the contrasts between the two: heartlander vs. gentle expatriate birth, cop vs. intelligence careerist, gun collector vs. fisherman who made his own lures. Most telling, Angleton was a Yalie who fitted into the OSS mold, whereas, of course, Harvey was from a state-run university out there beyond the Hudson River.

Certainly the two clashed at times, but each was an emperor in his own bailiwick. They saw to it that they seldom encroached on each other's turf. And, at the end, just before Bill Harvey died, they shared knowledge of a matter that to this day remains a mystery.

John Barron sums up: "There was no real animosity between the two of them, Harvey and Angleton. It all just goes back to Philby. Angleton was crazy in a sinister way. He never recovered from the Philby affair."

4

BAPTISM IN BERLIN

My first recollection of Bill Harvey is of an evening cocktail-cum-dinner buffet at the end of 1952 given by the outgoing chief of the Berlin Operations Base (BOB), Lester Houck, a transmuted Office of Strategic Services (OSS) type who had served in Italy during World War II and was later in charge of Agency operations in Africa. The evening was surprisingly balmy, and BOB officers bunched around the swimming pool of the chief's luxurious villa at Lepsius Strasse 16 in the posh suburb of Zehlendorf, scrutinizing a radically mismatched pair. Houck, perhaps six feet four inches tall, cadaverous, sallow, a gaunt, recovering academic, shuffled along in his gangling way, pushing forward a man who needed no propulsion, a guy who looked totally out of place, Bill Harvey. Harvey was conventionally dressed, perhaps even still in FBI gabardine. He had thinning, silvery-blond hair and a pencil-line mustache. He looked somewhat shorter than his six feet because of his shape—which made us gasp under our accustomed nonchalance—round in the middle, but really round, like the halves of two avocados glued together. About the only thing that united the two bosses was their addiction to nicotine, but Houck's habit was more advanced.

Harvey did not fit the BOB swashbuckler mold in which many of us felt we were cast. He was dowdy where we were dashing. He was solid midwestern, with what today might be called old-fashioned values. We were sophisticates who relished being part of Berlin, which had been in the 1920s, and was now once again, far naughtier than Paris.

We downed our generously poured drinks and nibbled Army-issue canapés. We eyed Harvey's ungainly figure skeptically as he circled the eerily lit pool, grasped each of us firmly by the hand, and took our measure in an instant of deep eye contact. In those first moments, we, as so many others, vastly underestimated Bill Harvey. We had no inkling of the surging quality of the man, nor how he would affect our lives, let alone the impact he would have on CIA. Nor did we have a clue about the plans Harvey had for the base, much less that he was in Berlin to mastermind a huge and most-delicate operation, the Berlin Tunnel.

The nuts and bolts of BOB's late 1940s, early 1950s operations were reams and reams of railway documents, clandestinely photographed in the East, which we passed on to economic and military analysts. The case officers who concentrated on political matters were more often frustrated than not: it was extraordinarily difficult to suborn anyone in the East German government or Community Party offices, let alone in Warsaw or Prague. But occasionally our people were able to recruit someone who had access to political information, which was, of course, the most prized intelligence of all.

We routinely gathered clothing, all sorts of documents, and other very ordinary materials from refugees, for shipment to the CIA's techies who refitted them for use by agents going back into various denied areas. We also had a standing requirement to gather cans and boxes (with their contents) from the East, to be made into concealment devices. Everyone knew there was a $25,000 reward (later increased to $50,000) for any pilot who brought over one of the new MiG 17 (later, MiG 19) fighters.

But we felt that a surge of incoming, nit-picking administrative types was corrupting the trust the CIA had previously placed in us. While we once had casually endowed agents with bottles of Rémy Martin, brown paper bags of bean coffee (a very highly prized item in both East and West Germany in those days), and very occasionally, a carton of American cigarettes (too incriminating to be handed out often), now we had to force our border crossers to sign receipts.

Harvey's arrival in Berlin was symptomatic, too, of a sea change in personnel within the CIA itself. With the Korean War in June 1950, the administration's demand for intelligence (and political warfare) increased exponentially. The CIA broadened its base of recruitment. People with degrees from Illinois and Tennessee, even California, began to appear in Berlin. The glamour-draped Main Line–New York–New England figures who had made their reputations with feats of derring-do during World War II knew they would soon be outnumbered.

Symbolically, Harvey, the ex-Bureau midwesterner, had maneuvered himself into the CIA's choicest overseas assignment. Berlin, though isolated, was tested, tough, and proud. Berlin and Harvey were made for each other. Neither was subtle nor smarmy. That Harvey got BOB at all is a comment on the expansion of the Agency. Once he had it, he needed to reshape the base in his image.

Harvey was canny enough to know that he had to win the core officers of BOB pretty much on their terms, at least until they disappeared by attrition. Despite the force of his personality, Harvey could not easily revamp BOB. His supply of time was not inexhaustible, and he was already working twenty-hour days. Still, he succeeded. And over time Berlin gave Harvey stature as an innovative and daring intelligence operator and as an executive, albeit an unconventional one out on the cutting edge. Berlin was the place to be.

Tom Polgar, who during the early 1950s, was Gen. Lucian K. Truscott's personal assistant in Frankfurt, recalls how Bill got to the outpost: "From November 1947 through January 1948, Harvey and I shared a office in Temp L Building along the Reflecting Pool [perhaps the same office Adam Horton's friend claimed to have observed that dusky evening]. . . . I saw Harvey again, when I was back in headquarters on a couple of occasions. . . . After one memorable cocktail reception, Harvey offered to drive me back to the Hay Adams hotel." He wanted to pick Polgar's nimble brain. "It was clear to him that he was at a disadvantage. The leaders of the Clandestine Service . . . had all been abroad. They had different social backgrounds from his. . . . He had to seek an overseas assignment." But where?

"There were two concrete opportunities: chief of base, Berlin, and chief, Austria. Which would I recommend? I said Berlin was the greater managerial challenge, and he would be dealing with the U.S. military, where his FBI background would carry great prestige. . . . Furthermore, I explained, in Vienna, the chief was physically separated from the bulk of the operational personnel, who were under Bill Hood.

"Hood was Allen Dulles's favorite, Helms's favorite, and he had continuity and control of the base. Bill Hood wouldn't give you the time of day. And you probably wouldn't get along very well with the ambassador, either!"[1]

Tom's advice was sound, but it's also probable that Harvey was mining the well-clued-in Polgar for information, while in no way revealing that he was already knee-deep in tunnel planning. It would have been a very typical Harvey ploy.

OUTPOST BERLIN

West Berlin in 1952 was truly an island, ringed by more than twenty divisions of the Red Army. Not only was BOB well behind enemy lines, it was less than fifty miles from Soviet-dominated Poland, through which the rest of the Red Army could sweep at a moment's notice. In this isolation, our horizons shrank. But all was not gloom and despondency. We were the occupiers, and we were spoiled. A case of Beck's Best Bremen Bier cost $1.20. A bottle of Cutty Sark was $1.35 at the Army's Class VI liquor emporium. Chesterfields cost $1.00 a carton. We lived in requisitioned housing—the Army had taken care to seize the best, especially if it belonged to Nazis—and we were fattened by stocky housekeepers.

Going to an excellent restaurant run by the French military in the northern borough of Frohnau entailed weeks of excited advance planning, even though it was only forty-five minutes away by car, zigzagging to avoid crossing Russian-controlled territory. One could drive east to west within the Western sectors in about half an hour. Every once in a while, the Russians dourly shut down the city's lifeline, the Autobahn, from the west on the excuse that vital repairs had to be made. Each time they did so, the U.S. Army got very tense.

The Western sector's most popular political cabaret performed in a black-painted, bare-bones nightclub called Die Insulaner (The Islanders). The troupe was made up of ribald, sharp-tongued young iconoclasts, whose show was broadcast into East Germany by the official American radio station, Radio in the American Sector (RIAS). Die Insulaner was heavily patronized by off-duty BOBers, one of whom the players insouciantly named Der Gami (the Germanized American). Maybe we helped to inspire the troupe's irreverence, or maybe it gave us attitude. We shared with them a comradely bond of bawdy skepticism. Subsequent writers cottoned to Berlin and its frontline aura; some, notably Norman Mailer and Robert Littell, even co-opted Bill Harvey as a central character in their fiction.

Berlin's only rival at the time was Bill Hood's Vienna. In Vienna, things were always earnest but never serious, and there was always that mellow soupçon of "*Schlampigkeit*," one of those German words that is impossible to translate but, very roughly, means "easy come, easy go." Vienna was the soft underbelly of Cold War confrontation, which only occasionally constricted and rumbled.

There was unspoken rivalry between the two cities and their base chiefs. But when Austria's occupation was lifted and the Four Power status of Vienna disappeared, Berlin became even more where the action was. In no other place was the Cold War fought as deviously and as intensely, nor did the CIA have a better training ground for its comers. All this, of course, was in the days when intelligence was primarily gathered by humans rather than by electrons.

A SHORT HISTORY OF BOB

When I arrived in November 1951, West Berlin was still gaunt and haggard, yet with the airlift in 1948 and 1949 it had begun to flourish a gutsy, near-tangible spirit as a taunt to the much drabber, even-worse-battered East. Peter M. F. Sichel, one of the outstanding intelligence officers of his time, tweedy but debonair, impatient, demanding but kind, was chief of base. He recalls, "Right after the war, Allen Dulles went home and Dick Helms left before Christmas 1945," after only two months as chief, leaving the base in the temporary charge of Sichel, who yielded to Dana Durant only to become chief in his own right in 1948. Sichel was twenty-seven years old at the time; this says a lot about the fledgling, brash CIA. Sichel was sniped at for his youth, and he also rankled Army Intelligence, which still considered OSS/CIA an upstart, amateur bunch of East Coast effete. In mid-1952, Peter Sichel was transferred back to headquarters.[2]

It was quietly decided that, pending Harvey's arrival, Lester Houck, PhD, GS-15 (a ranking rare in those days), should go to Berlin to hold the fort. Contrary to gossip at the time, Houck was not pushed out after only six months; Harvey's assignment to Berlin was decided before Houck arrived in Berlin.

When Bill got to BOB in December 1952, he walked into Sichel's exotic gentlemen's club of hardworking, hard-playing, experienced freebooters and at-times-untethered intellects. In early postwar BOB, compartmentalization was very, very tight; there were no overlapping operations, no admin sections, and no section chiefs. Everyone talked directly to the chief, if, that is, you could get through his primary guardian, his devoted secretary, Maggie Crane.

Harvey was clear in his own mind that the old order had to change, but making the changes was no easy task. The restructuring of BOB for the enduring Cold War was not congenial to the seniors who had produced solid intelligence for years, yet one never heard a derogatory word about Harvey from any of the veterans. They may have smiled privately at some of Harvey's quirks, but as they came to know him, they liked and respected him, even if they came from different worlds.

The men at the medium operating level were another story. They were younger, had been recruited by Peter Sichel, and they shared a particular emotional bond: they had been through the Berlin Airlift of 1948–49 together. During the blockade, when every piece of coal counted, the CIA's adventurous officers learned much about survival, courage, and humor in adversity from the city's people. The Berliners looked upon the Americans as saviors. That emotional link could never be broken.

When Sichel left, his crew stayed on, but the esprit that kept them going in the thin years dissipated. They were not sorry when their tours ended. Times had changed.

In 1954 Harvey told his new Soviet ops chief (and deputy chief of base), Dave Murphy, that the "wartime aura of OSS clung to BOB" and that Peter Sichel still kept "an eye on his old domain." Harvey had to cleanse BOB of its past. He recognized that the esprit de corps encouraged by Sichel was effective, and so, at first, he did not seek to destroy it but rather to co-opt it and remold it in his own image—at least at first. As he seeded BOB with his own choices, the days of the Cold War follies dwindled, then disappeared.

One important aspect of Berlin never changed: BOB was cutting edge, the Learning School. Beginning in May 1945, intelligence became target-of-opportunity work. Then, slowly, what is today called the intelligence community began to put together lists—called essential elements of information by the Army—of what the U.S. government had to know to assess the threat of hostile action or war. Deciding how to cover the assigned targets was BOB's job, although the base's work was, of course, always under the gaze of Washington. At that time junior case officers did not learn their trade from a manual or Farm in Virginia. The streets of Berlin were our campus. With Harvey's hard-charging innovations and improvisations, BOB became by far the most productive CIA establishment in the world.

THE BOBers

No one has tried, in any of the books I have seen, to re-create the flavor of the Berlin Operations Base that Harvey took over. The case officers there at the time made up a remarkable gaggle of people.

One of my favorites was a marvelous, kind, funny guy who had gone to Northwestern University on a football scholarship, but whose passion was Shakespeare. It became apparent he was not suited for the clandestine life when he failed to grasp that he could not send an attachment—I think it was a Polish Air Force uniform—to a cable. His boss was another kind, gentle man who had been born in the old country and whose heart was constantly wrenched. He dispatched agents who could, literally, walk past members of his own family, but he could do nothing to bring his kin out from behind the iron curtain.

We had a former Royal Air Force pilot, an American who had adopted British ways and often seemed to be cruising at an ominously low altitude. When communications across the border between East Germany and Czechoslovakia shut down at one stage, he quite seriously suggested sending messages by crossbow. He also wanted the CIA to establish its own speedboat navy to zoom through Berlin's lakes and canals and thus infiltrate the East. He was the case officer who crashed his car against a stout tree and woke up in the hospital to see Harvey peering at him. Harvey asked his wounded officer what he wanted. "A promotion," quoth the Royal Air Force man. He got it.

We had a lawyer, a married senior case officer whose roving eye landed too often on female agents, dalliance with whom was strictly forbidden. Then there was the former FBI special agent, also a lawyer, who, after a night's carousing, took a wrong turn and found himself in East Berlin. Crossing the border was strictly against BOB rules. Sitting in his Volkswagen, he tried to eat his false identification, found it inedible, made a run for the sector border, and arrived safely back in the West. He confessed his erratic ways to Harvey, was read the A Team riot act, and was grounded for some considerable time. That guy was also part of a movable poker game that was rumored to shift cities and countries as its members circulated through the Agency.

There was a former lieutenant colonel in the Women's Army Corps of World War II who acted as informal den mother to the young ladies sent up to serve our secretarial needs, a tough-but-sweet, no-nonsense custodian of much touchy information. She was married to one of our best senior case officers, who affected an FDR-style cigarette holder and produced priceless intelligence on the East German railway system. The ex-lieutenant colonel outranked CG Follick when she later appeared on the scene; CG had made only major. We noticed a certain chill between them.

Another of our seniors was quiet, unassuming, even shy. He had been an OSS Jedburgh, part of a special program of officers trained to drop into France ahead of the D-Day forces. But you never would have known it by looking at him. Another was a prewar member of the leadership of the German Socialist Party youth movement and a double PhD in chemistry and mathematics.

Taken together, the Old Guard at BOB was a remarkable collection of intrepid, colorful people, not all of whom fit into Harvey's scheme of things.

THAT NICKNAME

Practically everyone who has written about Harvey notes that he was called "the Pear," and most think the nickname was intentionally derogatory. It wasn't. Rather, it was coined in the almost-boyish, skeptically scoffing vein with which we discussed almost everything in those days.

One afternoon, BOB's two exuberant young reports officers returned from a bistro in central Berlin where the *soupe a l'ognion* was justifiably renowned and the Beaujolais flowed gently. As we regained BOB's terra firma, we glanced down the long hall and zeroed in on an unforgettable silhouette. One of us whispered, "Ohmigod, he looks like a pear!" We both tried to stifle our laughter as we slunk to our desks. From that modest beginning, "the Pear" became part of CIA legend.

Sam Papich swears that when Harvey left the Bureau for CIA in 1947, he was a mere hundred and fifty pounds. But by the time he hit Berlin, Bill must have weighed over two hundred, most of it distributed amidships. Why he was never dubbed "the Penguin" defies explanation, except that Harvey did not waddle; he tacked, especially around corners, and even more so after the requisite intake of martinis.

It's probable also that Harvey's habit of laying nicknames on everyone he met or dealt with stems from the BOB penchant, which was part fun, part doubletalk to conceal true identities.

THE BASE, JUNE 16–17, 1953

The three-story Berlin base that Harvey took over was hidden, well back from a main avenue, in the very upscale residential suburb of Dahlem. The Berliners had changed the boulevard's name from Kronprinzen Allee to Clay Allee in gratitude for American steadfastness during the Berlin Airlift. In many ways, the villa, once the property of the legendary Gen. Ludwig von Beck, who was executed for his leading role in the plot to assassinate Hitler in 1944, was an islet unto itself within the surround of West Berlin.

Since midday on June 16, 1953, the building on the obscure dead-end street had been at a high state of alert, while we tried to track what was happening in East Berlin and East Germany as unexpected, and, at first, inestimable, forces let loose their long-throttled rage against their Communist overlords. By that evening we were aware that something major was brewing across the sector and zonal borders. BOB surged into Wednesday, June 17, not knowing what the day might bring. By nightfall there could have been open rebellion against the communists, a tricky matter because, although the workers aimed their wrath at the East German government, its guarantor was the Red Army. We, indeed all of Western intelligence, were caught flat-footed. Tom Polgar remembers that day "vividly. General Truscott [CIA chief of mission], Assistant Chief Mike Burke, and I were in Nuremberg to discuss cross-border operations. [We] traveled back to Frankfurt late PM by train which stopped in Wuerzburg.

There I heard loud shouting and noticed commotion on platform. They were selling extra editions of the local paper, already reporting on Berlin events. That is how Truscott first heard about it."[3]

During the night and on into June 17, BOB's case officers were out in the streets in full force, questioning people, listening to conversations, sending agents over to observe, and then racing back to base to add their snippets to the picture we were building. One case officer, David Chavchavadze recalls, "I went up to Potsdamer Platz and was actually under fire by several tanks. I think they were blanks. I remember hitting the dirt and ruining my sports coat."[4]

Those agents who could come over from the East called in, in varying degrees of excitement. They were told not to reestablish contact with BOB until the dust settled. The Goon Squad—the base's footpads, drop servicers, hustlers, and odd jobbers—were over in the East, picking up whatever they could by mingling with the angry crowds.

Harvey sent Bob Kilroy off to spend the day at the Army war room. I hunkered in the office, churning out hourly "sitreps," bulletins with the latest information on the situation, which, because they had to be encoded and decoded, probably did not beat the wire services.

We had been sternly advised that the director of central intelligence (DCI), Allen Dulles, was at the White House passing our material directly to President Dwight Eisenhower. We were further advised that General Eisenhower would not read anything longer than one page; the advice brought knowing smirks to our faces.

Kilroy returned from the American Mission headquarters on Clay Allee at midnight on June 17 to a find a base meeting in full swing; the meeting went on until nearly three in the morning.

Chavchavadze: "The counter-intelligence guys had hatched a theory that the whole show was a provocation by the Soviets—'a plot to show how democratic they are.' I replied, 'I don't think any communist anywhere would ever stage a labor strike against himself!' I still remember Bill's deep bass voice saying, 'I'll buy that, Dave.' Bill never addressed a sentence to anybody without putting the person's name at the end of it."[5]

The question at that late-night conference was, what advice do we give Washington? The decision, after three hours, was that we could do little except follow the counsel we had given to our agents: lie low, stay watchful, and hope for the best.

HARVEY STEPS OUT OF LINE

By now, the Soviets had rolled their tanks into East Berlin. It was years before Budapest in 1956 or Prague in 1968. This was the first time ever, anywhere, that a Communist regime was boldly challenged by unarmed civilians. There was no question that the Soviets would defend their fiefdom against rebellion by the workers whose cause they so vocally trumpeted.

At about four o'clock on the morning of June 17, Harvey dictated to me, off the top of his head, a dramatic recommendation. I recall looking at him and asking, "You sure you want to say that?" He nodded emphatically. "Put it in words and let me look at it!" I banged out a draft, which he revised considerably.

In a lengthy cable (four pages, if I remember correctly), which bore the highest classification indicators, Harvey urged Allen Dulles, and through him, Secretary of State John Foster Dulles and, indeed, President Eisenhower, to make some plausible military gesture that would give the Soviets pause to think before the Red Army clanked further over the hapless East Germans. Bill suggested symbolic mobilization of the Sixth Infantry Regiment, the token garrison force in Berlin, on sector and zonal borders. He urged that American forces in West Germany, particularly the Eighty-second Airborne Division, be demonstratively put on combat alert and moved up to the iron curtain.

Harvey also bluntly told Washington something the policymakers did not want to hear: the East Germans would not have risen against their oppressors without open and covert U.S. support—specifically, the cries for liberation periodically issued by John Foster Dulles and transmitted over RIAS and the activities of our own "cousins"—the Office of Policy Coordination (OPC; later, PP), the psychological warriors who stirred up dissent in the East. The United States should, Harvey said, stand up to its responsibilities, even if it meant risking a showdown with the Russians.

In his fascinating biography of Allen Dulles, Peter Grose reports a garbled version of Harvey's bellicose initiative: "Reports of the rampage poured into the CIA base in West Berlin, headed by the OSS veteran Henry Hecksher, a man of imagination and aggressiveness in the kind of 'monkey business' that attracted Allen. . . . Hecksher drafted a cable to Washington reporting the mounting unrest and predicting a prompt and bloody Soviet reaction. He proposed that his networks start smuggling firearms to the East Berlin insurgents. Hecksher's cable arrived late Tuesday evening, June 16." The suggestion was knocked down by various lords of headquarters, backed up by Frank Wisner in Allen Dulles's temporary absence.

Dulles was back in his office the morning of June 17. "'It was the only time that I saw Allen angry and disappointed in me,' a senior officer remembered. A flash point for paramilitary covert action had come—and gone. The CIA has held back."[6]

Henry Heckshet, who gained notoriety as a case officer in Guatemala, had left BOB by June 1953. The chief of base, and very much in charge, was Bill Harvey. I suspect Grose's account is a garble of the cable I drafted for Harvey.

When Washington flatly rejected his plan, Harvey privately loosed limitless contempt for the pussy-footing cold warriors in Washington, who talked big but chilled when the chips were down, and for the brothers, Allen Welsh and John Foster Dulles.

With his June 17 cable, Harvey defied the CIA's standing dictum to stay out of policymaking. He was the FBI rebel at a higher level, and his cable marked him as a crusader—in some minds, as a loose cannon.

I think that Bill received an unofficial reprimand from Allen Dulles or perhaps from his number two, Frank Wisner, the head of Clandestine Services. But Harvey was unrepentant. Herb Natzke, a future chief of BOB, commented years later: "Something like that wouldn't bother him at all, even though he was way out of his own line of command and competence. . . . He was motivated. Very, very anti-Communist . . . and very patriotic."[7]

MANAGEMENT STYLE

Harvey could, if so inclined, be one of the most charming, considerate, and compassionate men in the CIA. It's a side of Harvey his critics never saw. Harvey unapologetically rode roughshod into what had been a gentlemen's club. Initially, he lacked sensitivity to the throbbing organism that was West Berlin and with which the airlift-era BOBers so deeply identified. For them, Berlin itself was a cause. For Harvey, Berlin was at first—but not later—a chessboard.

Right from the start, at the end of 1952, Harvey needed to remodel BOB in his image, into a many-faceted series of lances into Soviet Communism's engulfing empire. Upon arriving, he began questioning everyone, sketching the new, Harvey-look base in his mind. Then, he started to act.

Sichel had held staff meetings on Mondays at nine in the largest room in the building, the Reports Office, and had insisted everyone get out of bed to attend, regardless whether they had been working all night or carousing. He tolerated no excuses. Under Harvey, section chiefs crammed into his office early on Monday mornings. Once, three of the Old Guard showed up looking the worse for wear. In response to Harvey's biting sarcasm, Adam Horton exploded, "For Chrissakes, Bill! We work from seven at night until two or three in the morning! How about having these meetings at eleven or twelve?"[8] Neither Horton nor many of the others assembled then knew that Harvey consistently outdid their own hours. Bill had little sympathy for people who couldn't grind for eighteen hours a day or more.

The reformation of BOB took all the considerable wiles and personal charm Harvey could muster. As boss, he made it clear that while he encouraged our breezy informality, he expected us to play by his rules. Then, being Harvey, he proceeded to show us how to evade as many regulations as we needed to break.

THE SICHEL FACTOR

The person who most symbolized the strain of opposition to Harvey was Peter Sichel, whose emotional roots in Berlin go back to July 1945. Today, Peter diplomatically denies that he and Bill tangled.

Sichel briefed Harvey in Washington before Bill went to Berlin to take up his post. "I fully agree that Bill deserves to get credit for what he contributed to the common weal, which was plenty. I was head of EE [Eastern European] ops in Washington before [Harvey] went to Berlin and worked with him to get approval for the Berlin Tunnel. Though I had my reservations about his love of guns and gin, I had great respect for his ability and single-minded devotion to the cause.

"His alcoholism or gun toting never influenced his performance, nor his ability to run a base, or to get loyal support from his people. He also invited me to visit him in Berlin, when I was chief in Hong Kong."[9]

No Sichel loyalist is more outspoken than Adam Horton, the West Pointer who exploded at that staff meeting. Almost everything about Bill, starting with his appearance, rubbed Adam the wrong way.

> Bill was very fond of people who fawned. . . . I suppose he didn't like me because I was clearly—at least as far as he was concerned—akin to an East Coast Pinko. Also, he could not bear anyone who laughed at him.
>
> I was duty officer one night when he came in after a trip to Frankfurt. He had a large, suitcase-shaped briefcase, which he unlocked, and he took out six or so pistols, all fully loaded. He unloaded them there in the office. That was bad enough, but when he dumped on the desk some six more from various pockets, shoulder holsters, and the like, I burst out laughing, which he took very

> ill indeed. I asked him if he had been expecting some special trouble on the trip, and he said, no, that what I saw were his usual precautions! . . .
>
> Bill was not intellectually curious. I don't recall ever having seen him read a book or mention one. . . . At staff meetings, I cannot recall him ever coming up with an original idea.
>
> I was one of Peter's boys: this led Bill to think, probably correctly, that none of the old crowd thought much of him. . . . As a control freak, this bothered him.[10]

Horton wrote these words nearly fifty years after the two CIA officers parted company. They are indicative of the kind of dislike Harvey could provoke in those who disagreed with him, whatever the cause.

When Horton became chief of Polish operations, he ran into immediate turbulence from new subordinates, one of whom, according to Adam, searched his desk drawer, looking for evidence to damn Adam in the eyes of the boss. "They were incensed that all our Polish operations had been compromised by the UB [the Polish intelligence service]. I spent the rest of my time starting all over again."

The man who took over Polish ops was Ted Shackley.

POPOV

BOB under Harvey had its successes—many of them, in fact—in many fields of espionage, including scientific and technical intelligence, some political reporting, satellite operations, and economic information. But it also had a number of disappointments and some disasters, as is inevitable in the gathering of secret intelligence in hostile areas.

David E. Murphy, Bill Harvey's deputy from 1954 until he took over BOB in his own right, was one of very few people who were cut in on the Popov case, one of the Agency's most productive operations. Popov was a Red Army major—a Vienna walk-in penetration of the Soviet Army Intelligence Service (GRU)—who fascinated and absorbed an inner core of the CIA for several years in the early to mid-1950s. Popov required deft and agile handling by the senior case officer assigned, George Kisevalter.[11] After reporting extremely useful intelligence in Vienna for a time, Major Popov was reassigned in the Soviet Union. Perhaps he had been discovered; the case seemed to have been closed. Suddenly, Popov made contact with a member of the British Military Mission in East Germany, and the case revived. There are several versions of how it ended.

John Barron, the noted author of two comprehensive books on the

KGB, was a U.S. Navy lieutenant in Berlin at the time and came to know Bill Harvey well. Barron says, "Harvey blamed himself for the blowing and execution of Popov. Bill . . . foresaw and feared what actually happened." He took the arrest and execution of Popov, a disarmingly gallant officer who had risen from peasant roots, as a personal failing on his part for trusting headquarters.[12] It was the kind of episode that refueled Harvey's already deep distrust of Washington, a distrust that influenced much that he did thereafter and, in the end, contributed to his downfall.

HARVEY AND THE PSYWARRIORS

In Berlin, as in Washington, there was in the 1950s a self-reinforcing barrier between the two sides of CIA's Clandestine Services, which even shared field experience against a common opponent did not overcome.

Once in control of BOB, Harvey was absolutely determined to keep the cold warriors at arms length for several reasons. According to CG Follick Harvey, who had worked for the political and psychological (PP) chief in Frankfurt for a while, Bill had contempt for the political warfare people because, among other things, they bought Deutsche marks in Switzerland at a very favorable rate and sold them in Germany. The transactions were allegedly for operational use, but in fact, CG said, PP people "from the boss on down" had Swiss bank accounts and deposited proceeds of the black marketing to their own benefit. "Bill lived and breathed operations, and when these guys were stealing money from their operations, it really turned him off."[13]

Our psywar cousins were based out at Berlin's main civilian-cum-military airport. When the PP/OPC section chief phoned, Harvey would glance up from his desk with a theatrical sigh, "OK, Gerry, what is it this time?" If he absolutely had to see the chief of base, Gerry made the crosstown pilgrimage to see Bill, not vice versa.

OPC ran psywar operations into East Germany; this seemed flamboyant and risky to us. The cousins' agents were all-too-often rolled up, en masse, by the East German Staatssicherheitsdienst (later called the Stasi); they were even kidnapped from West Berlin. Our counterespionage (CE) officers and the footpads of the Goon Squad were regularly deployed to clean up the security flaps created by PP's showy capers.[14]

The psywarriors' thinking was exemplified for me during the Foreign Ministers Conference in Berlin in February 1954. Secretary of State John Foster Dulles had in tow C. D. Jackson, a former Time-Life executive who was President Eisenhower's political warfare adviser. At one high-powered briefing, when things did not seem to be going well for the Western Allies,

Jackson turned to Harvey and said, "Hey, how about organizing a demonstration outside the Soviet embassy in East Berlin, to show them the people aren't behind them?" Harvey was civil as he explained to the president's emissary that it was impossible to whistle up a few thousand people who would be willing to protest in a snowy street under the gaze of the Red Army and East German military and security. Jackson was not in the slightest concerned that people would be arrested, imprisoned, perhaps even sentenced to death, if his scheme were implemented.

Harvey had few friends among the psywar people. Tom Parrott was chief of base in Frankfurt, and had aspired to Berlin; instead, he became deputy to General Truscott's successor, John Bross. He gained a window into Harvey's thinking by reading correspondence flowing among Harvey, Truscott/Bross, Wisner/Helms, and Dulles.

A few years later, in 1962, Parrott was secretary of the Special Group Augmented, the Kennedy brothers' interagency board that sat on clandestine efforts to topple, even to assassinate, Fidel Castro. He was one of several sources for David Martin. More than forty years later Tom Parrott says, "Oh, I got along with Bill all right," and indeed, he expresses compassion for what befell Bill at the crux of his CIA career in October 1962.[15] But during the 1950s in Germany, Stan Gaines, a senior foreign intelligence operations officer in Frankfurt who was highly sympathetic to Harvey, comments succinctly, "Parrott was envious of Bill. He thought he was as big as Bill."[16]

The case officers at BOB watched Harvey carefully, at first with snickering amusement, then with growing respect, especially during the taut days of the uprising. Bill, in turn, learned under pressure that he could trust people he still did not yet entirely understand. After June 1953 BOB was a cohesive, smoothly functioning unit, one that would have been called "professional" before that word became synonymous with "mediocre." I know of no one in those years, with the exception of those who had deep personal reservations, who could seriously fault Bill on his performance.

BOB officers niggled that Harvey sat on dispatches too long; he was always in a hurry, brusque, and he seemed at times almost indifferent to our concerns. When one of us went in to see him, we were as brief as possible; Harvey rarely said so, but we knew we were poaching on time he needed for other matters. If Bill realized a message was important, he dealt with it as speedily as he could; any serious muttering in the ranks could lead to suspicions and perhaps even to subtle nosing around by subordinates who knew all the devious tricks, and Harvey wanted knowledge of his other major activity severely limited.

It may seem odd, but the intensity with which BOB worked was such that little thought was ever given to what might happen if the superpowers lurched toward hostilities. Two crises illustrate the mood of the base under pressure: In October 1956, at the time of the Hungarian uprising, John Barron offered the U.S. Navy's C-47 to evacuate CIA wives from Berlin. None of them accepted the invitation.[17] Later, as tension rose around Krushchev's Berlin ultimatum, at Thanksgiving 1958, BOB had to give some thought to the possibility that the Soviets might push into the Western sectors of the city. Preparations were scant. Some members of BOB who had military backgrounds were issued uniforms. They also practiced firing machine guns on the range in the Grunewald. Jack Corris, a Navy captain and BOB administrative officer, recalls, "We weren't sure what we would have done if they'd come in."[18]

CAREER MOVES

June 16–20, 1953, was the first defining moment of Harvey's Berlin career, his baptism in the font of foreign intelligence. From then on, Harvey was indisputably CIA Berlin. And the time was right for Harvey to make Berlin the most important and biggest single CIA installation in the world—devoted to aggressively penetrating the bailiwicks of Soviet Communism that were reasonably close at hand but nonetheless difficult to pierce.

The East German Uprising could have been a serious stumble in Harvey's surge to the top, but it turned out to be a stepping stone. Once he was past the uprising, he could get on with the big job, the actual installation and activation of the Berlin Tunnel. By the time Bill left Berlin, his path was clearly headed upward, although some who watched him from the wings harbored doubts, even nurtured grudges, and were, perhaps even then, ready to dig traps along his path.

Harvey was nearly as high in civil service rank as he could go at the time, a GS-15, maybe a GS-16, roughly equivalent to a brigadier general in the Army. About this time, too, Harvey began to think about becoming deputy director of plans, the most equal among equal deputy directors of the CIA, i.e., the man in charge of the Clandestine Services. Perhaps he even contemplated the chair of DCI.

POLISHING THE BRASS

Donald R. Morris, a Navy officer attached to BOB in 1958, recalls, "Behind Bill's desk was a poster of the statue of Greco-Roman wrestlers in the Uffizi Gallery, in which one brawny wrestler lifts the other off the ground and is about to hurl him over his shoulder, unaware the victim has a firm grip on the victor's penis. Harvey had attached a large brass shield to the frame which read, 'Headquarters Guidance.'"[19] It adequately summed up Harvey's attitude toward the establishment.

The DCI, Gen. Bedell Smith, had sent Gen. Lucian K. Truscott III to Germany to bring order into the CIA's diverse activities in the still-occupied country. Because of his war record and his rank, Truscott could also gain cooperation from an otherwise-unenchanted military; such cooperation was vital because the military still ran the American zone of occupation and the American sector of Berlin. Truscott soon bristled at what he perceived to be a loose chain of command, even insubordination, in Agency ranks, which was especially evident in Berlin where his man didn't show fitting deference to the brass.

After a while as chief, Harvey simply refused to attend meetings at the Office of the Commanding General, Berlin. He told Jack Corris, "You go. Just don't make any promises, and don't let those people know what the hell we're doing. But you report back to me what they're up to." Outranked by several grades, but backed by the shadow of Truscott, Corris now ran courteous interference for Harvey with the commanding general. "Somehow, it worked. We could get just about anything we wanted out of the Army."

There were other ripples.

> Once, we had a group of Army brass come up from U.S. Army Europe headquarters. I said, "Bill, do me a favor. Please put your gun in the drawer instead of laying it on top of your desk." He just laughed.
>
> So while he was giving them his number one speech, my God, there was the revolver right out on the desk! I could see the generals staring at it. But after Bill had talked for about five minutes, he had them. They even apologized for asking questions. "You may not be able to answer this, but how many people do you have?" "Oh, I'd say we have around fifty. Right, Jack?" [It was more like two hundred.]
>
> They were so grateful. . . . But they kept looking at that pistol! He never apologized.[20]

Neill Prew, who handled a number of tricky assignments for Harvey, recalls, "Bill developed a routine. The frequent visitors from Washington and Frankfurt would invariably be plied with martinis during the long cocktail hour at Bill's house and served copious amounts of wine with dinner. Dinner over, Bill would call me to take the guest[s] to the Harnack House [the official U.S. Army hotel and officers club in Berlin]. Guests out of the way, Harvey then departed for the tunnel. Bill even handled General Truscott the same way!"[21]

A final Corris lament: "I tried to stop him from carving his initials on his desk. Told him, 'That belongs to the U.S. government!' Bill Harvey answered, 'You trying to tell me how to use my desk? I don't give a shit who it belongs to, I'll carve where I want to.' End of discussion."[22]

THE MARTINI RITUAL

Practically everything ever written about Bill Harvey mentions his devotion to old-style martinis—no frills, no color additive, no fruit salad—a man's drink with gin and a whisper of vermouth, maybe a twist of lemon or an olive or a pearl onion. The Harvey Martini Ritual was part of the fitness-for-promotion testing for those whom Bill wanted to evaluate outside the normal course of work, a challenge to his subordinates to prove their manhood, and for others it was a rite of passage and a Bogartian symbol of virility.

In Berlin, the ritual took place in the spacious front living room of the Harveys' Milinowksi Strasse villa, which seemed to have little furniture except for two roomy, comfortable armchairs, which faced each other in front of the fireplace. Behind the boss's chair was a butler trolley, popular at the time, which held the essentials: a bottle or two of gin (Gilbey's, if I recall), Noilly Prat vermouth, an ice bucket, and bird-bath martini glasses, the kind that came back into vogue with the new millennium.

Harvey's style of mixing was rapid, businesslike, not show time. The first drink went down fast on both sides. It acted as lubrication for the synapses and vocal chords. The second drink was slower, reflective. It allowed the participants time for mellowing and for the layers to begin to peel away. The third brought on intimacy, at least on the part of the guest. After three, it was time to go back to work.

What lingers in my mind from these sessions is how much Harvey revealed of himself, even more so when I was no longer in the official loop. Then, Harvey showed me a warmth and humanity I barely suspected. He knew the most intimate details of his officers' lives, their marital problems, their fears for their children. He talked about his people with what can only be described as love. They were family, even though he didn't dare show his affection, most especially not to those for whom he was most concerned. This vulnerable side of Harvey, which many of us only sensed, made him the leader he was. And this side came out most poignantly when he was able to relax with a trusted confidant over a bucket of martinis.

Stan Gaines, the senior officer who anchored BOB in Frankfurt and whom we regarded as a Berliner by adoption, unlike most of the Frankfurt headquarters people, says that he went to Bill's one lunchtime when he was in Berlin. "As I recall, we had about five drinks in large glasses and then ate something! Then he drove me to the airport, where I clumsily boarded the plane and went to sleep. And he went back to the shop to work!"[23]

Clarence Berry: "I don't remember much about the furniture except he had a very comfortable, Archie Bunker type, easy chair. The coffee table adjacent to the chair had an 8 x 10, black and white picture of Bill on it [which showed] the inevitable wreath of smoke curling from a cigarette in his hand. CG commented to us that it was her favorite photo of him."[24] The photo is Wally Driver's character study of Bill, taken about 1957, which appears, in part, on the dust jacket of this book.

Dave Murphy brings the story to Bill's later years: "When we lived near the Harveys in Chevy Chase Village, I . . . would often drop by to participate in the Irving Street version of the ritual. It was held in his den, which was dominated by a huge German *Schrank* converted to a gun cabinet, and two overstuffed chairs. The ritual had not changed from Berlin; the equipment was the same. The only difference I can remember is that I would refrain from a third monster glass."[25]

Two Washington lunch companions recall a session with Bill at the renowned Harveys Restaurant on Pennsylvania Avenue. The waiter by appointment had a water pitcher of martinis at the ready and kept Bill's glass topped up without even a flick of an eyelid from Harvey.

AND THE GUNS . . .

Once Harvey fell into the pond in the garden of his house in Milinowksi Strasse in broad daylight. He changed clothes and then sat in front of the fireplace, cleaning and oiling the guns he had been carrying. Finished cleaning, he twirled one of the revolvers, and according to CG, accidentally fired a round into the wall. A terrified maid appeared instantly, followed almost immediately by the Black Watch, the caped policemen assigned to guard areas where Americans lived. Harvey was apologetic but unrepentant.

Neill Prew was so discreet he at times seemed taciturn. Because of this quality, if for no other reason, he had Bill's complete trust. On one occasion, Bill caught a very early plane to Frankfurt, then called Prew back in Berlin, woke him up, and told him to go to Milinowski Strasse to remove two pistols from under Bill's pillow, so the maid would not have a heart attack discovering them. The guns, Neill says, "were his safety blanket."

Once Bill lowered his facade and allowed you into his inner sanctum, you began to realize that guns were part of his persona. Stan Gaines agrees: "The guns and all that. . . . It was all part of Bill's facade. Something he used to impress people—maybe to intimidate, or test them, too."[26]

EXPANDING THE BASE

By spring 1954, BOB was fast outgrowing Field Marshall Beck's mansion. Bill's liaison with America's top dog in Berlin, USCOB, traditionally a major general, was always sticky, but Harvey was tact personified. So, with the weight of General Truscott behind him, Harvey negotiated for one of the large buildings within the High Commission, Germany (HICOG), compound, perfect for BOB purposes because it had its own entrance and did not front on Clay Allee, the main and ceremonial entrance to Field Marshall Goering's old fiefdom.

The move was accomplished in August 1954 by GIs in grinding six-by-six trucks, lifting the very, very heavy safes into the new premises. Neill Prew rode shotgun on what the base finance officer "thought was far more important than any state secrets we might have"—the sizable amount of cash (in a variety of currencies) that the base maintained.

Dave Murphy recalls, "Think of all that stuff! We'd been in the same place since September 1945!" The half-mile move was symbolic as well as practical. When the CIA pulled out of the villa, a chapter of Agency history closed, to Bill's complete satisfaction.

At the same time, sixteen carefully selected and trained U.S. Army engineering sergeants started to dig the Berlin Tunnel. "During those summer days, Bill was running the base and supervising the move. And nights, he was overseeing the beginning of the very, very tricky excavation of the tunnel! No one else could have done that!" writes Murphy.[27]

But Bill was nowhere to be seen during the actual move. Neill Prew thought "he was probably at the Maison de France drinking martinis with the Dutch chief of base, who was a buddy of his."

THE HARVEY SCHOOL

All the posturing and the drinking and the guns were incidental to business. Sure, Harvey was gruff and irretrievably profane. And, sure, when he was truly (as opposed to theatrically) angry, he spoke through clenched teeth. Yet despite the facade, and within a year of his arrival, Harvey had the loyalty of all but the few on the base. In our eyes, his positive traits, most especially his loyalty to us, bulldozed the negatives.

First, he knew what he was doing, what he wanted done, and in general, where he was going. His vision was clear; his directions precise. He gave his subordinates a lead, a standard to follow and match, if they could. Second, he bent or fractured regulations and took risks that a garden-variety civil servant would never contemplate, in both operations and administration, a trait that appealed to us on the front line. Third, Harvey listened to his subordinates. If he agreed with an operational plan one of the case officers submitted, he supported it, even if it blew back on him. He won many, many more fights than he lost because his judgment was, then, very sound. Fourth, it dawned on us that we were being offered on-the-job training at its best—an exquisite postgrad course in intelligence gathering from a master. The corollary was, of course, that Harvey graduates were in demand at CIA stations all over the world. Thus, the clandestine services were seeded with Harvey loyalists, as Bill intended. Last, we quickly realized that Harvey consistently backed his people, recognized and lauded honesty, hard work, daring, and devotion.

Once Bill had taken your measure, and if his judgment of you was favorable, he pushed you for promotion (sometimes over opposition), and he did everything he could to ensure that you had a good assignment when you left Berlin.

THE BRANDENBURG SCHOOL FOR BOYS

Once settled in the new HICOG compound office, with a lot more space, Bill set about making the final moves to make Berlin the CIA's largest base and grander than most country stations. He established sections for East German, satellite, Soviet, and of course, counterespionage (CE) operations, each with its head and deputy head—all of whom, to the elders' way of thinking, knew far too much about each other's business.

By 1955 Harvey had in place the four men who would succeed him sequentially as chief of base. Tom Polgar comments, "They were an impressive bunch. One of them liked to call it the Brandenburg School for Boys." They were, and remained for the rest of their lives, Harvey loyalists.

Dave Murphy arrived in 1954 as Bill's deputy and head of Soviet operations. Murphy took over BOB when Harvey left in September 1959 and was followed by Bill Graver, who had run the East German operations group under Harvey. In 1966 Graver yielded to Ted Shackley, who had been chief of the Soviet satellite operations section and then had run the anti-Cuban base in Miami, JMWAVE. Shackley became famous in his own right. Herb Natzke, Shackley's deputy, was the last Harvey-trained BOB chief. He left Berlin in 1971, ending the Harvey era. Natzke was the last of what he refers to as "the Berlin Brotherhood."

DAVE MURPHY

David E. Murphy had been in the Army, had switched to what became the CIA, and was a Russian linguist. When he returned to Washington in 1953 from Munich, the grapevine told him the slot of deputy chief, Berlin, was open.

> The reason for this vacancy, I learned, was the personality of the chief, William King Harvey, who devoured candidates while waiting for his second double martini. Harvey would be in Washington in July 1954 (I later learned it was on tunnel business), and I could then press my case. Bill made his own appointments, regardless of what the secretaries in the front office told him. . . .
>
> Even though it was out of line for a brown bagger from the temporary buildings, we agreed to meet for lunch at a restaurant out on Connecticut Avenue. I had met Harvey briefly in 1948, after my return from Korea, so I was not unprepared for the physical appearance. Since I still thought martinis were great fun, I joined in the first two.
>
> Introductory pleasantries were, however, minimal. Bill subjected me to a very searching review. . . . When I said I wanted to have a crack at the largest concentration of Soviets abroad, those in East Berlin and East Germany, I sensed a positive response.
>
> Once in Berlin, and contrary to my hopes and expectations, it soon became clear that the last thing Bill Harvey ever needed was a deputy in the classical sense of someone who waits for the boss to go on home leave.

Murphy suggested that he be assigned to review all ongoing cases, concentrating on Soviet ops. "Since Bill was absent on tunnel business a good bit of the time as the spring of 1955 wore on, this seemed to him a sensible arrangement."[28]

As Harvey prepared to go home in July 1959, Murphy thought he might be superseded by John Dimmer or Bill Hood, sometimes called "the Vienna choirboys." The ripples subsided when high authority spiked the Austria desk's takeover of Berlin. Murphy became chief of BOB in September 1959 and stayed until June 1961. The Berlin Wall went up in the August after Murphy's departure, an event he feels was not necessarily coincidental.

TED SHACKLEY

Ted Shackley is the prime example of a Harvey boy. A controversial figure who was never, ever known as "Shack," Ted arrived in Berlin in June 1954, after a tour of duty at Nuremberg. Harvey, replacing Adam Horton, put Ted in charge of BOB's expanded satellite operations. Shackley and Horton could not have been more different or, in their ways, typical of the old and the new Berlin Operations Base.

> At first, Harvey held me at arm's length. He was developing his team . . . his boys. . . . He was their mentor, their tutor. They were disparate characters, each with a different story.
>
> I'll give you a vignette: We had made a pitch to a Pole who was in East Berlin in December 1954. I was the reception committee, to meet the guy at the Zehlendorf West subway station. Typical Berlin weather. Maybe six inches of snow. The wind blowing like hell. There I was, waiting outside the station . . . some of our cars off in the distance, just in case.
>
> Then I noticed a car cruising the area. 'Shit!' I thought, 'The Poles may be surveilling . . . or maybe the UB [Polish intelligence service] has come over to snatch the reception committee—me!'
>
> I looked at the cruising car more closely when it came around again, and I said to myself, 'That's Harvey! The son of a bitch! He's checking to see I'm where I should be!'
>
> I waited. Stomped around to keep warm, walked around, but didn't go away. That car came back again a couple of hours later to meet the next train. Of course the guy didn't show.
>
> Next morning we had a postmortem in the office. Harvey only says to me, 'Pretty cold out there, wasn't it?' That's all. Nothing more. But from then on, I was accepted. I was one of Harvey's boys.

Shackley says he at first did not want to be head of the newly combined satellite section. "When he hit me with it, I was kind of opposed. I told him, 'I'll end up spending more of my time with paper and managing other people, and less time doing what I want to do, which is run agents.' By then he was no longer holding me at arm's length.

"Bill said, 'The way the Agency is expanding, if you want to get ahead, you have to be an admin type as well as have ops experience.'"[29]

Herb Natzke adds, "Shackley and I together ran one illegal crossing operation from Berlin to Poland, and he was meticulous in training, briefing, and providing guidance to the agent, who was a volunteer, as they all were. We were, in fact, pioneers in this type of operation. . . .

"Several times, when Shackley met an agent at the border, I backed him up with my hand on a .38-caliber revolver in my trench coat pocket. He did the same for me, and I never doubted he would pull the trigger to support me, if he had to."

Natzke gets aroused about a charge, in David Corn's *Blond Ghost*, that Shackley fabricated intelligence from a Polish source. "My desk was within fifteen feet of Shackley's. . . . Ted did recruit some agents in Poland, which was an accomplishment in itself . . . [but] I cannot imagine Shackley jeopardizing his reputation and his career for the momentary gratification of seeing his name on a few additional intelligence reports. . . . [We all] regularly had to pass very tough lie detector tests on which questions about fabricating were always present.

"Don't forget, either, that Bill Harvey was a tough professional taskmaster who would let no one play around with the truth."[30]

Shackley sums up the Berlin of the mid- to late 1950s: "There were so many leads coming out of the East, so many opportunities, a case officer in Berlin learned in two years about the same as in eight or ten years of experience in the 1990s. It was a unique treasure trove of experience, and we developed a lot of management experience. That's one thing I give Harvey credit for.

"He saw himself as somebody who had a mission to not only run successful operations, but to try to develop a core of officers for future advancement in the organization and disposition to other posts."

Did Bill make it obvious that he was grooming his inner circle for higher things? "Only in the amount of time he spent with some of the guys. I didn't have the sense then to know that was what he was doing.

"In my early days in Berlin, Murphy and Woodburn were in on the tunnel. I wasn't. But I had been in CIC [the Army's Counterintelligence Corps] in Berlin and still had contacts, so sometimes he'd make strange requests. 'Hey, can you get me a special kind of something or other?' or, 'Hey, I need this in a hurry!'"

Was Bill shooting for DCI? Shackley pauses for a split second before answering, "I think he wanted to be deputy director, operations, but it was a nonattainable goal. During the Berlin period, he was always the guy who was bashing away at headquarters . . . not necessarily a great recommendation for high appointment. After Berlin, sure, they'd give him Staff D, maybe even the CI Staff, but they'd never have given him a shot at the top! It wasn't a realistic possibility."

Who were "they"? "Bissell, Tracy Barnes . . . that bunch. Helms was pro-Harvey.

"Bill had the capability of being a damn good DDO, even though he was not a bureaucrat in the conventional sense, and had little patience with paper pushing. He was a workaholic, no doubt about it. His intelligence-collecting operations were imaginative. He was always ready to go for the big enchilada. He had a high CI/CE [counterintelligence/counterespionage] quotient. . . . You could even call it his higher calling . . . more than any other quality. He had a higher intellect than was generally recognized. He could quote the German philosophers, for instance . . . Kant, Hegel . . ."

The negative side? "He was opinionated. If you were on his shit list, it was very hard to get off it.

"Personally, a very honest guy. Loyal to his friends. He was very interested in seeing the service develop, so he nurtured people."[31]

APPRAISALS OF HARVEY IN BERLIN

Bill was chronically underestimated by almost everyone who did not work directly with him, partially because of the physical and psychological barriers he erected to confuse and deter those not in his trust. Those whom he admitted to his confidence learned to read him correctly, but only at a level he stipulated.

John Barron: "Bill had a basic trait of being able to admirably and accurately define and illuminate . . . talent or character in an individual, and then he would stick with that person forever."

The down side? Bill's drinking? Barron answers elliptically, "I'm aware of the stories about his excessive drinking, of course. In Berlin, it was like a twenty-four-hour-a-day fraternity party, but I never saw Bill intoxicated.

"I didn't see anything wrong with him later, in Washington. I've known alcoholics. Bill didn't have to have a drink. . . .

"I can't remember whether he smoked a lot. But I was smoking at the time, too."[32] Barron's memory was kind to his old friend.

Henry Woodburn was one of the case officers on the tunnel, and he went on to serve the CIA in a clutch of senior capacities, including, years later, as Harvey's deputy in Rome.

> In the early days, Harvey had a clear hand and carte blanche to do what he wanted. That must have been heady stuff for an officer

> still relatively new to the foreign intelligence business, and also aware that he was not popular with the OPC/PP crowd.
>
> It was he who selected his Berlin people. He interviewed them and tagged them for BOB. They weren't the choices of personnel in Washington.
>
> His routine, which would have brought lesser men down, appeared to phase him not at all. His stamina was incredible for someone who got no exercise, existed on a few hours of sleep, smoked three, perhaps five packs of cigarettes each day, paid no attention to diet, and drank copious quantities of booze. I can't remember him ever once missing a day's work, or being sick . . . in Berlin or elsewhere. . . . He simply never showed the strain.[33]

Stan Gaines, who scrutinized practically all of Berlin's plans in Frankfurt, says flatly, "Nobody was Bill's equal. Bill Harvey was the best operations executive I've ever seen. Everything that BOB did cleared through Bill, which was quite a feat in itself . . . just the amount of paper he dealt with.

"He was essentially a trainer of young officers. He told them what to do, and how to do it."

The climate in Frankfurt vis-à-vis the unruly element in Berlin? "Johnny Bross, who replaced Truscott, had personal differences with Bill. . . . Johnny was a very proud feller. He didn't . . . couldn't . . . respect Harvey the way I did."[34]

Tom Polgar adds, "I do not know the motives for Bross's dislike of Harvey. Maybe Harvey tried to go around Bross once too often. Certainly they were as different as could be, even though both were lawyers. Bross personified upper-class elegance, connections, and old money. . . . [He was] a negotiator not a dishbreaker."[35]

Years later, when I was an itinerant correspondent in the eastern Mediterranean and elsewhere, I sometimes ran into still-serving CIA officers. To establish my bona fides, I none too casually let drop that I had worked under Harvey in the halcyon days of Cold War Berlin. "You were one of Bill Harvey's Boys?" A long beat, followed by a marked increase in respect. Wherever the Agency had people, the legend of Bill Harvey was well known.

POWER PLAYER

Here and elsewhere the question arises: Did Harvey lust for power? Ted Shackley touched on it. I have raised the question with several other people who knew him well. No one who worked closely with Bill thinks he was interested in power for the sake of power.

A host of Bill's detractors—both in the 1960s and when they really piled on in the 1970s and thereafter—think that Harvey was a single-minded megalomaniac, that having surveyed the Clandestine Services, he was driven to try for the top rung and heaven help anyone who stood in the way.

Harvey went to enormous lengths to do his job as he saw it and to do it well. That job was to provide the U.S. government with the best possible intelligence. He was ambitious and his ambition was a consistent, all-out effort to serve his country. Big Bill was first and foremost an operator. If his operations specifically excluded many whom he screened but found wanting, well, that's the way it crumbled.

Was, for instance, personal loyalty the price of admission to the Berlin Brotherhood? The answer is yes. But not for the reason his gainsayers would advance. He was as loyal to his subordinates, once they were proven, as they were to him.

Yet Harvey could be a disciplinarian, with humor. One of his case officers spent some considerable time bicycling around Berlin in penance for a major traffic violation, not because of the malfeasance, but because he had drawn attention to himself and the cover unit for which he worked.

Harvey was not an empire builder in the sense that the conventional bureaucrat seeks to bolster his own inadequacies and self-importance. Bill Harvey didn't need that kind of flatulence on command. He wanted strong, courageous, iconoclastic leaders in his own mold, not sycophants. Those who were tapped knew they were graced; they knew there was no better way to become professional foreign intelligence officers.

OBSTACLES

But obstacles littered Harvey's path. The mandarins of the CIA, among them John Bross, were not about to let Bill, the rough upstart from Indiana, into the tightest of tight inner circles, no matter what he had accomplished in the Bureau or in Berlin.

With his own rough exterior and his way of doing business—perhaps even because of the potent network that he had trained and that was poised in 1960 to disperse throughout the Agency—Harvey was a threat to the inner core, i.e, the CIA establishment that circled around Dick Helms.

In retrospect, Harvey never had a chance to make deputy director, plans, even before the trouble that was looming. He had simply made too many enemies as he fought and maneuvered to get his way—even if that way was eventually acknowledged to be the most brilliant and most accomplished available.

Dave Murphy cited an instance, in his long, retrospective 1993 conversation with CG Harvey, that underlines Bill's surging ambition to do the best job possible.

> Murphy: OK, the time is February 1956. The tunnel is going full blast. . . . We had made contact with Popov through the British Military Liaison Mission. . . . So Bill sent a cable to Helms and Angleton saying, in view of the large amount of daily input to our counterespionage effort, Berlin should become a major player in the development of CE [counterespionage] activity against the Soviet Union. Helms and Angleton almost died.
> CG: Nothing ever came of it. Angleton would not have any [administrative] input from anybody.[36]

Back to Tom Polgar:

> The Harvey I knew was overweight and drank quite a bit, but I never saw him under the influence of liquor and I never saw him fall asleep during a discussion. He never displayed or fingered guns in my presence. . . . He impressed one from day one with his fantastic memory, his ability to marshal facts to support his argument, his goal orientation and his ability to work with his subordinates.
>
> He had handicaps. He spoke no German and had a deaf ear for language. He had limited "feel" for local political situations and knew no German history. He was stubborn and tried to escape conventional staffing and supervision by putting normal operational and personnel matters into the [highly restricted, tightly held] Staff D cable channel. This led to controversies and at least two verbal reprimands by the then–deputy chief of mission, Gordon Stewart, and by General Truscott himself.
>
> There were other indications that his superiors had concerns about Harvey's personality. (1) In February 1954 Secretary of State John Foster Dulles invited General Truscott to meet with him in Berlin. Truscott asked me to accompany him. He did not ask Harvey, even though we were in Harvey's territory. (2) When John Bross, chief EE Division [in Washington], left that position to become

> chief, Germany, I asked him what made him accept that assignment? He said that taking the job himself was the surest way to block Harvey.[37]

Harvey's fiery descent less than a decade later is also foreshadowed in the following excerpt from a personal letter from Lt. Gen. Lucian K. Truscott III, USA (Ret.), to Frank G. Wisner, head of the Clandestine Services. It is dated April 20, 1954. The photocopy bears no secrecy indicator. It came to me from a former CIA officer, another retired foreign intelligence man, who bears Harvey no goodwill. The two pages discuss general matters regarding the future of the German mission, its senior personnel, Truscott's own replacement in Frankfurt, and war planning.

> So long as I am commenting on personnel, I might make one or two remarks concerning Harvey. I think I told you last Summer that I believed Harvey was doing an outstanding job in Berlin. So far as his relationship with other agencies and his own specialized knowledge are concerned, I think that estimate holds true today. Harvey has found it difficult, however, to delegate authority and to utilize subordinates. In consequence, he has been something of a bottleneck that has prevented administration and operational reporting from being as effective as might be desirable. Another characteristic is that Harvey does not always respond easily to direction. He is sure that Berlin views are superior and almost any suggestion from Washington or Frankfurt invariably calls for extensive argument, even though he accepts the decision in the long run.[38]

Truscott was not prepared to cut Harvey any slack. Nor did the general make allowance for the tremendous working burden Harvey was carrying in Berlin.

If Harvey had known of the letter, he would have shrugged and said something like, "So, what else is new?" And then he would have gone back to work, but his private sense of outrage might have been the more poignant because CG Follick Harvey had been pushed in his direction by the same Truscott.

BURNING THE FILES

In the Berlin base chief's office was a special safe that held all of Bill's notes going back to 1952, including dispatches and cables of the most sensitive classification between Harvey and the higher-ups, personnel notes, and stuff Bill had kept out of the ordinary filing system for one reason or another. Years later rumors started to fly around Washington that major secrets affecting American policy had been lodged there and that someone had burned the files to protect Harvey.

In 1967, years after Bill had left, Herb Natzke arrived to take over as the new chief of BOB. "I drove into the compound and parked in the slot right by the office door. Someone said, 'You can't do that! That's Mr. Harvey's spot!' . . . Eight years after Bill had left!" While Harvey's BOB had soared to a complement of 250 people, by the start of Natzke's tenure, it was on its way back down to a mere 70.

Ted Shackley, who was on his way to Southeast Asia, succinctly briefed Natzke. The safe in the chief of base's office, Shackley said, "contains all the secrets. . . . They're all there, anytime you want to see them."

Natzke started to read the files at night. "It probably took me the better part of a year. . . . All the files pertaining to the tunnel . . . Bill's conversations with Allen Dulles . . . everything. . . . That's when I saw that Harvey was not a fraud. He had a good, crisp, taut style of writing. Wasted no words on emotion. His analysis of the Berlin situation, and possible Russian actions . . . was masterly.

"But after a couple of months, I started to tear the papers out of their folders and send them down for destruction." Why?

> Berlin was always a dangerous place. In those days, in the late 1960s, there were mobs gathered at the Oskar Helene Heim subway station near the American headquarters compound. . . . [They were] anti-American . . . against our engagement in Vietnam. I wasn't afraid that they would attack and get into the offices, but I didn't want to leave the possibility open to chance. . . .
>
> I just didn't believe those files were necessary for me . . . for the work I was doing. . . .Unnecessary paper, just lying around. . . .
>
> Then there was the protective motive. Up till then, the slot of chief, BOB, had been in the Brotherhood . . . from Peter Sichel, through Houck, to Harvey, Murphy, Graver, Shackley, and then on to me. One of those days, someone who was not a Berlin guy, not one of the Brothers, would come in . . . and that stuff was almost holy . . . almost sacred. I didn't want anyone else poring through those papers.
>
> As it happened, my successor was a guy from Staff D, not a Berlin ops man at all.

Natzke concludes emphatically, "I did not burn the papers to cover anyone's tracks. I never felt sorry. . . . Until about 1963–64, CIA was the good guys. Then it began to change, to go the other way."[39]

Dave Murphy heard a somewhat different version during his lengthy conversations with CG Harvey in Indianapolis in November 1993. CG was aging and had spent the past thirteen years trying to defend Bill's reputation against the assault started by *Wilderness of Mirrors*.

> CG: Let me tell you what happened to a lot of records . . . stuff that he put into his cryptic notes . . . the kind he took down constantly. He kept a pad and pencil with him at all times, and he'd write things down, but nothing anyone could ever interpret . . . so cryptically that I'd look at it, and it didn't make any sense. . . .
>
> When Herb Natzke got to Berlin, they were doing a lot of reviewing of records. Herb decided he would purge the files. He took everything of [Bill's] period and burned it. . . .
>
> Murphy: He didn't burn everything!? Bill must have had a chief of base file.
>
> CG: He did. Bill burned a lot of his own stuff before he left. Nobody could have read it anyway. But there were still things that Herb felt the Church Committee would be very interested in getting hold of, and he said to me, "CG, I wasn't about to let that gang get hold of anything. I spent two days doing nothing but burning Bill's files."[40]

NORMAN MAILER'S BERLIN

Two books have appeared over the years that really irritated Harvey's Boys. One was David Martin's *Wilderness of Mirrors* and the other was Norman Mailer's *Harlot's Ghost*. Tom Polgar ripped into Mailer's novel for *Welt am Sonntag*, which is, roughly, Germany's equivalent of the Sunday *New York Times*.

"Bill Harvey was an important figure in the CIA for nearly twenty years and he is a central figure in Mailer's notional CIA, in which the real Harvey is maligned, ridiculed, and distorted." Harvey, Polgar noted, was "used by Mailer as a vehicle for opinions which . . . sound remarkably like those that Mailer has expressed over the years."

Polgar pointed out that no one ever defected from BOB, nor did anyone spill sensitive operational detail to the media. "Thus Mailer, having no sources, had to invent things. His Berlin chapters are weak, as anyone familiar with the scene would have recognized. . . . When he claims to write about historic events and real people, he should, however, have his facts right."

For example, the novelist assigned Harvey a Cadillac, which in 1950s Berlin would have drawn astonished attention from Americans as well as Germans. Then, Mailer "has Harvey talking about the tunnel on the car radio—the same Harvey Mailer describes as an expert on communications security." And incidentally, *Harlot's Ghost* places Bill's main office on the Kurfuerstendamm in the heart of downtown Berlin, far from the near-pastoral quiet of Dahlem.[41]

THE BERLIN EXPERIENCE

A summation of Bill Harvey as chief, BOB, comes from the woman he married in February 1954, when the tunnel op was at fever pitch. "One of the good things about Bill was his ability to bring out the best in people." Berlin officers told CG, "The thing we really like about working for Bill is . . . he asks what you want to do. . . . You always feel like you're working directly with Bill, that he's backing you up all the way. . . . He brings out the best in you. He knows just how to ask the questions and pass out the responsibility to make you feel like you were doing your job."

"The young guys! . . . They idolized Bill. That was one of the reasons I talked to Bill about the heavy drinking. I said, 'You're setting a terrible example for those young guys!'[42]

There is, in CG's summation, a hint of ruthlessness. Harvey could and did weed out people whom he felt were vulnerable to recruitment by the opposition, even if they had done nothing wrong themselves. Likewise, all of us realized early on that we had to prove ourselves to him, even as we were mutely challenging him to prove himself to us. In the end, he won us over with his sheer mental capacity, his ferocious ability to work, and the loyalty to us that he showed as time went by.

Because our work kept us in the office, we two reports officers saw more of Harvey than the street officers, and we came to appreciate what a friendly and decent a man he was, behind the forbidding facade. We were genuinely fond of him, as were almost all who served under him. Sure, he had a gruff, often bitingly sarcastic exterior, but we learned that it was a facade, just as we intuited that some areas of his life and his work were not, under any circumstances, open to discussion. In some ways, we modeled ourselves after him. And, yes, I would say that we loved him in the gruff, macho way of frontline males. We Harvey Boys were devoted to him, not just because he was good, but because he had those very public warts.

Dave Murphy draws a picture of Big Bill at his peak: "He was a master of the art of cable combat, and whereas most of us drafted our messages on typewriters, he dictated, squinting through a haze of cigarette smoke, pausing every now and then, not so much to collect his own thoughts as to invite contributions from the circle of branch chiefs and case officers who watched and listened.

"We all had a sense of participation, heightened by the fact that in most situations, Bill was taking the side of his troops."

This was Harvey fully in charge, knowing he had the devotion of the close circle of men around him and of their subordinates. When Harvey finished his seven years in Berlin and headed home for reassignment, he was on a roll.[43]

By the end of 1954, Bill had cemented in nearly half of the Harvey legend. He had nailed Philby, and he had revamped BOB so that it was the CIA's most aggressive probe of the Soviet Empire, constantly searching for weak points in the iron curtain, for crumbling in Communism's monolithic structure. The other part of the legend's first half came to light in 1955, with the exposure of the Berlin Tunnel.[44]

Harvey gained confidence in his ability to lead others. He had been a chief before, but of a staff, limited by the confines and the atmospherics of Washington's temporary buildings. In Berlin, he was on his own, and he deftly exploited his exposed position, way out there on the limb, face-to-face with the enemy, playing ultimate poker. He showed his mettle to other government agencies, most particularly the military, and to the CIA hierarchy, most specifically, Dick Helms, and he was recognized for his excellence.

5

HARVEY'S HOLE: THE BERLIN TUNNEL OPERATION

Everything Bill Harvey did while at the helm of Berlin Operations Base (BOB) from 1952 to 1955, and even beyond, has to be measured in light of the Berlin Tunnel. Harvey's day job as chief of BOB was prodigious and prestigious in itself. His night job was supervising the building, equipping, and operating of a clandestine engineering project, unknown to all but a few. Perhaps Harvey's dual roles were most comparable to those of the resident vice president of an imaginary American bank's vital Moscow branch during the Cold War. The American would have been charged with tunneling undetected into the Russian Central Bank's vault, and all the while, he would have had to act perfectly normally under unrelenting observation from all sides, without showing that he was operating on about four hours of sleep a night, over a protracted period of time.

The forthright reason for the effort and the, for-the-times, huge expense of the Berlin Tunnel was that communications are the most vulnerable link of any enterprise. Governments, military services, businesses, even sports teams have to convey their secrets to other recipients. Other governments or competitors try to tap communication links to gain advantage; conversely, organizations spend large sums to try to ensure the privacy of their messages. The U.S. government maintains the National Security Agency (NSA, established in 1952), which strives to keep official secrets secret and to learn what other governments, political movements, terrorist organizations, even businesses and individuals are up to.

Much of Harvey's and the Bureau's success against the KGB immediately after World War II had been a result of the Venona intercepts supplied by the Army Security Agency (ASA), the home of a legendary figure named Frank Rowlett.[1] When Harvey moved to the CIA, Venona was still running, but it was accessible to only a very few and was used mostly to track KGB activity in the United States. In other words, the United States lacked a window into Soviet activities abroad that would provide positive intelligence on military and economic, perhaps even political, matters. Harvey's eye fastened on Germany and the anachronistic island in the Soviet zone of occupation that was West Berlin. Harvey and Rowlett had a meeting of minds, and the concept of the Berlin Tunnel was born.

Harvey's Berlin Tunnel was a bold idea: to drive deep under an exposed wasteland of southern Berlin to tap a sheaf of transmission lines that carried a huge amount of traffic between all of Soviet-occupied East Germany, Moscow, and other parts of the Soviet Union. At its peak, the tunnel operation actively involved more than a hundred people, yet it never leaked, except in one very significant way: a shadow was cast over it, years later, with the realization that the British Secret Intelligence Service (MI-6) had again been penetrated by the Soviets and that the officer concerned, George Blake, a Brit born in the Netherlands who had been imprisoned and turned in North Korea, had sat in on early CIA–MI-6 tunnel meetings in London. Blake told his KGB case officer what was up. That case officer was Gen. Sergei Kondrashev, who later teamed up with David Murphy and George Bailey to write *Battleground Berlin*. Kondrashev is the authority for the assurance, decades after the fact, that the KGB knew of the tunnel but decided to allow the operation to proceed in order to protect Blake. Kondrashev's statement negates assertions of writers who alleged that the tunnel was primarily a source of Soviet disinformation; some of those assertions were, indeed, aimed more at Harvey than at the tunnel operation itself. A sidenote: if this version were true, think of the complexity of seeding disinformation in the enormous flow of electronic traffic the Americans monitored. It is possible, yes, but it would have been an enormous enterprise for the KGB, if they even contemplated it.

The tunnel cannot really be compared to other secret enterprises—the U-2s, for instance. The U-2s' high-altitude flights over the Soviet Union were more expensive and just as daring and as important, and they certainly involved risk to the pilots, viz. Gary Powers. But the tunnel was a massive undertaking that involved drilling right into a main artery of the Soviet Empire from a location that was under constant hostile surveillance. The success of the tunnel depended on humans operating under ticklish conditions, made, in this case, the more tricky because those involved knew that even their overt activities were under constant hostile surveillance. Unless someone comes up with a stunning, heretofore-untold story of huge Soviet espionage success in the years from 1945 to

1989, the Berlin Tunnel must rank as the most dramatic and important human intelligence-gathering operation of the Cold War.

Just the concept of boring through wet clay for the length of five football fields, under the very feet of hostile forces, is enough to fire the imagination and to hint at the tension of the task. Then there was the installation of the three taps themselves by a British technician working a few feet below the surface of enemy territory. Finally, there was the kick of eavesdropping on the first actual Soviet military traffic, as it was being transmitted. All these factors make the Berlin Tunnel a credit to its main protagonist.

The official record, amplified by the memories of several participants, provides some inkling of the enormity of the task and of the conditions under which Harvey and his men worked. Today, of course, the time, manpower, effort, money, and nervous tension that went into it would be largely unnecessary; we have robotic machines that grab out of the ether communications traffic that may tell us what we want and need to know about our friends and enemies.

Unfortunately, much of the drama of the Berlin Tunnel op is lost because so many of those involved are dead. The official files—those that have been declassified and are available—are written in government prose and record none of the actual sweat, the nervous tension, the exhaustion, the interminable waiting during the dig while Soviet and East German patrols passed overhead. They give no hint of elation when the taps worked, nor of the grinding but highly secret routine of processing the miles of recorded tape and interpreting/translating, disseminating, and analyzing the thousands of messages the taps produced.

In the documentation and the recollections I have used, there is no hint of the ferocious bureaucratic infighting that so often characterizes major projects, in or outside of government. Indeed, and perhaps partially because it was cleared at presidential-NSC and Joint Chiefs of Staff level, the tunnel op seems to have been a rare model of government efficiency on a project that had to flow flawlessly.

One of the main participants says, flatly, the tunnel "would never have gotten off the ground without Bill constantly pushing it." The tunnel certified Harvey's inspiration, his drive, and his stamina, perhaps, indeed, at some lasting physical and mental cost to himself.

GOADED BY BRITISH SUCCESS?

In 1951 the Soviets conveniently shifted the bulk of their military communication from wireless radio to landline. At the same time, CIA technical staff, probably working on information gathered primarily by a notable Berlin case officer, Sig Hoxter,[2] from German scientists returning from the USSR, "became aware of a principle which, when applied to target communications, offered certain possibilities. . . . Exploratory discussions were held in Washington."[3]

Bob Kilroy, who played a background role in the early days of tunnel planning, comments, "Harvey and Frank Rowlett," of whom more later, "probably knew the kind of job they were contemplating was possible, because the Brits had done it in Schwechat, Vienna. Thus, MI-6/SIS [Secret Intelligence Service] had acquired the technical expertise in Austria. . . . Additionally, MI-6 had shared some of their stuff with us, too, and we're all gentlemen, aren't we?"[4]

The Vienna op may well, in turn, have been an outgrowth of the occasional successes intrepid British prisoners of war had in tunneling out of several prison camps during World War II. One of the problems the POWs faced (and solved ingeniously) was secretly disposing of the dirt they accumulated digging their exit route. The same problem faced the Brits in Vienna, and Harvey in Berlin.

In his memoir, Dick Helms skips over the maneuvers necessary to get the Berlin Tunnel op into gear, but he makes some interesting observations: "Within the Agency, cover stories within cover stories had to be invented. . . . We were well along with our research in Austria when our Vienna office learned that the British independently had . . . made considerable progress in tapping into the underground cables. . . . There was too much at stake to risk any overlapping effort. . . . The British agreed, and we each cooperated to the hilt at all times."[5]

The Berlin Tunnel inevitably became a joint operation. Apart from the early consultations in London, and after the tunnel had been dug, when all else was in place, the actual taps were made by John Wyke, a British expert. Since the British Vienna Tunnel had been called SILVER, Berlin became GOLD, a name that was subsequently used in public.[6] The official cryptonym used inside the CIA for GOLD remains classified. Clarence Berry, a soft-spoken Virginian who these days plays bridge and sings in a barbershop quartet, speculates that the moniker "maybe derived from the dirt they dug up and brought out from the tunnel itself."[7]

The extreme security in all aspects of GOLD worked. From the first culling of necessary infrastructure information on through the construction and exploitation phases, no one at Berlin Operations Base, except those who absolutely had to know, had a clue about the elaborate operation down there at the American sector–Soviet zone border on the southernmost rim of the city.

FRANK B. ROWLETT

Sometime, perhaps even in the late 1940s, the legend goes, Frank B. Rowlett and Bill Harvey—who was then still head of Staff C, Counterintelligence—were commiserating over the dearth of the kind of communications intercept material Rowlett's people had produced during World War II and the British Enigma machine had also delivered. Rowlett—described by James Bamford in *Body of Secrets* as "beefy and round-faced with rimless glasses . . . a high school teacher from southern Virginia [who] received a degree in math"—has sainthood in the intelligence world, even today. According to a military website, Rowlett, who had been hired for the Army's Signal Intelligence Service in 1930, was the central figure and the last surviving member of a team that solved Japanese code and cipher communications before and during World War II.[8]

Clarence Berry suspects that Harvey organized Rowlett's transfer to the CIA from the NSA in 1952. If this is true, it means Harvey already swung enough weight in the Agency to push for such a major personnel move. Rowlett became chief of Staff D, which was elevated to division status during the tunnel op, so he could backstop Berlin with the weight of his knowledge and prestige. It was a slick Harvey move.

Clarence recalls, "Frank was a southern gentleman, a country-boy type, well respected. . . . Quiet, soft-spoken, never mad, a very smart mathematician . . . a behind-the-scenes kind of guy. . . . Harvey and Fleetwood [see below] referred to Rowlett as 'Our Father.' I always called him 'Mr. Rowlett.' . . . He had an aura."

Because of the extent and depth of his very sensitive knowledge, it is unlikely that Rowlett ever went to Germany, although he did meet the British in less-exposed London. Berry: "I was at a meeting on the tunnel in Frankfurt, between Allen Dulles and Harvey. But [I was] never in Frankfurt with Rowlett. . . . I doubt seriously Rowlett was the prime mover in the tunnel operation. I give Harvey a lot more credit."[9]

SELLING THE OPERATION

Once Rowlett and Harvey had cooked up the concept, they had to produce an operational plan, which must have been a fairly elaborate document, going into manpower requirements, the need for no-questions-asked support from the Army, training of the tunnel diggers, provision of construction and electronics supplies, recruitment of support personnel in Germany —on and on. The wealth of planning over several years had to be accomplished in far more than the usual CIA secrecy. One relatively huge item was for a large corps of transcribers and linguists to handle the enormous volume of intercept traffic. It was no easy task to find (and then clear) not just native Russian speakers but people who knew Russian dialects and the jargon that is always part of military communication. The back end of the operation in Washington (and London) was, however, not Harvey's worry once he got the tunnel op approved.

Peter Sichel was in on it from the very beginning, without, at first, being briefed on what was up. One of BOB's Washington-imposed targets in 1951–early 1952 was to recruit post office officials who knew the telecommunications wiring, both local and long distance, in all Berlin.

"We were extremely successful. Henry Hecksher [then Peter's deputy and BOB chief of operations] was the main supervisor on the effort." Henry was a close friend of the West Berlin Police president, Dr. Johannes Stumm, who had stood up to the Communists in 1948, then set up the separate West Berlin force and who in turn introduced Hecksher to high-ranking postal officials. "Remember, there was no wall at the time and still only one German postal system. The network established through Hecksher and Stumm brought in reams of material on the whole telephone and other wiring under the streets of Berlin."

Sichel deduced that the idea was ultimately to put a listening device onto one or more of the lines whose diagrams Hecksher's sources had purloined. "I had no idea, however, that it involved us trying to put a major listening post into the Soviet sector, and I doubt that that idea had germinated at the time."

In early 1952 Walter O'Brien, a former infantry captain and lawyer, arrived at BOB and took over the preparatory work from Hecksher. Sichel also soon departed, to be replaced temporarily by Lester Houck. Harvey, then working out of Staff D, needed the Eastern Europe Division (EE), in whose bailiwick Berlin fell, to sign off on his project. So, says Sichel, "When I became ops chief of EE in Washington, I was finally brought in on the tunnel." Sichel thinks Harvey preferred to deal with him rather than with John Bross, since Harvey and Bross did not get along.

Still Harvey-Sichel was an odd alliance. Peter notes, "I am foreign-born, about as strange an animal as he could ever think of. . . . I was everything he seemed to disapprove of, yet somehow, he made up his mind that he was going to be my best friend . . . probably from the minute that he decided he wanted to go to Berlin and that I could probably do something to prevent it.

"Harvey was very clever about it. But if somebody likes you, what are you going to do? I knew he had four dry martinis at lunch. I knew he was strange. . . . But he was very perceptive. Later, when he was in Berlin and I was on the desk in Washington, I never had a fight with him, and that was extraordinary!"

Sichel was under the impression that he was brought into the secret in order to get Allen Dulles's approval. He had known Dulles "rather well and saw quite a bit of him when he was a lawyer, after leaving OSS [Office of Strategic Services], and before he came back as director. I was in touch with him and Wisner in New York on my periodic trips back to the United States and used to lunch with both of them on Wall Street."

Sichel also "knew Dick Helms, Wisner's second in command, very well, from a long time back. So I was part of the inner circle. It was very easy to find my way around back in headquarters . . . very easy to get things done." Sichel and Wisner had been colleagues in OSS; Peter had a closer bond with Dulles because both served in Berlin after the end of hostilities.

Harvey briefed the new head of operations for EE on the plan. Then, with Dick Helms's blessing, he and Sichel went to see Allen Dulles in the red-stone building at 2430 E Street to ask for his approval. Sichel comments flatly, "Bedell Smith was nowhere around when the tunnel matter came up. Bill had pretty well worked out the whole project with the people who had done the groundwork. Approval was quickly given. It was just the kind of thing that Dulles went for. I have no idea if he checked it out with the president or anyone else.

"I, for one, took it all as just another operation. Only when I saw the enormous recruiting of translators, etc., did I realize that this was indeed a different sort of project."[10]

The question of who knew about the tunnel and who didn't may seem academic today, but it was not irrelevant then. Harvey needed the active support of Gen. Lucian Truscott because the Army would inevitably be involved in the tunnel op in a number of supporting roles, and Truscott had the stars on his shoulder to ensure military cooperation. Tom Polgar comments that Harvey had a number of meetings in Frankfurt with General Truscott, often on Friday mornings; this gave Harvey the chance to dally over the weekend.

The exclusion of Polgar was a departure from normal. Polgar found himself being invited to leave the room on a number of occasions, not just during the Harvey meetings. "It was obvious to me that something was going on in Berlin because of these incidents and the big build-up of personnel in Berlin base, which was not warranted on basis of ops developments known to me."[11]

FLEETWOOD

Once they had the go-ahead from on high, Harvey and Rowlett had to find the specialists they needed. Their first priority was a telecommunications man who had experience in clandestine operations. The choice was a man who was forever after called Fleetwood. He was an Army major who came to the CIA in the spring of 1951, on direct field transfer from an ASA (Army Security Agency) unit in Germany. He was papered as an Air Force colonel to give him the rank he needed to deal with the military. Fleetwood was Bill Harvey's soul mate. They worked almost literally hand in glove. Clarence Berry, who watched both from his perch in Frankfurt, says, "I don't believe Bill felt as easy with anyone else in Washington, London, or Frankfurt."[12]

When Dave Murphy approached Fleetwood's family while researching *Battleground Berlin*, they requested that his identity be concealed. "Fleetwood was Cadillac's top-of-the-line brand, the American Rolls Royce. Harvey thought it was a suitable nickname for his main partner on the tunnel," notes Clarence Berry, thus Fleetwood he remains.

After the CIA's German headquarters moved from Karlsruhe to Frankfurt, Fleetwood became chief of Staff D, Germany, a four-person unit. As time went on, he delegated most routine Division D tasks to Berry. "He was a nonconformist in many ways, but he took his job very seriously and was very close-mouthed about it. He was a very private person . . . very circumspect in his dealings with other German Mission people. But he could also be very outgoing with those he came to trust.

"During Harvey's visits to Frankfurt, when they worked out a multitude of details relating to tunnel support, they were like a couple of young colts kicking up their heels together. They were quite a team!"[13]

INCEPTION

Walter O'Brien caught Fleetwood's eye because he spoke serviceable German. O'Brien was detailed to Berlin as head of a nonexistent counterespionage section; his real mission was to take over from Hecksher the recruitment of agents in the West Berlin post office, thereafter in East Berlin, to collect information on Soviet communications landlines. He was under the tight direction of Fleetwood in Frankfurt and Harvey, still in Washington. In May 1952 Peter Sichel was replaced by Lester Houck, who was kept in the dark about O'Brien's primary mission.

Harvey moved to Berlin in December 1952. The move was the very quiet signal that the tunnel op was ready to move into a more vigorous exploratory stage. The operational outline had been OKed, and enough money had been allocated to allow further probing.

Bob Kilroy was in on it almost from the beginning. Even though we were close friends in the early 1950s and all of his tunnel activity took place, almost literally, under my nose, I didn't learn that he was involved and how deeply until I started to piece the story together for this book. Kilroy's account of his participation details one aspect of the painstaking complexity of the entire operation—all of it ticklish, and all of it conducted in the deepest secrecy. Kilroy refers to his participation as "moonlighting" because he still had another, full-time Agency job as a reports officer. This is his story.

In the early of spring of 1952, an East German post office telephone circuit expert defected, was brought to Frankfurt, and was turned over to Fleetwood, who could, however, not communicate with his new recruit. Kilroy: "Fleetwood accosted me. I was bored to tears but bilingual. He asked if I would be willing to do an interpreting job for him. Fleetwood added that the assignment had already been cleared higher up, and my office had no need to know. I was the only linguist Fleetwood could find whose parents were not recent immigrants. I had no idea who Fleetwood was. I knew only that he was involved in the most sensitive operations."

A day or so after the first encounter, Kilroy and Fleetwood went to an apartment to meet a German who had been a fairly high-level technician in the Reichspost during the war. The three of them huddled around a microfilm viewer on which could be seen a maze of lines with numbers attached to them. Fleetwood had specific questions about these telephone or teletype circuits. The German had all the information in his head. None of it made much sense to Kilroy, but Fleetwood seemed satisfied.

"Within the week I was fetched to yet another evening *à trois* with more microfilms. From *Battleground Berlin* I know now that these were the circuit drawings for landlines, which O'Brien was photographing at BOB and shipping down to Frankfurt."

Before too long, Fleetwood was dispatching Kilroy to unchaperoned meetings with the German. Finally, Fleetwood asked if the agent would like to go to Berlin to renew some old acquaintances and added that Kilroy would accompany him to ensure his safety.

Fleetwood was at Tempelhof when Kilroy and the agent came in on a military flight. Fleetwood, Kilroy, and the German went to a safe house where they were joined by O'Brien and two or three West Berliners who worked for the Deutsche Post. "A great time was had by all, so great that the four old Reichspost buddies went off on a pub crawl."

The junket to Berlin was a reward for a job well done. Fleetwood had found what he was looking for. By July 1952 he had determined that cables numbered 150, 151, and 152 probably carried Soviet traffic and ran close enough to the American sector to be reached by tunnel.[14]

Kilroy was transferred to BOB. Shortly after his transfer, Fleetwood needed the most detailed possible maps of Berlin. "I came up with a list of military maps of the entire Fatherland, made in the 1930s . . . a cartographer's dream, something only the Germans would do . . . perfectly to scale (1:25,000, as I recall), with every street, alley, highway, and byway . . . and best of all, with the location of all buildings carefully blacked in. The problem was finding the actual maps.

"After some calling around, I found a firm that was struggling along in a partially burned-out building in the British sector. They said they might still have some of the maps lying around but were sure that they had no complete set (which numbered literally thousands of sheets)."

Kilroy and a case officer posing as a diplomat went to the store. The officer announced that the U.S. government would purchase as complete a set of the maps as was available. "The owners' joy was heartwarming because, in their eyes, the maps were flawed: not only an incomplete set, but many of the buildings shown no longer existed. The case officer showed typical American disdain for what the incomplete set would cost."

Back in Frankfurt, Fleetwood told Kilroy to take two or three sections of maps and have them enlarged as much as possible, securely and exactly to scale. "I was not about to question Fleetwood's reasons or motives." He insisted that Kilroy, a streetcar man, take taxis wherever he went and not ask for receipts.

An art supply store told Kilroy the solution to his enlargement problem was a pantograph. Fleetwood provided another wad of Deutsch marks. Bob bought and then set about assembling the machine in a safe house. It was not easy.

Once the machine was set up, "the enlarging took about two days. At the end of each day, Fleetwood rolled up everything in a large tube and took it back to his office. When I was finished, he pronounced himself satisfied with the results, and back I went to Berlin.

"I never spoke of my moonlighting to anyone. Nor did I discuss or allude to it with Bill Harvey, who probably knew about it, except the day the discovery of the tunnel was broadcast by the East Germans. I took the need-to-know caveat seriously, as I think we all did."

FINAL PREPARATIONS

By now, Fleetwood knew exactly where the various major landlines in the East were. Next he had to determine which circuits carried traffic of major interest.

In Berlin, Walter O'Brien was replaced by Henry Woodburn, who recruited yet more post office types, presumably to ascertain which cables were worth the effort. Finally, the extremely risky patch operation, described in both *Wilderness of Mirrors* and *Battleground Berlin*, verified the lines of most operational interest.

Once the lines had been verified, Harvey called Neill Prew into his office. Harvey told Prew to deliver a tape to Gordon Stewart, who was then chief of the German Mission. It was probably one of the first tapes made in the fraught patch operation by O'Brien's East German Post recruit to test the traffic on the lines in which Harvey and Fleetwood were interested—one of the lines in the Soviet zone accessible to tunneling. Prew was considerably frustrated by weather delays, but he eventually got an Air France plane to Frankfurt and presented himself, with the tape, at Stewart's apartment at one o'clock in the morning.[15]

By August 1953 the tunnel group was able to present a detailed plan of operation to Allen Dulles, who took it under advisement. The tunnel planners were ready to put the project together. Harvey attended a December 1953 conference with the Brits in London, during which plans for Anglo-American cooperation were finalized, and finally, on January 20, 1954, thanks mainly to Bill's staunch advocacy of the operation, Dulles gave his approval. In February 1954 the technical details were ironed out at another conference in London.

Bob Kilroy adds, "Thereupon, work on construction of the 'ELINT [electronic intelligence] warehouse,' and then the tunnel itself, began." Once the decision was finally made to dig, the tunnel op became Operation GOLD.

SUPPORT

It's time to backtrack, to follow another skein that led to the Berlin interface between the American sector and the Russian zone.

By mid- to late 1952, Harvey knew there was no easy way simply to siphon key Soviet communications into West Berlin, so he had to push the envelope—to dig a tunnel, as the Brits had in Vienna to get at the most important cables they could reach.

Even the concept—tunneling a remarkable distance into denied territory—took daring. Questions must have arisen. Who could be trusted in the Agency procurement offices? How much did they need to know? What were the specs for the six-foot diameter steel tubing needed to prevent tunnel cave-in? How in hell do we dig a tunnel under the feet of patrols and under a heavily traveled highway? How do we keep it from caving in?

Who's going to dig it? What kind of equipment do we need? How do we order the equipment so it's not traceable back to us? How many tape recorders do we need? Where do we buy the miles of recording tape and the transmission cables without arousing suspicion? How do we translate the take and disseminate it fast, if needed? How can we possibly keep the whole thing secure?

The CIA couldn't just go to Home Depot or Halliburton, nor even commission a jobber. Much of the purchasing and shipping for the undertaking must have gone through the Army, concealed in routine supply requisitions. Security had to be the paramount concern.

With the intelligence provided by the Berlin post office recruits, a technical staff under Frank Rowlett probably started to draw blueprints for the tunnel itself. Then Rowlett had to find someone who had the expertise to ramrod the dig, met all the security requirements, and could command the respect of the diggers, who would be working under miserable physical conditions, as well as under psychological stress. The Army produced Lt. Col. Leslie Gross, reportedly the only man capable of leading such an expedition. The actual grunts were combat engineers, GIs who could pass rigorous security screening and who might reasonably be projected not to go out on the town and talk boisterously or to flip out under the pressure and isolation.

Regrettably, I have not been able to trace Colonel Gross or any of the combat engineers who were the actual diggers to gain their accounts of the actual tunneling or their version of Harvey's oversight of the operation. That in itself is a mark of the security surrounding the operation, even fifty years after the fact!

After the diggers finished, technically qualified GIs from the various military communications/cryptological services had to be selected and revetted.

With the preparations well in train, Harvey moved to Berlin to be on scene. Unable to use his Staff D bully pulpit from that distance, he had to rely on Rowlett and others at home. For a guy of Bill's energy and ambition, the slow-moving development process must have been agonizing, but he used the time to establish himself as chief of BOB and probably to size up the difficulties he would face when the digging and, later, the operation of the tunnel were in full swing.

An official account of the operation, probably written years later by Vyrl Leichliter (of whom more later), amplifies drily, "A group of U.S. Army personnel set about building what they thought was a fairly large warehouse about 300 feet from the East Zone in southern Berlin. Among other specifications, the plans called for an unfinished basement with a 12 foot high ceiling. The officer in charge questioned this specification, but what he didn't know was that this basement later would be used to store about 3,100 tons of dirt."

An array of phony radar and electronic intelligence gear mounted on the warehouse looked "real sexy" to one participant. This gear was intended to catch attention, to dupe the Communists into believing it was signals intercept/ELINT equipment aimed at the Soviet (later East German civilian) airport at Schoenefeld. The Russians and East Germans may even have laughed condescendingly at the Amis because they had just switched their main transmissions from radio to landline.

OPS SUPPORT

Clarence Berry was spotted and recruited in mid-1948, while still in the Office of Naval Intelligence (ONI), by Harvey, who even then was thinking communications intelligence. Over the next five years Harvey farmed Berry out to several cryptological agencies for seasoning. For the last years of his indenture, Clarence was assigned to the Armed Forces Security Agency (AFSA), primarily to "procure certain 'dated' intelligence material in support of on-going CIA clandestine operations and to help flesh out the files of CIA's Central Reference Section." In blunter words, the CIA was building its knowledge on the accumulated wisdom of other outfits. When Clarence returned to the home fold, Frank Rowlett wrote him a letter of commendation.

Berry arrived in Frankfurt in July 1954 and quickly became involved in tunnel support activities. "Fleetwood was pretty close-mouthed at first . . . not the talkative type. But I soon learned what was going on from our own cable traffic. And I kept my ear to the ground whenever Harvey came down to visit with Fleetwood.[15]

The members of the Frankfurt Staff D element knew how to operate CIA cipher machines so they could encode and decode Staff D messages buried in the normal flow of encrypted CIA traffic. This supersecret channel allowed Harvey and Fleetwood to keep their correspondence even more sacrosanct than the usual flow of CIA messages.

Material for the tunnel came to Bremerhaven, the U.S.-controlled seaport enclave, in American military ships. It was offloaded onto freight cars to be attached to the American military supply train to Berlin. Berry recalls much of the plate and the rails necessary for tunnel construction came from the Norfolk, Virginia, area. The sensitive cargo also included 150 Ampex tape recorders "and jillions of miles of wire. . . . We even shipped in refrigeration equipment to keep the tunnel cool while they were digging."

Once, those in the know hit the panic button. "The heavy, curved steel plates . . . the sheathing for the tunnel . . . were loaded into two boxcars, which got lost somewhere between Bremerhaven and Berlin. There was a hell of a scramble, as you can imagine," until the cars were found and shunted to the right train. "But the equipment in the tap chamber itself, the stuff that was installed by John Wyke, that was British."

Berry continues, "If it was discovered, Bill wanted to blow the tunnel up, so we needed to rig dynamite in it. Fleetwood put the stuff in a suitcase and flew with it up to Berlin" in diametric violation of every regulation known to air transportation.

DIGGING

Soil analysts studied geological maps of southern Berlin carefully to check for water at the projected twenty-foot depth. They found a favorable-looking area next to a graveyard, which the maps showed was well drained.

Berry: "Lieutenant Colonel Gross and sixteen combat engineers went to the White Sands Proving Ground in New Mexico to test the techniques they would use because the soil there was similar to Berlin's. It was a pretty secure installation."

An official document confirms the digging team was to be sent to Berlin "in the normal manner as members of the 9539 TSU, [U.S. Army] Signal Corps. . . . These personnel will at no point appear as KUBARK personnel." The combat engineers arrived in Berlin in two groups in early 1954.[17]

Elsewhere there appear brief accounts of the actual dig, decribing hauling the dirt back from the tunnel face to the warehouse along a rubber-covered rail line; bolting the steel plates together; making slow, sweaty progress in extremely damp, uncomfortable conditions; and continuing, intense security precautions.

The Agency's file report continues matter-of-factly, "Without getting into detail about the multitude of security considerations and actual techniques used in the excavation, I will just say that during the next 5 months or so, those 16 GIs worked around the clock in 8 hour shifts. Starting in the basement floor, they dug down 20 feet, and then proceeded to dig a tunnel 6 1/2 feet high and 1,500 feet long—all by hand—and with the East Germany Police walking patrol overhead."

The engineers "lined [the tunnel] with circular steel plating, bolted together every 12 inches and pumped in concrete grout in the outside voids to prevent telltale settlement. . . . Very heavy air-conditioning equipment was installed to prevent giving away the location when it snowed.

"The Lt. Col. in charge did what could only be described as a magnificent job in all respects—engineering and command—and the 16 Sergeants could not have been a better group. They were terrific.

"When they reached what was judged to be the end of the tunnel and it was time to dig a vertical shaft up from the 20 foot level to within 18 inches of the surface where the cables were located, they hit the spot the first time. The three cables were right there where Harvey's sources said they would be."[18]

Berry adds, "I think it took John Wyke of MI-6 three days, on his back in the confined space of the tunnel, to make the taps on the three large target cables with over 150 pair, and complete the installation."

The GIs dug from August 1954 until February 25, 1955. When it was completed Harvey walked the length of the tunnel right below the main highway that skirted West Berlin and carried traffic from Soviet headquarters to Potsdam to East Berlin and East Germany. On the heavy steel door Harvey ordered be installed to block hostile entry into the tunnel on the day the operation would, inevitably, blow was a carefully worded sign that, in both German and Russian, said, "American Sector. Entry Forbidden by Order of the Commanding General."

Berry: "Colonel Gross and his crew came to Berlin in the dark, so to speak, and left the same way." ASA technicians quickly replaced the combat engineer sergeants to get the op under way. All were under tight wraps and were billeted on site.

VYRL LEICHLITER

References to Vyrl Leichliter, the "outside case officer," abound throughout the tale of the Berlin Tunnel. He must have been in Berlin when I was there, but I never knew of his existence, and I doubt very much whether anyone except those cleared for the tunnel did.

Leichliter was Harvey's day-to-day link with the tunnel. He operated as a loner and kept crazy hours. He accompanied Harvey on frequent, nocturnal visits to the dig. When necessary, he also met BOB's inside case officers—O'Brien, Woodburn, and one or two others—in a safe house. After the meetings, Vyrl continued his lonesome rounds.

Conventional BOBers could at least blow off steam with colleagues. Vyrl, the loner, had few chances to decompress. CG Harvey used to see a lot of him: "He came to our house every night, and they would sit there and drink and talk till practically morning."

CG, a motherly soul, recalled that the sergeants who did the digging had only three sets of clothing, which got filthy while they worked. "So Vyrl went out and bought a washer and dryer, and they washed and dried their clothes before they went out the door. . . . They were so careful about every single detail!"

Vyrl even censored the GIs' mail. Once he spotted a reference to Berlin in a letter from a combat engineer to his girlfriend on the U.S. West Coast. Staff D turned the possible security breach over to Army Counterintelligence, which assigned an agent to date the young lady. The young CIC man learned enough to erase Leichliter's and Harvey's unease.

Neill Prew had the chore of interceding with the Army provost marshal whenever one of the GIs broke loose from the discipline and the conditions in which they were working. "One time, one of the GIs was missing several hours after he was due to check back in. Vyrl was worried he might have been kidnapped and taken into the East, even that he might have defected. But it all turned out OK. The GI had had a fender bender and had been unable to contact his unit.

"The provost marshal, a Southern Baptist, hated the way the kids drank and used foul language and couldn't understand why a civilian was so solicitous about their welfare."[19]

In 1954 Vyrl's wife fell seriously ill; then Vyrl himself had a heart attack. Mrs. Leichliter died en route to the United States, leaving Vyrl with two children. When he recovered, the Agency sent him to the Far East to find a job that suited him. The tunnel story broke when Vyrl was in Tokyo, where he met and married his second wife, Ernie. Ernie says, "He never talked about the tunnel, except sometimes to tell funny stories . . . like how they disposed of the dirt."[20]

When Leichliter fell ill, Clarence Berry was summoned to Berlin. "Harvey drove my wife and me to his home, where CG was waiting. She was very cordial throughout, anticipating Bill's every want. She called him 'Daddy.'" The Martini Ritual ensued. "Bill tended bar and we had a pleasant time, far from the Cold War. I distinctly remember him relaxing in what was obviously his favorite easy chair.

"Certainly my most unforgettable character. A doer. We don't have them like that anymore."

Shortly thereafter, Fleetwood told Clarence that Harvey wanted him to take over Vyrl's job, which would have entailed separation from his wife. Fleetwood tactfully withdrew Berry's name from consideration, upon his request.

Shortly after the actual tap was made, Harvey got in touch with Charles

D. Arnold, who was stationed in Vienna during SILVER, and asked him to come to Berlin. Ted Shackley noted years later that Arnold had been in the FBI with Harvey. Arnold, said Shackley, was "very quiet, very self-contained." Dave Murphy: "Charlie . . . the Great Stoneface. That was what Bill called him."[21]

ROLLING

It was almost time to roll the 150 recording machines, covering the 172 circuits, each of which carried a minimum of 18 channels. The official Agency file continues:

> Once everything was wired up and in place, it was time to make the actual tap. This was the most critical part of the whole operation because for one thing the heavy rubber sheathing covering the wires was pressurized with nitrogen gas. This was to help East German repair crews locate water or other damage to the cables. Therefore it was necessary to install airtight doors at the bottom of the tap chamber so as to equalize the pressure when the sheathing was cut. Otherwise an alarm would be set off. There were about 170 circuits in the 3 cables and as each pair of wires was tapped they were connected to a bank of amplifiers which protected against line loss, so as not to alert the control station. It took the technicians three long days to complete the job, but it was accomplished without mishap.
>
> All of a sudden, we had 150 Ampex recorders spitting out magnetic tape at 15 inches per second. We were in business, big time. Recordings were made on 10 inch reels and were flown out daily. The voice tapes were transcribed immediately in London, while the teletype plain text and cipher was sent back to Washington for processing.
>
> Nothing moved in the Russian military that we didn't know about, and our knowledge about the Russian and East Bloc forces increased daily. Indeed, Harvey and his team were the toast of Washington and London.
>
> This went on for 11 months and 11 days without major incident, but then our world collapsed. We were aware that these three [Russian] cables were quite old and subject to breaks during heavy rainstorms, so it wasn't too unusual to see repairmen dig up a section along the line somewhere. However, on this particular day, following unusually heavy weather, a crew was spotted digging

> directly over the tap chamber. It wasn't long before a shovel hit the concrete slab which had been poured to reinforce the area over the cables, and we had a major flap on our hands.[22]

GEORGE BLAKE

For years after the tunnel became public knowledge, there was vigorous debate about the value of the operation to the Americans and the British. The reason for the debate was the perfidy of George Blake, the Soviet mole in MI-6, who had been in on the tunnel op practically from the start. Blake had been captured by the Communists in Korea, recruited by the KGB in the early 1950s, and returned to Britain.[23]

Blake describes the first meeting on the Berlin Tunnel between British SIS and CIA officers in his 1990 book *No Other Choice*. "In February 1954, the CIA sent a strong team of their experts . . . headed by (Frank) Rowlett, who at the time was Head of the Soviet section in the CIA [*sic*]. Also present was Bill Harvey the Head of the CIA station in Berlin. This Texan had a Wild West approach to intelligence and, as if wishing to deliberately draw attention to this, always carried a six-shooter in an arm holster with him. Its unseemly bulge under his too-tight jacket looked somewhat incongruous in the quiet elegance of Tom Gimson's office in the Carlton Gardens where the meetings were held."

Blake passed information on the tunnel to his case officer in London, Sergei Kondrashev. The KGB Center decided Blake had to be protected, practically at all costs. It therefore allowed normal military communications to flow through the cables Harvey's Hole was tapping, even though that volume yielded huge amounts of military, transportation, and industrial information. The KGB shifted its own traffic to other channels. Blake was, fortuitously or otherwise, transferred to the MI-6 station in Berlin. Years later, writing from Moscow, under KGB supervision, Blake continued,

> In the Western press, the tunnel operation was generally hailed as one of the most outstanding successes of the CIA in the Cold War. Although it was noted that most of the equipment found was of British manufacture [*sic*], there was no suggestion by anybody that the British had in any way participated in or had known about the project. This was too much for Peter Lunn. As soon as the news broke in the press, he assembled the whole staff of the Berlin station, from the highest to the lowest, and told the whole story, from its inception to its untimely end. He made it quite clear that this had been essentially an SIS idea, and his own to boot. American

> participation had been limited to providing most of the money and the facilities. They were, of course, also sharing in the product.

There is no hint of this claim anywhere else that I am aware of. The exaggeration was presumably dictated by the KGB as part of its continuing effort to sow discord among the Western partners. Blake continues: "Only in 1961 did SIS discover, as a result of my arrest, that the full details of the tunnel operation had been known to the Soviet authorities before even the first spade had been put in the ground."[24]

Harvey did not live to read Blake's book. His reaction to it would have been interesting to record.

What interests us here are two matters: How much did Blake really know? Did Blake deal directly or indirectly with Harvey?

Dave Murphy comments on *No Other Choice*: "I think Blake was asked by Kim Philby to include those comments on Bill as a gesture of personal revenge for Harvey's denunciation of Philby. . . . When I tried to get more from Blake, I got nowhere because Blake would admit to nothing that was not in his own KGB-cleared book!"[25]

I asked George Bailey, the third of the coauthors of *Battleground Berlin*, to query Gen. Sergei Kondrashev, who still, I knew, often saw Blake in Moscow. Kondrashev had earlier told Bailey that Blake was very difficult to handle, even though they were good friends.

Eventually, Kondrashev told Bailey he had talked to Blake about Bill "at least ten times. Blake says 'he knows nothing about Bill Harvey.' Harvey was at 'that big conference in London'. . . He saw Harvey there. . . . Other than that Blake has absolutely no impression of Harvey. He draws a blank." When Bob Kilroy learned of Blake's assertion, he exploded, "Blake has no impression of the Pear? What kind of a spook is he anyway? Who could ever have seen Harvey and forgotten him?"

Bailey commented, "Blake is a truly religious nut." Every report I have ever heard about George Blake describes him as being somewhat out of touch.[26]

JIGSAW, BY-PRODUCT, AND POWER PLAY

Bill's chief interest in the tunnel was to exploit its production. He had originally decided not to involve Murphy, but Dave was needed because BOB had amassed a pretty formidable registry of information on its prime counterespionage target, the KGB compound in Karlshorst. When the tapes began to roll in the summer of 1955, Murphy's people provided intelligence backup to the immediate-action transcribers who read the material for early warning of Soviet intentions. And then Lieutenant Colonel Popov, the former Vienna agent reporting on Soviet intelligence, resurfaced in East Germany after an agonizing silence.

There came next one of those exquisite Harvey moments. Bill, absolutely convinced he was right, charged into the Washington china shop. Murphy recalls, "In February 1956 . . . with the tunnel producing an unexpectedly large quantity of KGB personality identifications, much of it confirmable through our BOB information, and with Popov reporting as well . . . Bill recommended, in an eyes-only cable to Helms and Angleton, a new approach to counterintelligence responsibilities within the DDP [deputy director of plans, i.e., the Clandestine Service]."

On the surface, Harvey's proposal was eminently reasonable. Murphy: "Since BOB had by far the largest concentration of technical and human source reporting on Soviet intelligence in Western Europe, Berlin should assume headquarters responsibility," acting as controller and a clearing house for all RIS (Russian intelligence service, generic for both KGB and GRU) cases in the area."

Murphy continues: "We were all very excited about the prospect!" But the grandiose dream was foredoomed, if by no one else, then certainly by Jim Angleton, who couldn't possibly allow the locus of Soviet counterespionage knowledge to slip from his redoubt in Washington to Berlin. Quite apart from the base's exposed position in case the Russians decided to play rough, Dick Helms often turned to his old OSS friend Angleton to handle tricky assignments. Now, the upstart ex-FBI guy was making a power play from Berlin.

The gesture was more evidence of Harvey's faith in himself, his operators, and, sotto voce, his disagreements with the system. Murphy concludes, sadly, "Insofar as I can recall, the cable never even received a reply."[27]

THE TUNNEL BLOWS

Bill and CG were at the Murphy's house for dinner, along with Stan Gaines, who was up from Frankfurt, the night the tunnel blew. When the first disquieting calls came through, Harvey and Murphy raced out, leaving the ladies and Gaines to coffee and wonderment.

Henry Woodburn adds, "We learned of trouble about two or three in the morning."[28] In fact, the first alert must have come around, or soon after, midnight; it's doubtful the Harveys, Gaines, and the Murphys would have been dining and wining much later.

Harvey immediately thought of (a) damage control and (b) response. Clarence Berry was in Frankfurt. "I got a late-night call from Big Bill at my home. He simply said, 'BLACKIE (that's right, in capitals), you'd better get down there. There's a fast one coming.'" Berry said, "I'm on my way." He decoded the message from the Staff D cipher. He was the man on the spot because Fleetwood had returned to the United States, and his replacement had not yet been cleared by Washington to handle supersensitive material.

Berry recalls, "I vividly recall feeling like I had been hit in the belly with a sledgehammer. . . . Next thing I knew they were breaking through into the tap chamber."[29]

Continuing messages from Harvey reported that the microphones in the tunnel, still operating, indicated that the East German PTT (Post, Telegraph, and Telephone, the state-owned communications agency) officials were stunned by the sophistication of the chamber equipment. They expressed the loyal opinion it was a Russian tap on the American ELINT site, allegedly aimed at Schoenefeld Airfield.

But then uniformed Russians appeared on the scene. Everyone expressed amazement at what they beheld. The conversations picked up by the hot mikes still showed no indication that the break-in had been deliberate; rather the discovery appeared to have been the result of the heavy rains.

Henry Woodburn was there. "Bill was down there, sitting in the American end of the tunnel. We had set up a .50-caliber machine gun, and as time went by, the Soviets became somewhat bolder. Sitting back at our end, you could see their helmets with a large Red Star on the front, rather cautiously coming around the curve." And right at the border, the Soviets came up against Harvey's sign: 'Warning: You are now entering the U.S. Sector.'

"Bill said, 'I think it's about time to show these guys they're not welcome in this part of Berlin,' and he pulled back the bolt of the machine gun and let it slap forward. If you have ever heard the bolt of a .50-caliber machine gun slide forward in a confined space. . . . It's a noise you're not likely to mistake."[30]

Harvey was itching to blow the tunnel up with the prepositioned explosives. He sent Woodburn off to get permission from the commanding general in Berlin. USCOB, as he was called, "had no stomach for the proposal and nixed it" once he learned that some Soviets might also be blown up. Simultaneously, the Russian commandant was blowing a fuse, threatening dire consequence.

Berry learned that "officially, the U.S. commandant pleaded ignorance, asked, 'What tunnel?' and said no more about it."

Dave Murphy adds drily that, as the morning and day wore on, Bill got himself deeply involved in technical aspects of the tunnel's destruction. Remarkably, he kept his cool as he dominated "discussions with senior commanders whose only wish was to avoid a flap which might endanger their careers."[31]

As icy-cold furious as he ever permitted himself to be, Harvey returned to his office and once again went out of channels with a dramatic appeal to CIA headquarters for permission to override the commanding general and detonate the tunnel. Berry was still monitoring the cable traffic in Frankfurt. "The decision went all the way up to Eisenhower who vetoed it because we might kill a Russian in the explosion, and that would be serious. There was nothing anyone could do except stand around and wait for developments."

After a day or two, the microphones that had been so useful went dead. Harvey had the tunnel's opening concreted with available rubble and debris at the sector border.[32]

Woodburn: "All that was left was to retreat and block. Allen Dulles, called it one of the most daring and valuable operations ever."[33]

The inner circle at BOB gave much thought to why the tunnel had been discovered. A Russian, East German, even an American agent? Bill never bought the explanation that the break-in to the tunnel had been an accident. Dave Murphy recalls, "I never heard that he had any specific suspicions, but he was never satisfied, blaming it purely on luck."[34] The skepticism was pure Harvey.

Bill's suspicion was vindicated several years later when the Polish lieutenant colonel Michael Goleniewski defected and fingered George Blake.

TUNNEL PRODUCT PROCESSING

Even after the tunnel break-in, the CIA and the British still had an enormous amount of raw intelligence to sort through and disseminate. Processing the take was, in itself, a major undertaking. When the operation was running, the product was quickly scanned by linguists/technicians in Berlin for early warning danger signals and perishable items. The screeners paid particular attention to material from circuits of the Soviet High Command, the East German PTT, and the police. Harvey personally cabled hot material through the special Staff D channel.

Otherwise, parcels of tapes were brought into the BOB registry for shipment out on the regular courier runs to Frankfurt and Washington. To forestall curiosity about the large, heavy packages, the chief of registry,

Norman G., was told they were samples of uranium from East German mines being sent to headquarters for analysis.

Voice traffic was air pouched to London, where it was translated by dozens of white Russians and German-speaking émigrés. Nonvoice traffic, e.g., teletype messages, went to Building T-32 along the Potomac in Washington, where dozens of people printed transcriptions out on hard copy and sent them on for analysis. Enciphered messages went directly to NSA.[35]

BOB REACTION

BOB could have reacted to the Russians' discovery of the Berlin Tunnel with either jubilation or dismay. The actual reaction was total silence—for good reason.

Bob Kilroy heard the story breaking on East German radio. He raced into the office to see Harvey. "I said I knew it was our operation, but a lot of the others on the base did not. . . . The whole place would soon be buzzing. The sooner the lid was put on this, the better."

Bill held a base-wide meeting later that morning. It was one of the few times he issued a direct order to the troops: "Don't speculate! Clam up!" It worked. At BOB (if nowhere else in Berlin), it was as if the tunnel discovery had never been reported. Harvey's order was followed scrupulously by all despite the temptation to gossip and even to share some vicarious pride in what had been accomplished.

Harvey didn't know it then, nor did anyone else, but the peak moment of his life came then in April 1956, when, at the age of forty-one, he pulled back the bolt of that .50-caliber machine gun. It was Ultimate Harvey, a dramatic gesture of defiance and determination. He would have loved to have buried some Soviets in the demolition of the site, and the temptation must have been strong but discipline held. At the end, as always, Harvey took full responsibility for all that he did, even if he didn't entirely get his way.

FALLOUT

The Soviets invited Western correspondents to view America's shameful perfidy, expecting they would reap a huge propaganda coup from the discovery of the tunnel. Instead, much to Harvey's delight, the *New York Times*, *Washington Post*, and almost all the American media lauded the operation. For once, the Agency was given credit for doing something right. And, symbolically, this victory in the East-West propaganda war came not as the result of covert efforts but because of slogging, determined, undramatic foreign intelligence stick-to-it-iveness. Somewhat later came the sour-grapes argument, advanced mostly by KGB mouthpieces in the West, that the Berlin Tunnel had really been no big deal because George Blake had betrayed it at its inception to Soviet intelligence.

Questions arose. How much valuable intelligence had the KGB been willing to yield to protect Blake? Or how much disinformation did the Soviets play into the tapped cables to deceive CIA and NSA? Clarence Berry believes "the KGB did not engage in disinformation. The possibility was studied very carefully in a postmortem, and no particular evidence was found to bear it out.

Thanks to the tunnel, American and British analysts got a keen insight into the manner in which the Soviet military, logistical, and economic systems operated, and with that knowledge, they were able to estimate the strength of the West's opponent.

Berry: "Other than order of battle troop movements and the like, we also learned volumes about Soviet and East Bloc personalities and their MOs including who was dealing in black marketing and other rather interesting activities."[36]

KUDOS

When Harvey returned to Washington in 1959, he was awarded the thirteenth-ever Distinguished Intelligence Medal, which he was then told he could not take home for security reasons. He protested, and eventually the matter was resolved in his favor. Dick Helms, in his autobiography, wrote, "In retrospect, The Tunnel was an operational triumph. Bill Harvey, who pushed the operation through its innumerable, and sometimes apparently unsolvable, problems, deserves great credit."[37]

Forty years later, when Robert Hanssen, the FBI turncoat, was arrested, it became known that he had blown the FBI-NSA tunnel-audio surveillance operation at the Russian embassy in Washington. The two agencies had adapted the technique from Harvey's Berlin exploit. For all one knows, there may well be other tunnels elsewhere in the world even now yielding fascinating and valuable intelligence to the U.S. government, although the likelihood is that American communications intelligence today is more likely gathered by the less nerve-wracking method of catching and recording radio transmissions.

THE ROLE OF CARL NELSON

After Harvey and Rowlett received clearance to proceed, they urgently needed two very special men: a knowledgeable, technically versed executive on the spot, Fleetwood, and a top-flight electrical engineer. They found the engineer close at hand, in the person of Carl Nelson, the CIA's chief communications officer in Germany. Nelson was known as "Old Haah," for "Hot Air and Hyperbole," and as "Wafflebottom-1."

Clarence Berry got to know Nelson right after he got to Frankfurt. "Carl was always congenial and helpful, but he had nothing to do with phone taps, per se . . .

"All the commo people provided tech advice during the tunnel planning stages, and even when it came to processing the take in Washington. But their tech help did not mean that they were in the loop on operational matters."[38]

Some of the information about Nelson in *Wilderness of Mirrors* surprised Berry and others. Nelson probably attended at least one of the preliminary planning meetings in London, "but I find some of the statements in *Wilderness* about his role generally overblown and self-serving. . . . I don't recall ever seeing him in our restricted-entry Staff D office." And Berry comes down hard on the main point: "I certainly don't recall that Carl was 'the technical mastermind' of the tunnel, nor do I think he was the sole 'inventor of Bumblebee,'" the demuxing machine they used in T-32 to separate out the various teletype messages on a single transmission.[39]

Berry recalls that in the late 1970s, a fellow CIA retiree told him Carl was planning to write a book about the tunnel. "I was dumbfounded because, to my mind, that was sacred ground!" The summing up: "I have often thought Carl felt he had been slighted by the operational types and didn't receive appropriate credit for what he may have considered his major contribution to the success of the tunnel op."[40]

Wilderness of Mirrors came out in 1980 and quoted Nelson extensively.

THE ROLE OF THE GEHLEN ORGANIZATION

Another consistent legend has it that the Gehlen Organization was the brains and the organization behind the Berlin Tunnel. Gen. Reinhard Gehlen ran a section of the Wehrmacht in World War II that kept tabs on the Red Army on Germany's eastern front. When the war was ending, Gehlen farsightedly moved his intelligence files to a safe location in Bavaria to use as high-value bargaining chips. The U.S. Army took Gehlen over, kit and kaboodle. In 1948 the CIA became the sponsor of Zipper, the Agency's in-house name for the Gehlen Org, which became the Federal Intelligence Service—*Bundesnachrichtendienst* (BND)—with the return of German sovereignty in 1955. Throughout its early history, former German military people dominated Zipper.

In *Gentleman Spy*, the biography of Allen Dulles, Peter Grose credits Zipper with early reconnaissance for the Berlin Tunnel. It is possible that the incident Grose mentions—a blown Gehlen operation that attempted to place a cable in East Germany across the Heidenkamp Canal—may have led to the considerable misunderstanding that GOLD was actually German. Grose says that after the canal op crashed, "Gehlen then contacted Allen [Dulles] in Washington, according to German accounts of the operation, and the CIA director approved the ambitious idea of a man-sized tunnel from the American sector to the edge of Soviet East Berlin."[41]

Clarence Berry has a possible explanation for speculation that Gehlen was involved in the tunnel. Berry ran a communications intelligence op near Nuremberg, with very experienced, wartime German army personnel who had been recruited by Fleetwood in the early 1950s. They intercepted Morse code messages, mainly from Czechoslovakia and Poland; did preliminary analysis; and located by triangulation the site of the target transmitter. Another Agency staff officer ran a similar German navy group. Berry says, "Neither operation had anything to do with Zipper, which upset General Gehlen greatly. . . . It's possible that the rumors about Gehlen and the tunnel arose from the activities of the two radio-monitoring operations which employed German veterans."[42]

Jim Critchfield, the long-serving CIA base chief at Pullach, the Gehlen headquarters, adds that there was not "a thread of truth in any of the stories of Gehlen's involvement in the tunnel, which occurred during my time. Fleetwood doubled as my SIGINT officer in Pullach and for some months divided his time between Berlin and Pullach. I have no recollection of Harvey ever meeting Gehlen, or in fact visiting Pullach."[43] Thus, no face-to-face meeting between Harvey and General Gehlen at Pullach ever took place, except in *Harlot's Ghost*.

Bob Kilroy gives another possibility. "We used Zipper transcribers on wiretaps which came out of the Berlin post office. It's possible some of the transcribers may have indulged in some understandable preening. It's possible, too, that Gehlen's people didn't deny that they had been involved in the tunnel from day one."

BRONZE

Harvey was a man of appetites, inclined, perhaps, never to have enough of a good thing. Even before GOLD blew, he was working on something else.

Clarence Berry says that Bill wanted to press on and dig another tunnel, which came to be known as BRONZE. Berry sent Washington lists of Germans to be name-traced, "including some phony name checks on nonexisting people to cover the ones we were really interested in."[44]

Peter Grose: "David K. E. Bruce had become ambassador to the newly sovereign West Germany. Upon learning that the CIA men in his embassy were contriving to build another Berlin Tunnel, he ordered the station chief not to put 'a shovel in the ground without telling me first.'"[45]

Bill finally gave up the new op, but only after repeated refusals from Washington. Berry: "As ever, headquarters were a bunch of chicken-livered bureaucrats!"[46] Anyone who ever associated with Harvey can almost hear his none-too-dulcet tones expatiating on the myopia that so thoroughly afflicted headquarters' vision.

A footnote to Bill's involvement with communications intelligence procurement while still in Berlin: For years, decades even, the Russians had relied on the old-fashioned-but-very-secure one-time pad for their sensitive communications, a system that was basically unbreakable, but tedious, because it required hand encoding and decoding. In the 1950s the Soviets started positioning at their outposts something referred to elliptically as "Albatross," an encoding-decoding device that was, of course, a highest priority procurement item for the entire American intelligence community. The new cryptographic equipment was a severe challenge to NSA. Harvey, while still in Berlin, and later, in the United States, regarded procurement of an Albatross—referred to as "the Bird acquisition dream"—as one of his main priorities. Years later, the *Glomar Challenger* spent considerable time hovering over a sunken Soviet submarine, hoping to raise Russian nuclear technology and communications expertise from the depths of the Pacific.[47]

SUMMING UP

GOLD was Harvey's personal and professional triumph. Clarence Berry feels Harvey "was an outstanding intelligence operations officer . . . one of the best in the history of the CIA in accomplishing a given mission . . . assuming he considered it worthy of pursuit. . . . Of course he may have ruffled some feathers at times, but Bill was tailor-made for the multitude of problems which faced the United States during the Cold War. I think it's unfortunate we didn't have more like him."

Tom Polgar, who was not always charitably disposed to Harvey, judged the chief of BOB as "a full speed ahead type of guy who was on top of his career. . . . The tunnel experience may well have contributed to Harvey's overeagerness in Cuba ops."[48]

Peter Lunn commented to me years later about his American opposite number. "Once one had come to like and trust him, you couldn't have had a better friend. He held you closely in his heart, as I did him in mine." Lunn's comments reflect the closeness of two men of diametrically different backgrounds who, working under intense pressures on the tunnel project, had their disagreements, some of them probably flaming, but overcame them. "Bill was somebody whom I both greatly liked and admired. He was certainly a tough character who would tell the truth as he saw it and damn the consequences. But as a friend, he was very relaxed and easy-going, so that it was a great pleasure to be with him."[49]

6

HARVEY'S SUPPORT SYSTEM: MARRIED WITH CHILDREN

After the triumph of the tunnel, Bill Harvey's workload in Berlin eased to something approaching human level. Of course, he still worked crazy hours; he drank; he smoked; he twirled revolvers; he pared his nails. That was the image of the CIA's top maverick in those days. Those who accepted this facade without question neglected Bill Harvey's attachment to his family, which was a rich and rewarding counterbalance, when he allowed it into his schedule.

Harvey's divorce from Libby was sad and bitter. David Martin notes that locals in Maysville blamed Bill for, in effect, keeping Libby subjugated by plying her with booze. Some accused him of domestic abuse and violence. Within the CIA, the gossip was that Libby had been unable to keep up with her surging husband. And there were the never-proven-but-juicy allegations of Bill's repeated infidelity.

Whatever the truths and lies of the gossip, as Bill wrote in an application for admission to the D.C. bar in 1967, "On January 26, 1954, I was divorced from Elizabeth Howe McIntire (Plaintiff) by order of the Circuit Court of Fleming County, Kentucky. . . . [The] attorney for the Defendant was William K. Harvey. The grounds were cruel and inhuman treatment. . . . Custody of a minor child was granted to the Defendant." The divorce came less than two years after Harvey met CG Follick in Frankfurt.

WOMANIZING

But what about the persistent rumors that Harvey—despite his ungainly appearance and often-obnoxious habits—was a legendary womanizer? What better cornerstone to the Harvey facade than the story that he had been caught having his way with a secretary on a desk in L Building?

It's highly probable that Bill, a wily-but-often-heavy-handed joker, cultivated his image as a rake. In the late 1940s, when Harvey arrived at the CIA, America was still in puritanical mode. Hollywood affected twin beds and pajamas; there were girls who did and girls who didn't. Harvey would have loved to tweak the Ivy League effete who, in his eyes, invariably married anemic graduates of the Seven Sisters colleges and whose affairs were usually kept well within the charmed circle. If they assumed Bumpkin Harvey marched to a rougher social drummer, Bill was only too happy to provide them gossip.

No one I have talked with has been able to shed any light on Harvey's alleged sexual adventures and not because they were polishing his reputation. Dave and Star Murphy mention Rita Chappiwicki, who was Harvey's BOB secretary after Maggie Crane.[1] Star once happened upon CG "shrieking" at Rita at a Berlin party. Maybe, indeed, there was more to Harvey's relationship with his secretary than pure business, but CG's jealousy may well have been about business because Rita knew all the secrets, including the tunnel, which were denied to CG.

With the exception of Adam Horton's story, which I have also heard third- or fourth-hand elsewhere, no one has ever described Harvey in anything but sexually monastic terms. Those who knew him, even in the 1940s, cannot imagine him womanizing flagrantly, if only because he was so devoted to his work.

CG FOLLICK

Bill and CG (Clara Grace) Follick first met in the late 1940s, when she was a personnel officer at the young CIA and Harvey was the new transfer from the Bureau. Sally Harvey, the couple's daughter, years later commented of their first meetings, "She called him a 'pompous jackass.'"[2]

CG told Dave Murphy in 1993, "At first, he was so serious, pompous, and arrogant, and all the other things I didn't approve of! . . . Such a bear! I used to have to check my double agents with him, and I just hated even to go to [Bill's] office in Staff C!"

Who was the woman Harvey, despite the rocky start, came to love deeply and to whom he remained married for more than twenty tempestuous years? What manner of woman could have tolerated, and later adamantly sought to defend, a man who might have said, as others before him, "I'm indefensible!"?

CG was viewed with awe by people who met her in Frankfurt in the early 1950s, or, later, when she became Berlin base den mother. Henry Woodburn, who knew and observed her over many years in various locations, describes her as "tough-minded, intelligent, and a very determined woman who supported her husband through thick and thin."[3]

Clara Grace was a daunting, chunky figure, a perpetual enthusiast, a cheerleader for the home team. She bubbled constantly, but she was also tough, efficient, and not inclined to tolerate any form of malingering, much less opposition. In Germany, we maintained happy face in her effervescent presence and then ducked into our fusty nooks and crannies for relief from all that enforced good cheer.

Sally Harvey takes up the story. "My mother loathed being called Clara Grace. We children changed CG to 'commanding general' because her personality was bigger than life, but really, it was a term of endearment."

CG was born in a log cabin on February 9, 1914, in Morgan Township, White County, Ohio. She was the first of three children born to Roscoe C. Follick and Josephine Tibbatts Follick. The obstetrician had a terrible time getting to the cabin on horseback through half a foot of snow, and CG's mother had had a difficult birth—so difficult that she became unconscious. When the doctor asked Ross for the baby's name for the birth certificate, CG's father blurted "Clara" and "Grace," the names of two old girlfriends. When Josephine came to, she was none to happy, but she called the baby CG, it stuck, and from that day on, there were never any periods between the initials.

CG's father was a horseman. Josephine had to work two jobs to make ends meet because Ross bet on his own ponies. By the age of eighteen months, CG was riding. In time, she took on the role of mother. "She was driving at the age of twelve—what else?—a Model T Ford!" says Sally.

Ross's fortunes didn't improve. CG scrubbed floors for wealthy neighbors. In 1932 she finished high school in Hamilton, Ohio. Her mother wanted her to stay home to work, but Ross saw her potential and sent her to Ohio State, where she got a scholarship. There, she chauffeured a family in return for room and board. She graduated with distinction in 1935 with a BS in chemistry and physical education. She also greatly admired her classmate, Jesse Owens.

CG understandably had her sights on financial security and social stature. "Mom wanted to be a doctor but could not afford all the required tools and books; instead she got an MS in psychology from OSU in 1937 and began work on her doctorate in international studies." The switch in emphasis came after she led a Youth Hostel bicycle trip through Europe in 1936. In Berlin, she saw Jesse Owens win, then be denied, his Olympic medals. The injustice became a driving force in her life.

Back home, she had to be content in the academic world until World

War II gave her a chance to move out. In July 1942 she joined the Women's Army Corps, became a lieutenant, and was assigned to the Army adjutant general's office in the Pentagon. For a while, she was an aide to Eleanor Roosevelt, whom she greatly admired. She was the first woman to attain the rank of major.

In 1945 she was in Santa Barbara, California, debriefing Americans who had been in Japanese POW camps. Sally: "Years later, tears still welled in her eyes when she described the tortures the prisoners, many of them women, endured in those camps. The salt-in-the-wound stories were unbearable; she described them as 'beyond ghastly.'"

Out of the service, CG applied to the State Department, in hopes of being stationed overseas. But State assigned her to the Central Intelligence Group. While interviewing new entrants there, she first met and formed an instant impression of Bill Harvey.

CG finally went abroad in a personnel job on the staff of the U.S. high commissioner for Germany. Then she was assigned to a temporary position with General Truscott.

Sally Harvey says that during all this time "she always sent money home to her family.

"Mom is listed in Marquis *Who's Who of American Women*. She is also listed on the WWII Women's Memorial in Arlington."[4] Years later, after CG's death, Sally added, "She was more than remarkable in her own right. I miss her so."

UNDER THE MISTLETOE

At Christmastime 1952, Harvey traveled down to Frankfurt to meet with General Truscott. Bill's marriage was over, although he was not yet divorced. He had custody of but was separated from his son, who was in the care of Harvey's mother.

Sally: "Truscott felt sorry for how lonely my father was, and said to CG, 'Take this guy in hand!' Remember, she still thought he was a jackass."

CG, talking to Dave Murphy years later: "I thought, 'God, he's going to ruin my Christmas,' but of course, anything General Truscott told me to do . . . Well, 'Yes sir!' I said. . . .

"I had a really heavy holiday schedule because I was having the time of my life. . . . I was dating the lieutenant colonel who was in charge of the Military Police in Frankfurt. Since he was head of the MPs, I had a car and a chauffeur at my disposal, and I was treated like the colonel's best girlfriend." She simply brought Bill along. "I took him to all the cocktail parties, to the dances and the dinners . . . had him scheduled over the whole holiday." The MP officer's reaction has not been recorded.

"By the time the holiday season was over and he'd gone back to Berlin, he decided I really liked him!"[5] Sally adds, "He began to think she was chasing him, on orders from Truscott. Still, they soon fell in love."

Peter Karlow, who years later was one of the victims of the internal CIA witch hunt conducted by Jim Angleton, had dated CG Follick casually in Frankfurt, where he was head of the branch that manufactured intelligence gadgetry. Karlow claims credit for having introduced CG and Bill at a party at Christmas 1952[6]—so does Tom Polgar, who adds, "I believe I took first photo of them, kissing under the mistletoe."

The romance was very discreet. Bill rarely, if ever, discussed his private affairs with anyone. CG was outwardly garrulous, even overwhelming, but, she, too, well knew how to remain silent. After the 1952–53 holiday season, CG went to Heidelberg to do two weeks' reserve military training. "Bill called from Berlin every single day. . . . That's when it really started."

When CG was back at her roost in Frankfurt, Harvey took to flying down from Berlin early on Friday mornings, conferring for a couple of hours with Truscott, Fleetwood, and others, then spending the weekend with CG. Sometimes, CG came up to Berlin for the weekend, "But I wasn't interested in getting tied down."

The proposal doesn't sound very romantic, but these were two pretty pragmatic people. "Bill asked if I would consider leaving Gen. Truscott, coming to Berlin and working for him, and then we would be married. I told him I would." So Bill went in to ask the general for CG's hand. "I'd just like to have your blessing and permission," he said. Truscott replied, "Well, I'm not sure you deserve her, but I'll give you my blessing."

"Bill and I had been going together for two years before that [It was actually just over a year.]. . . . I was thirty-nine and I always wanted to be married before I was forty." The wedding was on February 3, 1954.

Bill's mother had brought Jim, who was about seven years old, to Berlin. Sally Harvey: "In Berlin, it was tough on Jim. Dad was always in a hurry . . . in a rush to get back to the office. Jimmy thinks of his early childhood as 'formal.' He had no resentment against Dad. I guess he just accepted it."

CG loved Jim right from the start, and she made "a very conscious effort to explain that Bill was doing really important work. Jim and I really hit it off. . . . I really loved him. . . . The day Bill and I were married, he was standing at the foot of the steps with some flowers, and he said, 'CG, now that your name is Harvey, may I call you Mommy?' That was the best thing that happened to me on my wedding day!

"When Bill arrived in Berlin in December 1952, he had two suitcases and $750 in debts. He didn't care about money. He had nothing when I married him, whereas I had a house, a car, and a bank account. . . .

"I had to work if I was going to get things [at BOB] straightened out. . . . I tried to make the base feel like a family."[7]

"OUR CHEERLEADER"

When CG took charge of the domestic side of Harvey's life, she wanted more substantial premises than the art deco villa at Lepsius Strasse, and she found them at 18/20 Milinowski Strasse, which was almost in Dahlem, Berlin's social equivalent of Greenwich or Beverly Hills. It was a large, rambling house not too far from the office, and it had a pond, which later became a swimming pool. CG could coop her chickens and raise her vegetables on the premises. Periodically, Mrs. Harvey brought eggs around to other base wives.

Part of the role CG took on, once married and settled in Berlin, was keeping a benevolent eye on base families. In the mid-1950s, Star Hellmann Murphy arrived in Berlin with her then-husband. "Someone whisked him away, and someone else took me and my children away to the Harveys. . . .

"CG scared the hell out of me with stories about spies being everywhere . . . even the men working on the U-Bahn subway tracks. . . . I don't think I spoke for days afterward, for fear of saying something wrong. . . . I was terrified of her at first, but later we became great friends.

"She was a bundle of energy. . . . She would do anything for you. . . . A complete teetotaler. Not even wine. . . . [She was] preoccupied with her health, a hypochondriac. . . . She ignored Bill's drinking in public." Dave Murphy adds, "CG could get on Bill's case, but not when subordinates were around."[8]

Herb Natzke agrees: "She was always tolerant of Bill's fondness for alcohol. . . . Well, maybe she would say, afterwards, by way of explanation, 'Bill had had a few drinks, you know!'

"She was an excellent cook. Solid, all-American, meat-and-potatoes food, but very, very good. She was like a midwestern farm woman. Kept an immaculate house. Self-confident . . . Very bright . . . Very likable."[9]

CG HARVEY AND BOB

CG Follick Harvey was not born to be a stay-at-home, pinafore'd wife. In

Harlot's Ghost Norman Mailer makes much of her role as a sort of BOB sergeant major den mother, and to some extent, Mailer is correct. She became, de facto, the base real estate officer, renting, staffing, and supplying safe houses. She recalled in 1993, "I made the deliveries, put in all the supplies, assigned the houses to case officers."

Then there was the matter of the East German scientists whom the United States badly wanted for their expertise on rocketry and other defense hardware. BOB's Sig Hoxter brought a number of such Germans to the West, out of the grasp of the Soviets. CG mused, "These were the guys who were going to get us to the moon. But they were scared to death. . . . General Truscott thought that if I got them onto a military plane and flew with the families to the States, it would reassure them that they weren't going to be pushed out over the Atlantic. We used to have some wild flights. I made twenty-six of them between 1951 and 1955."[10] The tale may have been a slight exaggeration.

ENTER SALLY

Something happened on August 20, 1958, to change the man behind Harvey's belligerent, take-no-prisoners image, even if the facade itself didn't alter. A year later, Bill's mother, Sara, the professor, handwrote a comprehensive account of the complicated and touching affair.[11]

On the evening of August 20, Bill and Dave Murphy were called away from a party. CG took Dave's wife, Marion, home. When they arrived at the house entrance, in heavy rain, they noticed a brown cardboard shoebox on the doorstep. Marion picked up the carton and shrieked. Through air holes in the box, they could see a baby's head. The baby, cold and wet, awakened and yawned. Cops arrived on the scene shortly after CG and Marion and told Marion she could not take the German baby. But the two women took off—fast. By the time they got to the Harveys', CG had claimed the baby.

CG telephoned friends, and in a surprisingly short time and although it was nearly midnight, they supplied the baby with a bed, clothes, formula, and everything else she needed.

When Dave Murphy got home from the office, he found a posse of policemen, waiting to arrest him for kidnapping. The baby's mother didn't know that Murphy was CIA. "She had come over from the East, registered as a refugee, and been sent to a maternity home near our house. She cased the neighborhood, and spotted what she yearned for—obvious signs of reasonably well-to-do occupants."

At Milinowksi Strasse, CG Harvey said to Bill as he arrived, "'Come in and look what the Lord has sent us! The little girl that we really wanted! Can we keep it?' and he said, 'Of course we can!' and right then and there, Sally had a good American home."

When Murphy got to the Harvey house, "Bill was flustered, although he tried to conceal his bubbling excitement. More cops came . . . and Bill told them to get lost. Thereafter, he pulled all the strings he knew how to. He was absolutely determined they were going to keep Sally, and the hell with what German law said."

The police were, at first, equally determined to take the baby to a children's home and were also inclined to bring charges against CG. The U.S. Army provost marshal arrived to mollify the police. At some point, Murphy told a U.S. Army MP liaison officer "that he would resent any interference on the part of the police"—probably not in such formal language.

The Germans didn't know what to do. The baby stayed.

For the next twenty-four hours, chaos reigned at Milinowski Strasse. Grandmother Sara noted, "a continual procession through the house: police, the mayor of Zehlendorf [the borough in which the Harveys lived], welfare workers, the Army chaplain, doctors, friends, newspaper men, photographers. It took almost strong-arm methods to maintain a measure of quiet for the child."

The official English translation of the German precinct report reflects some of the confusion. "Mr. Harvey contacted, it is assumed, Col. Salisbury, which, on the other hand, Mr. Gilardi [the liaison officer] did, too, who received orders by Col. Salisbury to step off the case immediately." Thereupon, the local precinct, by now realizing this was a very, very sticky, no-win matter, tried to buck the case up to criminal police at headquarters, but the Kripo, as they are known, wisely "refused to have any German detective officer take charge of the case, in view of the circumstances surrounding it."

A criminal exposure of a helpless person report was filed. A puffy note of Teutonic frustration crept into the stilted translation. "Since the American parties involved did counteract the efforts of the police concerning an investigation into the case, going so far as to avail themselves of Col. Salisbury's good offices, no further action on the part of this bureau [the local station] should be taken into consideration, Germans having no jurisdiction over the said American parties involved.

"Rules of procedure would have required, under normal circumstances, that the infant child be taken to a hospital immediately.

"A Special Events Teletype was issued on the part of the 164th Precinct."[12]

Police identified the father and reported that he felt he could not leave the East without jeopardizing his parents in Leipzig, so the mother, Christa, came alone, determined to have her baby in the West. Thereafter the legal struggle began in a country not known for the flexibility of its official attitudes. Sara King noted that Henry Woodburn was a tremendous help because his "mastery of German was an invaluable aid."

Christa was imprisoned on child-abandonment charges for three weeks, and then she was paroled to face trial. Bill ensured that she had the best available legal counsel. The lawyer testified that "not one German baby in 10,000 is as fortunately situated as [Sally]." Christa got a six-month suspended sentence and two years probation, but she wanted to see her child. "She came to the Harvey home. . . . She was much moved. Still she conducted herself with great composure and great dignity."

She told the Harveys her father was an executive in a pharmaceutical company and that Franke's dad was a professor of social studies at Leipzig University. "Obviously, Sally comes of fine stock."

The now-defunct *Washington Star* ran the story on Sunday, August 24, 1958.

> **Diplomat Gets a Baby from Berlin Doorstep**
>
> Berlin, Aug 23. (AP) The William Harveys of Washington D.C. went to a friend's party the other night in West Berlin and came home with a baby girl.
>
> "It's a strange feeling to become a mother overnight without knowing it," said Mrs. Harvey.
>
> "It's all very, very simple," said Mr. Harvey, a 42-year-old diplomat in the United States mission here. Mr. Harvey has served in isolated West Berlin for five years and knows "this city is seldom dull."

The German media were flooded with tear-jerking reports that were not entirely favorable to the Harvey's insistence that Sally was theirs. The mass-circulation *Bild* covered the trial under the headline, "I Was So Ashamed!" The *Tagespiegel* clucked, "Our sympathy lies with the baby, for whom we hope that the humanity and readiness of a strange mother can replace the lost love of her true mother."

Nowhere in the German or American press was there even a hint that Harvey had been the mastermind behind the Berlin Tunnel only a few years earlier.

FAREWELL, BERLIN

On July 1, 1959, the German authorities issued a birth certificate in the name of Sally Josephine Harvey.

Almost exactly a year after the doorstep incident, the Harveys left Berlin. One of the city papers splashed their departure with an emotional farewell and a shot of Jimmy Harvey embracing the year-old baby. Another ran a photo of a grinning Pan Am stewardess and CG with Sally between them.

As soon as Bill and CG checked into headquarters, Harvey wrote a lengthy memorandum to the chief of the CIA Security Office, dated September 30, 1959. "It should be noted that this incident and the publicity which ensued did not cause any political or other embarrassment either to undersigned or to the American occupying forces and, in fact, the German public reaction . . . was universally favorable, sentimental and sympathetic."

He closed with a stern request "that any pertinent excerpts [of this memorandum] be placed in [Harvey's] administrative personnel file." Bill also asked that any senior officer of the Agency who needed to know be shown the memorandum, "after which it is requested that the copy be destroyed." The Agency's Alien Affairs Staff quickly indicated that there would be no problem in the naturalization of young Sally.

In August 1968 CG brought Sally back to Berlin, and once again the Berlin press turned out to cheer. A tabloid accorded them front page and centerfold. *Berliner Morgenpost* ran a shot of CG pointing out the very spot at which she and Marion Murphy had found the shoebox. CG told the reporter, "I had to get together 160 documents before everything finally was cleared up . . . and everyone was satisfied I would be a good mother." *Morgenpost* also ran several photos of the ten year old, in sneakers, reading German comics with some difficulty "because she barely speaks a word of German."

More than four decades later, Sally Harvey, a once-divorced mother of a now-grown son, a devoted innercity teacher, and a PhD candidate, leaves the room where she has been dispassionately discussing the turbulent events of her birth and adoption. She returns with a nondescript brown cardboard shoebox and some other items: German-manufactured baby powder and ointment and the like. Sally looks at the familiar objects with detachment. I find them moving in the extreme.

"I was found in that shoebox. CG always told me she wanted a child more than anything else, and I was the answer to her prayers.

"Christa had several requests of my parents. She wanted me raised a

Lutheran, wanted me to play the piano, and never wanted to see me again. It would have been too painful for her, and she wanted a chance to start a new life.

"I've never heard from her. I'm still not intensely curious about her, nor passionate to locate her. The only real reason I would have to locate my birth mother is just to get medical history.

"CG always answered all my questions with information and truth.

"As far as I am concerned, I only had two parents. They are the ones whom I mourn and celebrate. I thanked Mom for bringing together and so fiercely loving our ragamuffin family!"

7

INTO THE CAULDRON: MONGOOSE AND TASK FORCE W

Before Bill Harvey returned to CIA headquarters in triumph in September 1959, he and CG went on an extended duty tour of Europe and the Middle East. I have found no reason for the trip. Bill liked history and literature, but his taste was Elizabethan, not Biblical; and it's difficult to imagine him taking several weeks off to admire old stones. Jim Critchfield, who had come back from Germany, "had no recollection of Harvey making a trip to any part of the Middle East at that time. . . . I became quite involved in both the U-2 flights out of Turkey and all of the intercept stations in Turkey, Iran, and Pakistan in my early months in Near Eastern Division. . . . [There was] no evidence that Harvey had been there."[1]

Upon their return from abroad, the Harveys bought a house at 28 West Irving Street in Chevy Chase, Maryland, which they rented out when they later went to Rome and reoccupied when they came back from Italy. Sally Harvey later commented, "I loved Chevy Chase. But the house was *huge*," even compared to the palatial housing in Berlin and Rome.

Harvey collected his Distinguished Intelligence Medal from the hand of Allen W. Dulles and took over as chief of Division D, succeeding Frank Rowlett. Harvey's very confidential appointment was a sign that he was highly regarded and trusted on the quarterdeck of the CIA, despite General Truscott's misgivings of years earlier, despite the clashes with political and psychological (PP) officers, despite his reputation for flamboyance and boozing.

Formerly Staff D, Division D ranked with Jim Angleton's Counterintelligence/Counterespionage Staff as the most secretive of the Agency's Clandestine Services. In my day, for instance, one required special clearance and documentation to enter Angleton's suite of offices; lacking that, you shoved your piece of paper through a slot in a forbidding door and retreated as if pursued by howling banshees. Staff D was simply off-limits and rarely mentioned—not even in the sardonic jokes that rippled along the temps' fusty corridors.

Throughout 1960 Harvey stayed deeply dug into Division D, conducting its obscure business without leaving any accessible paper trail. On the political warfare–executive action side of the Clandestine Services, though, things were far from routine, even for the CIA. Political, Psychological, and Paramilitary Warfare (PP/PM) erupted in April 1961 at the Bay of Pigs in Cuba, a failure that shortly brought East and West to nuclear confrontation.

The upper reaches of the CIA were in a metaphorical sweat. Richard Bissell, a knight of Camelot, the man who ramrodded the U-2 project and who bore the responsibility for the Bay of Pigs, was soon on his way out. Toward the end of November 1961, Bissell called Harvey in and gave him the most secret assignment in the Agency's quiver.

Simultaneously, a broken and rapidly aging Allen W. Dulles resigned as director of central intelligence (DCI), effective November 28. John F. Kennedy selected a surprised businessman, John McCone, as the new DCI.

With the reputation Harvey had so carefully cultivated, it's no wonder Richard Bissell chose Bill to do some heavy lifting.

THE BAY OF PIGS

Many books have been written about the Bay of Pigs operation, and even though it now is medieval history, it's still one of the most searing miscalculations in all U.S. foreign policy history. Suffice it here to quote Dr. Arthur Schlesinger Jr., the eminent Harvard historian and one of JFK's inner circle, reflecting aloud at a Bay of Pigs conference held in Havana, Cuba, in March 2001: "In the long annals of U.S. foreign policy, no fiasco was more complete, no miscarriage more total, than the Central Intelligence Agency's attempted invasion of Cuba at the Bay of Pigs in April 1961. Historians call it, 'the perfect failure.'"[2]

Tension had long been simmering between Bissell and Dick Helms. Many foreign intelligence (FI) officers had simply refused to take part in the Bay of Pigs operation. It was, said Jim Critchfield years later, as if the two branches of the Clandestine Services, FI and PP/PM, were living in two different worlds. "Just a few days before [the invasion], Helms invited Jim Angleton, Lloyd George, Tom Karamessenes, and me [his top staff] into his office and said that Bissell had just called him in and apologized for not staying in close touch and told Dick the Cuban operation was about to kick off."[3]

"Helms didn't give Tracy [Barnes of PP] the best people," said Al Ulmer, who had been moved from the Far East to a European station. "But Tracy wouldn't have known them anyway."[4] All of the CIA took the rap for the Bay of Pigs fiasco. It was the worst, most flagrant, most costly of many disasters that the PP side of the Clandestine Services sponsored during the Cold War.

CRITCHFIELD'S ACCOUNT

It's worthwhile pausing to glance at the internal working of the CIA from the point of view of Jim Critchfield, the gallant former U.S. Army tank commander/colonel who was for many years chief of Pullach Operations Base, the CIA liaison element to the Gehlen Organization, which in 1955 became the Bundesnachrichtendienst (BND, Federal Intelligence Service).

Critchfield was from North Dakota, a quiet operator who let his deeds speak for themselves. Harvey's bluster and theatrics were intended to achieve the same end. The two barons respected each other, though they were worlds apart. Bill had a sardonic nickname for almost everyone, but I cannot recall that he ever called Critchfield by anything other than his real name. Jim lacked any idiosyncrasy that Bill could have latched onto.

Critchfield was also one of the few senior FI officers who got on with Bissell. Before becoming head of the Near East Division (NE) and after his service in Pullach, Germany, he had recommended military backup for any CIA amphibious operations based on his experiences in the Sicilian invasion. In March 1960, as head of NE, Jim attended a high-level conference in Athens. While in Athens, he and Bissell dined at a sidewalk cafe. "He told me that Eisenhower had approved a paramilitary operation against Cuba. . . . Bissell asked me to assume responsibility for it." Critchfield refused, politely but firmly. The amphibious operation had no military backup.

Months later Dulles and McCone met with Attorney General Bobby Kennedy and Brig. Gen. Edward Lansdale on Dulles's last day as DCI, November 28, 1961. In that meeting, Lansdale told Bobby Kennedy that he would like Dulles and McCone to agree that Critchfield be assigned as Agency rep on the new task force Kennedy had created to dispose of Castro. Once again Critchfield dodged the bullet. "I talked with Dulles an hour later and pointed out that I was deep into the NE assignment, which he had created, and thought it wholly in the U.S. interest that I stay with it. At a dinner that same evening, Dulles told me he had stopped by to see Bobby Kennedy at home on the way to dinner and told him that it was his firm recommendation that I not be re-assigned.

"I must admit that I had no desire to get involved in Bobby Kennedy's operation to dispose of Castro.

"That is the full story on my involvement in Cuba. I stayed away from Task Force W. It was a busy time in the Middle East."[5]

A MYSTERIOUS TRIP

To reiterate, Harvey returned to Washington in late 1959 to take over the cryptological intelligence section of the Clandestine Services, Division D. Given Bill's feelings about paper trails and the nature of D's activities, the record of his tenure at the post is sparse and likely always has been. Figuring out exactly what Harvey was up to from October 1959 until November 1961 is almost impossible. There are, however, some indications of his activities.

A year after he took over Division D, but well before he became the official head of ZRRIFLE, the Agency's assassination program, Harvey took a trip to Europe, probably to vet, although not (yet) recruit, European criminal lowlife who might be useful in Division D's clandestine procurement operations. At least that's what the trip appeared to be.

I have come across only one document that even by implication puts Harvey into direct contact with criminals, apart from Johnny Rosselli, whom we will meet later: a heavily censored CIA internal dispatch from a station abroad to Washington, written October 13, 1960. The geographical names and pseudonyms that appear in the dispatch have been redacted. Originally graded top secret—a surprising classification for what otherwise looks to be a routine dispatch—it is addressed to Division D, Attn: [ ]. from Chief [ ]. Subject: Envelope For [ ].

"Forwarded herewith is an envelope of [ ] notes based on his discussions in the [ ] Station. Please hold for his return." The signature is blanked.

The notes are a page of typed, terse comments, which might be spotting notes, presumably dictated by Harvey to a secretary. The focus of the notes is the Trieste region of northern Italy, but there are subtle hints that Harvey had been elsewhere on the trip.

> Source: [ ] 11 & 12 Oct 60:
>
> [ ] Interpol Rep as source and spotter for Corsicans.
>
> [ ] to pick his brain and pinpoint his ability to do this job for us, but once selection made, [ ] to be eliminated. [ ] believes KUBARK [CIA] handling as matter of convenience in behalf of

Narcotics Bureau [Department of Treasury predecessor to the Drug Enforcement Administration] [ ] to follow up with [ ] on word from Hqs. Purpose is selection of one or two Corsicans as entry men to be teamed with Triestino safecracker.

[ ] Chief of Detective [*sic*] [ ]. Thoroughly acquainted Trieste picture. Appears to have on tap safecracker, lockpicker type, ca. 40 years old, whom he had once mentioned to Rowlon [pseudonym for an unknown CIA case officer].

[ ] outside man in Trieste, to follow up with [ ] after briefing by [ ] and [ ]. Purpose is selct [*sic*] Triestino for teaming with Corsicans, split them after job done. Possible find Triestino speaking German as well as Italian. Possible German documentation.

(1) Siragusa, Asst Deputy Narcotics Commissioner, as source on Corsicans and Sicilians; query him whether District #2 [New York, New Jersey, New England] has West Indian colored contacts suitable for our purposes.

(2) [ ] contact: [ ], Rome, American citizen, has clearance, good potential PA, experienced with criminals; educated England and US.

(3) [ ] offers good possibilities of finding safecrackers and document-suppliers.

(4) [ ] contact Florence: bar owner, speaks Italian, German, English, has thorough knowledge underworld Antwerp and Brussels, working knowledge underworld Frankfurt, Cologne, Nice.

(5) [ ], Chief of Criminal Investigation Branch, [ ] has two expert safecrackers who were introduced to [ ] on 19 July 60 in Barcelona.

(6) [ ] born 11 May 1910, Antwerp; stateless [or Russian descent]. Alias "[ ]," "[ ]." Knowledgeable northern underworld. Possible spotter. Has worked for CID, [ ] Narcotics Bureau, and RCMP. Speaks English. Can locate through CID Fran, or thru desk clerks at Frankfurter Hof, asking for [ ] and using [ ] name as reference with him.

For trng purposes: French commercial film *Rififi* can be obtained through [ ] Interpol; excellent detail on planning and execution of safecracking job.[6]

We'll come back to this curious matter later.

A BRITISH VIEW

As he took hold of Staff D, Harvey needed help wherever he could get it, although he would have been loath to admit it.

In October 1961, two years after Harvey returned to run Division D, one year after his known spotting trip in Europe, and a year before the Cuban Missile Crisis, the National Security Agency (NSA) called a conference on code breaking to which the British were invited. Peter Wright, a former British counterintelligence (MI-5) officer who wrote a vivid tell-all book about his experiences, found, as expected, that he and his colleagues were met at the NSA conference with suspicion—even hostility—by their CIA opposites, particularly by Harvey. Guy Burgess's cartoon of Libby and Kim Philby's perfidy had "left [Harvey] with a streak of vindictive anti-British sentiment," even despite his close cooperation with the Brits on the tunnel and a bond of genuine affection between him and Peter Lunn, the MI-6 station chief in Berlin.

It was an awkward time. The Brits were intent on working their way back into full partnership, to overcome the blotches on their record caused by the still-hovering Philby-Burgess-McLean mess, which had by this time expanded to "the Cambridge Five." Wright had the uncomfortable job of briefing the Americans on yet another delicate matter: the case of Gordon Lonsdale, a deep-cover Soviet agent who had gathered Royal Navy secrets. At a briefing, Wright talked about the Lonsdale case, which nearly brought the conservative government down because of his dalliance with a couple of party girls who had very high social and political connections. Harvey let Wright feel the sting of his scorn over what he considered slipshod British security.[7]

During his trip to America for the NSA conference, Wright agreed to meet Jim Angleton and Harvey for dinner one night. He was driven out to a rustic site in northern Virginia, where Angleton and the head of the Western Europe Division were already present. Harvey arrived shortly thereafter with a bottle of Jack Daniels. The evening did not start auspiciously. Harvey waxed profane as he accused the Brits in general of trying to get money for their projects from Uncle Sam, while harboring another deep penetration in their midst.

"Harvey was all puffed out and purple like a turkeycock, sweat pouring off his temples, his jacket open to reveal a polished shoulder holster and pistol, his gross belly heaving with drink. It was now four o'clock in the morning. I had had enough for one night, and left."

The following day Angleton apologized, saying Harvey "drinks too much and thinks you have to give a guy a hard time to get the truth. He believes you now." Angleton said Harvey wanted to meet Wright to discuss Cuba.

Wright agreed to meet Angleton and Harvey at a Washington restaurant the next day. Harvey arrived looking "well-scrubbed and less bloated than usual, and made no reference to the events of two nights before." He wanted to hear Wright's experience as a counterinsurgency officer in Cyprus during the EOKA troubles, the right-wing nationalist Greek effort to throw Britain off the strategic Eastern Mediterranean island in the 1950s. Harvey wanted to see if British experience could be valuable in the American effort to get rid of Castro.

Bill saw interesting parallels: Cyprus and Cuba were both islands with dominant guerrilla forces headed by forceful, media-savvy leaders. So he asked Wright what the Brits might do in Cuba, if they had to deal with the Castro problem. The man from London was careful to stress that he was not giving official advice, but he speculated that Whitehall would probably do all it could to nurture a native resistance, "'whatever assets we had down there—alternative political leaders, that kind of thing.'

"'We've done that,' said Harvey impatiently, 'but they're all in Florida. Since the Bay of Pigs, we've lost virtually everything we had inside. . . .'

"'How would you handle Castro?'" Angleton asked.

"'We'd isolate him, turn the people against him. . . .'

"'Would you hit him?' interrupted Harvey. . . . I realized why Harvey needed to know I could be trusted." The meeting was about a month before Bill was officially given the "Kill Castro" assignment. He and Angleton obviously suspected the order was coming down from Bissell. Wright also realized that Harvey's bravura performance at the Virginia dinner several nights earlier had been, at least in part, a test.

"'We'd certainly have that capability,' I replied, 'but I doubt we would use it nowadays.'"

Harvey was most interested in the use of poisons. He said, "We're developing a new capability in the Company to handle these kinds of problems, . . . and we're in the market for the requisite expertise." Bill was referring obliquely to what became ZRRIFLE. This statement might also be regarded as a veiled offer, should Peter Wright even vaguely want to consider coming over to join the CIA enterprise.

"Whenever Harvey became serious, his voice dropped to a low monotone, and his vocabulary lapsed into the kind of strangled bureaucratic syntax beloved of Washington officials. He explained needlessly that they needed deniable personnel, and improved technical facilities—in Harvey jargon, 'delivery mechanisms.'"

Bill also expressed interest in the British Special Air Service (SAS), the equivalent of the Green Berets. Wright said that SAS could not be hired out, but he indicated some retired SAS personnel might be available to freelance, if Harvey could get clearance for their use from the British Secret Intelligence Service (MI-6).

"Harvey looked irritated, as if I were being deliberately unhelpful." Wright cordially suggested that the French might be useful, unaware that Bill had made at least one spotting trip to Europe a year earlier.

"'You're not holding out on us over this, are you?' asked Harvey suddenly. The shape of his pistol was visible again under his jacket." Wright made a feeble joke about being the junior partner in the great transatlantic alliance, but "Harvey was not the kind of man to laugh at a joke. Come to that, neither was Angleton."

It is evident from these quotations that Angleton was intimately involved with Harvey, at least in the early stages of ZRRIFLE. And it's interesting that Wright suggested that the CIA might look for talent in France.

THE SIMMERING POT

Much has been made, in a number of books, of Harvey's role as the CIA's point man on Cuban operations. He was the man Bissell and the Kennedy brothers turned to to avenge themselves for their loss of face in the Bay of Pigs debacle. The framework of the Cuban Missile Crisis is well-known; the role that Harvey and his close associates played during the period from late 1961 until Harvey's removal in October 1962 is not.

During the build-up to the crisis, Gen. Maxwell Taylor, the Kennedy's designated top man on Cuba, was determined that whatever might yet come would not be as horrendously embarrassing as the Bay of Pigs. One aspect was to ensure that the CIA committed itself to paper. General Taylor and others did not make a distinction between the Bissell's PP operators, who had been responsible for the Bay of Pigs, and the FI mindset, typified by Dick Helms, which took control. To outsiders, then and later, CIA was CIA, period.

General Taylor told Brigadier General Lansdale to come up with a master plan to wreak havoc, death, and destruction in Cuba. Sam Halpern recalls that Lansdale's resulting directives became infamous for their grandiosity and their sheer lack of comprehension of Cuban reality. "The first thing was to collect intelligence. We all knew we were writing the book as we went along."[8]

SOMETHING SPECIAL

Cuba was something special, and the CIA's Cuban operations were way, way out of the routine. Even despite the reckless Bay of Pigs calamity, the Kennedys urged that normal cautions on matters relating to Cuba be disregarded; this neglect in itself was an insult to Harvey, a man steeped in the clandestine mode who would take risks, sure, but only after he had calculated the odds very finely.

Bill's precept had always been that he would not share his activities with others, especially those outside the CIA, except as absolutely necessary. Yet Task Force W, although a creature of the CIA, was directly beholden to Attorney General Bobby Kennedy, the administration's restless anti-Cuban crusader, and to the heavyweight interagency committee he created, the Special Group Augmented (SGA).

The SGA held forty meetings from January to October 1962. This was an extraordinary number given the stature of its members and an indication of the priority the administration assigned to Cuba. The group rode herd on Operation MONGOOSE, a pseudonym intended to point away from Cuba. Harvey generally considered meetings a waste of time unless he was able to attune them to his own purposes. If they took place after lunch, well, he might have stopped at Aldo's on the way into town.

Bill writhed under the irksome goading of Brigadier General Lansdale, who had captured the Kennedys' attention for his James Bond–style activities in the Far East. Lansdale, who had been an ad man before he found purpose in a life in uniform, was racking up chair time in the Office of the Secretary of Defense when Bobby Kennedy decided he needed a surrogate. "To Harvey, Lansdale was worse than wacky. He was a security risk. 'Harvey seldom really talked to me,' Lansdale said. 'He would never initiate conversations. It was very hard to get information from him. . . . I'd ask for a full explanation, and I'd get one sentence back. . . . It used to burn me up. . . . If I was talking to Harvey, and he got a phone call, he'd start talking code. After a while, I caught on and realized he was talking about me. The son of a bitch. Why couldn't he have just told me he had something he wanted to discuss in private, and ask me to step out for a moment? I would have understood that.'"[9]

Part of the problem was that Lansdale took himself seriously, whereas the men in the Langley basement called him "the Man Who Walked on Water." Sam Halpern had known Lansdale in the Philippines. "He could sell refrigerators to Eskimos, but it was inevitable that Lansdale and Harvey would clash." And it was even more inevitable that Harvey and the president's brother would tangle.

INTO THE OVAL OFFICE

President Kennedy's curiosity had been aroused by what he had heard of the tunnel maker, and he asked to meet Harvey. The story goes that Harvey and his shepherd were waiting for the signal to enter the Oval Office. The escort leaned over to Bill and said, "You carrying?" Bill is alleged to have grunted and to have reached into his shoulder holster. He very slowly proffered his revolver to the Secret Service duty agent, butt first. Everyone relaxed. A few moments later, Bill grunted again, shifted his bulk, reached behind him, under his suit jacket, and extracted another, smaller weapon, which he also offered to the security man. In a few moments, the pair was called into the office. The chaperone is alleged to have said, "Mr. President, I'd like to introduce you to America's James Bond." Harvey later told a fascinated listener that he actually had a third weapon on his person when he went into the Oval Office.[10]

PRESSURES

The Kennedys made no bones of the fact that they did not trust military or intelligence professionals, but Harvey was intriguing, and maybe useful, even though he didn't fit their stereotype of the clean-cut fighter for the American ideal. An Ian Fleming character? No book could have prepared them for the Pear.

The Kennedy brothers had little patience with an irascible civil servant who did not know how to bow gracefully to his political masters. For his part, Harvey, at least at first, may have reveled in the appointment. He once told CG that when the going got really tough, the president had to turn to the only guy who could handle such a hot potato. Harvey quickly made it clear that he was the professional and that he was underwhelmed by the brothers' concept of personalized clandestine warfare. Yet here he was, the imperial tunnel master, suddenly beholden to a rainbow of rank amateur bosses: the president and his brother, a new Catholic DCI, the Boy Diplomat, and from over across the Potomac, a full general and the Ugly American, not to mention assorted cabinet-level high rollers, like Bob McNamara and Ed Murrow. Harvey was on stage in heady company, but showing awe would have been out of character.

CG Harvey commented to Dave Murphy, years later, "Fifth Avenue cowboys, that's the way Bill used to describe the Bobby Kennedy group. It hurt me when they made all those derogatory statements about Bill and his backwoods upbringing."[11]

I suspect Harvey secretly loved the theatrics of the role into which he was thrust. It had everything: conspiracy within secrecy, headline players, international intrigue, a high-risk factor, drama. But I also suspect that, if someone had put Harvey on a couch, he would have growled a bit, maybe farted blatantly, but finally said, very deliberately and very profanely,

"I wanted to do the best job possible under God-awful circumstances. Not, you understand, to save the Kennedys' asses—they got us into this—but to do what I could to save the country from embarrassment, and maybe even disaster. I saw everything I did as my duty to my oath. Afterward—well, afterward, I didn't want to see all the bastards who contributed to the mess get away with it. They tried to dump on me, but I tried to set the record straight in front of the Church Committee." Had Harvey spoken for himself, the vocabulary would have been more colorful and emphatic.

GETTING STARTED: TASK FORCE W

Richard Goodwin, one of President Kennedy's key staff members, wrote a White House memo, effective November 30, 1961, calling for a "command operation" under the attorney general "to unify the U.S. Government against Castro . . . get rid of Castro and the Castro regime." The classification of the memo was so restrictive that DCI McCone had to ask JFK to relax the restrictions from eyes only so he could let his operators know what was afoot.

The architect of the Bay of Pigs fiasco, Richard Bissell, briefed Harvey in November 1961 and hinted that Bill would take over the entire range of Cuban operations. When Helms succeeded Bissell as deputy director of plans, effective February 1, 1962, Harvey was appointed head of what became a supranational, all-out anti-Castro effort.

One of the memorable figures of the CIA at the time is Sam Halpern, who has testified at length at innumerable hearings, contributed to television analyses, and been a source for countless articles and books. He is as close to a living encyclopedia on the Cuban Missile Crisis as exists. Sam has also discussed those fraught days with Russians who were sitting in war rooms just as tense as the White House Situation Room or the tank in the basement of the CIA's new Langley headquarters. Sam is one of those indispensable people who make things really work, not one of the self-enthralled chiefs who duel for rank and parking spaces. In November 1961 he had just come back from temporary tours of duty in Tokyo and Saigon to find himself, to his considerable surprise, named the new deputy chief of the Cuban Branch.

Dick Helms asked Sam Halpern, upon his return to Washington, whom he thought might be right for the Cuba chief's job. Halpern scoured the list of FI heavyweights for a senior intelligence officer, not a political action figure. But Helms rejected the names Halpern and others came up with. "Tom Karamessenes was in Rome or Vienna and was too valuable to move.

Jim Critchfield was important as head of another division, etc., etc.

"Then," says Sam, "I'm thinking like a bunny, hippety-hop, and I say, 'Oh, shit! Bill Harvey is sitting in FI/D, and no one cares about Staff D any more.'

"Helms said, 'I'll get back to you!'" A few days later Harvey phoned Halpern over in Quarters Eye and said, "When's a good time to come over to see you guys?"

But before Harvey arrived, sometime in December 1961 or January 1962, Helms himself went to Quarters Eye to visit Halpern. Sam gave Helms a list of the Bay of Pigs headquarters staff still housed in the ramshackle, ex-Navy temporary buildings along the Potomac that had earlier housed the Berlin Tunnel processing operation. "Helms was appalled [at the list of names] . . . but tactfully." Sam later reproached Desmond FitzGerald, his former boss in the Far East and a PP man: "You ought to be ashamed of yourself. You didn't give the Bay of Pigs operation a fair share of good people!"

Now, in Quarters Eye, Helms said to Sam, "We don't know what we're going to be asked to do, but we need the best men around." Halpern later thought, "To the White House, it was just pressing buttons. They didn't understand how long it took. Spies don't grow on trees." Helms upgraded the Cuban operation to task-force level; this gave Harvey priority on anyone in the Clandestine Services.

Halpern says he was actually warned off working with Harvey because Bill was reputed to be anti-Semitic. Halpern says, "He didn't give a damn what color you were, or what religion. His criterion was, simply, could you get the job done?"

Harvey and Halpern went to see Dan DeBardeleben, a West Point graduate and former chief in London who was now head of the Career Management Section, and requisitioned a list of all the people who had just been promoted and those recommended for promotion. The next day Harvey had a stack of personnel files on his desk. All division chiefs in the Clandestine Services were required to cut loose their best people, if they were tapped for Cuban ops. "Bill consciously played the heavy role; he used people's fears. He knew when to yell and when not to yell at people," says Halpern.

Harvey named his bailiwick Task Force W. The "W" was Bill's memorial to another maverick, William Walker, a colorful freebooter who could not stay away from Central America in the 1840s and 1850s. Walker mounted three expeditions of adventurers from San Francisco; fought in and over Baja California; became president of Nicaragua; and tangled from afar with New York power brokers, particularly Commodore Vanderbilt, and with the laws of the United States. He was eventually executed by American soldiers because he refused to reclaim American citizenship, even as he was facing a firing squad.[12] The reference took Halpern by surprise; he had had no idea that Harvey was a student of history nor that he was widely read.

The naming of the task force could have been a hint that Bill knew he was in a no-win situation, an indication that he was prepared to accept criminal prosecution, even a death sentence, for his role in ZRRIFLE. Farfetched? Perhaps. But Harvey had a vivid, if secret, imagination, and he was above all a thorough-going patriot, as well as the ultimate pragmatist.

Task Force W officially came into existence on February 1, 1962, and at about that time, the group moved from the dank and crumbling Quarters Eye into the basement of the new building Allen Dulles had planned and built out at Langley, Virginia. The task force offices took up about a quarter of the Langley basement floor, which had originally been designed as a storage area for the Map Division, whose low, flat metal cases ranked against the wall.

PERSONNEL

In the Langley basement, Task Force W gelled quickly. Harvey's deputy was Bruce B. Cheever, a colonel and a decorated member of the U.S. Marine Corps Reserve who was recalled from Paris because Bill needed someone who could talk with the Pentagon. Halpern was the executive officer. Covert action was the province of Seymour B.—who had been an Agency contact to Willy Brandt, first when he was lord mayor of Berlin and later when he was chancellor of the German Federal Republic—and Dave M., whom Halpern described as "Big. Huge. Not quite as hefty as Bill, but close to it. . . . He was the case officer who was trying to work with Cubans to take Castro out." Art Maloney, an ex-Army colonel who had been wounded in World War II, handled paramilitary matters.

And then there was Skip. "Middle-aged, plain looking, hard as nails, precise, but a good worker. She probably had a last name, but I never knew it. She wouldn't even give Helms the time of day. Not even tell us if Bill was in his office, or if he had gone out to lunch. They seemed to work together by osmosis. If Bill told her to file something securely, she might have used her own body cavities. . . . That's how loyal, and how secure, she was."

Skip was the latest in a select line of secretaries who served Bill with ferocious fealty. In Berlin, it had been Maggie Crane of Mobile, Alabama, who sat on the floor when she drank martinis "so she wouldn't fall off the carpet." Rita Chappiwicki succeeded Maggie. And then, in the Langley basement, it was Skip. The three knew all the secrets, but they never, ever betrayed Bill's trust.

As always, Harvey compartmentalized. Sometimes he'd tell Cheever something, but not Halpern. Sometimes it was the other way around. "Most of the time, he didn't tell either of us. We didn't compare notes, of course."

Once the pressure was on, Harvey worked his accustomed twenty-hour day. The stacks of PSM ("Please see me!") and OSOD ("Oh shit, oh dear!") cables that passed over Halpern's desk? "By the time you got in to see Harvey, he had taken care of them all."

> He could be a rough SOB, but he had a heart of melted butter, and he would defend his officers to the death. Once Col. J. C. King, the head of Western Hemisphere Division, chewed me out on the phone. Bill picked up his phone, and told JC flatly, 'Stay away from my people. If you want to talk to them, you talk through me!'
>
> I learned to do my business with him in the morning. . . . From time to time, Bill stuck his head out his door, and said, 'Lunch?' and we'd go over to Aldo's on Washington Circle at New Hampshire Avenue, a pleasant Italian place with a garden and above average Italian-American food. Bill always ordered pasta, and he would have two double martinis and one single. Afternoons, he'd nod off. I'd tell the secretary not to wake him. In the evening, he took his gun off, and he'd sit there, twirling it.
>
> When the situation got hairy and we didn't have time to leave, we went up to the executive dining room for meals. There was the equivalent of a small community hospital in the building, which had beds we could use, if we needed to.

HARVEY'S M.O.

There was another aspect of work at Task Force W. Halpern notes emphatically, "The record was amended, even at the time, to make things look good. Even Des FitzGerald later said he didn't want to know and told us to fill out the documents any way we felt like. It was such a combustible project, no one—even back in those days—wanted to leave much paper lying around where subsequent investigators might find it." Harvey was a master obfuscator. He could, when he wanted to, spend pages of typescript saying absolutely nothing. The good stuff, that which was vital, he kept to himself or passed on to whomever needed to know; he put it on paper only when he absolutely had to.

Harvey was also, as ever, elusive. "Right from the beginning, Bill went off on his own." Most of the division chiefs had open travel orders, but they checked with the front office before they did something unusual. "With Harvey, we never knew where he was or where he was going. He could run as many vest-pocket operations as he wanted, and he didn't have to worry about touching base with grandma every time he made a move.

"Then," Halpern recalls fondly, "there was this memo which he headed 'Girth.' Just that. He sent it to the travel office. Took two paragraphs to explain the size of economy-class airline seats and how difficult it was for him to sit in one. So he got a blanket authorization to fly first class from then on."

Harvey, of course, never explained his frequent absences to anyone. Maybe he was on a quick trip to Miami to talk with his people there, or even to spend a few hours relaxing at sea. Or maybe he flew to Europe.

Almost immediately after Bill's appointment to be overlord of Cuban ops, headquarters sent out a book message to CIA posts throughout the world announcing that William K. Harvey was in charge. Headquarters, under the assumption that some of them were penetrated by Soviet agents, specified that liaison services should also be informed of Harvey's appointment.

Halpern: "We *wanted* the KGB to know that Bill was running the show! The Sovs knew Bill well. They immediately realized we meant business over Cuba. So they started hanging tough." Halpern thinks the Soviets decided to put missiles into Cuba as a direct response to Task Force W and Bill's nomination as its chief. For them, "It was a matter of face!"

JMWAVE

By early spring 1962 Task Force W's headquarters staff was in place. Bill's throne room during the fraught Cuba days was, of course, in the Langley basement, but his empire was in Miami, masquerading as Zenith Technical Enterprises on two thousand acres of CIA-leased property. In the Agency the Miami station was called JMWAVE, and it was the largest operational base ever theretofore assembled by the Agency, bested only by Saigon during the Vietnam War and by the CIA's operations base in Baghdad during the Iraq War.

JMWAVE was a body of men and women, case officers, contract agents, administration and support personnel, mostly in and around Miami. But

Cuban operations were not confined to Florida. Considerable activity originated in the American embassy in Mexico City, which had its share of CIA personnel, and Task Force W had officers all over the world, milking air crew, merchant seamen, diplomats, and other intelligence services.

Star Murphy, who went to Berlin in the 1950s, when her husband was assigned to BOB, has a vivid personal recollection of Harvey's main outpost.

> It was almost run by Berliners . . . Ted Shackley, Jack Corris, who ran admin, and a lot of others.
>
> We were all issued jumpsuits and told we would only be in Cuba for six months after the American takeover. Headquarters actually thought that it would only take that long; case officers were assigned to various Cuban provinces for eventual take over. . . . We were some two hundred in number at the actual headquarters.
>
> Some other wives and I were given the joyous task of indexing all the voluminous files and records from the Bay of Pigs times. . . . Nothing had been carded. . . .
>
> In November 1963, a year after the missile crisis, President Kennedy was to visit Miami and speak to the Cuban refugees. I was asked to list those Cubans we thought untrustworthy or suspicious. JMWAVE and Secret Service officers babysat them during the president's visit. We all heaved an enormous sigh of relief when [Kennedy's] plane left Miami without incident.
>
> Then, when it was announced that Lee Harvey Oswald had been arrested, I ran down to the registry card files. Sure enough, there were two cards on Oswald from Mexico City station. Both were from liaison and cited Oswald as having entered the Soviet embassy in September 1962. This scared the hell out of me, and I scurried to get [the information] to those in charge of communicating to headquarters.[13]

JMWAVE's priority was intelligence gathering. This priority was emphasized by the appointment of Ted Shackley as base chief, which automatically implied that Bobby Kennedy's boom and bang would be subordinate to the scrutiny of a hard-eyed executive. Halpern comments drily that Shackley in turn "vacuumed the European stations" to get the people he wanted. Harvey and Shackley did business double-talking on a normal, commercial telephone line that didn't go through the Agency's secure switching system, and they also bypassed the Agency's cable secretariat, which otherwise saw everything.

TED SHACKLEY AT JMWAVE

Neill Prew—the man who took the pistols from under Bill Harvey's pillow, who in the early 1960s recruited agents in the Cuban community, ran raids, and landed equipment in Cuba—offers a caustic view of JMWAVE: "Bill and Shackley tried to bring BOB people to JMWAVE because they trusted them. . . . But our people in Miami were scared shitless of Shackley, because he simply went too far. I thought the whole thing was an exercise in treading water by a bunch of jerks."[14]

Years later Shackley set the record straight: "JMWAVE was actually six hundred people [some estimates ran as high as one thousand], but it was not particularly dominated by former Berliners. Sure, some of them had been at BOB and in Germany, the FI people. The PP and PM guys were mostly from Latin American operations, plus the professional PM group.

"There was a lot of standard FI stuff going on . . . networks, singleton operations. . . . We were reasonably successful. Our communications with the island were good. The product was sound.

"All Bill wanted was to get the job done!"[15]

The stories about JMWAVE are legion. Among them is the tale of a visit by Bobby Kennedy to JMWAVE—an incursion that in itself must have put Harvey into something south of a slow burn because CIA operating premises were off-limits to non-Agency personnel, regardless of rank or stature. As Kennedy roamed the building, he heard a telex machine chattering away. He ambled over to it, ripped the message out, and began to read it. Incensed beyond courtesy, Harvey, in turn, ripped the copy from the attorney general's hands and thundered words to the effect that Kennedy was not cleared to read classified Agency correspondence. Both smoldered. The incident naturally became legendary and was symptomatic of relations between the two men.

Shackley recalls, his voice rarely changing from dry reportorial, "With Bobby Kennedy, Bill had a multiplicity of issues. There was irritation at the Kennedy level. Bobby was demanding, arrogant. Bobby's personality and Bill's were never destined to match. But Bill wasn't always venting when I saw him. He'd complain . . . 'I need authority. I need guidance, but I can't get it by myself from the political level.'

"[Harvey] came down to Miami every four to six weeks, mostly to see Johnny Rosselli. I went to Washington, mostly just for the day, maybe every two to three weeks." In Florida, Bill sometimes went deep-sea fishing with Shackley to unwind from the Washington tensions. "He badly needed the breaks from the tensions and demands of President Kennedy's team.

"By the time of JMWAVE, [Harvey] was a binge drinker. We'd go out on a boat, and he'd drink all morning, and by one or two o'clock, he'd be drunk. But then he'd sleep it off in the afternoon and be ready to go again." Ted makes the comment matter-of-factly; there is no criticism in his voice. Harvey drank. Period.

Some of Ed Lansdale's requirements, imposed in response to General Taylor's misgivings, drove Harvey up the wall. "There was always pressure on us to develop schedules . . . plans. In April we had to schedule for June, which didn't take into account any of the variables, like the nature of the team to go in, the length of time they had to be in isolation, the type of transportation, the weather, the condition of the beaches. . . . All those things that went into an operation. And we had to submit detailed plans . . . thirty to forty pages. An inch-thick document. In detail! . . .

"In some cases, the guys were actually in the boats, near to landing when the operation was canceled, and no reason was given . . . no explanation. Maybe someone realized Castro's patrol pattern had changed. . . . The whole thing was not a sparkling success!" Whether Shackley was referring here to a particular wave of landings or to boat operations in general is not clear.

"Bobby was being besieged by Cubans. Everyone had access to him. The guys from Brigade 2506 . . . they were always whispering in his ear and influencing him." Shackley is not specific, perhaps he cannot be; his tone is flat, not bitter.

"Eventually, Bobby was running stuff parallel to the Agency. Every Cuban in Miami had ideas about killing Castro. Two or three of them together and you had a plot. . . . 'Let's kill him!' and Bobby listened to them." Shackley adds enigmatically, "Americans don't think that way."[16]

Another popular JMWAVE story is the U-Haul truck deal. Writers like this one because, to them, it proves that the CIA and Harvey provided arsenals to the Mafia. The only known witness/participant to the event is Shackley.

"Bill came down with a list . . . four or five pages . . . of equipment he wanted. Nothing particularly out of the ordinary in that. We turned the list over to the JMWAVE warehouse manager, who loaded the stuff into watertight containers. All very standard procedure. I rented a truck through three or four cutouts and drove it into the JMWAVE compound. The stuff was manifested in and manifested out. I drove the truck out of the compound and turned it over. Bill and I followed it to a parking lot in South Miami. The driver of the truck took a hike and caught a cab. Bill and I waited, maybe up to an hour."

Again, Shackley's account is precise and phlegmatic. "It was no different from any other odd request for equipment."[17] With so much weird stuff going on around Miami, and especially because Harvey made the requisition, Ted Shackley did not question the consignment. Indeed, it probably never occurred to him to do so.

During the last days of Task Force W, at the climax of the Cuban Missile Crisis, it looked as if the United States was going to war. Shackley: "Bill was in Washington, but he was maneuvering to go into Cuba.

"American military teams were ready to be infiltrated . . . pathfinders and people like that. I was to be in a plane with the airborne commander. The presumption was that the American military would pacify Cuba, and then J-2—military government—would take over. I guess I would probably have been Havana station chief.

"Then Bobby heard there was a commando team on the water, which he had not authorized, and he called them back."

Herb Natzke saw Harvey in Indianapolis in about 1973, and Harvey said to him that he had been on a plane to Guantanamo when President Kennedy called off a "thirteen-day invasion."[18] But Shackley says, "Bill Harvey was never on a plane that was called back from a flight to Gitmo during the peak of the tension or when the invasion was near reality. He was not in any boat headed for Cuba, either." The surprise in the anecdote is that Bill persisted in embellishing his legend, more than a decade later, even though it was unnecessary for him to prevaricate, especially to someone he liked and who admired him.

WARREN FRANK

As JMWAVE heated up, Shackley needed to find a strong, proven FI man. He called Warren Frank, who had been in Czech operations in Germany while Shackley was at BOB and who later became deputy chief of BOB under Herb Natzke, down to Miami. "I wanted to go back to Germany, where things were civilized . . . maybe to Bonn, but then Shackley asked for me, and that was that." The man Warren replaced as FI chief at JMWAVE in the summer of 1962 "went out in a strait jacket." Frank adds wryly that JMWAVE counted as overseas service for retirement, so a lot of administration types sought cushy berths there since they needed five years abroad on their records."[19]

> What was JMWAVE like?
>
> Bill Harvey hardly ever came to the FI element of JMWAVE. He was preoccupied with the PM staff. That's where the politics were. That and the Mafia stuff.
>
> PM/PP went their way. We went ours. The base was constantly being reorganized.
>
> It wasn't hard to get agents in Cuba, but a lot of them weren't effective. . . . At the time of the [missile] crisis, we had about forty agents reporting from Cuba.
>
> We had one-way and two-way radios in there. Every afternoon at 3:30, we got the messages ready for one-way transmission. Upwards of thirty on any one broadcast. We had eight radios going until early in 1964.
>
> Around the time of the crisis, we had many incoming reports about 'palm trees'—that's what the Cubans called the IRBMs [intermediate-range ballistic missiles]. Anyone who was half awake in Havana would have noticed them. Once [the Russians] had to get the post office to take out a mailbox because they were so awkward to move through the streets.
>
> The reports certainly sounded genuine. Hell, the Soviets had their men wearing sports shirts but still sitting rigid in rows in military trucks!
>
> We pinpointed the missile sites through a network we ran with a whole bunch of subsources. No one knew their names, but they were giving us real-time information: the Sovs built a long antenna, maybe about a mile long.

Confusion and politics entered the CIA's reporting on the missile sites. The FI element of Task Force W had hard evidence that the Russians were installing IRBMs—weapons capable of hitting major targets in the United States. But the head of the Intelligence Analysis Directorate (DDI) and the scientific and technical officers couldn't agree on what FI's reports indicated.

Warren Frank continues,

> Around March or May 1962, the National Intelligence Estimate [the CIA's considered consensus on a given country] said 'it was most improbable' that the Russians would bring missiles into Cuba. They were trying to fit the facts to their theories.

> We were told, 'HQ doesn't want any reports from Cuban sources! That statement became dogma. Our reports officer was told not to [disseminate] what we had! I guess it reflected pressure from the top . . . and everyone had to toe the party line. . . . Everyone in the DDI skewed their reports to fit headquarters' position. Otherwise you didn't get ahead in the DDI. It was like a university faculty. People signed off on reports knowing they weren't true.[20]

Years after the frustration and anger, Frank recounts the deceit coolly, betraying no hint of the emotion of the times.

Shackley: "We had a belt-buckle series of reports which we reevaluated. The trapezoid [launching site] had been identified by human sources. But the Kennedys only believed in photos. That's all they wanted, even though we had the intelligence they had demanded. Then came the U-2 photos." Intelligence analysts always prefer documentary evidence.

Frank shifts to a different subject: "My star agent was Juana Castro, Fidel's sister. Fidel let her come out to Mexico to see a sister. . . . I contrived a story to meet her . . . [and] met her for three days, during the missile crisis, then broke off. I didn't talk with her about anything too deep. Mexico was studiously neutral. . . . Des FitzGerald, who had replaced Harvey by then, wanted more meetings, but I told him, we couldn't treat her like an Opa Locka refugee.

"She passed on a lot of family gossip, but she wouldn't take money. So we bought a box of Cuban cigars from her for something like $7,000, and I later heard JFK was passing them around in the White House."[21]

TENSION BUILDING

David Martin wrote the only account I'm aware of describing the tension between Bobby Kennedy and Harvey, about a decade and a half after the events. In it, he underlines the confusion and the crossed lines of action created by the attorney general as he asserted his mastery of operations.

> Kennedy browbeat Harvey and his aides so relentlessly that after one session, [General] Taylor turned to [Kennedy] and said, "You could sack a town and enjoy it!" The Attorney General seemed to delight in cutting across channels. He would call a junior officer in the Task Force W bunker at Langley, bark out an order, and hang up, leaving the CIA man wondering whether he had just talked to the President's brother or a prankster. [Kennedy] gave one officer the name of "a man who was in contact with a small group of

> Cubans who had a plan for creating an insurrection." When the officer reported back that the Cubans did not seem to have a concrete plan, Kennedy ordered him to fly to Guantanamo and "start working and developing this particular group." The officer protested, saying that the CIA had promised the Defense Department not to work out of Guantanamo. "We will see about that," Kennedy snapped.
>
> Sometimes, the Attorney General would take things into his own hands, and the CIA would not find out about it until after the fact. He sent Lansdale down to Miami in a futile effort to form a cohesive government-in-exile, and kept the trip a secret from the CIA. . . . The Attorney General frequently dealt directly with some of the Cuban exiles who were supposed to be Harvey's agents. They would troop in and out of the Justice Department, bearing firsthand reports of CIA ineptitudes.[22]

Predictably, Harvey took Bobby Kennedy's interference and the fawning support the attorney general received from Lansdale as a professional and, increasingly, as a personal affront. Harvey had never had much use for diplomatic niceties, nor for the established chain of command, and here was a young man with no intelligence background, but with money and a record of crusading domestic politics, trying to tell him exactly what to do, not only out of channels but as if the attorney general had the operational background of, say, Dick Helms—or Harvey.

> For Harvey, it was all too much amateurish meddling. [Harvey] . . . began suggesting that some of the Attorney General's actions bordered on the traitorous. It usually happened after he had been drinking and it made his friends wince. . . . In short, a friend said, "he hated Bobby Kennedy's guts with a purple passion."
>
> For his part, Kennedy thought that Harvey was "not very good." The Berlin Tunnel "was a helluva project," Kennedy conceded, "but . . . then he ended in disaster. . . . " Stories began to circulate. One had it that Harvey had flatly refused a direct order from Kennedy, then slapped his gun down on the conference table and spun it around so that the barrel pointed at the Attorney General. The story was almost certainly apocryphal, but its very existence signaled that something was disastrously wrong. . . .
>
> Harvey displayed his contempt in other ways as well. At meetings he would "lift his ass and fart and pare his nails with a sheath

> knife," Helms's aide, Walt Elder, once said. One day at the Pentagon, Harvey took his gun from his pocket, and began playing with the bullets in an elaborate show of boredom. The incident caused such a ruckus that the CIA issued new regulations regarding the carrying of firearms by employees.[23]

Halpern provides the other side. When Harvey came back from his frequent, taut meetings with Lansdale, the SGA, or Bobby Kennedy, he was "uptight . . . steaming. . . . He clenched his jaws . . . shifted his weight from side to side. He blew off profanely . . . but nothing specific. He let you know he didn't like what was going on at the high levels. It got so, that Skip, the secretary right outside his door, didn't blush any more."

The CIA man who bore the brunt of Bobby Kennedy's impetuousness was Helms, who was by that time head of the Clandestine Services. But Helms did not want to know too much about what was going on. He had put his trust in Harvey, his chosen operator. The arrangement gave Helms plausible deniability.

Harvey was loyal to those he considered of like mind, up as well as down. Despite the "Boy Diplomat" nickname he pinned on Helms, Halpern recalls, "Bill never made any derogatory comment on Dick. He respected Helms, not as another case officer, but as an administrator. . . . A good politician, who kept his fences mended. But Bill didn't think Dick would make good DCI material.

"Bill didn't share his personal comments or views on Dick Helms and RFK, but he felt strongly [that] the Kennedys should not be in charge."

And Helms at the time was unwilling to see, and/or deal with Harvey's growing drinking problem.

"WASHINGTON POLITICAL OPERA"

In mid-February 1962 Lansdale produced a game plan that he claimed would lead to the violent demise of the Castro regime by October—just in time for the midterm congressional elections. Lansdale demanded a weekly listing of agents of all varieties landed and operating in Cuba, and he wanted frequent accounting for arms and ammunition supplied to clandestine infiltrators—all very much in the manner of charts for a marketing campaign and very much against CIA custom. Lansdale applauded the thought of using "gangster elements" to further his operations. Predictably, Harvey reacted negatively to the Kennedys' volatile impatience and to Lansdale's attempts to control Agency activities.

Halpern: "Everyone was happy when the SGA turned down Lansdale's timetable of requirements and said it needed hard intelligence. That gave our spirits a big lift."

Partially in response and partially as a preemptive strike, Halpern tried to write a paper for the SGA on behalf of Harvey, who certainly wouldn't have written as tactfully. Halpern's paper said, in effect, "Sure, we'll do what you want, boss! But we have to be honest about the limitations on us."

As the Kennedy domination of Cuban operations became more pronounced, Halpern developed the feeling that "this whole thing had nothing to do with the security of the United States. It was a Washington political opera, which had everything to do with saving face after the Bay of Pigs fiasco. . . . Our drafts were kicked back to us all through the holiday season, 1961–62."

The approved gem out of the basement was "Operation MONGOOSE—Appraisal of Effectiveness and Results Which Can Be Expected From Implementing the Operational Plan Approved at the Meeting of the Special Group on 16 March 1962, William K. Harvey through Richard Helms to DCI McCone, 10 April 1962." The substance of the intragovernment debates is thoroughly covered in the postmortems on the maneuvering that led up to the Cuban Missile Crisis. Harvey and the CIA argued that nothing of an overt nature, such as landings or encouragement of insurrection against Castro, should be undertaken unless and until the Agency had developed a strong and reliable intelligence-gathering network inside the country. The professionals in the Langley basement spent days explaining to their superiors outside the CIA what intelligence gathering was all about and emphasizing, repeatedly, that covert intelligence could be won only by following meticulously planned steps.

Tom Parrott, secretary of Bobby Kennedy's SGA, talked to David Martin for *Wilderness of Mirrors*: "'Nobody knew exactly what they wanted to do. . . . What was our policy toward Cuba? Well, our policy toward Cuba was to keep the pot simmering. Over and over the phrase was used, 'Keep the pot simmering.'"

Harvey resisted the brass. He griped that the demand for detail was "excruciating." Kennedy's lieutenants, in turn, found Harvey to be an appalling spectacle, especially after lunch. JFK's national security adviser, McGeorge Bundy, told Parrott, "Your Mr. Harvey does not inspire great confidence."

Martin continues, "The SGA even wanted to know what rations the raiders would carry. 'It was almost as if Bill and the rest of us were accused of trying to sucker them into another Bay of Pigs,' Harvey's paramilitary aide said. 'It was an insult to our professionals.' Sam Halpern added, 'and it was a useless exercise. What difference did it make if they were carrying a .38 or a .45?'

"Exasperated, Harvey complained to McCone. 'To permit requisite flexibility and professionalism for a maximum operational effort against Cuba, the tight controls exercised by the Special Group and the present, time-consuming coordination and briefing procedures should, if at all possible, be made less restrictive and less stultifying,'" he wrote in typically longwinded fashion.[24]

It's not hard to picture Harvey, sitting at a polished conference table in which he yearned to carve his initials, defensively offensive as senior members of the government pressed him for details and explanations they had no need to know. Harvey would rebel internally, rumble, then explode in a fury of thin-lipped frustration or retreat into obfuscating governmentese.

Bill probably respected some of the SGA members, like General Taylor, as men of accomplishment and integrity. Others, like Lansdale, he scorned, too openly. And for Bobby Kennedy, he had nothing but loathing because the attorney general was, in Bill's eyes, an undisciplined opportunist who would sacrifice any principle, as well as security and the lives of people he did not know, to score brownie points of personal revenge against Castro.

For a while, the episodes were funny to Harvey's staffers in the Langley basement. There was Bill, the dragon slayer, out tilting at windmills. But gradually, people like Sam Halpern realized that Bill was increasingly, and sadly, beginning to run out of control.

BOOM AND BANG

The cynical war cry in the Langley basement was (taken from a Kennedy demand) "boom and bang." That was what Bobby Kennedy wanted, and that was what Ed Lansdale was determined to give him. Support for deposing Fidel Castro came, of course, from the noisy enthusiasts in Miami's Cuban exile community. Every CIA officer who dealt with the exiles noted that they hatched assassination plots every other day, yet the Cubans were notoriously unable to keep secrets. And they seemed to have that open line to the attorney general's office.

By October 14, 1962, as the missile crisis loomed, Bobby was urging "massive activity" against Castro, a broad program of sabotage that would hit the Soviet military presence in Cuba, by now estimated to include, according to Cecil Currey's biography of Lansdale, "20,000 Soviet military,

1,300 field artillery pieces, 700 anti-aircraft guns, 3,250 tanks, 150 jets—all poised and waiting. U-2 spy planes then confirmed that the Soviets were constructing some half dozen launch sites for the surface-to-surface intermediate-range missiles."[25]

Shackley's people at JMWAVE estimated forty-four thousand to forty-five thousand Soviet troops on the island. The actual number was forty-two thousand. Harvey's appointment to head Cuban operations had provoked the Soviets to reinforce their presence on Castro's island.

The days and nights in the CIA basement were grueling. Halpern whips out a battered Hallmark wallet calendar for the year 1962, which he still carries.

> Bill didn't leave the office much after October 15. He was working flat out. We were all dead on our feet. No one ever told us we couldn't go home. Pretty much everyone just stayed.
>
> Whether you were making any sense or not, only someone else could tell. . . . With Bill Harvey, you just stayed there and worked until he sent you home. You might have fought him because he was still there, but he just said, "Out!" and you had to go.
>
> October 20 was a Saturday. Bill threw me out of the office. I had been working continually for seventy-two hours . . . no shower. I hadn't shaved. Bill said, "You're out on your feet. Go home, get some sleep. I'll call you when I need you." He even took my badge, so I couldn't get back into the building without him escorting me.
>
> My phone rang at noon on Sunday. I had slept straight through. "You're my last fresh troops," he said. So I got up, shaved, and went back in.
>
> We at the working level knew on the fifteenth [about the IRBMs], when we got the photos from the photo interpretation people. JFK knew on October 16. Our crisis lasted from then until the twenty-second.
>
> If it had continued much longer after October 22, all of us would have really been out on our feet.

The official end of the Cuban Missile Crisis was on Sunday, October 28.

How close did we come to nuclear war?

> I was very concerned in the first few days. But then, in the days right after, we were getting NSA material which told us there was no Soviet military build-up. They didn't call up their reserve classes

> of conscripts for the armed forces . . . there was no sudden change in orders or disposition for railroad box cars . . . or supply ships . . . or aircraft. . . . The Russian forces in Germany went on a higher state of alert. . . . But that was the only thing. The Russians weren't getting ready to fight a war!
>
> The Kennedys ordered Defcon 2. SAC [Strategic Air Command] was in the air, communicating in the clear [i.e., basically telling the Soviets we were prepared to bomb Russia if necessary]. In our office, we were wondering what the hell was going on! Of course, we didn't know then that the Russian general had tactical nukes at his disposal, and the authority to use them . . . until Khrushchev took that authority way from him.
>
> Then Major Anderson was shot down on October 27, and the Russians threw in the towel on the twenty-eighth.

The Kennedy brothers most certainly had not reckoned with the possibility of offensive nuclear weapons in Cuba. From Moscow, Col. Oleg Penkovsky told the CIA that the missiles in Cuba could be readied to strike the United States in less than a day.

BLOW-UP

There have been various accounts of the maneuvering that brought the Cold War to flashpoint in October 1962, but there have not been many that told of an intense clash—indeed animosity—between Attorney General Bobby Kennedy and the man appointed to carry out the Kennedy brothers' revenge on Castro for the humiliation of the Bay of Pigs, Bill Harvey.

Harvey tried valiantly for nine months to bring some order to Cuban operations, and as an FI man, he continued to stress the need for solid intelligence before military vengeance was sought by the administration. And then he got into career-destroying trouble by once again thinking that his way was the best way, despite what his overlords thought and said.

It all came unglued on the afternoon of Friday, October 26, 1962. Halpern: "We heard that Bobby said to Harvey, 'I could train agents at my house in Virginia!' And Harvey retorted, 'as baby-sitters?'"

To this day, there is still no absolute clarity about all that happened in the culmination of friction between Bobby Kennedy and Harvey. We do know that during that afternoon or early evening, DCI John McCone decided Harvey had "outlived his usefulness." There most definitely was a meeting of the MONGOOSE principals across the Potomac, in the Joint

Chiefs of Staff Operations Room at the Pentagon, starting at 2:30, i.e., after lunch. The minutes, dated October 29, written by the Special Group Augmented's secretary, Tom Parrott, and originally stamped "SECRET—EYES ONLY," survive and are predictably bland, almost more interesting for what they omit than for what they say. The official record gives no hint of tension or rising tempers, even though everyone in the room, even those who were highly disciplined, must have been somewhat on edge and close to exhaustion in the full spate of the Cuban Missile Crisis. It was a time when the United States military was rapidly preparing for war.

Much of the discussion dealt with a plan to launch nine covert teams, details further unspecified, into Cuba. "Lansdale disavowed any responsibility for, or information of, the proposed infiltrations. General Taylor stated JCS had not established any such requirements, nor had they outlined requirements toward which they could contribute." Lansdale would canvas several agencies. "After this examination it will then be decided what the best use of these assets actually should be."

Then comes the discussion of the three agent teams which Bobby Kennedy had recalled while they were at sea en route to Cuba. The attorney general's action cancelled a mission that the CIA considered part of its responsibility under long-standing guidelines with the Pentagon. To RFK, the boats were an Agency end-run, an attempt to operate behind his back and without his authority, a flagrant violation of political control of the government, especially when he was involved in separate sensitive maneuvers to defuse the showdown.

The dry minutes reflect nothing of any open flare-up between Kennedy and Harvey. "Mr. McCone and Mr. Harvey said during the course of the discussion on agent teams that the action taken had represented a unilateral decision by CIA and was not in response to specific military requirements. CIA had felt that this was within its sphere of responsibility, and particularly with respect to the first three teams, had considered that it was a continuation of previously-approved operations."

McCone seemed to try to mollify the Kennedy side by commenting that Cuban security had improved noticeably within the last two weeks, "therefore agent activity on this scale will only be justified if the responsible departments specifically require it for intelligence purposes. . . . Mr. Harvey made the point that the proposed agent dispatches would not use up all existing assets."

At the end of the minutes: "It was reiterated that General Lansdale is the focal point for all Mongoose activities, that he is charged with their overall management and that he should be kept informed."[26]

Even though they are not elaborated in Parrott's memorandum, harsh words fitting the tensions of the moment must have been exchanged during the meeting. And it must have been galling for Harvey to have Lansdale's authority over MONGOOSE operations confirmed, even though Bill was well aware that Lansdale held the Kennedys' personal brief on clandestine matters to do with Cuba.

More than four decades after the searing events of the October days, Parrott does not recall a particular showdown on that day between Harvey and Bobby Kennedy. "Of course he had had a couple of martinis before the meeting. But I was the only one there who knew him and his habit. . . . Well, [Gen.] Max Taylor did say to me, 'Tell your friend Mr. Harvey to stop mumbling into his umbilical cord!'"

Parrott probably had little respect for Harvey while both were in Germany. Now, in retrospect, his view of Bill has mellowed. "I thought it was unfair to Bill that they fired him. He had dispatched the teams under the rules. . . . Of course he hated getting all the clearances [that the military and Lansdale] required, but he had gotten the approval of the principals. Bill did maintain that he had the authority to dispatch the boats."

And, again, for emphasis, Tom says, "During the missile crisis, everyone was told to stand [provocative acts] down, but Bill had no way to call the boats back."[27]

The boat mission might not have looked then, to anyone who knew Bill's record, to be another instance of Harvey pushing against established authority—going out on a risky limb to do what he considered right, despite the considered judgment of the U.S. government. Parrott underlines that Bill went by the book and was sure he had the authority to send the boats on their way. But, to a probably overwrought Bobby Kennedy, Harvey's behavior qualified as insubordination from a man who had been difficult and abrasive in the past; perhaps Bobby took it as a personal provocation, as well as a danger to the peace-making negotiations.

Bill had done only what he considered best, in line with Pentagon requirements, and he obviously had gotten himself into a tense showdown with Bobby Kennedy, even though this is not reflected in the minutes. Then, he had the rug pulled out from under him. The military didn't back him up when the crunch came, and Bobby, who may have been looking for cause, made it obvious that Harvey was a liability to the CIA.

Halpern's memory of a personal, eyeball-to-eyeball showdown is not reliable, but that is not Sam's fault. Perhaps his recollection of the circumstances of Bill's crash was embellished over time because it is based on what Harvey told him all those years ago.

When Harvey came back from across the water, back to the Langley basement, he likely was steaming even more than usual after an encounter with Bobby Kennedy and Lansdale. He may well be forgiven for having dramatized the circumstances of his dismissal from Cuban operations, transferring the showdown, in the telling, from the Joint Chiefs' Operations Room to the White House Cabinet Room. Halpern and his colleagues would not necessarily have known where the meeting was held, nor who had taken part in it, and they would have eagerly accepted Bill's version as just another indicator that the CIA was ever more under the control of the nation's political leaders, who had no understanding of and little respect for the professionals of intelligence.

If, indeed, Harvey embellished and dramatized the circumstances of his ouster from the Cuba chair, he was certainly forgiven by his loyal staff, who then, of course, spread the word in the Langley corridors. Halpern would not have invented a fiction to make Harvey look good. Here is Sam's version of that fateful day:

Harvey approved the dispatch of six three-man teams to Cuba, on either October 21 or 22, 1962, as the missile crisis heated up. The missions were launched at the specific request of the Pentagon, as part of the standing Interagency Command Relationship Agreement. The military was reckoning with an invasion of Cuba by air and sea; its forces needed support on the ground to help the landings. Harvey did what was right operationally and within the framework of the interservice agreement. The CIA dispatched the three teams of saboteurs or perhaps pathfinders for an American airborne invasion toward Cuba.

It is, of course, possible, given Bill's rambunctious, iconoclastic mindset, that he launched the three boats as a provocation, to force strong American action in response to the threat of the Soviet IRBMs. Remember the episodes in Berlin, when Bill urged the administration to take risks he considered justified, to face the Soviets down. Bill's humiliation—being shoved aside by McCone—was made all the deeper because Lansdale was reconfirmed as the point man on "all MONGOOSE activities."

Still, for Harvey the professional, dismissal was the final joust. The whole MONGOOSE effort had long been too personalized, the erratic pressures from topside had become too intense, the piddling requirements laid on Harvey by Lansdale too annoying, the Kennedy interference too obvious, too irrational, too far out of the line of normal operational procedure, too unprofessional.

Halpern says Harvey blew his cool, personally and with Harvey-esque obscenity, in the face of the attorney general. According to Sam, the climax came at a top-drawer meeting in the Cabinet Room of the White House on October 26. Whatever the immediate point of friction, says Halpern, Harvey chose to tell the Kennedy brothers what he thought of them and their handling of the situation. "If you fuckers hadn't fucked up the Bay of Pigs, we wouldn't be in this fucking mess!"

In itself, this version of the episode is interesting if for no other reason than that its source must have been Harvey, who did not usually give sensitive background to his subordinates—or to anyone. It's possible that a deeply wounded, even bitter, Harvey went back to Langley and gave his staff this version, inserting Jack Kennedy and setting the scene at the White House, in a forlorn face-saving grasp at credibility. The truth lies in CIA papers that have not been released.

Harvey's Lone Rangerism and its accompanying insubordination could not be tolerated in a government as top-down as the Kennedy administration. Harvey had crossed the line once too often. He had to go.

Was his self-immolation before the Kennedys simply the outburst of an exhausted man who had been given a series of impossible jobs, harassed by an image-conscious-adman-turned-soldier, overseen by politically driven, headlining people whom he considered incompetent meddlers? Was Harvey consumed by William Walker's story? Was the final blow-up simply a melodramatic drunken spasm? Or was there something more to Harvey's scathing personal denunciation of John F. and Robert F. Kennedy?

Halpern: "Everyone had expected something like this to happen one of those days. But we were all professionals. . . . We all knew when to keep our mouths shut. Bill was not embarrassed by his outburst, but he was censured for being 'disrespectful to the president.'

"Bill hinted that Helms saved his skin. . . . He was very stoic about it. I felt very sorry for Bill after he was removed."

Warren Frank recalls, "They chewed Harvey pretty bad. When he was relieved, all we could do was say, 'It's been nice working for you.' That was all. . . . They had him sit in the middle of all those desks and all that activity, doing absolutely nothing. . . . Just sitting in that damn office in Langley, twiddling his thumbs! . . . Just sitting there, as punishment! It took them a couple of months to transfer him to Rome."

Even Tom Parrott, who had not been overly friendly to Harvey years earlier in Germany, now says, "That meeting was the end of an era, really. I thought it was unfair that they fired Harvey. He had dispatched the teams under all the rules. Bill did maintain that he had the authority to dispatch the boats, but he couldn't get them back.

"No, there was no obvious tension between Bobby and Harvey at that meeting . . . no showdown. But it was convenient to get rid of Bill.

"Everyone was fed up with Bobby. He was a dreadful little guy. I didn't see any saving grace in him. . . . He would come into meetings with his necktie down and his shirt unbuttoned when everyone else was formally dressed. He was always picking, picking. Bobby affected everyone. No one wanted to deal with him if they didn't have to. . . . He was abrasive."

Still, "after the meeting, driving back to the White House, Mac Bundy said to me, 'Bill doesn't inspire confidence, does he?'"

THE MAN WHO NEVER WAS

The trouble with Bobby Kennedy was the start of Bill's decline from the peak of power and capability. Whether what happened on October 26 crushed the inner Harvey is moot. Suffice it that within the next few years, his drinking became a huge, visible problem, and reasonable questions were raised, even among friends, about his judgment.

Harvey accepted the consequences of his actions. The consequences of his work in Berlin had been praise and a medal. In Washington and Miami, they were argument, frustration, fury—shaming and reassignment. He had held sway over his empire for nine hectic months in 1962, a huge, nearly overt yet clandestine juggernaut aimed at Fidel Castro's Cuba.

The "First Intelligence History Seminar" run by the Agency's Center for the Study of Intelligence on October 19, 1992, dealt with the CIA and Cuba. Not once was Harvey mentioned in all the panel discussions, nor in written handout material.

Decades later Bill's boss in the 1960s, Dick Helms, observed in his memoir that Harvey was "an aggressive officer and a demanding and conscientious executive, and he had a good knowledge of the operations personnel he could count on."[28] The Boy Diplomat, then at an advanced age, chose to ignore the friction between Bobby Kennedy and Harvey.

The various accounts above leave out what else was going on in Harvey's bailiwick, two related matters that later led to much questioning and soul-searching: the ongoing political assassination operation, codenamed ZRRIFLE, and the association between Harvey and Filippo Sacco, aka Johnny Rosselli.

8

PLOTTING ASSASSINATION: ZRRIFLE

Whether or not he agreed with its objectives, the ungainly Bill Harvey ran the Agency's hit squad, the designated instrument of the Kennedys' revenge on Fidel Castro, from November 1961 until his degradation in the midst of the Cuban Missile Crisis in October 1962. He performed the assignment in his customary clandestine fashion, which called upon all the skills he had accumulated during his years of covert practice and required secrecy that almost made the Berlin Tunnel look like an open book.

Right out of the gate, Bill decided he would have to be the only person who knew precisely what was going on in the assassination operation. If the case blew, Harvey would take the rap. The tactic afforded plausible deniability to the U.S. president and his brother, the attorney general, as well as to Bill's own underlings. It was tradecraft very much in keeping with the code of the intelligence service.

In what follows, I have had to rely almost exclusively on official documents, with the exception of a few comments from people who worked with Harvey during the period. The reason for this is simple and typical Harvey: he consulted no one, not even, in many cases, his boss, Dick Helms, or his closest associates, among them Ted Shackley and Sam Halpern. Part of his reserve was the conspiratorial persona of Harvey; part of it was his realization that he was playing with dynamite; part of it was his acceptance of the rote that the ball stopped with him. He did not want to involve his subordinates in matters that might become messy. Harvey accepted total responsibility for matters which, later, others did their utmost to shrug off or to lie or plead ignorance about.

ACCEPTING RESPONSIBILITY

Richard Bissell, CIA's deputy director of plans, carried the can for the humiliating failure of the Bay of Pigs operation. A brilliant, Ivy League, staunch PPer, Bissell, the man behind the U-2, had become a personal and political embarrassment for the Kennedys. He knew he was on the way out when he intimated to Harvey, toward the end of 1961, that the Cuba portfolio, and all that came with it, would be his.

The first time the U.S. government had become involved in foreign assassination planning and/or execution was in the botched, seriocomic 1960 attempt on the life of Gen. Rafael Trujillo, the Dominican Republic's dictator at the time, undertaken at the behest of President Eisenhower, who felt the world would be a better place without the Caribbean dictator. The attempt on Trujillo happened to coincide with the interests of the Mafia, which had gambling investments in in the Dominican Republic. "There was some talk about it but that was it. All talk. I think people got cold feet," says Sam Halpern. The Church Committee later exonerated the CIA of any responsibility in Trujillo's death in 1960. In 1960 there was also the Lumumba affair, dealt with below.

Now the target was Cuba. Helms says in his memoir, "At the Agency, the impression was that Robert Kennedy, whom none of us knew well enough to judge, would serve as his brother's vengeful hatchet man. . . . It was easy to imagine the probable result—an upending of the Agency with the espionage and intelligence production elements blistered in the heat generated by the failed covert action [of the Bay of Pigs]."[1]

At their meeting in November 1961, Bissell designated the tight-lipped Harvey as the CIA's executioner of Fidel Castro, specifically. The appointment to run what became known as ZRRIFLE was a logical one. Harvey was the only CIA executive who had both the leadership ability and the street smarts to handle this diciest of operations—undertakings that ran against the spirit of everything upon which America's free society was based. Leading ZRRIFLE was, at once, the most explosive and the most unenviable assignment on the Agency's books. If asked, Harvey probably would have grunted, "That's what I get paid for," and bleakly discouraged any further speculation. Refusal of the assignment probably never occurred to him.

What he got paid for got very, very messy. And because Harvey did not enlighten anyone, a number of latter-day gainsayers have sneered that power lust drove him to commit and to sanction dishonorable acts. Few, if any, of these gainsayers ever bore responsibility for covert presidential directives involving the lives and careers of others, and few, if any, understood the Intelligence Service. I doubt Bill ever considered refusing the assignment, even if it was likely to blow up in his face.

If Harvey allowed himself to savor the appointment at all, he probably grinned sardonically at the thought that the Ivy Leaguers had to turn to the roughneck from Indiana to handle something that was way beyond them. Bill could not have wished for a more powerful slot, except for the deputy director of plans berth itself, yet he may well have known his new assignment was doomed from the start. He also undoubtedly knew through verbal-only warnings from Helms (perhaps from Bissell as well) that Cuba and Fidel Castro were very, very personal matters to Bobby and his brother.

Neither Bruce Cheever nor Sam Halpern, Bill's closest subordinates during the Cuba operation days, even knew the ZRRIFLE cryptonym. "It was Bill's personal responsibility. His very own vest-pocket operation. Skip, his secretary probably knew, but he created it and kept it to himself. . . . Bill had a phobia about committing sensitive matters to paper."[2]

Bill strongly felt that Cuban operations should be left to professionals and removed from the politics of ego. He personally took over ops that were so touchy—specifically, but not only, the Agency's dealings with Johnny Rosselli, the mafioso who had been involved in the Trujillo assassination attempt—that they had potential to wreck the CIA as well as to besmirch an administration he disliked.

Bill's own pithy and profane views of ex post facto posturing on the matter of assassination plotting by senior CIA officials and Kennedy apologists appear in his margin notes on the report of the U.S. Senate's Select Committee to Study Governmental Operations with Respect to Intelligence Activities, which was otherwise known as the Church Committee, after Senator Frank Church, a liberal agrarian from Idaho. Harvey received a draft copy of the Church report on November 22, 1975. The timing—right around Thanksgiving—might have brought an ironic smile to his now-gaunt face.

Harvey set about poring over the document's close-set 339 pages, and he left behind at his death, less than seven months later, his comments on the committee's conclusions, most searingly, on the testimony of those who found it convenient to bend history.

Bill made it clear that he thought Senator Church gravely harmed American national security in holding the hearings at all. The fact that Bill privately made his margin notes, and kept a few other classified documents after his retirement from the CIA, hints that Harvey might have been thinking of writing a book to clear the record and his own name. Some years later CG Harvey said she thought Bill had been planning as much, even though such a memoir would have been in stark contrast to his decades of conspiratorial secrecy.

WHAT WAS ZRRIFLE?

ZRRIFLE is a digraph some writers have thrown around recklessly. The Castro assassination effort was contained in and covered under an existing activity. ZR was the digraph for Division D, Cryptological Procurement. It seems to have served purposely to confuse the Castro hit ops with Earl Harter's closely held series of operations to procure cryptographic materials by breaking-and-entering target premises. Very few, even in D, knew what Harter's boys did: their activities were far less generally known in foreign intelligence (FI), even less in the other Clandestine Services, and not at all in the whole of the CIA; this was exactly how it should have been. Precisely because Division D was so secure and already involved in matters gentlemen preferred not to know about, it was the logical administrative compartment in which to house CIA's newest and touchiest activity, the projected assassination of political leaders whose further existence impinged on U.S. interests.

That ZRRIFLE quietly became another element in Division D's ultrasecret activities was nobody's business. The cryptonym and the activities it concealed became the personal duchy and responsibility of the chief of division, Harvey.

THE SECOND-STORY MEN

The National Security Agency (NSA) had been established to tap the communications of anyone, anywhere. It did a fine job of capturing communications and decoding material on its own supercomputers. But its task could be made much easier if someone provided it with codebooks and other materials on which encrypted messages were based. Procurement of such cryptographic materials was the original raison d'etre of Staff D.[3] For the sake of clarity, let's deviate to look briefly at this procurement endeavor.

The team that provided such documentary gold was part of Division D, where they were referred to jovially as the Second-Story Men, CIA's licensed burglars. They were run by Earl Harter, a CIA legend in his own right. Their feats are to this day highly classified, but the members of the team were greatly admired among those few who knew them. When they dropped by Staff D's offices, the acquisitors responded to the admiration they received in kind, retailing severely bowdlerized versions of some of their exploits.

In a report prepared in 1967, the CIA's inspector general (IG) noted that the Second-Story Men were recruited precisely because they knew how to "break into safes and kidnap couriers." Evan Thomas, author of *The Very Best Men*, adds, "They were a very rough bunch with strong ties to [if not full-fledged membership in] the underworld. 'We had to keep the FBI informed when one of them traveled,' said Sam Halpern. Bill Harvey knew where to find men of this caliber."[4]

Clarence Berry, the former Berlin Tunnel support officer, knew the team casually.

> I interacted with our Second-Story bunch, which was a super group. . . . [They] had a small building south of Alexandria, inside a U.S. Army warehouse compound. . . . They had a pretty good security setup.
>
> Those guys were a very tight, fearless group, with absolute confidence in each other's ability . . . not a motley crew, true professionals. Basically top-of-the-line locksmiths, photo experts, and building tradesmen. . . . They were very good . . . and were always getting more commendations and spot, in-grade promotions, probably, than any other unit in the Agency. They were without peer in opening and resealing one-time [cryptographic] pads, which were wax-sealed and grommeted. . . .
>
> They did not work on anything inside the States, only abroad. Overseas, they depended on station chiefs to help out as appropriate. When they went on a job, they utilized station personnel in support, making sure that all target people were accounted for at all times, otherwise there was an abort. They ran probably dozens of crypto missions and, to my knowledge, never came close to being caught in the act.[5]

Halpern recalls, "Earl Harter was absolutely wonderful. His boys were very, very good. They never talked. . . . No one will ever know the number of embassies all over the world that they entered and relieved of crypto materials."[6] The very secrecy in which Harter operated was an obvious attraction for Harvey, who needed to hide any trace of the CIA's attempts to assassinate Fidel Castro.

THE CIA'S STRUGGLES WITH THE ASSASSINATION MANDATE

As 1960 turned to 1961 and his personal charter expanded, Harvey had to find hit men to carry out the ZRRIFLE assassination mission. I asked Halpern if Harvey objected to assassination in principle. "He may have objected to the practice, but he didn't object to it in principle."

In 1960 Patrice Lumumba, a left-leaning, charismatic political star in Central Africa was killed, allegedly while trying to escape from custody. His killer was Sese Seko Mobutu, one of his rivals for supreme power in the part of mineral-rich Africa that became Zaire. The order for the Lumumba hit came from Richard Bissell, authorized by President Eisenhower. In fact, a lengthy history about the CIA's involvement in the affair indicates that, although Lumumba's death came at the hands of a political rival, who was perhaps supported by the CIA, the Agency was itself prepared to kill Lumumba.

Harvey's notes in the margins of the Church Committee's report confirm that he knew of the Lumumba assassination planning, though he was not directly involved in the operation. He appears to have been uncomfortable with his knowledge of the undertaking.

In his memoir, Dick Helms asserts that political killing, for the CIA as a whole and for FI officers in particular, is morally repugnant. "The Agency had no influence in the action whatsoever. . . . Lumumba . . . was by any standard unfit to rule the Congo. That said, in peacetime, the assassination of troublesome persons is morally and operationally indefensible."[7] That ambivalence meant that each such authorization had to be signed by the president in a "finding."

Helms succeeded Bissell as deputy director of plans effective February 1, 1962. He didn't then know that the Castro assassination effort would consume an inordinate amount of time in his future. The Church Committee notes, "Office of Security files reflect that Mr. Allen Dulles had approved the entire operation against Castro. . . . Our files reflect that *six* Agency people were [at the outset] aware of the operation—Allen Dulles, William Harvey, Richard Bissell, Sheffield Edwards, Col. J. C. King and Jim O'Connell."[8]

When, in 1967, Helms demanded his own internal investigation of ZRRIFLE, the CIA's inspectors general reported,

> IG Comment: After Harvey took over the Castro operation, he ran it as one aspect of ZRRIFLE; *however, he personally handled the Castro operation and did not use any of the assets being developed in ZRRIFLE.* He says that he soon came to think of the Castro operation and ZRRIFLE as being synonymous. *The over-all Executive Action came to be treated in his mind as being synonymous with QJWIN, the agent*

> *working on the over-all program.* He says that when he wrote of ZRRIFLE/QJWIN, the reference was to Executive Action Capability; when he used the cryptonym ZRRIFLE alone, he was referring to Castro. [Emphasis added.][9]

THE LANSDALE FLAP

The CIA IG's report, cataloguing the Agency's actions regarding the Kennedys' passion for the assassination of Castro, concludes with a section titled "Discussion of Assassination at High-Level Government Meetings." There were two such discussions: one "was in the Secretary's Conference Room at the Department of State on 10 August 1962" and the second meeting was on July 30, 1964, and it did not include Harvey.

The purpose of the Special Group Augmented (SGA) in 1962 was to overthrow the Castro regime in Cuba. The CIA's own analysts had concluded that the United States could not expect indigenous revolt to overthrow the Cuban dictator. Defense Secretary Robert McNamara noted privately that a degree of hysteria marked the Kennedys' anti-Castro posture.

The SGA meetings on MONGOOSE, the external code name for anti-Castro operations, were about as high-level as a U.S. government meeting could get without the presence of the president and his brother. The cast included Secretary of State Dean Rusk and his deputy, U. Alexis Johnson, as well as Richard Goodwin, a high-level national security adviser; the White House sent Gen. Maxwell Taylor and McGeorge Bundy, pinch-hitting for Bobby Kennedy; Robert McNamara, his deputy, Roswell Gilpatric, and chief of the Joint Chiefs of Staff, Gen. Lyman Lemnitzer, attended by Brig. Gen. Ed Lansdale, came from the Pentagon; Edward R. Murrow was present from USIA; the CIA weighed in with Director of Central Intelligence John McCone and Bill Harvey. Tom Parrott of the CIA was secretary of SGA. McNamara, General Taylor, McCone, Murrow, Bundy, Goodwin, Lansdale, Helms, and Harvey were present at the explosive August 10, 1962, meeting.

At the meeting Lansdale presented "the touchdown play" that he thought would eliminate Castro. It involved the use of all conceivable pressures—diplomatic, economic, political, and psychological warfare—everything short of full-scale military intervention. There was discussion of a possible Castro assassination, perhaps mentioned first by McNamara. After the meeting, McCone, at Harvey's urging, called McNamara. "The subject you just brought up. I think it is highly improper. I do not think it should be discussed. It is not an action that should ever be condoned. It is not proper for us to discuss, and I intend to have it expunged from the record." McCone also told those close to him—perhaps only half jokingly—that if he even contemplated assassination, he feared he would be excommunicated.

On August 13, 1962, Lansdale, showing his poor judgment, committed McNamara's thoughts to paper in a memorandum to State, Defense, the CIA, and the USIA that outlined the game plan for Cuba. David Martin reported in *Wilderness of Mirrors*, "There, in black and white, Lansdale wrote: 'Mr. Harvey: Intelligence, Political (including liquidation of leaders), Economic (sabotage, limited deception), and Paramilitary.'"[10]

Halpern was by then well used to Harvey's profane dismissal of those on the policy level who couldn't leave messy matters to the pros. He fills in the details: "Harvey [read the Lansdale memo mentioning assassination and listened to McCone's angry protests] with a straight face, then stormed back to his basement office, scratched out the offending words from the memo. He raged against the inadmissibility and stupidity of putting this type of comment in such a document. All mention of the liquidation of leaders had to be expunged from the official minutes of the meeting."[11]

The next, thunderous step was an understated memorandum to Helms, a photocopy of which exists in Harvey's personal papers.

> MEMORANDUM FOR: Deputy Director
> SUBJECT: Operation MONGOOSE
>
> 1. Action: None. This memorandum is for your information.
>
> 2. Reference is made to our conversation on 13 August 1962, concerning the memorandum of that date from General Lansdale. Attached is a copy of this memorandum, excised from which are four words in the second line of the penultimate paragraph on page 1. These four words were "including liquidation of leaders."
>
> 3. The question of assassination, particularly of Fidel Castro, was brought up by Secretary McNamara at the meeting of the Special Group (Augmented) in Secretary Rusk's office on 10 August. It was the obvious consensus at that meeting, in answer to a comment by Mr. Ed Murrow, that this is not a subject which has been made a matter of official record. I took careful notes at this meeting on this point, and the Special Group (Augmented) is not expecting any written comments or study on this point.
>
> 4. Upon receipt of the attached memorandum, I called Lansdale's office and, in his absence, pointed out to Frank Hand the inadmissibility and stupidity of putting this type of comment

> in writing in such a document. I advised Frank Hand that, as far as CIA was concerned, we would write no such document pertaining to this and would participate in no open meeting discussing it. I strongly urged Hand to recommend to Lansdale that he excise the phrase in question from all copies of this memorandum, including those disseminated to State, Defense and USIA. Shortly thereafter, Lansdale called back and left the message that he agreed and that he had done so.
>
> William K. Harvey
> Chief, Task Force W

The stifled bureaucratic prose of the memo masks Bill's outright fury that senior government officials—namely subcabinet and cabinet officers—could be so naïve as to mention (and then commit to paper) the U.S. government's consideration of the liquidation of the head of a foreign state.

The Agency's IG reported in 1967, "Harvey told us that Lansdale repeatedly tried to raise the matter of assassination of Castro over the next several weeks. Harvey says that he always avoided such discussions. Harvey estimates that five persons in Lansdale's office were generally aware of the sensitive details of project Mongoose and of Lansdale's interest in assassination as an aspect of it."

Lansdale later recalled "he had only one brief conversation with the CIA agent after the 10 August meeting. At that time, Harvey stated, 'he would look into [the assassination of Castro and] see about developing some plans.' Not surprisingly, Lansdale insisted that was the last he ever heard about assassinations." On August 30, after another session with Bobby Kennedy, Lansdale was back to talking up revolt against Castro and attacks on Soviet bloc personnel that could be blamed on Castro's regime.[12]

The discomfort of some senior government officials over the matter of Castro's assassination was real, even though they could not then even begin to guess the ramifications of the CIA's involvement with the domestic Mafia on ZRRIFLE. What follows is complicated and obscure, but it is an essential part of Harvey's, and indeed, the nation's story.

PLANNING PROJECT ZRRIFLE

Even though plans for the elimination of Castro were among the U.S. government's most sensitive secrets, the CIA had to record at least some aspects of the operation.

The ZRRIFLE project name first appears, as far as is known, in May 1961, six months before Harvey was given the Castro assignment, but while Bill was chief of Division D. The first page of the file is in Harvey's own scrawl. Dated January 25, 1962, i.e., after he had assumed ZRRIFLE but before he officially took over responsibility for all Cuban operations, the paper contains some Harvey-esque doodles, as if it had been written while Bill was in a meeting. The notes were the precursor to a project outline that formalized ZRRIFLE. Although they are not specific, I assume that the handwritten documents refer to the spotting and possible recruitment of one or more foreign gangsters who could be used to assassinate Fidel Castro. Helms might have strongly urged Harvey to abandon this approach, so he could better concentrate his efforts at finding a liquidator in the domestic underworld.

The photocopy from which I made the notes below does not cover the margins of the original document. I have included some of the notes for the flavor they give of what was about to be undertaken.

The text:

25/1 Exec meeting [possibly a meeting between Helms and Harvey]
"The Magic Button"
. . . for a living—RIS 201 cover [RIS = KGB; 201 = personnel file]
. . . utions—Bankruptcy—No Star
. . . eyes—Jim A—Contradestruct [Jim A = Angleton]
. . . a TSD problem from U-2
[TSD = Technical Services Division]
. . . last resort beyond last resort &
a confession of weakness—
—El Benefactor—[illegible]
Elint R & D—Memo [Elint = electronic intelligence]
basic sound project
—AS—Fanfani—[Arnold S?—the Luxembourg Second-Story team's case officer? Amintore Fanfani was an Italian politician and prime minister.]
never mention word assassination

1. Select proper officer to run
2. Place & cover Max 2/3
3. Security—Rules B—WKH—A[rnold]S (?) -
4. [illegible] lives Sid—Reserv[ations?]
5. Last resort—Brakes Substitute what [illegible]
6. No other agencies.

7. No project on paper except for cover.

8. Principal Agent [blacked out] AF Project draft LCH [probably CIA general counsel Lawrence Houston] travel—1500—from "RB"

9. Disposal [Disposal of an agent at the end of an operation is always a consideration; it is not necessarily hostile.]

10. Targets who where Must know before we can spot

11. Case officering

12. Cover file—Create from RIS [Russian Intelligence Service—KGB] *or* abt it—non-Sov

13. Note dangers of RIS counter-action & monitor if they are blamed.

7d. I list—*Remember*[13]

The gist of Harvey's notes—but not all of their nuances—was translated into a formal project outline dated February 19, 1962. The formal document referred only to the Earl Harter style of cryptographic procurement, but it is sufficiently flexible to cover the admininstrative needs of the Castro assassination undertaking.

Project ZRRIFLE

1. Identification: The purpose of Project ZRRIFLE is to spot, develop and use *foreign* agent assets for Division D operations. Agents will be spotted in several areas, including the United States, but for operational security reasons will probably not be used in their countries of residence. *Present developmental activity is being conducted in the WE and EE areas*, but it is anticipated that this will be extended to other division areas. The project will be operated against third country installations and personnel.

2. Objectives: The objective of this project is the *procurement of code and cipher materials and information concerning such materials, in accordance with requirements levied on the Clandestine Services, primarily by the National Security Agency.* Since these requirements are subject to frequent revision, no listing of targets would be valid for the duration of the project. Specific operations will be mounted on the basis of need and opportunity. The project will be conducted by Division D with assistance from area divisions and stations as needed.

3. Background: In response to the increasing requirements for the operational procurement of foreign code and cipher materials, Division D in 1960 began the spotting of [words are illegible] as a

developmental activity. During the same period, requirements from NSA became more refined and in many respects, more sensitive. Because most [overseas] stations are not equipped to conduct this type of operation and because of the desirability of completely centralized control over this entire effort, it was determined that Division D, which is in closest touch with NSA on procurement requirements, could conduct the activity. The spotting activity has now advanced far enough to justify removing from the [exploratory] category.

4. <u>Operational Assets</u>: 1) <u>Personnel</u>: *QJWIN is under written contract as a principal agent, with the primary task of spotting agent candidates.* QJWIN was first contacted in [nearly two lines heavily redacted] in connection with an *illegal narcotics operation into the United States*. For a period of a year and a half, he was *contacted sporadically by Luxembourg, on behalf of the Bureau of Narcotics.* Files of the Bureau reflect an excellent performance by QJWIN. In October 1960, [page ends abruptly and is not followed by a sequential sentence.]

The next page in the Harvey papers is the ZRRIFLE budget:

QJWIN annual salary	$7,200
Travel and ops expenses for QJWIN and other agents and agent candidates	2,000
Fees for services by and standby of agents and agent-candidates	2,000
Travel of staff employees engaged in ZRRIFLE activity [i.e., Bill Harvey]	2,500
Hire of safehouses, automobiles, and other operational expenses	<u>1,000</u>
	14,700

<u>Pay for agents on completion of jobs</u>?[14] [Emphasis added.]

ZRRIFLE: CRYPTO PROCUREMENT OR POLITICAL ASSASSINATION?

Next in the file are some grimly fascinating notes specific to political assassination, not to crypto procurement operations. They are not in Harvey's handwriting; rather, I suspect the writer was Seymour B., of Harvey's Task Force W staff, or perhaps Justin O'Donnell of Division D.

I have seen two versions of the same tough, even ruthless, memorandum and have tried to combine them. One was apparently the original working draft; the second was a rewrite. Combining the two conveys the thoughts and apprehensions of Harvey's closest staff member on a breaking-and-entering cryptographic procurement operation. If the memo is actually about assassination, it's apparent, as Halpern said, that Bill did not tell his most-trusted lieutenants what he was really engaged in.

The document was originally stamped, "Reproduction prohibited"; one version is stamped, "Approved for release 28 Aug 1985; the other version is stamped, "Approved for release CIA Historical Review Program 1993." How the notes came into the possession of CG Harvey remains a mystery.

1) Legal, ethical-moral, operational problems; political; non-attributability.

2) Our own experience (Bangkok) (& effect on DDP) and experiences w/ KGB (Crossup, Bandera group, Khokhlov [i.e., KGB assassination operations])—require most professional, proven operationally competent, ruthless, stable [could also be "sterile," as in securely compartmented], CE-experienced ops officers (few available), able to conduct patient search & w/ guts to pull back if instinct or knowledge tells him he should, and w/ known high regard for operational security, assessment and [illegible].

3) Maximum security: (highest not secure enough) & within KUBARK [CIA] only (e.g., how much does Siragusa [the senior Bureau of Narcotics official for whose needs QJWIN had originally been recruited] need to know?) Limitation on number code clerks for enciphering and deciphering. Guise of [illegible] objective. No approach to other Govt agencies.

b. Within Kubark, one focal point for control, search, training, case officering, etc. DDP authority in this focal point mandatory. DCI officially advised?

c. *Max. security cable commo for innocuous cables only; no restrictions on travel; possibility of one-man overseas (Europe) control base with own (non-Station) commo—word-of-mouth & no bashfulness re trips.*

d. (Every operation to be rigidly case-officered. No silk-shirt PA's [principle agents]) No PA's except for search or intermediaries. . . .

e. No approach to officials of foreign govts. (Non-attributability; no American citizen or American resident for direct action. Possibly for approach to foreign elements.) No criminal who tainted by use by another American agency. Use of case officers who can pass as foreigners—and limited official reference. No chain of connection permitting blackmail. Don't [ ] any [ ] as home territory. Avoid discussion with foreign officials until all possibility of search through [ ] has been examined.

f. No approach to any agent who ever [worked for] a U.S. Govt agency. Training by opposition would reveal.

g. Use of <u>already</u> tested assets (e.g. [blanked-out—probably QJWIN]) in the search.

h. Stand-by list of Kubarkers [CIA staff members] who can pass as foreigners.

i. Pretext: Kutube/D [FI/D] search; this established (e.g. *Rome*) [Note: It is interesting that Germany is not listed specifically as a recruiting ground; it could and should have provided a considerable pool of potential break-and-enter crooks, and/or assassins of various, even indeterminate, nationalities. Perhaps for that very reason, and because of the large American presence there, it was excluded as too obvious a source.]

j. No discussion in [CIA] stations.

k. No "team" until ready to go, if at all.

4. Blackmail:

a. <u>No</u> American citizens or residents or people who ever obtained U.S. visas.

b. No chain of knowledgeable [?—*sic*]. *Strictly person-to-person; singleton ops.*

c. No meeting any candidate in home territory.

d. *Exclude organized criminals, e.g. Sicilians, criminals, those w/ record of arrests, those w/ instability of purpose as criminals.*

e. Staffers involved—selection.

5. Cover: planning should include *provision for <u>blaming</u> Sovs or Czechs in case of blow . . . organization criminals, those with record of arrests, those who have engaged in several types of crime. <u>Corsicans recommended. Sicilians could lead to Mafia</u>.*

6. Testing of nominees essential: re following directions, security, blackmail.

7. *Former resistance personnel a possibility. Period of testing, surveillance, etc. for each selection.* All Kubark personnel should have some CE experience.

8. *Use <u>nobody</u> who has never dealt w/ criminals*; otherwise will not be aware of pitfalls or consider factors such as freedom to travel, wanted lists, etc.

9. *Should have phony 201* [personnel file] *in RI* [Central Registry] *to backstop this*. All documents therein forged and backdated. Should look like a CE file.

10. *Possible use of defectors* for these actions.

11. Silverthorne and stable in [*sic*—?]

What are limits on team or individuals selected? No "team" until ready to go.

Danger of standbys.

Keeping of files[15] [Emphasis added.]

If we did not now live in such a chilling age, the relentless, ruthless qualifications Harvey was looking for would be startling in themselves. Yes, the project outline can be read to apply only to break-and-enter crypto procurement. But it could also have applied to the recruitment of assassins. At any rate, it was obviously intended to provide absolute maximum security for one or more very nervy operations.

In light of what comes later, paragraph 4d is particularly interesting: "*Exclude organized criminals, e.g. Sicilians, criminals, those w/ record of arrests, those w/ instability of purpose as criminals.*" Followed by paragraph 5: "Cover: planning should include *provision for <u>blaming</u> Sovs or Czechs in case of blow . . . organization criminals, those with record of arrests, those who have engaged in several types of crime. <u>Corsicans recommended. Sicilians could lead to Mafia</u>.*" And, finally, paragraph 7: "*Former resistance personnel a possibility. Period of testing, surveillance, etc. for each selection.*"

A significant question arises from the mention, immediately above, of Sicilians: Why was Harvey concerned that investigation could "lead to the Mafia"? There is the barest hint here of explosive connections among the CIA, the American Mafia, and its Sicilian parent group. We'll look at the possible connection later.

Also in the personal file left by Harvey, and later, CG, is a memorandum dated less than a month later that carries no classification stamp but has a handwritten note from Harvey: "Skip, Pls file securely." This memo was Bill's license to proceed.

February 1962
MEMORANDUM FOR: William K. Harvey
SUBJECT: Authorization of ZRRIFLE Agent Activities

1. For the purpose of ZRRIFLE activities, you are hereby authorized to retain the services of Principal Agent QJWIN and such

other principal agents and sub-agents as may be required. This authorization will continue to be in force through 31 December 1962, subject to renewal at that time.

2. As established by contract with him, QJWIN's salary will be $7,200 per annum. Accounting for the expenses of QJWIN and other agents involved in this activity will be in the form of receipts for funds received by them, and these receipts will be retained in the ZRRIFLE covert operational file. Because of the sensitive nature of this activity, accounting for funds will be by general category and by your [portion illegible]. In addition to the salary payable to . . . QJWIN, you are authorized the expenditure of $7,500 through 31 December 1962. If further funds are necessary, they will be provided.

3. This memorandum is to be considered *in lieu of project and constitutes authorization for all travel, per diem, operational and other expenses.*

4. *It is requested that this activity be handled strictly on an EYES ONLY basis.*

/s/
Richard Helms
Deputy Director (Plans).[16]

[Emphasis added.]

The memorandum says nothing about the purpose of QJWIN's engagement, nor about the scope of ZRRIFLE. It also recognizes that the activity authorized in the memo was so sensitive that the operation(s) would not be subject to the usual project review and disbursement approval procedures. The amount of money discussed in the documents was not lavish at the time.[17]

Harvey may have demanded the memo to cover his ass; he was one of the most security-conscious people in the CIA and would not have held documents of this sensitivity outside the office without good reason. Did he anticipate rough going ahead? Did he think some people might find his presence inconvenient? Or maybe he kept the papers simply as the basis for that unwritten book?

It seems obvious that Bill wanted to protect himself by keeping a written copy of his orders as proof of Helms's authorization of ZRRIFLE. He wanted this insurance to be where someone would find and know what to do with it after his death. It is most likely that Harvey felt strongly that his reputation, perhaps his pension, and maybe even his life might be in jeopardy at some future time.

Still, a couple of other puzzles remain. First, we have Sally Harvey's word that, almost immediately after her father's death in June 1976, CG, on her husband's instructions, burned a lot of very sensitive paper that had been in Harvey's personal safe. Second, how did the handwritten notes, cleared for release only on August 28, 1985, ten years after Bill's death, and Dick Helms's memo authorizing ZRRIFLE, which seems to be based on the handwritten project outline, find their way into the Harvey family files while CG was still alive? Even if CG had used the Freedom of Information Act, the CIA likely would not have released them.

One must also wonder whether these ZRRIFLE memos were among the papers thieves were after when they broke into the Harveys' house in Indianapolis after Bill's death. The burglars were interrupted when CG heard them, and they fled after having started to ransack Bill's ground-floor-rear study.

CASE OFFICERING

For the Castro hit, Harvey needed a senior case officer whom he could trust as much as he had trusted Vyrl Leichliter, Clarence Berry, or Charlie Arnold back in the Berlin Tunnel days. Division D had its own case officer in Europe, described by Clarence Berry: "There was an individual in D . . . Arnold S., who had been stationed in Luxembourg or Hamburg. He just floated in and out of D, like O'Donnell. I never knew what he was about." Arnold S. was the Luxembourg case officer for QJWIN. "[He] struck me as being a sort of dandy in dress, with blow-dried hair and a perpetual sun-lamp tan. I was not impressed with him professionally, although to be fair, I was not around him much."[18]

Harvey undoubtedly considered those involved in crypto procurement, including Arnold S., and found no one who met his exacting bill of particulars. Thus he felt duty and honor bound to handle the most sensitive parts of ZRRIFLE himself. Harvey felt he was one of very, very few CIA officers who could run QJWIN satisfactorily on the really dicey matters that Bissell handed him. So in effect, in the true sense of the silent service, he alone bore the responsibility for the assassination operations, which were called "wet affairs" by the Russians. He himself could hardly murder Castro, but one man to whom he was drawn, Johnny Rosselli, could. We'll look at that relationship shortly.

EUROPEAN MOBSTERS AND HARVEY

Harvey had abundant reason to be sensitive on the matter of ZRRIFLE, and his sensitivity was heightened by the other pressures he was working under from the spring into the fall of 1962: all the ramifications of running more conventional operations, as head of Task Force W; his potentially explosive relationship with Johnny Rosselli, the mafioso in whom J. Edgar Hoover's FBI had a near-pathological interest—quite apart from his persistent feud with the attorney general of the United States.

Overlooking his leaden ear for languages, Bill considered himself an operator, not a headquarters type. He would have felt obliged to look at the very foreign and very different playing field that now was of major interest to him. Harvey would have especially wanted to meet QJWIN, out of sheer curiosity, bordering on magnetic attraction; indeed, he might have been drawn to QJWIN in the same way he was drawn to Johnny Rosselli.

QJWIN AND WIROGUE

Other foreign intelligence agencies may cooperate routinely with the underworld, but American intelligence is expected by a puritanical Congress and the easily shocked media to hew to lily-white standards of ethics, even as it deals in a very nasty world.

There is considerable circumstantial evidence that the Europeans who smuggled heroin into the United States in the 1950s and 1960s were of operational interest to the CIA. Some of this group of primarily Marseilles-based hoodlums were associated with Santo Trafficante, the Miami Mafia capo. They were rough and unscrupulous, but they operated by a singular code. Recall that Harvey took at least one spotting trip to Europe, apparently on the lookout for underworld talent for the crypto procurement operation, in October 1960.

For our purposes, the agent referred to as WIROGUE seems the less interesting of the two surfaced criminal agents. QJWIN deserves more attention. The Agency hired both men precisely because they lacked scruples and were familiar with the illegal life.

During the Lumumba operation, different case officers, thanks to an administrative snafu, lodged both WIROGUE and QJWIN in the Regina Hotel in Leopoldville. In a moment of delicious comedy, WIROGUE tried to recruit QJWIN for the Lumumba operation in the hotel bar one evening. QJWIN did not know that WIROGUE was CIA and refused the invitation. Stephen J. Rivele has it that QJWIN appears as an older, trusted colleague, and though of criminal background, not of unsavory reputation. The distinction between the two men is clear: WIROGUE was a cheap young hood; QJWIN was a high-placed criminal operator who had come from the world of sensitive secret work.[19]

The senior case officer who had flown in to be on the spot, Justin O'Donnell, and the local officers must have either groaned or laughed hysterically when they heard of the episode, which sounds like something out of *The Maltese Falcon*. WIROGUE took the opportunity of the chaos in the Congo to engage in money-making propositions for personal gain, and in July 1961 he departed Leopoldville under a thunderhead.

The circumstances of Lumumba's death were eventually fairly well determined. While a CIA employee did not actually pull the trigger, the Agency certainly seems to have encouraged Mobutu to eliminate his rival. The denouement began on January 13, 1961. At that time, Harvey had been in charge of ZRRIFLE for fewer than six weeks. As mentioned above, he knew about the Lumumba-connected operations as chief of Division D, but he was probably more than content to allow Justin O'Donnell to represent D's interest on the ground in the Lumumba affair.

TERMINATING QJWIN

O'Donnell denied that QJWIN had anything to do with Lumumba's murder in early 1961. Still, a message Harvey wrote to the CIA's finance division at the time says simply, "QJWIN was sent on this trip for a specific, highly sensitive operational purpose which has been completed."

The CIA put QJWIN on the polygraph in April 1961, after Harvey had taken over Division D. The agent was then described as "a 44 year-old Luxembourg citizen who has been utilized by this organization since the end of 1960 in several sensitive operations"; this makes it sound as though he helped the Second-Story Men on cryptographic procurement ops.

QJWIN appears to have been the kind of law-dodging cutthroat with whom gentlemen don't readily associate, but of whom intelligence agencies at times have need. In 1962 QJWIN "was about to go on trial in Europe on smuggling charges." He probably lived in Cologne, Germany, in 1963–64 and may have opened a shop there. According to the IG's report, while Harvey was clearing out his desk prior to his transfer to Rome, he wrote a memorandum to the chief, FI Staff, dated June 17, 1963, five months before the Kennedy assassination, stating that the original justification for employing QJWIN no longer existed.

> I believe the original purpose for which QJWIN was continued and sent on his present undercover assignment is no longer of sufficient validity. . . .
>
> QJWIN . . . is a competent, usable agent who is capable of operating in certain circles in Europe where we have very few as-

> sets. . . . He is not being used at the present time. He is being paid but he is on ice. . . .
>
> If after [discussions with other offices] a sensible framework for the operational use of QJWIN can be established, I would recommend we continue him. If not, I would recommend that he be terminated at the time his present contract expires.
>
> As far as the ZRRIFLE aspects . . . except for one precautionary "life line," aspects of this case have been terminated.

After an anonymous case officer noted that QJWIN was unstable and perhaps inclined to hedge his bets, QJWIN's contract of employment with the CIA was allowed to lapse on February 29, 1964. Nothing in the file indicates that the executive action capability of ZRRIFLE/QJWIN was ever used. At the time the agent was terminated, Harvey was in Rome.

Researchers into the John F. Kennedy assassination have spent countless hours trying to pin down the identity of QJWIN. Their search has taken them deep into the legends of the French intelligence and security services, the underworld, and France's political seethings of the 1960s. Various names have cropped up from that rainbow of interests and attachments, each of them belonging to fascinating characters, but none of them indubitably the name of QJWIN. His identity remains elusive, though tempting, because he was part of Harvey's story at a key juncture and because he just might have had something to do with JFK's death.

The QJWIN/WIROGUE/ZRRIFLE questions and complexities will not be decisively unraveled until, and if ever, the CIA decides to open whatever files it has on the JFK assassination.

SUMMING UP

Dick Helms acknowledged to the Church Committee, "I had very grave doubts about the wisdom of [the Castro assassination operations]. . . . We had some few assets inside Cuba at that time. I was willing to try almost anything."

Harvey summed up the liabilities of this "damned dicey operation" for the Church Committee by saying that it carried the "very real possibility of this government being blackmailed either by Cubans for political purposes, or by figures in organized crime for their own self-protection and aggrandizement."

The CIA IG's report of spring 1967 states:

> This reconstruction of Agency involvement in plans to assassinate

> Fidel Castro is at best an imperfect history. Because of the extreme sensitivity of the operations . . . *no official records were kept* of planning, of approvals, or of implementation. The few written records that do exist are largely tangential to the main events, or were put on paper from memory years afterwards. *William Harvey has retained skeletal notes of his activities during the years in question, and they are our best source of dates. . . .*
>
> *We cannot overemphasize the extent to which responsible Agency officers felt themselves subject to the Kennedy Administration's severe pressures to do something about Castro and his regime. The fruitless and, in retrospect, often unrealistic plotting should be viewed in that light.*
>
> . . . After some discussion of the problems involved in developing an Executive Action Capability, Bissell placed Harvey in charge of the effort. . . . Harvey states that after the decision was made to go ahead with the creating of an Executive Action Capability, and while he was still discussing its development with Bissell, *he briefed Mr. Helms fully on the general concept, but without mention of the then-ongoing plan to assassinate Castro.* [Emphasis added.]

Recall Harvey's statement to the Church Committee that "I would like to make as clear as I can that . . . this was an ongoing matter which I was injected into." This statement implies that the entire undertaking was out of control and that Harvey was brought in to try to make some sense out of a sorry catalogue of misjudgments made under nearly intolerable political pressures. The explosive potential of the operation was so great, Bill did not brief his boss in detail. This was his way of protecting Helms and, again, evidence that Harvey was prepared to take the fall for a matter he did not believe in, but for which he had assumed responsibility.

LONG-RANGE EFFECTS

In late 1962 and early 1963 those seniors in the know in the CIA drew the obvious conclusions from the Kennedys' desire for insurrection in Cuba and for the assassination of Fidel Castro: the flamboyant, iconoclastic individualism that had flavored the CIA since World War II and the Office of Strategic Services had no place now in the gray pinstripe bureaucracy. The CIA had become a major agency, with all the bureaucratic appurtenances of the Department of Agriculture, and as important, if not more so, it had become an instrument of the president's political will. The CIA could have tried to achieve the independent status of Britain's MI-6, but from Eisenhower on, it didn't stand a chance. The American system is results oriented; the CIA simply had to produce or, bluntly, its budget would have been—and later was—emasculated.

In 1962 part of the trouble was that, after the Bay of Pigs, the administration felt it could not rely on the spooks. When it came to the crunch, Lansdale and the Kennedys sent U-2s to check on the pinpoint-accurate intermediate-range ballistic missile reports JMWAVE's agents had sent.

Only Harvey knew the lengths he went to to arrange Castro's demise because only he knew the extent of ZRRIFLE. But people who knew Bill knew he could be ruthless in fulfillment of his duty. The anomaly of dealing with the underworld people Bobby Kennedy had vowed to exterminate was certainly not lost on Bill and others. In fact, many seasoned CIA hands became aware, in some cases only vaguely, of the Castro Thing, and they disliked it—even more so, as word spread—and it did, despite compartmentalization—that the mafioso, Johnny Rosselli, was cut in on the deal.

The final report of the last group to look into the Kennedy assassination, the 1992 Assassinations Review Board, had this to say:

> William Harvey was intricately involved in . . . the various assassination plots against Fidel Castro. The Review Board received a query from a researcher concerning the possible existence of "operational diaries" that Harvey may have created. CIA searched its Directorate of Operations records and did not locate any records belonging to Harvey.
>
> The introduction to the 1967 CIA Inspector General's (IG) report on plots to assassinate Castro notes that Richard Helms directed that, once the IG's office produced the report, CIA should destroy all notes and source material that it used to draft the report.
>
> CIA may have destroyed Harvey's alleged diaries in response to Helms' directive. . . . Despite its efforts, the Review Board did not locate any diaries.

Harvey's position was undeniably delicate. He had learned much about the way the Kennedys' Round Table worked. He was in a position to dent, perhaps to shatter, the shining white knight image. The Kennedys—Bobby, in particular—may have felt that Harvey's knowledge of their passion to eliminate Fidel Castro was a threat to the dynasty. To lance Harvey at the weakest chink in his armor, his drinking, and to let it be known that he was no longer reliable was to subvert anything he might later say about the Kennedys' addiction to violent vengeance. Recall that McGeorge Bundy of the JFK White House remarked to a senior CIA official, "Your friend doesn't inspire confidence."

If nothing else, Harvey left Task Force W and ZRRIFLE having utterly baffled most of his superiors. The illustrious star had dimmed, even imploded. Many years after the fact, one of Bill's closest associates, Dave Murphy, said, "After Cuba, Bill was a shell." But Harvey lived on, and even if discredited, he had a storehouse of knowledge that did the Kennedy name no good.

BILL'S MOTHER, SARA KING HARVEY, EARNED HER DOCTORATE IN ENGLISH LITERATURE FROM THE UNIVERSITY OF CHICAGO AND AT OXFORD. SHE LATER WAS A PROFESSOR AT INDIANA STATE UNIVERSITY. *SALLY HARVEY, HARVEY FAMILY PAPERS*

CG HARVEY (THEN MRS. ROBERT D. HAN) PICTURED ON THE DAY SHE ENLISTED IN THE WOMEN'S AUXILIARY ARMY CORPS (WAAC), JULY 1942. *SALLY HARVEY, HARVEY FAMILY PAPERS*

BILL HARVEY (TOP LEFT CORNER), SIGMA CHI FRATERNITY, INDIANA UNIVERSITY, 1934. *CHUCK COFFIN, DBM*

Alex ("Silver Fox") MacMillan, pictured in 1961, left the FBI for the Office of Strategic Services and in 1947 became one of the Central Intelligence Agency's first officers. *Susan McCone MacMillan*

Jim Critchfield, a decorated Army colonel and tank commander who transferred to the CIA and became chief of base at Pullach from 1948–55. In those years, he presided over CIA support for and relations with the Gehlen Organization, later the Federal German Intelligence Service. *Lois Critchfield*

Peter M. F. Sichel was stationed in Berlin from October 1, 1945, until May 1952. At first, he was acting chief of the CIA's Berlin station, then deputy chief of base until 1949, when he was appointed chief of base in his own right, while still in his twenties. He was succeeded in May 1952 for a short time by Lester Houck, Bill Harvey's immediate predecessor. When Harvey became chief of base, he butted heads with some Sichel loyalists. Harvey, however, formed a realistic working relationship with Sichel, who had become head of the CIA's German desk. Photograph dated 2000. *PMF Sichel*

David E. Murphy was Harvey's deputy chief in Berlin from December 1954 to June 1959. Murphy became chief of base, Berlin, in his own right, from June 1959 to June 1961, after Harvey returned to Washington. Murphy specialized in Soviet operations. He was the prime mover and coauthor of *Battleground Berlin* in 1997. This photograph was taken in 2000. *David E. Murphy*

This photograph shows an actual section of the Berlin Tunnel, now on display at the Allied Museum on Clay Allee in Berlin. *Alliierten Museum /von Kostka*

Ted Shackley, a gung-ho agent recruiter and a tough administrator, was Bill Harvey's best-known protégé. He arrived in Berlin in 1954 and, working satellite operations, quickly caught Bill's eye. As chief of the CIA's JMWAVE station in Miami from 1962 to July 1965, he was Harvey's right-hand man for operations against Cuba. Shackley rose to become the assistant deputy director, operations, of the Agency, after tours of duty back in Berlin as chief of base and later in Laos and Vietnam. *Hazel Shackley*

Warren Frank, deputy chief of base, Berlin, July 1965–July 1970. *Warren Frank*

An Ampex tape recorder used in the Berlin Tunnel. *Alliierten Museum/Polizeihistorische Sammlung*

Herb Natzke was a World War II prisoner of war who later served with the CIA in Berlin from 1954 to 1959 and returned as chief of base from 1966 to1969. *Herb Natzke*

Dave and Marion Murphy, Bill and CG Harvey, in party mode, 1954. *Author's collection*

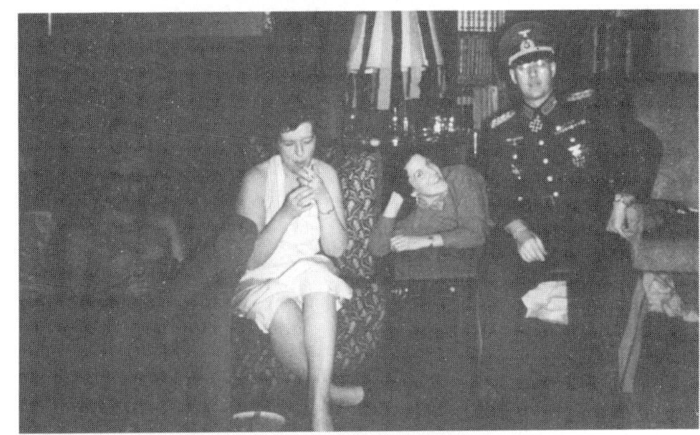

The Berlin Base Halloween party, 1955. *Author's collection*

"The Pear" on display at the Milinowski Strasse pool, July 1955. Maggie Crane, Bill's very discreet secretary, is in the black bathing suit. *Author's collection*

Bill Harvey, grillmaster, at a Berlin Base pool party, July 1955. *Author's collection*

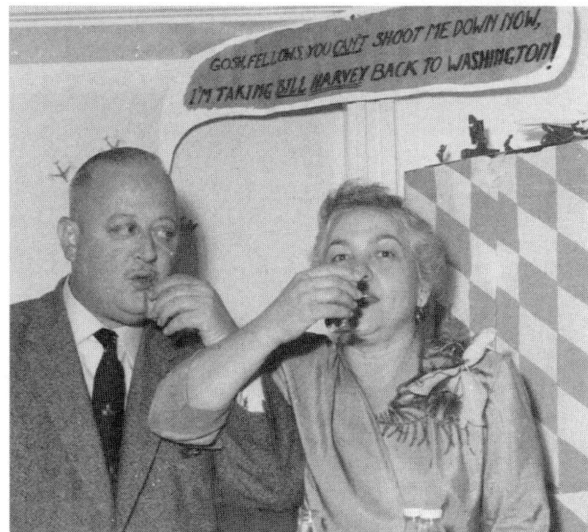

Bill and CG lift one at their Berlin farewell party, 1959. The sardonic cartoon bubble reads: "Gosh, fellows, you can't shoot me down now, I'm taking Bill Harvey back to Washington!" *Author's collection*

Bill and CG dancing on board ship on the way home to the United States, September 1959. *Sally Harvey, Harvey Family Papers*

A caricature of Bill Harvey relieving himself of his pistols at the last minute as he enters the Oval Office to meet President John F. Kennedy in 1961, when he took over the CIA's Cuban operations. *David Suter*

A slimmed-down, almost-haggard Bill with CG in Florida. The photo is undated, but it was probably taken about 1972. *Author's collection*

Sam Halpern, the indispensable staff man, loyal, knowing, and incredibly discreet. After the Cold War, Sam often compared notes with high Soviet officials on what the two sides had done, or not done, during the Cuban Missile Crisis, which he lived through, mostly with Bill Harvey, in the Langley headquarters basement. *Halpern Family*

Marajen Chinigo, owner of the *Champaign News-Gazette*. Marajen was a socialite who had residences in Champaign, Illinois; Palm Springs, California; and Sorrento, Italy. She was a friend and confidante of Johnny Rosselli, and she was a law client of Bill Harvey after his retirement from CIA. News-Gazette, *Champaign, Illinois*

Michael Chinigo was probably a CIA contract agent and liaison to the Sicilian Mafia. During World War II, he was a Hearst News correspondent, and after the war he married Marajen. He died a most mysterious death in Rome in 1974. News-Gazette, *Champaign, Illinois*

An ID from Bill's Indianapolis days in the 1970s. The ID listed Bill as a "security officer" but his final job at Bobbs-Merrill was checking legal decisions. *Sally Harvey, Harvey Family Papers*

9

BILL AND JOHNNY

The individual most deeply involved in the attempts to assassinate Fidel Castro, even before Bill Harvey, was Johnny Rosselli. The story of Bill and Johnny is complex and sorry. Only some of it can be reconstructed.

The fifteen-year relationship between Harvey and Rosselli is the source of some fascination, but so too is the considerable speculation that Harvey was somehow involved in the assassination of President John F. Kennedy. If there is a link between Harvey and the assassination, it almost definitely runs through Rosselli.

From the beginning, their relationship was a twaining of yin and yang, a bonding of men from different sides of the moral tracks. In the end, Bill's loyalty to Johnny contributed much to his own downfall, yet it was very, very Harvey.

Rosselli was more than a gunsel. He was a player on various stages, some of them overt and visible, others deeply private, conspiratorial. He had killed for the Mafia, early in his career, yet he fancied himself a gentleman and a diplomat, as well as a devoted patriot.[1] Businesswise, Rosselli had been involved with Al Capone in Chicago. He became the Chicago Mob's ambassador to young and restless Los Angeles and was deep in LA's popular gambling scene from his very first days on the coast in the 1930s.

Rosselli's path crossed those of Jack and Bobby Kennedy in various ways. The Kennedys' father, Joe, did business with the Mafia during Prohibition and again in Chicago during World War II. The Mafia, particularly the Chicago family, helped finance Jack Kennedy's 1960 election campaign, but Bobby Kennedy, both as chief investigator for the U.S. Senate's Kefauver Committee of the 1950s, and then as attorney general, galloped roughshod over his family's ties with and debts to the selfsame Mafia. At one point, Rosselli asked Frank Sinatra to get Bobby to lower the pressure on the Mob.

Rosselli went to parties thrown by Peter Lawford, the Kennedy in-law. He was an on-again-off-again boyfriend of Judith Exner Campbell, who had affairs with Sam Giancana and John F. Kennedy. He knew Marilyn Monroe, although probably not carnally. He also knew, perhaps at first only in passing, a couple who played a part in the latter stages of Harvey's story, Michael and Marajen Chinigo, who had a sprawling villa in the expensive Thunderbird Heights enclave of Palm Springs. Mrs. Chinigo was the owner of the *Champaign News-Gazette* in Illinois. She also spent some of her time in Rome and Sorrento, Italy. The Chinigos attended parties at which Sinatra provided the glitter.

And, from 1961 on, Johnny Rosselli was an ever-closer friend of Bill Harvey.

GENTLEMAN JOHNNY ROSSELLI

Rosselli was born Filippo Sacco on July 4, 1905, in a village midway between Rome and Naples, which was Camorra territory, not the Sicilian Mafia's turf. He and the rest of his family came to join Sacco Senior in Boston in September 1911. Johnny's first arrest, for delivering drugs, came in September 1922. Soon thereafter he was nailed for robbery; he may even have caused the death of a government informant and was shot in the leg. He skipped to New York, collected points in the bootleg trade, and then migrated to Chicago, where he became a sworn, or "made," member of Al Capone's syndicate during Prohibition and where he also became John Rosselli, a name he took from a Renaissance artist he found in an encyclopedia. (In another version of the story, he took the surname of a murdered Boston mobster; in still another, he copied the name from a tombstone.) Throughout his voluminous FBI records, his name is spelled "Roselli," whereas his business cards and other references prefer the double "ss" version.

Johnny's lungs couldn't take gusty Chicago, so Capone personally dispatched him to the sprawling village of Los Angeles. He quickly became LA-suave, endearing himself to various gangsters. He even once piloted a speedboat with a load of booze in a getaway that may have resonated with him years later when he was aiming for the shores of Castro's Cuba on behalf of Uncle Sam.

Rosselli did some foreshortened World War II military service at Camp Cook near Santa Barbara, and for years thereafter, he was a frequent patron of the Sansum Clinic there. He was excused from the military; was tried and convicted on charges of racketeering in Hollywood unions; was sent to Atlanta, one of the Feds' most ancient prisons; but was soon transferred to the more modern and comfortable pokey at Terre Haute, the town where Sara Harvey was then still prodding Indiana State students.

After he was released from prison, Rosselli renewed prewar connections. Soon he was accepted as the true Hollywood article. Johnny was a dandy, the epitome of a salon mobster, the kind of guy who sent shivers up and down the spines of more-or-less wellborn ladies and who compiled a notable bedding record. He became a recognized rim figure to the Frank Sinatra Hollywood/Palm Desert entourage. Indeed, persistent rumor has it that Rosselli was instrumental in securing Sinatra the lead role in *From Here to Eternity*.

Rosselli's admirers considered him "gallant" and "loyal." In his later career, his sponsor—the guy who could provide the muscle if Rosselli needed it—was Sam Giancana, who ran the Chicago Mob from the 1950s until his unseemly death two decades later.

When Las Vegas's time came, Rosselli was there. His official position in Vegas was unassuming. He had the concession for the ice-making machines on every floor of every hotel. If Johnny was short of folding green, said one observer, he simply walked up to a cashier's window, signed a marker, and walked away with a bundle.

Rosselli was also a passionate patriot of the country he had adopted, which had done him well, even though he had not bothered to become a legal citizen in good standing. The FBI bitterly disagreed with all the glowing characterizations of Gentleman Johnny.

TICKLISH CONTACT

The CIA's Office of Security, with a view toward the assassination of Fidel Castro, made contact with Rosselli in 1960. According to the Church Committee report, once Harvey was appointed head of Division D, he got in touch with the CIA's director of security, Col. Sheffield Edwards, and asked "to be put in touch with Rosselli. Edwards says he verified Helms's approval and then made the arrangements. . . . Harvey states that thereafter he regularly briefed Helms on the status of the Castro operation."[2] Rosselli and Harvey met at a turnover meeting at the Savoy Plaza Hotel in New York on Sunday, April 8, 1962, in the company of several others.

From then on, the official record—what there is of it—is straightforward. Less than two weeks later, on April 21, 1962, Harvey and Rosselli met in the cocktail lounge at Miami Airport. The bulbous Harvey gulped his double martini while the sleek Rosselli, wearing a custom-tailored suit, alligator shoes, and a $2,000 watch, sipped Smirnoff on the rocks. Harvey is alleged to have suddenly slapped his revolver down on the table between them. From now on, he commanded, Rosselli would work only for him. Rosselli was to maintain a particular Cuban contact but have no further dealings on the existing Castro assassination operation with Robert Maheu, Sam Giancana, or Santo Trafficante.

From the beginning, Harvey was well aware of the ticklish nature of his contact with Rosselli, and he fully understood the blowback risk. ZRRIFLE "was truly a vest-pocket operation," says Sam Halpern, who knew next to nothing about the Johnny connection. Bill wanted to be the only person who could answer questions, should they arise. He had no assistants on ZRRIFLE, and his closest, and apparently sole, confidant was, as it later turned out, Rosselli.

After the Kill Castro phase ended, and before his transfer to Rome at the end of June 1963, Harvey continued a close relationship with Rosselli, which later made Bill the object of deep suspicion in the upper echelons of the CIA. Was it anchored in their shared antipathy for the Kennedys? And what tipped the balance between the two to give Rosselli control over Harvey? I have a strong suspicion that Johnny, less than a year before his death, may have involved Harvey in a murder contract. Whatever it was that locked the two together, their tight association in later years made life difficult for Harvey and kept both under official scrutiny.

Bill's attachment to the mafioso was reciprocated. Rosselli was the first non–family member to call CG Harvey only a few hours after Bill died. It must be assumed that Rosselli knew about Harvey's passing so quickly because he had kept a phone watch on the Indianapolis hospital. Not content merely with expressing his deep and obvious condolences, Rosselli offered CG and the family "any help you need. Anything. You just tell me. You need money? You let me know, no matter how much."[3]

And then, only a couple of months after Bill died, Rosselli himself wound up dismembered in an oil barrel in a Florida swamp, a victim of his pals' displeasure.

GET CASTRO! CUBA AND THE MOB

During the reign of the tough little Cuban dictator, Fulgencio Batista, organized crime openly ran gambling and prostitution on its properties in Havana. In the mid-1950s Rosselli began to find his way around the Mafia-owned-and-operated casinos on the island. At about that time, he also became friendly with a CIA officer named Dave M., the notable figure mentioned by Sam Halpern as a member of the Task Force W staff in the Langley basement. Dave M. soon joined up with Johnny in the Florida Keys, where he was one of the mafioso's frequent drinking buddies.[4] Earlier assignments had earned Dave a reputation as a man capable of violence.

When Castro came to power, he closed Havana's casinos and jailed, albeit comfortably and without rancor, Santo Trafficante, the Mob's proconsul. Trafficante was released and decamped to Miami, leaving the impression that he would eventually return to Cuba. In August 1960 Sam Giancana boasted, on an FBI intercept tape, that Meyer Lansky, the father of Mob gambling interests in Cuba, had put a million dollar price on Castro's head. Such was the syndicate's upset at its eviction.

So, both the U.S. government and the Mafia shared an interest. President Eisenhower regarded Castro as enough of a bother to authorize an attempt at his overthrow and even his murder on March 17, 1960.

OFFING CASTRO: THE EARLY STAGES

If the CIA was to have an assassination capability specifically for Cuba, as distinct from roving commissions elsewhere in the Caribbean and in Africa, it needed better-qualified assassins. To fill this need, the Agency's Office of Security got in touch with an FBI academy classmate of Harvey, and later front man for Howard Hughes, Robert Maheu, who had a portfolio of interesting contacts.

In his testimony to the Church Committee, Harvey agreed that Richard Bissell, the deputy director of plans, and Col. Sheffield Edwards, the director of the Office of Security, were the ones who originally decided to reach out to the Mafia. The CIA's Mafia contact was assigned to the chief of the Operational Support Division of the Office of Security, Big Jim O'Connell, who had become "close personal friends" with Maheu while dealing with him on other matters. O'Connell was told that the top brass were looking for someone to "eliminate" or "assassinate" Castro.

O'Connell testified (and Harvey agreed) that it was actually Maheu who suggested using Rosselli. Maheu recalls, "the CIA was my first steady client, giving me 'cut-out' assignments [those jobs in which the Agency could not officially be involved]." Now in his eighties, Maheu professes not to recall any involvement in CIA's Cuban activities, unless provided with specific dates.[5]

Maheu had known Rosselli since the late 1950s and was well aware that the mafioso could get things done in the fertile oasis of Las Vegas and in the Mob's broader cosmos. The Church Committee report said,

"The Support Chief [O'Connell] had previously met Rosselli at Maheu's home." Harvey's marginal comment was that familiar OSOD ("Oh shit, oh dear!"), probably written with a deprecatory smile over the transparency of the admission.

In late August or early September 1960, before Kennedy became president, O'Connell asked Maheu to ask Rosselli "if he would participate in a plan to 'dispose' of Castro." Maheu overcame any moral qualms and introduced Big Jim to Rosselli. O'Connell told Johnny he represented unspecified corporate interests that might find the elimination of Fidel Castro advantageous.

On the Senate committee stand, Maheu and O'Connell each righteously claimed that the other had suggested using an unseemly citizen like Rosselli to perform an unspeakable deed and then carefully noted that the contract was worth $150,000. Maheu brought big-time mobsters Momo Salvatore (Sam) Giancana, the Chicago boss, and Santo Trafficante, who had by now settled in Miami, into the operation.

Of course Johnny didn't buy O'Connell's cover explanation, but he also didn't make an issue of the sponsorship. He was eager and happy to engage in a plot to dispose of Castro. Rosselli, say his biographers Rappleye and Becker, was "a bedrock conservative, [he] considered it his patriotic duty . . . a matter of honor and dedication" to heed the government's call to action.[6]

The formal account of Rosselli's accession to ZRRIFLE is in the 1967 report of the CIA inspector general (IG):

> 6. The pitch [to join the assassination plot] was made to Rosselli on September 14, 1960, at the Hilton Plaza Hotel in New York City. Mr. James O'Connell, Office of Security, was present during this meeting and was identified to Rosselli as an employee of Maheu. O'Connell actively served as Rosselli's contact until May 1962 at which time he phased out due to an overseas assignment. Rosselli's initial reaction was to avoid getting involved, but through Maheu's persuasion, he agreed to introduce him to a friend, Sam Gold [Giancana], who knew the Cuban crowd. Rosselli made it clear that he would not want any money for his part, and he believed that Gold would feel the same way. Neither of these individuals were ever paid out of Agency funds.
>
> 7. During the week of September 25, 1960, Maheu was introduced to Gold at the Fontainebleau Hotel, Miami Beach. During this meeting Maheu also met an individual identified as "Joe" who was sup-

> posedly a courier operating between Havana and Miami. Several weeks later Maheu saw photographs of both of these individuals in the Sunday supplement *Parade*. They were identified as Momo Salvatore Giancana and Santo Trafficante. Both were on the list of the Attorney General's Ten Most Wanted Men. Giancana was described as the Chicago Chieftain of the Cosa Nostra and successor to Al Capone. Trafficante was identified as the Cosa Nostra boss of Cuban operations. Maheu called this office immediately upon ascertaining this information.[7]

Giancana advised the small assembly at the Fontainebleau that guns might not be the preferred tools of execution; rather he suggested some kind of "potent pill which could be placed in Castro's food or drink." Giancana even had a possible agent, a corrupt Cuban official who had been on the Mafia payroll, "who still had access to Castro, and was still in a financial bind."

THE SECOND FONTAINEBLEAU MEETING

O'Connell requisitioned six pills "of high lethal content" from the CIA's Technical Services Division. The operation crawled along until details of the first attempt on Castro were firmed up at a second planning meeting on March 14, 1961, at the gangster-chic Fontainebleau, home of the Boom-Boom Room. The reason for the time and place was a world championship heavyweight boxing match pitting Floyd Patterson against Ingemar Johansson, a must-attend social event. Patterson won in the sixth; Johansson was noticeably past his prime.

This all took place well before Harvey took over ZRRIFLE. If Bill had been in charge, such a large confabulation of Mob kingpins would not have come close to discussing a matter of top-level national concern. Too many people, especially people whose reliability was open to question and over whom the Agency had absolutely no control, were in the know.

At the second meeting "Maheu opened his briefcase and dumped a whole lot of money. . . . [He] came up with the capsules, and he explained how they were going to be used. As far as I can remember, they couldn't be used in boiling soups and things like that, but they could be used in water or otherwise they couldn't last forever. Maheu said, 'this was Johnny's contract.'"[8] Giancana later was alleged by a Church Committee witness to have recalled, exquisitely, "I am not in it, and they are asking me for the names of some guys who used to work in the casinos."[9]

J. Edgar Hoover now weighed in, just to tell the Agency he knew what was going on. The Bureau's tap on Giancana had caught him talking about the Castro contract with some pals. "It would occur in November. Moreover he allegedly indicated he had already met with the assassin-to-be on three occasions." A month after the second Fontainebleau get-together, on or after April 20, 1961, Edwards told the FBI to lose interest in Maheu because Bureau persistence "might reveal information relating to the abortive Bay of Pigs invasion," which had just blown up.[10]

The Mob's Havana contact allegedly made a few attempts to slip the pills into Castro's food, but then he chickened out and instead nominated someone else "who made several attempts without success." The new hit man never got the word to proceed, or he lost the job that had placed him near Castro. He eventually, and honorably, returned both the pills and payment.

The timing of the pill operation is unclear. The CIA thought, officially, that it was in March–April 1961, before the Bay of Pigs, but after Eisenhower's watch had ended. The witness quoted above placed it at the time of the heavyweight title fight, i.e., around March 14, 1961. Bissell said the effort was canceled after the Bay of Pigs in April. Harvey simply underlined that passage and noted "No" in the margin. Maheu said he was not involved in the Bay of Pigs. O'Connell was certain the pill operation took place in early 1962. So many operations against Castro's life failed, were aborted, or were misconceived that even the Church Committee had trouble keeping track of them.

Then, on April 21, 1962, a year after the Bay of Pigs, Harvey and Rosselli met at the Miami airport, and the Get Castro enterprise took on a new life. "The second phase [i.e., after Harvey took over] appears to lack the high-level gangster flavor that characterized the first phase. Rosselli remained as a prominent figure in the operation, but working directly with the Cuban exile community, directly on behalf of the CIA"[11] and directly under Harvey. In fact, immediately after he took over the ZRRIFLE portfolio, Harvey cut Giancana and, most especially, Trafficante out of the operation. It would be rational to assume, however, that Rosselli kept them informed, as a matter of Mob tact and diplomacy.

In an internal memorandum dated May 14, 1962, Sheffield Edwards noted a phone call from Harvey, who said "that he was dropping any plans for the use of [Rosselli] for the future." The comment may have been an accurate indication of intent at the time, but it was not factually correct. Rather it was a conclusive, deliberately misleading signal, obscuring the fact that Bill was tucking the Rosselli/Get Castro operation into his vest-pocket.[12]

Also in May 1962 Bobby Kennedy demanded to know what the hell the CIA was doing playing footsie with the Mob. Bobby was understandably irate because he had been prosecuting the Mafia for years, first as the lead counsel on Senator Estes Kefauver's Senate Committee investigating organized crime and then as his brother's attorney general. The Mob was, in its turn, even more irate because they felt that Jack Kennedy would not have been resident at 1600 Pennsylvania Avenue had it not been for considerable sums of untraceable money and for votes provided to Chicago's Daley Machine by the Mafia. The Mob felt it was being persecuted, unreasonably and unfairly.

Bobby's demand flew in the face of the principle of plausible deniability, but the attorney general was not to be denied. The CIA responded with a straight tell-all memorandum, dated May 22, 1962, a week after Harvey took control of Rosselli. The sequence of events from Spring 1962 until Harvey's dismissal (and even for a while thereafter) became the stuff of much investigation years later because it seemed as if it might have bearing on the assassination of President Kennedy.

ROSSELLI'S NEW CASE OFFICER

When Harvey learned that he was to take on the Castro assassination assignment in November 1961, he had to digest many new matters quickly.

He needed a principal agent who was used to the ways of the covert world. He could not use an Agency employee because the risks for blowback were too great. And he could hardly trust a foreigner with this one. Rosselli was already on the books. In March 1961, well before Harvey was involved in Caribbean matters, Rosselli went to the Dominican Republic, accompanied by Howard Hunt of the CIA. Rafael Trujillo, the Republic's dictator, was ambushed and killed on May 30, 1961, but the CIA was cleared of involvement in the assassination.

Bill probably got in touch with one or more of his former colleagues at the Bureau, met them somewhere for a drink or two, and pumped them discreetly. The FBI man or men would have told Harvey, completely off the record, that Hoover had a tap on Giancana and that he was notoriously garrulous. They would have given Rosselli a good recommendation as an operator: his criminal record wasn't all that egregious, and where Giancana spouted constantly, Johnny knew not to talk, except to the right people. What better solution to Harvey's problem than a man who had lived his whole adult life as a member of a secret organization with very, very strict rules, enforced by the discipline of *omerta*?

Another of Johnny's advantages was that he was sincerely, almost touchingly, grateful to the country that had given him so much, even if the acquisitions had been illegal. And he needed brownie points in case his citizenship was questioned, which it subsequently was and, indeed, if the Feds got onto him for other malefactions.

All these factors contributed to another sine qua non of clandestine operation: control. It looked as if Rosselli could be controlled by his case officer, Harvey. Still, Bill must have thought that the operation was sticky from the outset. He was sensitive to the potential for eruption; he was also cynically savvy to the ways of Washington and to the scavenger ethic of the media, even in those relatively innocent days. What if it became public that Jack Kennedy's CIA had recruited elements of the Mafia to carry out an assassination contract on Castro?

HARVEY TAKES OVER

The actual transfer of Rosselli from the Office of Security to ZRRIFLE started out at the Savoy Plaza Hotel in New York on that April 1962 Sunday evening and then developed into a scene that, despite the IG's official prose, is vaguely reminiscent of what would have happened if Jack Nicholson and Robin Williams had met the Marx brothers. Or it might have played better as a scene from *Guys and Dolls*.

> After discussions, Maheu suggested dinner at the Elk Room, a fashionable restaurant in a nearby hotel. O'Connell says that Maheu picked up the tab [i.e., Howard Hughes paid.]. They finished dinner about 9.30 or 10.00PM. Rosselli wanted to buy the group a nightcap, but since it was Sunday night, nearly all of the bars were closed. They walked around the neighborhood looking for an open bar and finally wound up at the Copacabana [a famous, celebrity-drenched nocturnal watering hole of the time, much frequented by gossip columnists and their stringers].
>
> They were refused admittance to the bar because of a rule restricting admission to couples, so they sat at a table where they could watch the floor show. Rosselli found himself facing a table at "ringside" at which Phyllis McGuire was sitting with Dorothy Kilgallen [one of the mainstream gossip columnists of the time] and Liberace for the opening night of singer Rosemary Clooney. To avoid Phyllis McGuire's seeing him, Rosselli got his companions to change their seating arrangement so his back was turned to Miss McGuire.[13]

EARLY CONTACTS

Not surprisingly, Rosselli did not at first feel comfortable with Harvey. After the Copacabana caper, an overlap continued during which Jim O'Connell sat in on Harvey-Rosselli meetings in Washington on April 14, 1962. Thereafter O'Connell was assigned to Okinawa, and Harvey dealt with Rosselli alone.

Joe Shimon, the former Metropolitan Police officer whose background remains obscure and whose presence on the periphery of the Castro operations is inexplicable, segued into Harvey's circle, at least after Bill retired. Years later Shimon reminisced about the early 1960s and CIA Cuban operations to the investigative journalist and author Anthony Summers.

> The thing [the Castro assassination plot] wasn't going too well. They sent a few teams and they never came back. Well, then Harvey was assigned to direct the show instead of Jim O'Connell, then he came [to Washington] and . . . Johnny was in a safe house for about six weeks with Harvey. . . . You see, Harvey . . . you got to give him credit . . . this was one of the greatest investigators in the world. He was very good. He had sources all over the world. He's the guy dug the tunnel.[14]

Joe Shimon, according to Summers, "loved to be a source." His daughter, to whom Joe was something of a mystery, says that Mob figures, including Rosselli, often came to the Shimon family home in Arlington, Virginia, and that Harvey was a visitor from time to time.[15] Joe also may have loved to embellish the truth, just a tad.

After the last joint meeting with O'Connell, Harvey headed out of Washington by car on April 19. There is no record of how and when Rosselli went to Florida. According to Rappleye and Becker, Rosselli, another CIA officer, and perhaps later, Dave M. set up shop in the Kenilworth Hotel—not the Fontainebleau—in Miami and also "in a motel in an upscale section of Key Biscayne."

Harvey told the CIA IG's investigators that "he arrived in Miami on April 21, 1962, and found Rosselli already in touch with Tony Varona, the Cuban exile leader who had participated in Phase One [of the assassination operation]. . . . Harvey described the manner in which [some poison pills provided by the CIA's Technical Services Division were] to be introduced into Castro's food, involving an asset of Varona's who had access to someone in a restaurant frequented by Castro. We [the IG officers] told Harvey that Edwards had described precisely the same plan. . . . Harvey replied that he took over a going operation—one that was already 'in train.' Edwards denies that this is so. O'Connell says that Harvey . . . is right."[16]

Shimon alleged that Harvey kept Johnny incommunicado for six weeks, probably in Florida, in the spring of 1962. Bill probably figured that Rosselli would present a handling problem, that he might be loath to accept discipline from a Fed. Harvey would have wanted to determine such vital factors as Rosselli's motivation, his loyalty, and the extent to which he was under control of or in close touch with (a) Mafia figures and (b) any other intelligence or security service (including the FBI and the Immigration and Naturalization Service [INS]). To satisfy himself of Johnny's bona fides, Bill probably conducted an interrogation himself or had it done by a trusted lieutenant, perhaps Dave M. It's almost a given that Harvey had Johnny polygraphed.

When Johnny emerged clean from the various preliminary inquiries, Bill or, more likely, the robust Dave M.—not trusting the usual trainers to meet the mafioso—gave Johnny a crash course in intelligence tradecraft, particularly the need for security and perhaps most especially the use of the telephone, countersurveillance, the use of cutouts, recruitment requirements, and name checking—the usually boring but vital aspects of intelligence work. Most probably, as circumstance permitted, the two men from worlds apart felt each other out, probed each others' vulnerabilities and weaknesses—often over a bottle or two—and gradually formed the basis for an enduring palship.

According to Ted Shackley, Harvey came to Florida periodically while Shackley was head of JMWAVE, primarily to see Johnny. Rappleye and Becker say that in Miami Johnny "frequented JMWAVE . . . sometimes attending the staff briefings, but more often engaging in demolition exercises with Ed Roderick, in rounds of cribbage, or heading off with Dave M. for drinking bouts."[17] Dave M. was assigned to Johnny's raiders to exert day-to-day control over a group of buccaneers who could have turned a messy situation into a disastrous one. It's more than possible that the U-Haul resupply caper recalled by Shackley in chapter 7 was actually a resupply mission for Johnny's ops base in the Keys.

Various accounts place Rosselli physically—sometimes in the uniform of a U.S. Army colonel—at the JMWAVE headquarters. Shackley, who was known by the Cubans as "El Rubio," "the Blond One," vigorously denies that Rosselli ever came close to JMWAVE.[18]

Warren Frank and Star Murphy, who was in the JMWAVE office, have absolutely no recollection that Johnny ever appeared at the operation's headquarters. Indeed, Star Murphy knew nothing at all of Johnny's activities for the CIA until they became public in the 1970s.[19] It is highly unlikely that Rosselli did, indeed, come onto the base. Such a visit would have been a severe violation of basic security and would have been anathema to Harvey.

Whether Rosselli actually sauntered Miami's boulevards in bird-colonel uniform, as has been alleged, is also subject to doubt. Johnny's CIA contacts/controllers probably tried to keep Rosselli as entertained as possible at the raiders' camp in the Keys. Recognition of such a well-known figure, especially in an American officer's uniform, could have led to embarrassing repercussions.

ROSSELLI'S SUBBASE IN THE FLORIDA KEYS

The only description I have found of Rosselli's paramilitary activities against Cuba comes from Richard Mahoney. Once Dick Helms personally cleared Rosselli for the assassination operation, the mafioso was covered as a colonel in the Army and Dave M. moved from the Langley basement to Florida. Toward the end of May 1962 the CIA built a small base for Rosselli's unit on Point Mary, Key Largo, clearing out an acre or so of the thick mangrove forest for rough-hewn sheds and two crude structures. A floating dock was anchored on coral reef. The purpose of the base was to train snipers.[20] Mahoney continues:

> Rosselli . . . was the only person who could make the incendiary [Dave] M. laugh. They would drink until the sun came up, usually joined by Rip Robertson, the hard-bitten Texan and decorated veteran of World War II who was the favorite "boom and bang" guy among the exiled Cubans [because he had actually participated in the Bay of Pigs landing operation]. A favorite bar was Les Deux Violins where, according to one of his Cuban operatives, "Johnny knew all the help by their first name, tipped hugely, and would tell farcical stories about his days with Al Capone." Throughout his criminal life, Rosselli had befriended men more dangerous and sociopathic than these. . . .
>
> . . . According to [a Cuban commander under Rosselli], Colonel Rosselli used the team from time to time for raids and other operations. Rosselli was one of only two Americans authorized to go into Cuba on clandestine missions.[21]

Elsewhere in the accounts of JMWAVE's activities in Florida is mention of considerable CIA activity in the Keys, where live firing exercises could be conducted without fear of compromise and fast boats could slip out to sea and return without question. These accounts may all be based on the same source, a colorful account attributed to Col. Bradley Ayers.

Back in the mangrove, Rosselli wanted action. Recall that he had not served his country during World War II because the Feds had yanked him out of uniform to stand trial and then to serve his sentence for extortion. He had missed Korea. Now was his chance to prove his mettle, as well as his loyalty to Uncle Sam. Johnny's yearning would have touched a responsive, perhaps even envious, chord in Harvey who, himself, had never served in uniform or fired a shot at any U.S. enemies.

Rosselli and Dave M. separately kept Harvey informed of the operation's progress. Sometime in May 1962, Johnny reported that the lethal pills and guns had arrived in Cuba. On June 21, only a month after Harvey took over, Johnny told Bill that a three-man team had been dispatched to Cuba. The IG's report described the team's mission as "vague."

There is no hard, documentary evidence to suggest that Rosselli ever put to sea or came close to Cuban shores on hostile missions, but there is at least this account of his derring-do, again according to Mahoney. Late in the summer of 1962,

> [Rosselli] Led his first nighttime mission across the Windward Passage in a pair of swift V-20s. The V-20 was the workhorse of the CIA fleet, admirably suited to its unique tasks. With its gun mounts and twin 100-horsepower Graymarine engines concealed by fishing nets, the boat looked like any other medium-sized craft plying the route. . . . The V-20's top speed was 40 knots. . . . [A] Cuban patrol boat spotted Rosselli's raiders and gave chase, ripping the bottom out of Rosselli's boat with machine-gun fire. Rosselli jumped into the water and swam to the second craft, which managed to make it back to camp.
>
> On his second run toward the coast of Cuba, Rosselli's V-20s were again intercepted and the lead boat was sunk. Rosselli managed to get aboard a small dinghy before the speedboat went under. He drifted alone for several days in the boat and was given up for dead back in Florida until an American patrol cutter rescued him and brought him back to camp.
>
> Giancana, for one, thought he was crazy to risk his life, but Rosselli had always been an over-the-top type.[22]

Mahoney's source was likely Bradley Ayers, who might have heard this story one night at Les Deux Violins—unless, of course, he participated in the op. I have seen no confirmation of these incidents, but they are in keeping with the Rosselli legend and thus may be a subsidiary part of Harvey's story.

If the story is true, Bill would certainly have conducted post-op debriefings when possible, to ascertain facts, perhaps to reprimand Johnny for recklessness, and then killed a bottle or two. Undoubtedly a few meetings during the summer of 1962 went uncatalogued—perhaps target practice in the Keys and drinking bouts—as the palship between the two deepened. Johnny was nearing sixty years of age and had given up a soft bed, but not booze, for a flamboyant existence dedicated to paying back a country that had given him the good (if illegal) life, and in so doing, acting at the behest of a man who had pursued him and his ilk for years. It's not hard to imagine Harvey admiring Johnny for having put his life where his mouth was.

There is, too, considerable irony that the CIA made an instant Army colonel out of an illegal immigrant who used a false name for most of his life, was a professional criminal, and was on unpaid leave of absence from the Mafia. The idea for the field-grade commission probably came from Johnny, who must have coveted the rank and the uniform as signs that he had, at last, made it in the world to which he so yearned to belong.

The Church Committee report said that in late summer 1962 the CIA was preparing to send in another three-man team to penetrate Castro's bodyguard. Harvey saw Rosselli in Miami on September 7 and 11, 1962, although no record indicates that Bill went to Johnny's base in the Keys then. Johnny told Harvey that the lethal pills for Castro were 'still safe' in Cuba. "Harvey testified that by this time he had grave doubts . . . and told Rosselli that 'there's not much likelihood that this is going anyplace, or that it should be continued.'"

The October missile crisis intervened, and in its midst, Harvey was officially removed from Task Force W. Bill's handwritten marginal note on the committee report at that juncture says, "Actually, the termination [of the operation] started, then was expedited 11/62," after Bill was removed from Cuban operations. The final, official termination of the CIA's contact with Rosselli came in February 1963. But that was in no way the end of the relationship between Bill and Johnny.

For all the reasons cited earlier, there is almost no paper on Johnny's activities, or on the Johnny-Bill relationship. Harvey would not have written memoranda for the record to himself. His superior, Helms, did not want to know much about ZRRIFLE. And Scott D. Breckinridge and Kenneth E. Greer had to depend on interviews with CIA officers when they put together the IG's report for Helms.

The Church Committee report bends over backward to underline that Rosselli conducted all of his activities for CIA out of his own pocket, so no accounting records exist. "He paid his own way, he paid his own hotel fees, he paid his own travel. . . . He never took a nickel. He said, enigmatically, 'No, as long as it is for the Government of the United States, this is the least I can do, because I owe it a lot.' [Harvey's note: 'True!'] Edwards agreed that Rosselli was 'never paid a cent,' and Maheu testified that 'Giancana was paid nothing at all, not even for expenses, and that Mr. Rosselli was given a pittance that did not even begin to cover his expenses.'"

The committee, perhaps a bit prissily, added, "It is clear, however, that the CIA did pay Rosselli's hotel bill during his stay in Miami in October, 1960. The CIA's involvement with Rosselli caused the Agency some difficulty during his subsequent prosecutions for fraudulent gambling activities and living in the country under an assumed name." Harvey noted, "Inaccurate," next to this item but provided no further comment.[23]

Harvey spent the 1962 Christmas holiday, after Director of Central Intelligence John McCone had relieved him of command of Cuban operations and after the rapid termination of the Rosselli Cuba operation, in Florida. Bill saw Johnny "several times" while he was there. He gave Rosselli $2,700 to be passed on to the three "militia men." Rosselli probably spent the holidays with his sister at Plantation Key, outside Fort Lauderdale; he and Harvey discussed the operation on the phone several times between January 11 and 15, 1963. They agreed that "nothing was happening. As far as Harvey knows, the three militia men never left for Cuba. He knows nothing of what may have happened to the three reported to have been sent to Cuba."[24]

Harvey was in Miami again February 11–14, 1963, well after he had been officially removed from Task Force W. He left a message for one of the Cubans that "it now looked as it if were all over." With Helms's approval that Rosselli be terminated as a CIA asset, Harvey flew in February or March 1963 to Los Angeles, where the pair "agreed that the operation would be closed off." Rosselli would remain in loose contact with the principal agent, Varona. Thereafter, Harvey told the investigators, he had a couple of phone calls from Rosselli, who, because of the time difference, called Bill in the evenings at home.

During another set of meetings in Florida in April, Harvey and Rosselli agreed on official termination and Johnny signed a quit claim. Bill and

Johnny went out to sea in a chartered boat on two consecutive days, April 18 and 19, 1963, during which time they presumably discussed matters of mutual interest under circumstances that made surveillance of any kind almost impossible. During this period the pair had dinner with a third person, perhaps Johnny's sister, Edith Daigle, or perhaps someone else. The dinner was official enough business for Bill to charge it, something he would not have done merely to recoup an out-of-pocket expense.

According to some expense account records for ZRRIFLE/QJWIN from April 13 to 21, 1963, Harvey was at the Plantation Yacht Harbor motel/marina in Plantation Key, Florida. "John A. Wallston" (one of Rosselli's known aliases was John A. Ralston), who listed his address as 56510 Wilshire Boulevard (the Friars Club) in Los Angeles, was registered in the next room, which was also charged to Harvey's bill.[25] This stay occurred well after the Rosselli aspect of ZRRIFLE was supposed to have been shut down and as Harvey was reading into his upcoming assignment in Rome.

Bill submitted precise accounting to a financial officer with an apologetic note, "These piled up on me while trying to figure out whether [ ] shouldn't write to [ ] to tell them to address these differently. . . . Hope this late receipt of receipts hasn't upset your book-keeping." Harvey then listed his expenses, "all chargeable to Ops Expenses QJWIN/ZRRIFLE." (Not all amounts are visible on the scratchy photocopy of the accounting.) First there appears a series of phone calls within Florida and to Los Angeles.

17/4	Drinks and dinner for 2 (1 unofficial American and self) Eden Roc Hotel, Miami Fla.	26.00
18/4	*Boat charter fee for ops purposes*. No rcpt available. Islamora [*sic*—Islamorada?] Fla.	75.00
19/4	Ditto above	75.00
20/4	*Ops hotel room*—day Plantation Yacht Harbor, Plantation Key Fla	22.00
	Phone call, Plantation Key to Miami	
	Miami, Fla. Dinner for 3 (*2 unofficial Amis and self*) Fontainebleau	45.00
20/4	Reimbursement to ZRRIFLE/MI for ops-related rooms at Eden Roc Hotel, 3 days. No rcpt.	200.00
	Reimbursement ZRRIFLE/MIR trip *1 class plane ticket Miami-Chicago* No rcpt available	200.00
	Termination payment ZRRIFLE/MI—No receipt	1,000.00

It became necessary or advisable, perhaps as a result of the conversations listed in the above expense report, for Rosselli to visit Chicago. In an unusual move, Harvey paid for Johnny's ticket. Perhaps during this trip Rosselli brought Giancana up to speed, relaying to him the news that the CIA connection was finished. Or perhaps Rosselli, who by now might have seized upon Harvey's disgrace to gain the upper hand in the relationship, went to Chicago to discuss certain matters involving Harvey with the head of the Chicago Mob. Rosselli might have also visited the newspaper owner Marajen Chinigo in Champaign, Illinois, during the trip.

Also, note that in the accounting, Harvey gave Rosselli (or, conceivably, a third party) a $1,000 termination payment; this one instance might contradict previous assertions that Rosselli paid all but limited operational expenses out of his own pocket.

Last for now, around the middle of June 1963, Bill picked up Johnny at Dulles Airport. He "remembers having suggested to Rosselli that he bring only carry-on luggage so there would be no delay at the airport awaiting baggage." Harvey had closed his own home prior to leaving the country and was staying in the house of a neighbor who was out of town. Rosselli spent the night with the Harveys in the neighbor's home. That evening, Rosselli, Harvey, and CG went out for dinner. While dining, Harvey received a phone call from Sam Papich, the FBI liaison officer to the CIA, asking if Harvey knew the identity of his dinner guest. Harvey said that he did. Harvey speculated that he was picked up by the Bureau's surveillance of Johnny and was identified through his car license number.

"Harvey met Papich the next morning and explained that he was [in June, still] terminating an operational association with Rosselli. Papich reminded Harvey of the FBI rule requiring FBI personnel to report any known contacts between former FBI employees and criminal elements. Papich said that he would have to report to J. Edgar Hoover that Harvey had been seen with Rosselli. Harvey said he understood. . . . Harvey . . . asked Papich to inform him in advance if it appeared that Hoover might call Mr. McCone—Harvey's point being that he felt that McCone should be briefed before receiving a call from Hoover. Papich agreed to do so. Harvey said that he then told Mr. Helms of the incident and that Helms agreed that there was no need to brief McCone unless a call from Hoover was to be expected."

The IG's 1967 report concluded, "This was Harvey's last face-to-face meeting with Rosselli, although he has heard from him since then. The later links between Harvey and Rosselli are described in a separate section of this report."[26]

What the IG's report does not answer, or speculate on, is why Rosselli flew in from the West Coast only days before Harvey was due to take up his new post in Rome. To say good-bye to an old pal, whom he had been telephoning at home, but not in the office? To pass along some parting words of wisdom? Perhaps to ask that Bill perform certain very delicate services when he got settled in Italy? We shall never know.

ROSSELLI CONVICTED

The FBI had been trying to nail Rosselli for years. Then Immigration started breathing down his neck. Johnny figured he had markers he could call in. On May 12, 1966, he told Col. Sheffield Edwards that he was facing federal charges for being an illegal alien but promised that he did not intend to bring up his CIA activities.

Yet Johnny began to feel the heat. In January 1967 Drew Pearson, the *Washington Merry-Go-Round* columnist of the day, learned from Rosselli that, a few years earlier, the Agency had engaged the Mafia to assassinate Castro. Pearson held back until March 3, 1967. "Robert Kennedy may have approved an assassination plot which then possibly backfired against his late brother." On March 7, 1967, the same column reported, "A reported CIA plan to assassinate Cuba's Fidel Castro . . . may have resulted in a counterplot by Castro to assassinate President Kennedy." Pearson had taken his story to Chief Justice Earl Warren and from there it spread in a tight circle.

Almost simultaneously, on March 1, 1967, Jim Garrison, who had been looming on the periphery of the JFK assassination investigation, submitted an indictment in New Orleans that named fourteen CIA officials as conspirators in the murder of Jack Kennedy. The FBI heard whispers that the Mob had a contract ready for Bobby Kennedy if he got close to the Democratic presidential nomination the next year.

Dick Helms, as DCI, had to know what the extent of the CIA's Rosselli problem was. He asked the IG to get at the unvarnished truth. Harvey was "recalled from sick leave" to testify to the inspectors in the late winter, early spring of that year.

In 1968 the Feds finally got their vengeance. Johnny was tried and, after six months in court, was convicted on December 2, 1968, of skimming winnings from high-stakes gambling at the Friars Club in Los Angeles. He was also sentenced to five years plus six months on immigration charges.

Before he started to serve his time, a judge ordered Johnny to attend his mother's funeral. Rosselli asked Joe Shimon to accompany him to

Boston; they were there in June when Bobby Kennedy was killed in Los Angeles. According to Rappleye and Becker, Johnny showed little interest in the murder.[27]

AGENCY POSTMORTEM

The CIA IG's report is the primary source of information about the CIA's and Harvey's role in the Castro assassination maze. The IG's investigation, conducted under great time pressure, was written and typed by two officers, Kenneth E. Greer and Scott D. Breckinridge.[28] The one "ribbon-copy" report was "delivered to the Director, personally, in installments, beginning on April 24th." Helms returned his copy to the IG on May 22 with strict instructions that one copy only be retained in the IG's eyes-only file. The report was finally released for public scrutiny under President Clinton's "JFK Act" on February 3, 1999.

The IG report winds down with this analysis:

> a) If Drew Pearson has a single source . . . then Bill Harvey emerges as the likely candidate. He was the only person we found in the course of this inquiry who knew all four of the key facts at the time the Pearson columns appeared. *We preferred not to think that Bill Harvey was the culprit. We could find no persuasive reason why he would wish to leak the story deliberately and we doubted that he would be so indiscreet as to leak it accidentally. Further, if he were the source, we could expect Pearson's story to be completely accurate because Harvey knew the truth.* [Emphasis added.][29]

Thus Harvey was cleared of direct suspicion that he had leaked efforts to enact the Kennedys' wrath against Castro. The inspectors strongly implied that they suspected Rosselli of passing the information to a lawyer, Ed Morgan, who was tight with Drew Pearson. It is doubtful that Rosselli would have taken such a thunderous step unless it had been approved at the highest Mafia level. Still, Rosselli was a patriot and wanted to be recognized as such. And there may have been other considerations as well.

SUMMING UP

Harvey testified to the Church Committee, "It is quite conceivable that [the Rosselli plot to kill Castro] had been penetrated." There is considerable reason to believe that Santo Trafficante was a double agent and continued to ingratiate himself with Castro by reporting on the CIA and Cuban exile activities. Ted Shackley recalled pointedly that JMWAVE had nothing to do with Trafficante during Ted's tenure as chief.

In mid-February 1963, as Harvey was in transit from the Langley basement to Rome, the obsessively fixated Jim Angleton fingered S. Peter Karlow, one of the Office of Strategic Services stalwarts who had carried over honorably into the CIA, the man who might have introduced Bill Harvey to CG in Germany, as the possible KGB mole in the Clandestine Services. The investigation came when Anatoli Golitsin and Yuri Nosenko defected in 1961 and 1962 and crippled the Agency with devious information, at least some of it presumably hatched in the brain of Kim Philby.[30] The FBI handled the case with deliberate indelicacy, and although Karlow came out clean, the CIA behaved reprehensibly to him as an officer and a person for decades thereafter. Helms was one of several in the CIA who did not show any particular loyalty to Karlow during the investigation, although much else was going on at the time to preoccupy the beleaguered DCI. Others who played parts in the handling of his case were names familiar in this account, men at the top of the CIA pinnacle who appeared, in retrospect, to cherish their stature more than honesty and loyalty to an old friend.

Thus, in the winter of 1963, the top tier of the CIA was dealing with the fallout from the Cuban Missile Crisis, the Kennedys' alarms and excursions, and the seemingly real possibility that a senior staff member might be a KGB penetration. Too, the Agency was beginning to get involved in Indochina. Plus whatever else may have been going on around the world. The atmosphere in the halls of Langley was not conducive to trust and good-fellowship. Harvey would have been aware of the stratospheric writhings over the Karlow case. He knew Angleton, even if they were not close. He also still had friends in high places in the FBI, which handled the interrogation and investigation of Karlow. One can almost hear Bill saying to himself, "If this is the way they treat a guy who has been a loyal officer for more than twenty years . . . " It's possible that such thoughts led him to fraternize with Rosselli more than he might otherwise have. The two were of like, restive mind about bureaucracy and about the Kennedys.

PEAS IN A POD?

Harvey was the senior handling officer for Rosselli during nine months of intermittent, official association under highly conspiratorial circumstances. Together they ate, drank, and went out to sea, where no one could overhear their conversations.

Johnny was the kind of guy whom Harvey's FBI training would ordinarily have taught him to hold in contempt. The mafioso was also an iconoclast, a guy who rejected the system, a buccaneer, a man of guns, who had shown that he was willing to risk his life for his adopted country—whose government had imprisoned him once and still hounded him—a guy whose tell-it-like-it-is, four-letter-word, forthright manner clicked with Harvey's own approach to life. The only personal attribute on which they diverged, and even here, there may have been some compatibility, was on women. Johnny was a Ladies Man, in capitals; Harvey was not. But Bill had had that reputation as a womanizer before he married CG.

After ZRRIFLE lapsed, Bill may well have figured that Johnny could be a useful contact, as well as a buddy. In spring and early summer 1963, in the last days before Harvey went to Rome, the pair set the stage for speculation that stretched over the next decades: that they had come to be involved in considerably more than raids on Cuba and the attempted assassination of Fidel Castro.

The intangible that brought the two closest together was their shared, intense dislike of Bobby Kennedy, a dislike that tarnished the president because Jack backed Bobby. Bobby had betrayed the family's debt to the Mafia in particularly vicious ways. Harvey, for his part, was appalled by the Kennedys' wholly unprofessional need to make Cuba a matter of personal revenge, regardless of the cost.

The consequences of Harvey's dismissal from Task Force W and ZRRIFLE might, in retrospect, have been truly disastrous for the nation. Bill's pride must have been badly damaged. In the winter of 1963, or soon thereafter, after their official business should long have been settled, Johnny may have taken subtle control of their relationship and used that control in ways that may have influenced history.

Harvey almost certainly felt he had, in blunt terms, been screwed, and he probably made no secret of his feelings to Rosselli when they talked privately; in the flights of fantasy that alcohol can inspire, who knows what might have developed. Rosselli may have even deliberately plied Bill with booze to gain control over the CIA officer. He undoubtedly recognized Bill as a useful contact for the future, whatever it might hold. In his world, it was always useful to have a friend to watch your back or perform other favors.

Harvey's assignment to Rome opened up various possibilities. It's not beyond imagination to think that Rosselli introduced Harvey to the right people. Johnny had, for instance, visited Lucky Luciano, who had helped the United States invade Sicily, in his retirement near Naples.

These things mattered. Rosselli may have discussed certain French and Corsican underworld types with Harvey, from his knowledge of the international drug trade; or Bill might have mentioned some names of people on the rim of ZRRIFLE to Rosselli.

Whatever they chatted about on land or sea, a subtle, gradual reversal of roles took place. And when they renewed contact after Bill's return in 1966 to Washington—if, that is, they had not been in touch during Harvey's term in Rome—Rosselli assumed the upper hand. In the Agency, Bill was in disgrace, in recovery and therapy, on the ropes. No longer a henchman, Rosselli became the leader and even threw Bill some legal work, despite Harvey's official protestations that he would not do law for Rosselli. Most dramatically, as we shall see, Johnny introduced Harvey to Marajen Chinigo.

An FBI memo of May 4, 1967, the day after the CIA cut all official contact with Rosselli, says the CIA IG told the Bureau liaison officer "that CIA has instructed Harvey to avoid contact with subject if possible. CIA realizes that Rosselli may force a contact and it will be impossible for Harvey to evade the subject. . . . If contact is made, Harvey is to furnish the results which will be passed on to the Bureau. . . . Harvey on sick leave [pending] retirement. . . . CIA is in an extremely vulnerable position."

Convicted on the skimming and immigration counts in 1968, Johnny was first sent to a chill, dank prison on an island in Puget Sound, and later, he was moved to a more salubrious big house in Arizona. He finished his term at Lompoc Prison, near Santa Barbara, and was paroled on October 5, 1973. Almost immediately after his release, he moved to the Miami area to be with his sister.

10

BILL HARVEY AND THE ASSASSINATION OF PRESIDENT KENNEDY

There are various complex theories about the events of November 22, 1963, some of which concern us here because they might have involved Bill Harvey, who was, however, demonstrably in Italy at the time of the assassination. If Harvey did play a role in the assassination, as some people have almost passionately suggested, it was almost definitely a passive one.

The major Kennedy assassination theories are (1) it was a Mafia operation, (2) it was the work of a group of renegade CIA psychological warfare/paramilitary officers in cooperation with right-wing Cuban exile students, (3) it was the work of a lone gunman, and (4) it was an operation guided by Fidel Castro, employing various entities in the United States to gain revenge on the Kennedys.

If it was a CIA job, Dick Helms, head of the Clandestine Services at the time, might have known, but if it was a Mafia hit, he would not have known unless Harvey knew and confided in his boss. Only Harvey could play a possibly credible, knowledgeable, senior-level role in the two major theories. In both theories, Harvey appears as an enigmatic, owl-like, before-the-fact bystander, not as an active participant but also not as a naysayer. His role might be described as "conflicted"; he was not tormented, but rather wary, silent, holding his own counsel—this would be very Bill Harvey.

Harvey left behind a hint that he had some knowledge of the JFK killing. After he had testified to the U.S. Senate's Church Committee in 1975, he commented, "They didn't ask the right questions," implying that he might have had some answers to more pointed questions regarding the assassination.

Countering all of the above, however, it must be said that as yet no convincing evidence suggests that the assassination was anything more sinister than what it appears to have been forty-plus years and countless hundreds of thousands of dollars in investigating expenses later: a one-man hit on the president of the United States. History may yet judge the veracity of the speculations of those theorists who doubt Lee Harvey Oswald, the only confirmed shooter, acted on his own.

THEORY 1: MAFIA HIT

The spokesman for theory 1 is G. Robert Blakey, a professor of law at Notre Dame University and chief counsel to the 1978 House Select Committee on Assassinations (HRSCA). Blakey believes that the assassination was a Mafia operation, specifically engineered by Santo Trafficante, the Miami boss, with the active support of Carlos Marcello, the New Orleans capo. Oswald was a dupe, recruited by Trafficante's or Marcello's people as a shooter and fall guy. One of Oswald's shots killed JFK and wounded Texas Governor John Connally. A second shooter, a Mob soldier whose job might have been to kill Oswald, was stationed on the grassy knoll along the parade route in Dallas. The Mob recruited Jack Ruby, a small-time crook, to eradicate Oswald when the second shooter failed to do so; Ruby was dying of cancer and so had nothing to lose by taking the assignment. No supportable evidence suggests that French or Union Corse gangsters were involved in the assassination; neither is there supportable evidence that Cuban exiles in Miami, including those of the Directio Revolutionario Estudiantil de Cuba (DRE), were directly involved in the assassination. Johnny Rosselli knew of the Mafia's plans and may, indeed, have been a co-conspirator.

If the Mafia plotted the assassination, Rosselli might well have confided the fact in Harvey. The question is, if Rosselli told Harvey, when did he do so: before November 22, 1963, or well after, perhaps in 1967, when he talked to Jack Anderson, a well-known Washington columnist? And, if Rosselli told Harvey, why did he do so? And, of course, was there a Mafia plot to kill John F. Kennedy at all?

THEORY 2: CIA PLOT

Theory 2, propounded by James Hiram Lesar, chatelaine of the Assassination Archives and Research Center in Washington, D.C., and supported by others, excludes the Mafia as participant but implicates the CIA very, very deeply. Lesar's theory is predicated on the assumption that restless Agency officers who had tasted political blood in Guatemala and the Dominican Republic and had suffered through the Bay of Pigs fiasco either plotted to murder the president or acquiesced in a plot devised by Cuban students in exile in Miami.

The key figure in theory 2 is a legendary CIA political and psychological (PP) officer named David Atlee Phillips. Further, the theory involves the right-wing, anti-Castro Cuban students group, the DRE, and the manipulation and use of the hapless patsy, Oswald. It implicates high-level Agency officers who were involved in paramilitary operations against Cuba, specifically Dick Helms, Tom Karamessenes, Ted Shackley, a case officer named George Joannides, and Dave M., the paramilitary officer who was at the Florida Keys base with Rosselli. The Lesar theory is anchored in a single question: Who had the capability to assassinate JFK? His proffered answer is: only the military and the Agency.

The Harvey connection in theory 2 is straightforward. Dave Phillips was a Harvey subordinate when he was in charge of CIA's covert PP operations out of the Mexico City, which fell under Task Force W. Phillips was in close touch with JMWAVE, and Shackley, chief of JMWAVE, was especially close to Harvey. Phillips later was head of the Western Hemisphere Division of CIA's Clandestine Services and was a founder of the Association of Former Intelligence Officers (AFIO), which to this day reveres his memory. When I talked to Shackley in 2001, he adamantly, even curtly, dismissed the possibility that he or the CIA had been in any way involved in the JFK assassination.

Just to complicate the theorizing, there is a possibility that Santo Trafficante recruited DRE members to conceal Mafia involvement in the murder. But that would not change Harvey's situation in the complex of relationships.

GLEANINGS

The biggest unresolved question in the still-simmering mystery is: What kind of role, if any, did Harvey play? Jim Lesar goes so far as to say that Harvey's role is "one of the last remaining, unexplored lines of inquiry in the JFK assassination."[1] Some additional important questions are: Was Bill witting, before the fact, of a presumed Mafia or DRE plot? And, if so, did he report his knowledge to a CIA superior?

It is possible that, while still in the United States and involved in Cuban affairs, i.e., before October 27, 1962, more than a year before the assassination, Bill might well have heard that a group of Cuban students in Miami was making threatening noises about Kennedy. If so, he probably would have dismissed the reports: the Miami Cubans were volatile and given to fanciful scenarios of revenge for their plight. They were not to be taken too seriously, at least not then and not by foreign intelligence (FI) officers.

If, indeed, the Mafia was scheming to take out the president, Harvey might have had some advance indication from Rosselli in spring or early summer of 1963. Harvey might even have briefed the Sicilian Mafia on behalf of its American nephews after he settled into his new post in Rome.

If he had advance information on either possibility, Bill would have been duty bound to report it to Dick Helms personally. Let's speculate that he did tell Helms that a plot was festering but that Helms did not give the tale much credence. Would Helms, then head of the Clandestine Services, but not yet director of central intelligence (DCI), have sent Bill abroad? Probably not; it would be logical to assume that Helms would have wanted the explosive Harvey on a short leash, close to home. In fact, Harvey held a reasonably prestigious job in Rome for some time and only truly became an object of suspicion to CIA brass in 1968.

Another important question: Would Harvey have borne the Kennedys so much animosity—because of their manipulation of the CIA and their treatment of him personally and of what he stood for—that he would have acquiesced in an assassination plot, if, indeed, it came to his attention? Harvey was a lawyer and a patriot, and he took his oath seriously. The real question in this case might be, did drink so impair Bill's judgment that he would have become a silent accomplice before the fact, had he known what was in train?

POSSIBLE LINKS

The unlovely Bill Harvey fitted some people's need for a heavy, a suspect, but no hard evidence links Harvey to the assassination of John F. Kennedy, or years later, to the killing of Kennedy's brother, Robert. That said, here is a summary of the theoretical links between Harvey and the JFK assassination:

a) We will shortly touch on the role of JMWAVE case officer George Joannides and the DRE. The DRE were in convulsed touch with Oswald. A tenacious writer continues investigations into this possible linkage. As this is written, that reporter, Jefferson Morley, who has been mining this lode for years, is proceeding in federal court in an attempt to force more documents out of the Agency. Harvey was two or three levels above Joannides in 1963 and would have known about DRE.

b) Harvey, as head of Task Force W, was overlord to elements of CIA Mexico City, which had Oswald and the Soviet and Cuban embassies under surveillance. Investigators later proved that an individual entering the Soviet embassy whom CIA identified as Oswald was, in fact, a French or Belgian criminal figure; despite this identification, some still feel the person caught on the surveillance tape was, indeed, Oswald. Does this confusion, or indeed, the possibility that CIA—and in effect Harvey—purposely misidentified the man, mean that Harvey was involved in the JFK assassination? It does not.

c) Bill's close personal connection with Rosselli, and his meetings with Rosselli in the spring of 1963, before Harvey's reassignment to Rome, could be considered suspicious. As mentioned above, Rosselli may have told Harvey of the Mafia plot against John F. Kennedy during these meetings, if, indeed, there was such a conspiracy.

d) Harvey was well aware of Santo Trafficante, a possible Castro double agent, and some of Trafficante's operations. Harvey strenuously avoided meeting Trafficante. Shackley, the boss of JMWAVE in Miami, also took a very dour view of Trafficante and actually took measures to ensure that the CIA's operations and Trafficante never collided. Still, because Harvey and Shackley knew Trafficante, theorists have speculated that they may have had ties through him to the assassination.

e) Once in Rome, Harvey might have contacted European criminals and/or the Union Corse, the Sicilian Mafia (with whom he had loose liaison), and the mainland Italian Camorra, on behalf of Rosselli. Thus, though it has not been proven, Harvey may have acted as a line of communication between European and American plotters.

THE RUSSO FACTOR

Gus Russo, a leading authority on the Mafia, argues trenchantly in his book, *The Outfit*, that the Cosa Nostra was not in any way involved in the Kennedy assassination. In an e-mail discussing this analysis, which came as this book was in the final stages of preparation, Russo expands,

> I was all over organized crime for *The Outfit* and knew that the mob, especially Rosselli, had nothing to do with Oswald or Dallas. . . .
>
> Over the years I have spoken with many who knew Rosselli, not to mention his sister and goddaughter, all of whom find it ridiculous that he would kill JFK, or anybody. Rosselli, a former boot-

> legger in Joe Kennedy's Boston crew, stopped being a thug after the union fights in Hollywood in the thirties. After that he was a mob deal maker who never got his $1,000 suit wrinkled. He was never charged with a violent crime in his life. He went to prison in the forties for receiving kickbacks from the Hollywood studios for whom he had been controlling the unions, and late in life for a card cheating scam that he had only a tangential connection with. . . .
>
> The reader should know that Rosselli was an admirer of JFK and even went to Florida to participate, at age fifty-seven, in Mongoose raids and to help broker the Castro assassination plots during the Eisenhower and Kennedy administrations, both free of charge; he felt it was his "patriotic duty" as he so testified and told friends (see both Rappleye's book and my *The Outfit*, pp. 384–393 and 426–427).
>
> Lastly, even Rosselli's biographers, who tried hard to get a Dallas headline from their book (Johnny knew somebody who knew somebody who knew somebody who knew Ruby, etc.), had to admit the tenuous links to Dallas: "These reports are fragmentary and inconclusive, falling short of proof that John Rosselli played a part in the Kennedy assassination." (Rappleye, p. 248)[2]

Russo, in a follow-up conversation, emphasized his conviction that the Mafia theory was based on shaky speculation, and that the mafiosi Russo had interviewed over the years scoffed at the possibility. Still, we must, even despite the expert view of Gus Russo, look at the possibility of a Cosa Nostra connection to the death of JFK.

THE TIMES

In the years of disabuse and anger stemming from the Vietnam War and, later, Watergate, people were prepared to believe anything about secret government. It didn't take much of a stretch to think that the enigmatic Agency, and Rosselli and Harvey, might have plotted to kill John F. Kennedy—although that suspicion, oddly, did not extend to the murder of JFK's brother, Robert.

Jack Anderson, long after the fact, made emphatic statements about DCI John McCone's visits to Robert Kennedy at his Hickory Hill residence on November 22, 1963, the day of the assassination, and the next day, to President Lyndon B. Johnson. Anderson said McCone stressed to both Kennedy and Johnson that, if the true story of the assassination came out, there was a real risk that World War III would start because Soviet Premier Khrushchev was irrational and might "press the button." McCone was relaying an immediate suspicion that JFK's death was not what it seemed to be and that the Soviet leader might seek to take advantage while the United States grieved.

The how and why of the assassination had to be dealt with openly and honestly. LBJ opted to appoint a commission, under Chief Justice Earl Warren, that could be relied on to upset no applecarts. As a member of the commission, Allen Dulles would make sure that anything the Agency believed to be of a too-delicate nature was sidetracked. To skeptics, these very facts are sufficient to cast the CIA in the role of, at the least, accomplice to murder of the president.

ROSSELLI AND THE MOB

Recall that after Harvey officially "terminated" Rosselli's contact with the CIA in Los Angeles in February 1963, while the Agency's bounty on Castro's head was intact, contact between the two continued, even flourished.

There are the receipts in Bill's financial accounting for his last official trip to Florida in April 1963. He and Rosselli stayed and/or ate at the Plantation Yacht Harbor Motel, Eden Roc, and Fontainebleau Hotels in Miami. Harvey paid for Rosselli's room and took him out on a boat, twice, then sent him off to Chicago. On at least one occasion, the pair was joined by another, unidentified person, who could have been Johnny's sister but likely was not; if it had been Edith, she probably would have been accompanied by her husband. A conspiracy theorist might suggest that the third person was Harold Meltzer, described, by the Church Committee in 1975, as "a resident of Los Angeles with a long criminal record."

A note about Meltzer surfaced in what little there was of Harvey's ZRRIFLE files. What the ZRRIFLE memo did not say was that Meltzer was a longtime collaborator and sometime shooter for Rosselli. Did Harvey meet Meltzer? Why?

Recall that Harvey picked Johnny up at Dulles Airport and that they dined, with CG Harvey present, the night of June 20, 1963, under the eyes of the FBI. Thereafter, Rosselli spent the night at the Harveys' temporary accommodation, an occurrence Washington Metropolitan Police Inspector Joe Shimon found odd, "unless they were doing business," because Johnny usually stayed at the Madison Hotel.

As mentioned in chapter 9, it is possible that Harvey may have maintained casual contact with Rosselli while he was abroad from 1963 to

1966, although in a 1967 statement to a senior CIA official, Harvey stoutly maintained that he had not *seen* Rosselli since before he went to Italy in 1963.

ROSSELLI, THE MAFIA, AND THE ASSASSINATION

Rosselli occasionally traveled with the Rat Pack, which overlapped, through Peter Lawford, with the Kennedys. Yet if Rosselli had had to declare his politics, my guess is that he would have opted Republican.

It may be conjectured that Johnny and his fellow mafiosi disliked the Kennedys for two reasons: their betrayal of the Mafia after it had supported JFK financially and with votes in the 1960 primary and general elections, and the personal hounding to which Rosselli and others were subjected by the FBI. Rosselli may have shared this dislike with Carlos Marcello of New Orleans, who had been forcibly exiled from the United States, and with Santo Trafficante, the Miami capo who had been a big shot in pre-Castro Havana.

Trafficante was probably of two minds. On one hand, he wanted to be back in business in Havana, but this was not possible as long as Castro reigned. On the other, he may have been a principal agent for Castro's intelligence service in Miami, keeping tabs on the exiles so that one day he might be more acceptable back in the Cuban capital. Whatever his allegiance, Trafficante may have disliked the Kennedys because, in addition to reneging on their obligations to the Mafia in general, they had—at the very least with the Bay of Pigs—interfered with the orderly running of his business in Cuba and then failed to oust or off Castro.

Rosselli, as the Mafia's roving ambassador, was often in Miami, and he knew and consorted with Trafficante before the time of Johnny's Cuban operations.

The first hint of Mafia involvement in the killing of JFK that I am aware of came from Ed Becker, who coauthored *All American Mafioso*. Becker reported that in his presence in September 1962 Carlos Marcello, the Mob capo in New Orleans, said that RFK "was going to be taken care of" but that first JFK would have to be eliminated.

THE ROSSELLI CONNECTION

The obvious hypothetical link between Harvey and the JFK assassination runs through Rosselli. Ed Becker, reminiscing in 2002:

> Everyone's still talking about Johnny as a gentleman. Hell, he wasn't a gentleman. When they were fighting [in the 1930s] over the

> offshore gambling out of Los Angeles, that was brutal . . . lot of killing, and Johnny was involved in it. . . .
>
> Yeah, the FBI lost Johnny [during the critical days of the JFK assassination]. He stashed Judith Exner in a hotel on Pico Boulevard. . . . And he talked on the phone about going to Finland. . . . The Bureau lost him. . . .
>
> Giancana, now he was nuts. He threatened to kill JFK. . . .
>
> Rosselli was involved. But not your guy, Harvey. . . . Johnny would never have brought anyone like that into it. . . .
>
> Of course, if Johnny Rosselli knew, Johnny would have told Bill, no question. After the fact, sure, they talked about it.
>
> The murder was committed by a guy who was in the scavenger business . . . Red Donergan.

Questioned again in a phone conversation nearly two years later, Becker said he didn't recognize the name of Donergan. It must also be said that I got the impression that Ed, who's getting on in years, enjoys talking to someone who is receptive to his memories.[3]

THE MAFIA AND THE JFK ASSASSINATION

Rappleye and Becker contend that Johnny Rosselli was in the picture, either shortly before the assassination, or more likely, shortly after. Professor Blakey speculates that Rosselli used his knowledge of the Mafia's hand in the murder of JFK as a bargaining chip in his dealings with Bill Harvey at some undetermined date and again, years later, with Jack Anderson.

Rappleye and Becker:

> Four years after the events in Dallas, [Rosselli] made the startling claim that he had inside knowledge of The Assassination. Over the following decade, he juggled his knowledge of The Assassination with his other great secret, the CIA-Mafia plots, paying out snippets of information. . . .
>
> John Rosselli's circumstantial ties to the Kennedy assassination extended beyond his various connections to Jack Ruby. He worked closely with Santo Trafficante, who made the firm prediction of Kennedy's impending death.[4]

Rappleye and Becker also delve into other possible connections between Rosselli and anti-Castro Cubans, including a Hollywood gossip columnist's report: "What I heard about the Kennedy Assassination was that Johnny was the guy who got the team together to do the kill . . . that 'the scenario was "fairly well-known" in the underworld but [the source] was reluctant to go into detail.'" Another report that the biographers uncovered places Rosselli in Dallas on November 22, 1963, and says he took the assassination weapon from the hands of a marksman—the second shooter—and was driven away from the infamous grassy knoll. Rappleye and Becker: "He knew what had happened in Dallas."[5]

Becker might not be an entirely credible source, however. For example, the conversation in which Marcello suggested the Kennedys would be "taken care of" took place in a Louisiana barbershop and was carried on primarily in Sicilian, a language Becker acknowledged he did not understand. It is highly possible that Becker, receiving the translated gist second- or third-hand, consciously or otherwise distorted what was actually said. A Becker associate at the time told Russo that Ed Reid might have been guilty of "using poetic license." Reid, a former FBI agent who later became a private investigator, "had employed Becker on occasion. [The PI] conceded that Becker was 'a controversial guy.'"[6]

Robert Blakey, in *The Plot to Kill the President*, treats Becker harshly: "We found that Becker, a former public relations man for the Riviera Hotel in Las Vegas, had been involved in shady transactions . . . [which] helped explain Becker's presence at [the September 1962] meeting with Marcello. . . . We were able to obtain substantial corroboration for Becker's presence in New Orleans . . . to discuss a promotional scheme with Marcello."[7] Blakey's source was also Ed Reid.

"I GOT SHOCKED!"

Gus Russo has ruled out Mafia responsibility for, or complicity in, the assassination of JFK primarily based on evidence taken from FBI wiretaps on members of the Mob.

> Johnny Rosselli was awakened at the Desert Inn [a legendary hostelry in Twenty-Nine Palms, California] by . . . an old friend named Jonie Tapps. . . . John thought he was dreaming. "I didn't believe it at first . . . because I was in deep sleep."
>
> When he turned on the radio, "I got shocked!" Rosselli told Congress thirteen years later, making a mighty effort to censor his language. I said, "Gosh Almighty, those Communists. . . . You know that was the first thing that crossed my mind because a few months before, Castro had made [a threat] in the newspapers, and it sounded just like he was threatening the establishment here."

> Johnny had expounded on his theory three weeks [after the assassination] with fellow-hood Jimmy Fratianno. . . . [They] lamented that the press was openly speculating [that the Mafia] was responsible for the hit. "You know, Johnny," Fratianno said, "the more of this bullshit I read, the more I'm convinced that we're scapegoats for every unsolved crime committed in this country! What's this mob the papers are always talking about. . . . It's against the fucking rules to kill a cop, so now we're going to kill a president?"
>
> Throughout the country, the FBI huddled around their illegal surveillance apparatus, trying to learn if Organized Crime had finally gotten even with the hated Robert Kennedy. What they consistently heard convinced them that the country's underworld would never even contemplate such an action.
>
> In Buffalo, local boss Stefanno Magaddino lamented, "It's a shame we've been embarrassed before the whole world by allowing the president to be killed in our own territory." He added that Kennedy was one of the greatest presidents and, as noted by the eavesdroppers, "blames the assassination on his brother, Robert Kennedy." . . .
>
> The Giancanas were glued to their TV set. His daughter remembered [Sam] saying in 1960, "Some day Jack will get his, but I will have nothing to do with it."
>
> Three days later, after the pro-Castro Oswald was charged with the murder, [one of Sam's henchmen] commented, "This twenty-four year-old kid was an anarchist. He was a Marxist Communist." To which [Sam] replied, "He was a marksman who knew how to shoot."

Based on all their wiretaps the FBI came to the firm conclusion that the Mafia was indeed innocent of the crime of murdering JFK.[8] Of course, the mobsters, aware of the Bureau's wall-to-wall coverage of their activities, might have developed into world-class actors, capable of a huge deception operation, but that's not a question for examination here. In light of Russo's persistent tracking, it does seem highly doubtful that the Mafia played any role in the killing of John F. Kennedy.

CASE OFFICER–AGENT: THE CONTROL FACTOR

That said, since we want to examine every possible link, if Rosselli indeed was active in a plot to kill the president, or knew, during the spring of 1963, that the Mob was intent on assassinating Jack Kennedy, would he have told Harvey? Did Rosselli recruit Harvey as an accessory before the fact, before Harvey went to Rome?

Did Rosselli reverse the balance of their relationship in late 1962, after Bill lost the Cuban portfolio, and then get Harvey to contact one or more European criminal elements on behalf of the Mafia? The European and American underworlds knew each other from Havana and from drug smuggling, but Bill could have provided a very useful, discreet, and authoritative communications link in delicate matters of mutual interest. Harvey had that very useful mobility, at least until he went to Rome. Perhaps he traveled far and wide, not just on the CIA's behalf.

Did Rosselli blackmail Harvey in later years? Could the mafioso's hold over Harvey have been Harvey's knowledge of the Kennedy assassination, which Harvey did not fully report to his superiors?

It is worth noting that Harvey, in his testimony to the Church Committee in the mid-1970s, which was otherwise blunt and to the point, never gave the slightest indication that he knew anything explosive about Jack Kennedy's death. He and Rosselli had discussed their testimony at some length in advance. Again, Harvey later gruffly and enigmatically commented that the committee simply didn't ask the right questions.

Was this complex of possibilities the reason Harvey was still so very cautious about personal and family safety after he retired to Indianapolis?

WISPS

Would the wisps indicating that Harvey was involved with Rosselli beyond the limits of CIA practice have been sufficient cause to indict Harvey as a conspirator in the murder of John F. Kennedy, if they had been known in 1963 or in 1974? The evidence seems to me insufficient. Yet, why did the CIA tell CG Harvey that Agency files on Bill would absolutely not be accessible until 2063? Why that particular year, one hundred years after the JFK assassination and Harvey's transfer to Rome? It seems as if the Agency had something to hide that would lose its effective half-life a century after the facts.

Also, what lies behind this thought-provoking statement in the Church Committee report?

> Harvey kept the [Castro] assassination plot "pretty much in his back pocket," Helms said. "There was a fairly detailed discussion between myself and Helms as to whether or not McCone should at that time be briefed concerning this," Harvey related. "For a variety of reasons which were tossed back and forth, we agreed that it

> was not necessary or advisable to brief him at that time. It appeared to be . . . a very real possibility of this government being blackmailed either by [anti-Castro] Cubans for political purposes, or by figures in organized crime for their own self-protection or aggrandizement, which as it turned out did not happen, but at the time was a very pregnant possibility.
>
> Helms explained that, "Mr. McCone was relatively new to the Agency and I guess I must have thought to myself, well this is going to look peculiar to him. It was a Mafia connection . . . and this was, you know, not a very savory operation."[9]

In his copy of the report, Harvey scrawled the following cryptic note: "When McCone was in Rome, long after he was 'officially in writing' ordered, no mention or hint of subject [presumably of assassination] came up in my many hours of discussion with him."[10] McCone might have flaunted his secrecy pledge but assuredly would have done so only if he did not suspect Harvey had been involved in the assassination.

CONSIDERATIONS

It's understandable that Harvey's name surfaced in the JFK investigations. Harvey had that gun-slinging reputation; he scorned his higher-ups; he had deep personal reason to dislike Bobby Kennedy; and as Carlos Marcello is alleged to have said, Bobby could not be killed until Jack was out of the way. Additionally, Harvey came from the darkest, most impenetrable, and therefore, most suspicious byways in the tortuous labyrinth that was the Agency. He was known for his vest-pocket operations. More to the point, he had that close connection with Rosselli. And he had been in charge of—no, had actually been—ZRRIFLE, which was specifically concerned with the assassination of political leaders.

Those who are suspicious point to ZRRIFLE's ultrasecrecy and say, in effect, "If those guys could keep their own boss, McCone, in the dark, it is certainly possible CIA officers were involved in the JFK assassination."

One of the key questions here is motive. Did Harvey so dislike the Kennedys that he abandoned his spectrum of training and experience, his lawyer's faith in the Constitution and in government, to engage in a truly horrendous act, in concert with professional criminals? If so, does this imply that Bill's mental balance had shifted? In the spring of 1963, when one has to assume that any Mafia plot would have slipped into gear, did Harvey, in his perhaps-delusional, overwrought, drinking state, give Rosselli a useful handle over himself?

Harvey was back in the United States after July 1, 1963, the effective date of his transfer to Rome, only for one or more routine consultations, until he was recalled for good in April 1966. If Harvey was truly suspect, the CIA almost surely would have hauled him back from Rome, perhaps in early 1964, for interrogation and for a polygraph examination conducted by the Office of Security. If Harvey had been fluttered as part of the internal JFK investigation, the CIA would understandably be reluctant to release that fact, much less the result.

It must be added, parenthetically, that, early on, the CIA's side of the JFK investigation was handled by Jim Angleton. Evidence suggests that Angleton and Harvey were in close and friendly touch just before Bill's death, which might not have been the case if Angleton had suspected Harvey of connivance in the murder of the president.

Would Bill's very patriotism, when confused by boozy vapors, have led him to complicity in the assassination? Did he believe that JFK was a menace to the nation? Could Harvey have disregarded his oath of allegiance to the Constitution sufficiently to take active part in such a plot?

If Harvey had favored the elimination of any Kennedy, his candidate would have been Bobby, but I have never heard even a whisper that he was involved in that murder.

HARVEY AND GUILT

Harvey disliked Bobby Kennedy intensely. In 1962 he felt strongly that the brothers were conducting a personal and very unprofessional vendetta against Castro. Harvey disagreed with but did not dislike Jack and may even have respected him slightly, in a sort of skewed, avuncular way. CG contended, years later, that Jack liked and admired Harvey. But had Harvey's judgment become so skewed over the years of boozing that he allowed himself to, in effect, become judge, jury and, by default, witness to the execution?

At least one operational point weighs against any direct Harvey involvement in the assassination, were DRE involved. From way back in the Berlin days, when BOB had had to spend so much time and manpower cleaning up blatant, ineffective, cowboy-style operations—which destroyed lives unnecessarily, or for minimal gain, in Harvey's eyes—Bill was always skeptical about political and psychological operations. That skepticism was borne out in the Bay of Pigs, in which two former Berlin PP officers played key roles. The DRE was supported by the Agency's PP wing.

During the Task Force W days, Harvey would have been appalled at the Cubans' flouting of tight security. Would he have simply written off hints of an assassination plot as more wild talk from Miami's Little Havana? Would Harvey have reported what he heard to Dick Helms? If Helms and company were actually involved, would Bill have kept silent? The answer to this last question is, yes, because of his own patriotism and his ingrained loyalty to the Agency.

If he knew that Dave Phillips and others were involved in an assassination plot, he would have been a dangerous liability to some persons in the CIA—someone to be handled with kid gloves since he could not be terminated with extreme prejudice. Inside knowledge of the assassination could explain Harvey's extraordinary security measures in Indianapolis: the watchful eye over Sally, the guns stashed all over the house, the belief that "the KGB was out to get him." Agency suspicion that he might have something in his files that was very embarrassing to the CIA might, too, explain the burglarizing of his houses in Chevy Chase and, later, after his death, in Indianapolis.

If he knew anything about the events of November 22, he never told anyone, save, maybe, CG.

AFTERMATH

The CIA conducted its own internal investigation of Agency involvement with the assassination in late 1963 and early 1964. As far as I know, the results of that scrutiny have never been released. It may be assumed that the investigation at some point looked into Harvey.

If the CIA's scrutiny established that Bill was knowledgeable of some aspects of JFK's death, Harvey, an increasingly loose cannon, hardly would have been allowed to remain in Rome for any length of time. Rather he would have been transferred back to the United States and tucked away somewhere, out of sight, but still employed, and thus under control, so that he could be dried out and then thoroughly interrogated. He might not have been prosecuted because a court case would have blown too many uncomfortable secrets wide open. Rather, after a certain period of time, he might well have been allowed to retire, quietly and having signed a severely binding secrecy agreement, hardly ever again to be mentioned by anyone in the CIA hierarchy. In fact, something fairly close to this script did happen, except Harvey stayed on in Rome for more than two years after the assassination.

All of the Agency alumni I have talked with about the matter emphatically exclude any possibility that Bill was complicit, even passively, in the JFK assassination. Several, when I said I was going to examine Bill's entire life, obliquely urged me to deal only with the times when Bill was at his peak. They didn't warn me off; their unspoken concern was for what Bill might have done in the depths of his drinking. Still, they did not, could not, believe their Bill was involved in one of America's most unsettling crimes. I sympathized then with their feelings, and I share them now. But the wisps remain, floating loosely in air.

Some speculation is permissible. A heavy, consistent drinker can become contemptuous of the rule of law and of the codes by which others live. Indeed, one revels in the sense of liberation one feels, with the first couple of drinks of the day, from the dictates of conformist, mundane society.

Only in 1966, after Bill had made such a shambles of his posting to Rome, did the CIA send him into a form of alcohol rehab—in his case, periodic visits to a cleared psychiatrist or counselor. Bill remarked to friends that he was not impressed by the treatment, and indeed, it didn't get him off the booze at the time.

A couple of other tangential matters: When I started my inquiries, Sally Harvey was wholly cooperative. A year or so later, she sent me a formal letter saying, "the family" wished me well in my endeavors but had decided to cease cooperation because public discussion of Bill's life would not be what he or CG wanted. Sally's statement runs directly counter to the twenty-plus page letter handwritten by CG Harvey in 1983 that gave me abundant leads and every encouragement to write a book that, as originally envisioned, would have been a rebuttal to David Martin's *Wilderness of Mirrors*. I must conclude that Sally's flip-flop came as a result of pressure from Jim Harvey, the keeper of some papers and at least one artifact from his father and stepmother's home in Indianapolis, who, perhaps not surprisingly, prefers reserve to open discussion of his father. My several attempts to secure Jim Harvey's cooperation proved fruitless.

Until, or if ever, documentary evidence is available, there can be only conjecture. A Harvey connection to the assassination cannot be proved or disproved. It's like an Etch-A-Sketch—any fanciful picture therein can be erased with a vigorous shake. Or, if you prefer your imagery more classic, it's like trying to find your way out of a labyrinthine cave, following the string you have played out behind you, only to find that the cord crosses itself and goes in circles and knots, leaving you hopelessly lost.

THE FRENCH CONNECTION

Although neither the Blakey nor the Lesar theories suppose that French or French-Corsican gangsters were involved in the JFK killing, others suggest that they were and that Harvey may have been involved with them.

In 1960, immediately after taking over Division D, Harvey, with his unlimited, unchallenged travel warrant, made one or more trips to Europe. He may even have traveled abroad as late as 1962. He was allegedly interested in locating and perhaps assessing professional criminals who might help obtain cryptographic materials. With his FBI background, Harvey could talk fraternally with European cops, including French officers who became major figures in the Europe-American heroin trade. Maybe, from that pool of candidates, he was able to draw a potential assassin for the CIA's wet affairs. Bill might not have met any criminals personally, but he was certainly privy to information on European drug gangs. It may be assumed that Arnold S., the Division D European case officer based in Luxembourg, arranged for Harvey's access to European police officials.

According to the one set of notes available, Harvey's inquiries during his trip to Europe seemed to center on Trieste. The highly-sensitive, amended, handwritten draft project outline transcribed in chapter 8 shows clearly that ZRRIFLE was intended to be carried out by non-American criminal elements. Note, again, these two excerpts from Bill's stipulations for ZRRIFLE:

> *Exclude organized criminals, e.g. Sicilians, criminals, those w/ record of arrests, those w/ instability of purpose as criminals.*
>
> But then:
>
> *. . . organization criminals, those with record of arrests, those who have engaged in several types of crime. Corsicans recommended. Sicilians could lead to Mafia.*
>
> And:
>
> *Former resistance personnel a possibility. Period of testing, surveillance, etc. for each selection.*
>
> *Use nobody* [as a case officer] *who has never dealt w/ criminals*; otherwise will not be aware of pitfalls or consider factors such as freedom to travel, wanted lists, etc.

Is it possible that Harvey, probably posing as something other than a CIA officer, might have met some European criminal, assessed and perhaps recruited him, perhaps using the interpretive services of a trusted intermediary? Did Harvey meet QJWIN, with or without his handler, in Europe in the winter of 1960–61 to assess him for ZRRIFLE, prior to the planned attempt on Lumumba and thus gain what might have been his first direct insight into the European criminal milieu?

Recall that Harvey met Rosselli in Washington around June 21, 1963. On June 27, Harvey, winding up his headquarters responsibilities prior to departure for Rome, wrote a memo stating that the original justification for employing QJWIN—"asset developed for the original ZRRIFLE project"—no longer existed, and he raised the question of QJWIN's termination. QJWIN was not finally let go until February 14, 1964. Note that executive action against Cuba was officially terminated by Bobby Kennedy on October 30, 1962, but some efforts continued beyond that date. Again, inconclusive evidence suggests that French criminal elements were in Dallas on November 22, 1963. I am aware of no further indications of direct European involvement in the assassination, but let's examine the possibility further.

Even if we accepted, for the sake of argument, that Harvey met and assessed QJWIN or WIROGUE, or both, on the 1960–61 Europe trip, it is still a considerable leap to assume that he recruited one of them to participate with either the CIA or the Mafia in the JFK assassination. Stephen J. Rivele, a contributor to a book on Oliver Stone's *Nixon* and author of a lengthy expose on the French Connection, asserts that QJWIN was "a Luxembourg-based smuggler" named Jose Mankel and that WIROGUE was "a Soviet-born Paris bank robber named David Dzitzichvili [also spelled Tzitzichvili], alias David Dato." Rivele says flatly that he never came across any definitive connection between Harvey and the French underworld figures who may have been involved in the events of November 22, 1963.[11]

ROME AND THE ITALIAN CONNECTION

Did Harvey play any role in the assassination plot after his arrival in Rome in early July 1963?

By the time of the JFK assassination, Harvey had been stationed in Rome over four months. On November 22, he was at a Mediterranean island stay-behind training site. "Bill Harvey . . . was unconscious. His drinking had progressed from habit to disease after his exile to Italy. . . . When the telex noting Kennedy's murder was received by his deputy, Harvey had to be awakened from a late-day martini stupor. The man who hated the Kennedys . . . staggered to his feet." (The news would have hit Italy sometime after seven in the evening.)

"What he is reported to have said to his deputy should be taken with Harvey's condition in mind; the auditor recorded it for posterity: 'This was bound to happen,' blurted Harvey, 'and it's probably good that it did.' Soon, when Harvey discovered that his deputy was spending time helping local officials with condolences, he sent the deputy packing for the U.S. 'I haven't got time for this kind of crap, Harvey told him.'"[12]

Mark Wyatt, Harvey's deputy in Rome who may have been the source of the above account, told me forty years later, "One night, we got the call that JFK might not live. Bill was so pie-eyed drunk, we could hardly get him on his feet. The Italians were saying to him, 'Mr. Harvey, we have to get you back!' It was a stormy night, so we had to get back to the mainland by ship." I have also heard that a high officer put his personal plane at Harvey's disposal to get him back to Rome.

Wyatt, again, enigmatically: "Harvey said to me later, 'Mark, we tried so hard, but no one will ever know who shot JFK!' Bill interpreted it as the Mob getting to Oswald. I felt terrible about it."[13]

CG Harvey's recollection not surprisingly contrasts sharply with Wyatt's. At the time of the JFK assassination, CG claimed, "Bill was in Sicily, on an operation with the Mafia, trying to stop the drug trafficking. He had to get back to Rome immediately. The Mafia gave him a wooden thing which allowed him safe passage throughout Sicily." (It was a three-inch carving that was bolted to the front of the car, or perhaps displayed on the dashboard.)[14]

Intermittent, top-level liaison with the Sicilian Mafia, maintaining an American intelligence contact dating back to World War II, was probably among Harvey's responsibilities while he was stationed in Italy. In this role Harvey likely met Michael Chinigo, who had served in the Office of Strategic Services (OSS) and played a minor but key role in the American landings in Sicily in 1943, and then probably handled mundane, routine contact between the CIA and the Mafia. Chinigo was an ideal candidate for CIA recruitment, if, indeed, he had ever been out of the employ of OSS and its successors. Harvey and Chinigo may also have been in touch with the Camorra, the Italian-American dominated criminal underground of southern Italy, based around Naples.

What these wisps add up to is unprovable, of course. But it seems certain that Bill Harvey had direct or indirect contact with various European criminal elements; that he dealt with unseemly elements through Chinigo, who was a CIA contract agent; and that, if the American Mafia was involved in the Kennedy assassination European elements might have been implicated.

LEE HARVEY OSWALD

Did Harvey have anything to do with Oswald's defection to the Soviet Union? Was Oswald a CIA agent, dispatched to the Soviet Union for some intelligence purpose? Did Harvey hold a watching brief or have anything to do, directly or indirectly, with Oswald after his return to the United States from the Soviet Union? Is it conceivable that Harvey might have fingered Oswald for the mafiosi who needed to divert attention from their role in the actual assassination? I have come across no evidence to substantiate any of the above speculation.

Harvey, as chief of Task Force W, was lord over much of the CIA's Mexican activities. David Atlee Phillips, a man who fascinates Kennedy conspiracy theorists, was the initial case officer on DRE, served in Cuba, and later was the Cuban desk chief and a PP officer at Mexico City. Violating the CIA charter that forbade domestic operations, Phillips may have run anti-Castro agents in the United States, specifically in the New Orleans area, where Oswald operated for a while. Assassination analysts have long been intrigued by some evidence that suggests that the CIA (possibly purposely) misidentified photographs of an individual entering the Soviet Russian and Cuban embassies in Mexico City in 1963, calling the man Oswald, when in fact he was an impostor, subsequently identified as a French or Belgian criminal.

A side note: Jack Whitten, alias John Scelso, who later provided congressional investigators with scathing testimony on Harvey, was head of the CIA's Mexican Branch at Langley in 1963 and was therefore privy to some, but not all, of the operational traffic between Mexico City and Harvey, as head of Task Force W.[15]

Is it conceivable that Harvey fingered Oswald as a possible patsy for the Mob murder of JFK? This is one of many vague possibilities in the tangled skeins that weave around the JFK assassination. But only a remote possibility.

THE WHITTEN/SCELSO TESTIMONY

The person who cast the most direct suspicion on Harvey, by outright bitterness and also by carefully phrased innuendo, was a man who spent his working career in the OSS and CIA, John (Jack) Whitten, who chose the alias John Scelso when he testified to the HRSCA in 1978. Whitten's true identity became public only after he died in 2002.

Michael Goldsmith, staff counsel for the committee, who conducted the interview with Whitten, commented nearly twenty-five years later,

"We really focused on the CIA . . . trying to determine the quality of the product the Agency had given the Warren Commission. . . .

"We had five or six staff members, among them, two conspiracy theorists, who were really pushing on Harvey. . . . Harvey was *a* central figure, not *the* central figure. But we were unable to pin anything on him."[16] Goldsmith bored in while he had Whitten on the stand.

> Q: Do you know whether Harvey was running any operations outside the ordinary course of business?
>
> A: I did not know at that time. I just heard about this assassin he had on the payrolls and so on. . . . I would like to say first, among officers of my grade, and I was a super-grade, and I had as broad a view as anyone of Agency operations, the thought of, or engaging in, assassinations as distinguished from guerrilla warfare or coups d'etat . . . setting out by stealth and surprise to kill an important foreign person . . . was abhorrent to the standards of the clandestine service. . . . In the Lumumba case, they refused to carry out the order, but they were guilty of conspiracy to commit homicide. . . .
>
> The consensus of officers, including the greatest cynics, was that we would never do anything like that, as indeed we did not, as far as I know.
>
> Q: You just characterized Mr. Harvey as a thug.
>
> A: I do not like to speak that way of him, but Harvey . . .
>
> Q: Mr. Harvey is the central figure in the Committee's concern here. I would like you to be as candid as you can be.
>
> A: Harvey was not the kind of personality who appeals to me and I certainly was not the kind of personality that appealed to him. I have wondered—I wonder if the government has ever looked into the possibility that Harvey did not knock off Giancomo [*sic*, Giancana]. He lived in the same area, when he was retired. He was a great one with guns.
>
> I read it in the newspaper. I was overseas and I said to myself, I wondered if they look into Bill Harvey.
>
> Q: This question may come to you out of right field, but *do you have any reason to believe that Mr. Harvey himself may have been involved in the President's assassination?*
>
> A: I do not have any reason to believe it. . . . [17]

Whitten is one of very few professional CIA officers who criticized Harvey openly, venomously, on the record. He may have reflected a feeling common to that of some of CIA's Ivy Leaguers, those who still believed in the romantic OSS-style ethic.

Whitten made the following comments, in a more personal vein, almost as if he were seeking revenge. Note that Whitten had been Helms's first choice as head of the JFK investigation, but he was then sidelined in favor of Angleton.

> Harvey was a really hard-boiled, unsubtle, ruthless guy who was, in my opinion, a very dangerous man. I had run-ins with him several times. I also had to investigate one of his big cases and although I was always on friendly terms with him—we never slugged it out with each other—he never liked me and I never liked him. . . .
>
> The very thought of Helms entrusting Harvey to hire a criminal to have the capacity to kill somebody violates every operational precept, every bit of operational experience, every ethical consideration. And the fact that he chose Harvey. . . .
>
> Harvey could keep a secret, you see. Harvey could keep a secret. This was one way to make sure that nobody ever found out about it.
>
> I just cannot understand Helms doing this.
>
> But Harvey, in my opinion . . . the whole thought of Helms appointing Harvey . . . the very thought of [Harvey] using a former criminal for anything, let alone to assassinate people or to be on a standby basis to assassinate people—here Helms cannot turn around . . . [after] low-rating people for deviating from certain principles, and so on. . . . He cannot turn around, just because he is the DCI, and appoint a thug like Harvey to hire some criminal to commit assassinations. The best thing you can say was [Harvey] was a buffoon for doing it, or perhaps he never intended to use it and just would be able to say he had the capacity. That is the kind of interpretation I put on it.[18]

Whitten, however, supplied no evidence implicating Harvey in the assassination, either with Rosselli and the Mafia or with Phillips and the DRE students.

JACK WHITTEN

In early 2003 the determined investigative reporter, Jefferson Morley, became interested in the elusive figure of Jack Whitten and found a reason, in Whitten's HRSCA testimony, for Whitten's dislike of Harvey.

> Whitten: Then I investigated a famous communications intelligence case that Harvey was mixed up in when he was the Chief of the Communications Intelligence, the Deciphering Staff, [Division D] and so on. This turned out to be one of the biggest hoaxes in our history.
>
> Mr. Goldsmith: What happened there?
>
> Whitten: For a number of years, the Agency had been running a source in Austria who was to procure for us the Soviet codes, and so on, Soviet intelligence, say for instance. And I, as a polygraph operator, had to polygraph this guy a couple of times.
>
> By that time, we had spent a fortune on the operation and they have never been able to crack this guy. He was interrogated at length. He was on drugs, hypnosis, under the polygraph by the Blue Bird team and he beat them cold. And they gave him to me to interrogate for the second time, and I cracked him and made him admit that it was a hoax which made them all look bad.[19]

A definite note of triumph marked Whitten's claim that he had beaten the Agency's top gun by showing that one of Division D's prime sources had been a fabricator.

I asked a former top CIA FI officer for his view of Whitten. The officer, who chooses to remain anonymous, replied,

> I knew Jack from couple of cases in the '50s and '60s. He was bright, rather acerbic in nature, had high opinion of himself. Was polygraph operator in early days after World War II. Highly security conscious to point where he would sometimes type own dispatches rather than let secretaries do it. . . .
>
> It's strictly speculation on my part, but I think he probably was not suited for managerial role in view his acerbic personality and this probably impeded his career.
>
> I know nothing of any dispute [he may have had] with Bill Harvey. . . .
>
> I would guess that using another name when testifying at congressional committee was Jack's idea of being secure. . . .
>
> I remember once he bragged to me about what a great operator he was which I thought was a bit heavy.[20]

THE INVESTIGATORS

Of the many official investigations of the Kennedy assassination, the most thorough, the most compelling, and the last was that of the HRSCA, the House Select Committee on Assassinations. In his book about the case, G. Robert Blakey, chief counsel of the committee, says, "We concluded from our investigation that Organized Crime had a hand in the assassination of President Kennedy. We had come to the investigation predisposed to conclude that Organized Crime figures would not have taken the considerable risk entailed in plotting the assassination of the President. The reasoning process that led us to change our minds only becomes explicable when the myth and folklore are put aside."[21]

Expanding on these thoughts, Professor Blakey replied to my direct inquiry as follows:

> [There was] the connection between the Agency and Rosselli, who, as *The Plot to Kill the President* points out, arguably had inside information on the assassination (shots from the front, not, early on, a major question, that he shared with Anderson).
>
> Harvey was no fan of JFK and a "cowboy" during the period when he was in our focus. . . . Even if he were involved, I don't read it as Agency-sponsored; it would have been on his own, though with his clients.
>
> I once thought that the Agency was as reasonably candid with us as could be expected, but now there's recent information [about George Joannides], who . . . turns out to have headed a Cuban desk in New Orleans at the time of the assassination, a fact not shared with us at the time. . . .
>
> In short, a conspiracy existed; it was most likely Mob connected; the Agency was connected with at least one possible Mob player, if not a person who had inside information; and your guy was that connection. . . . The committee staff people who looked into him swear that he was involved.[22]

CIA INVOLVEMENT?

The supposition—what I above call the Lesar Theory—that the CIA was somehow involved in the JFK plot is based on the Agency's links to anti-Castro groups in Miami, New Orleans, and elsewhere and on the possibility that the Agency was in touch with Oswald.

Right-wing Cuban exiles in Miami whispered about a momentous event due in mid-November 1963. Some of them were students grouped under the banner of the rabidly anti-Castro Directio Revolutionario Estudiantil de Cuba. If the DRE students knew something, their gossip would have spread through Little Havana like an oil fire on water. According to David Corn, "Shackley's station did not unearth any significant information in this regard. . . . Shackley believed that since the CIA did not have primary responsibility for probing Oswald and the assassination; his station only had to collect information 'in a passive way' from existing sources. . . . In 1979, the House Select Committee on Assassinations judged Shackley harshly, without naming him. His station ought to have debriefed thoroughly all its sources."[23] In his autobiography, Shackley dismisses the DRE without mentioning the Kennedy assassination aspect.

But the possibility remains that Oswald was in touch, in one way or another, with the CIA, and the murky relationship between Oswald and the Cuban students remains unclear.

None of these intimations of CIA foreknowledge of the assassination have to do with Harvey directly; he would have seen operational traffic detailing the CIA's link with the DRE leadership as a matter of routine, up until his ousting from Task Force W in late October 1962. Most of the heat that has built up around DRE surrounds its activity in 1963, at least six months after Harvey was removed from Cuban operations. Still, it is worth pushing the examination a bit farther.

DAN HARDWAY

Dan Hardway, was a first-year law school student when he joined HRSCA in July 1977, although he didn't actually get to work on the case until September. Although Hardway was youthful, he played a role which in later years assumed considerable importance.

In conversation in 2002, Hardway readily admitted he was gunning for Harvey from the get-go. "What little I could do on Harvey was on my own, and only insofar as I could relate it to what was officially being investigated.

"I had placed him in the middle of a web of intrigue. Harvey was central to everything that went on. . . . Harvey was a natural suspect. He had the assassination teams. He was in charge of JMWAVE. I was convinced that Bill Harvey was involved in the assassination.

"I wanted to investigate Harvey vigorously. . . . I was determined to prove his complicity in the assassination, if I could."

At first, Hardway and another investigator were given a secure office at CIA headquarters in Langley. "The deal was we could see any document we wanted, provided we left our notes in that room. They provided us with the unexpurgated documents. We had remarkable access." This was heady stuff for a law student on a case that had made world headlines.

"We had operational action information . . . operational criteria which didn't fit into the rules of evidence but, I thought, were enough to make probable cause."

Hardway now says, with the skepticism of years of contemplation, "It was an active disinformation operation. [The CIA] moved so fast after the assassination. Must have been planned in advance."[24] Suddenly, the scent he had been following so avidly dissipated when the Agency simply shut down Hardway's access to documents of the time. He was reassigned to Mexico City to look into CIA links with Oswald there. He spent nine months on that job.

The key to the sudden shutdown was the CIA liaison officer who had at first been so forthcoming to the young investigators but then stonewalled them. The officer's name was George Joannides.

THE STRANGE CASE OF GEORGE JOANNIDES

The story of George Joannides and his possible involvement in the Kennedy assassination is the result of many years' work by Jefferson Morley, the *Washington Post* reporter. More may well be revealed as a result of a federal court case that Morley and Jim Lesar of the Kennedy Assassination Archives are pursuing to force more documents that they now know exist, out of the CIA. Those documents may indicate that Joannides knew of an assassination plot by students of the DRE against John F. Kennedy. Such a sensational revelation will certainly lead to more speculation that Harvey was knowledgeable as well because he was Joannides's superior, albeit several levels removed.

Morley provided me with a copy of his exhaustive piece documenting the link between Joannides and the Cuban exile group in New Orleans. It contains much information that was only partially available to Dan Hardway in 1978 and makes bleak reading for anyone who wants to believe there was no CIA involvement in the JFK assassination. The details are complex and are not overly relevant here, but they are part of the Harvey background, and so deserve some attention.[25]

Morley credits his knowledge of the link between Joannides and the JFK assassination to Oliver Stone's movie *JFK*, which caused a stir when it appeared in 1991 and led to the JFK Assassination Records Act, which "created an independent civilian panel with unique powers to declassify JFK files, even over the objections of federal agencies. Between 1994 and 1998, when its funding ran out, the panel, known as the Assassination Records Review Board, dislodged four million pages of classified documents."

The tale began when the HRSCA started to work in 1978. "Officials at the Agency grew concerned. How could they filter the questions? The CIA's deputy general counsel, Scott Breckinridge [who had been one of the two inspectors to write the 1967 inspector general's report for Helms], thought Joannides would be just the man to handle requests for records. . . . 'He was a good man with a good reputation,' Breckinridge recalled [in a 1999 interview]. He knew his way around. . . . He could find things in a hurry." In July 1978 Joannides came out of retirement to handle liaison with Hardway and other congressional investigators.

The crux of Morley's accusation is that Joannides was the CIA case officer on the DRE, which was at one time "the single most popular exile group in Miami. . . . It had been receiving funding, training and logistical support for its leaders, thanks to a CIA officer named David Atlee Phillips. . . . The Agency was giving the group's young leaders $25,000 each month."

The DRE students were difficult. Morley quotes Joannides's predecessor as saying, "they were scarcely less hostile to the President than to Castro." Ted Shackley wired Washington "that DRE's attitude toward US policymakers 'was one of contempt, repeat contempt.'" Yet DRE happily continued to accept the CIA's subsidies.

Then DRE got into a publicity flap that went to Helms personally. Morley: "For [DRE case officer], Helms selected up-and-coming political action officer, George Efythron Joannides, who had been transferred to Miami earlier that year, and was working as deputy chief of psychological warfare operations against the Castro government. . . . "[26]

As CIA case officer on the DRE, Joannides had knowledge of Phillips's operations in New Orleans in 1963–64. Thus, if Phillips were involved in a JFK assassination plot, Joannides had a personal as well as a professional interest in covering up what really happened. Again, all this transpired after Harvey had been sacked, but it had roots in the time when Bill had been in charge.

"As [Joannides] worked with congressional investigators [Hardway among them], he betrayed nothing about his own participation in or knowledge of the events of 1963 . . . nothing to suggest he knew of the DRE's contacts with Oswald."

"'I worked closely with Joannides,' says G. Robert Blakey, former general counsel of the HRSCA. 'None of us knew that he had been a contact agent for the DRE in 1963.' Another investigator, Gaeton Fonzi, told Morley, 'We got the run around, from day one, on the DRE.'"

IN-HOUSE AGENCY REACTION

The Joannides story is a classic example of the deep schism between the Agency's FI and PP branches. Yet former FI officers find it extraordinarily difficult to think that their PP cousins could have been involved in such explosive operations as those touched on here or that the icon they worshipped, Dick Helms, was personally and in detail knowledgeable, and indeed authorized some of the activity. FI men to this day cannot believe that PP could have dealt with, even supported, such a flagrant, undisciplined rabble as DRE. Or maybe they just don't want to believe in yet another conspiracy theory that denigrates the CIA.

For background, it's useful to bear in mind that, according to Morley, "in April 1964, Joannides . . . was transferred to Athens with a job evaluation that praised his performance as 'exemplary.'" And, "when Ted Shackley became CIA station chief in Saigon, Joannides followed him there and ran covert operations against the Vietcong in 1970 and 1971. He returned to CIA headquarters to work in the General Counsel's office until he left the Agency in 1976 to start an immigration law practice in Washington, DC." Joannides was recalled from his law practice to the CIA to deal with the congressional investigators in 1978.

In the article about his petition to open CIA's records, Morley says, "Tom Crispell, spokesman for the CIA, insisted that the Agency is 'absolutely not stonewalling.' While declining to answer questions about Joannides actions in 1963 and 1978, Crispell said the CIA has made public 'all known records' about Joannides that are relevant to the Kennedy Assassination story"[27]—at least in the CIA's judgment. Later developments proved this and previous statements were false.

REBUTTING JEFFERSON MORLEY

After I first heard of Morley's work and read his *Miami New Times* piece, I got in touch with Warren Frank, who was pulled down to Miami to head the FI section of JMWAVE, then was deputy to Herb Natzke in Berlin in the late 1960s, and later was a senior FI officer. Warren replied, "I am sure that there is no factual info connecting Bill H. to the assassination."[28] Warren's flat denial was symptomatic of the faith Harvey's subordinates—and not just the Berlin Brotherhood—had in their erstwhile leader.

Joannides gets mixed marks from CIA/FI officers who knew him. Frank, again: "I knew George Joannides quite well in Miami. I recall that he was definitely there in 1964 when he headed up the publications side of the project. Always a dapper dresser, and I remember that he was always very wrapped up in his writing; not the type to go out and do a lot of street work. . . .

"I don't ever recall that he was in New Orleans. There was never an ops base there. Maybe something in Domestic Contacts, which kept changing its name every few years."

In a later e-mail, Warren notes, "I found a note I made of a call from a *Washington Post* reporter on 19 August 1999. . . . The *Post* guy reminded me that George was brother-in-law of George Kalaris, longtime Agency hand who replaced Angleton as chief of CI [Counterintelligence] Staff and later headed SE [Soviet-East Europe] Division."[29] Both Kalaris and Joannides are now dead.

Frank checked his recollection with Shackley shortly before Ted's death. Shackley emphatically denied any connection between Joannides and the JFK assassination. Finally, Frank talked with another former CIA officer, who preferred to remain anonymous.

> Jack said he could not say positively since he was not in chain of command but also thinks Morley account most unlikely. He said he had absolutely never heard anything about George [Joannides] being involved in anything in New Orleans. I noted Morley's comment that Helms had personally put [Joannides] in charge of DRE group. It is conceivable that Morley has some document which would indicate this, but I doubt it. I doubt that Helms ever knew the names of the various Cuban groups in Miami.

Frank's assertion is the reflex action of a long-serving FI officer, steeped in the discipline and tradition of compartmentalization.

> Like all the various and changing groups which we supported at one time or another, there was little direct control over what DRE did, except [their publications]. There is similarity to our support in '50s of various East German anticommunist groups in Berlin, which you will recall.
>
> The groups, both in Miami and Berlin, were sizeable, consisted of very active, often zealot types, presumably penetrated by the East Germans, Soviets, or Cubans, so it is almost inconceivable that the Agency would have used DRE for any sensitive activity in the United States or elsewhere for that matter.
>
> Helms never to my knowledge visited JMWAVE when I was there. Also, Helms was always careful to distance himself from PM

[paramilitary] activity, I think both from lack of interest in it and his preoccupation with regular intelligence.

As you probably know, Helms and Bissell literally did not speak to each other prior to the Bay of Pigs, partly personal, but also because of Helms's tendency to avoid PM stuff.

Also, while I guess Helms somehow was technically in the chain of command, we always heard about Harvey [bypassing Helms to confer with McCone], or that Harvey was meeting with Bobby Kennedy. McCone was interested in Cuban activity and he is on record at the time of the missile crisis about his distrust of Castro. . . .

I only recall Harvey visiting JMWAVE twice, maybe three times. I think he came on very few other occasions to Miami to confer with the Chicago types. Ted drove him on one occasion but did not participate in any discussions which Harvey may have had.[30]

CONCLUSIONS: THE DRE CONNECTION

I suspect the CIA is to this day so embarrassed by its slipshod dealings with DRE that it remains reluctant to confess its laxity, especially because the Agency has again become a target of criticism in the fraught atmosphere of the Iraq War. But sloppy case officering is not enough to link Harvey to the JFK assassination.

I simply cannot conceive of any reason the PP warriors and David Atlee Phillips, a highly regarded officer, would have collaborated with the DRE students in killing the president. More likely, it seems to me, is the possibility that Joannides heard excited talk in DRE circles in, say, late summer or early autumn 1963 but discounted it as just another wild Cuban fantasy and didn't report it to higher levels with any degree of emphasis or urgency.

I wrote Morley, "PP were, basically, such bumblers, I can't imagine them ever carrying the assassination off, even if they had wanted to. If it had been their caper, you can almost bet someone would have forgotten to give Oswald the ammunition . . . or it would have been the wrong caliber.

"Next question: was the Joannides–David Atlee Phillips–Oswald link a cover—a diversion—organized by Trafficante and Rosselli, with, perhaps, some early assistance from Harvey, to attract attention away from the real plot?

"Possible. But. again the CIA I knew . . . would never, repeat never, have contemplated assassinating the president."[31]

GUILTY?

So, does all this prove anything about Harvey's conjectured participation in, or knowledge of, the plot to assassinate John F. Kennedy?

The forthright answer is: No. There are filaments in the glow of suspicion that Harvey was somehow connected with the events of November 22, 1963, but those suspicions are based, to a great degree, on people's reading of the unpolished character of Harvey—which serves to confirm their own dark suspicions that the CIA and the Agency's Bad Boy were somehow involved.

To sum up, let's stipulate that Harvey knew of DRE before Joannides appeared on the scene. Recall that Harvey was a detail man. He worked through, and signed off on, stacks of paper daily. In those stacks were undoubtedly correspondence, maybe project outlines, recruitment proposals, and the like, from the PP side of JMWAVE. Recall that Bill was ultra-security conscious and, with his Berlin experiences in mind, that he would have looked at PP ops sternly for potential security breaches and flap potential.

DRE started as a Phillips operation but apparently began to use its $25,000 monthly CIA subsidy in ways that made the Agency uncomfortable. The students ran an apparently freelance raid against Cuba on August 25, 1962, at a time when Bill and Johnny were still in close touch and when Rosselli may have been involved in the same type of activity. Ted Shackley acknowledged that he was aware of DRE's activities; this is perfectly normal. It is possible that Shackley and Harvey earlier discussed DRE, as they did much else, face to face, perhaps even out at sea on a fishing trip, and/or in their many telephone conversations of the period. The two pragmatic old FI hands probably decided to give the DRE operation the rubber-glove treatment—to stay as far away from the students as they possibly could.

In late 1962, after Harvey had been removed from Cuban operations and a year before JFK was killed, Joannides worked two levels under Shackley at JMWAVE. Shackley's prejudice against PP would have held, even with Bill out of the picture.

Joannides did not become the DRE case officer until after the student leadership went public at the time of the October missile crisis, trying to force an American invasion of Cuba. When Joannides took over responsibility for DRE, it was on direct order of Dick Helms, who told the Cubans that Joannides would report out of channels directly to himself. Again, however, this was after Harvey had been removed from the Cuban scene.

In Little Havana, everyone knew about everyone else's plots, so it's highly probable that Johnny Rosselli was aware of the Cuban students in exile. He may have asked Harvey to have someone seine the DRE pool, to look for people for his raiding parties and perhaps to spot students who might be useful as decoys. Too far-fetched? Much surrounding the murder of the president on November 22, 1963, is so strange that all possibilities must be at least aired.

Every time I raise the question of CIA involvement in the assassination with former CIA officers, the reaction is disbelief, horror, and/or absolute rejection. And in most cases, these are men who look at their former employer with some loyalty but also with skepticism verging on cynicism.

DAN HARDWAY REDUX

Let's return to the recollections of Dan Hardway. After Joannides shut down the House Select Committee team's access to CIA files in 1978, "we moved back to the HRSCA offices, and started requesting documents, which gave the CIA time to be careful. Previously, they hadn't had the time to vet the documents.

"One of the documents was Sheffield Edwards's debriefing of Johnny Rosselli. It was two inches thick. When I first saw it, whole pages of it were blanked out . . . not blackened as they usually are. Blanked. We never got that version. When we finally got it, it had been totally retyped."[32]

When I asked the CIA in May 2002 for a copy of the interrogation report under the Freedom of Information Act (FOIA), I was told that a search of the files had failed to reveal any such document. Perhaps, indeed, by 2003, the interrogation no longer existed.

Back to Hardway, recalling 1978:

> In my opinion, the Agency was obstructing justice. After three months . . . we were stymied in trying to prove conspiracy. Then I was assigned to Mexico City.
>
> If we had had six months more, we would have had enough evidence to go to a grand jury, or to Justice Department prosecutors.
>
> I wrote a memorandum on Harvey. . . . He had motive and opportunity . . . probable cause. The memo was written in [the Select Committee's] secure room. You couldn't take anything into or out of the room. Everything stayed there. Bob Blakey saw it, read it. . . . The memo doesn't exist any more. . . .
>
> I proved that Harvey was the pivotal connection. . . .

> The assassination was a Mob hit, but it wasn't a Mob hit like the ones they had done previously. They used a different MO. . . . In JFK, they used a patsy, and they used disinformation, both of them techniques they had learned from the Agency. . . . You have to look at the JFK assassination as an operational plan . . . and disinformation.
>
> Phillips was no slouch, a master of disinformation. . . . He was very, very good at what he did.
>
> My analysis, based on a lot of material from the FBI, was that a significantly large proportion of the assassination could be traced back to Phillips. But I didn't have any support. . . .
>
> [At a session with the Select Committee] Philips admitted he had lied. The chairman, [Rep.] Louis Stokes, called a break for lunch, and that was that.
>
> By the time we had proof of a conspiracy . . . the senior staff on the committee was winding up. They weren't interested. . . . Said "it could be coincidence." . . . They didn't have time or money to look into it. . . . I'm not sure I would have found anything . . . except for the full debriefing of Rosselli by Sheffield Edwards.[33]

Somewhere in the more than three hundred thousand pages of documents turned over by the CIA to HRSCA there may be one or more leads that connect Harvey directly to the murder of John F. Kennedy. The papers have not been fully indexed; perhaps they never will be. To put it mildly, the CIA is disinclined to be helpful. And it is increasingly doubtful that the Agency actually did turn over everything in its files on the JFK assassination.

It must be added that even former CIA/FI officers feel very strongly that David Atlee Phillips, a PP man, was a straight and honest Agency officer. They cannot conceive that Phillips operated outside his charter or was in any way involved in the Kennedy assassination.

BLAKEY ON THE MOB AND ROSSELLI

Robert Blakey's book, written in 1980, dispassionately details the Mafia's tradition of silence, loyalty, and bloody vengeance if its rules are broken. As Blakey winds down his take on the Mafia, he turns to Rosselli's role in the assassination.

> Rosselli, according to Jack Anderson, confided in him what he knew about the Kennedy Assassination, on the condition that Anderson

not reveal his identity. . . . The details that Rosselli supplied in their face-to-face meetings, according to Anderson, linked the Mafia directly to The Assassination. It was the work of Cubans connected to Santo Trafficante, according to Rosselli, and Oswald had been recruited as a decoy. Oswald may have fired at the President, but the fatal shot was fired from close range.

Once Oswald was captured, The Mob arranged to have him killed by Ruby who, Rosselli told Anderson, had not been in on The Assassination itself. (Anderson told us that Rosselli had characterized Ruby as a "punk.")

Rosselli said it was also his theory that Castro was behind The Assassination, along with Trafficante. He said he knew that a team had been sent to kill Castro, had been captured and tortured, and he believed Castro may have formed an alliance with Trafficante to kill Kennedy.

. . . Certain aspects of Rosselli's account came tellingly close to what we knew to be the truth. . . . Rosselli could not have been aware of the fact of a shot from the knoll unless he had inside information, for up until the time of his death in July, 1976, the official view was that all the shots had come from behind. We knew from the acoustics evidence that there was, in fact, a close-range ambush in Dealey Plaza, as Rosselli said there had been. . . . Rosselli's report that Kennedy was killed by a close-range ambush, therefore, had the ring of inside information to it, information that could only have originated with the gunman himself. . . .

Taken together with the fact of the second gunman and the Rosselli account of how Oswald was recruited by Cuban agents of Santo Trafficante, the pattern of Oswald's Latin associations could be stitched, we believed, into a tapestry that depicted the true nature of the plot.[34]

HARVEY'S POSSIBLE PHYSICAL INVOLVEMENT

While I was looking into the various hints that Harvey was physically involved in the Kennedy assassination, I actually heard a rumor that Bill had been present in Dallas on November 22, 1963. While this rumor is patently absurd, some other potential physical connections to the event are not so easy to dismiss.

In late winter, early spring 1963, Harvey was coming out of the limbo of his awkward banishment to the outer office of what had been Task

Force W in the Langley basement and moving into the office of the chief of the Italian Branch of CIA's Clandestine Services. We don't know whether Helms curtailed Harvey's unlimited travel warrant after he was removed from the Cuban effort. Maybe not. So perhaps Harvey still had the freedom to travel wherever he chose, and in his accustomed style, perhaps he did not bother to tell anyone where he was going or had been. But he probably filed accountings, which might be somewhere in the CIA's records.

He might have traveled in the United States. We know of only that one trip to Florida from April 13 to 21, 1963, during which Bill and Johnny went out to sea for a couple of days.

From July 1, 1963, until April 1966, Harvey was stationed in Rome. He conducted vest-pocket operations, was senior contact to the Italian intelligence and security services, and was involved in the overall stay-behind program, in addition to many other duties. I believe Harvey was also the top American official liaison to the capos of the Mafia in Sicily, even though Henry Woodburn, his chief of operations at the time, denies the contact. I assume that Harvey was also in contact with the Camorra in the Naples area, perhaps indeed with Lucky Luciano, who had helped the United States with arrangements for the Sicily invasion in 1943. Perhaps the key go-between on routine matters was Michael Chinigo, the mysterious figure we examine fully in a later chapter. It is also possible that Harvey was in indirect touch with Rosselli after his arrival in Rome, through Mafia couriers or through some other communications system they had established.

On November 22, 1963, Harvey was either on the island of Elba, on Sardinia, or in Sicily. I think Mark Wyatt's story of Harvey returning to the mainland on a stormy night ferry is more plausible than CG Harvey's recollection, two and a half decades later, that Harvey was actually in Sicily, talking to the Mafia about smuggling drugs to the United States. I accept CG Harvey's recollection of Harvey's contact with the Mafia and his hasty return to Rome, but I think that trip (and others) did not take place on the day JFK was killed. Perhaps before.

No one in the CIA who knew Harvey at his prime believes, or believed, that he possibly could have been involved in the JFK assassination. No one. Not even those who had reason to dislike him. The very idea was and is to this day, among the still-living, anathema to them. It is also hard to imagine that CG Harvey would have so enthusiastically endorsed the concept of this book if she had the slightest inkling that her late husband had been involved in the crime of the century.

JOE SHIMON, SOUL MATE

And what about detective inspector Joe Shimon, a member, by his own admission, of Harvey's tight circle, especially after their respective retirements? Joe's daughter, Toni, finally got her stepmother to talk, a little bit, about Joe's relations with Harvey.

"Harvey used to come over, sometimes with Johnny Rosselli, and they'd sit in the kitchen. Joe was extremely fond of Johnny. It was like he was a soul mate, and that feeling extended to Harvey. Yes, they were soul mates. Joe liked Harvey very much."

Shimon would never discuss the JFK assassination with his family. Toni: "It was the only time I saw Dad afraid. He was actually afraid to talk about the Kennedy assassination. That was it. He was afraid of what he knew, and the consequences of it."[35]

Anthony Summers, the British investigative reporter, told me that "Joe Shimon was deeply involved throughout in the aftermath of the JFK killing. Harvey told Shimon . . . they were great pals . . . that Jack was killed as a result of a plot steered by Castro. . . . Harvey was sure Trafficante had JFK killed." Summers based his statement on the interview he conducted with Shimon on May 7, 1994, when Shimon was in his eighties. His memory seemed clear, but a certain amount of embellishment may have taken place between fact and narration. Some of the conversation is missing, lost when the tape cassette was turned over.

> Shimon: . . . working under Castro directly, the head man's name, the way I heard it, the way I understood his name, was Hernandez. . . . When he went back to Cuba, he disappeared.
> Summers: This is Harvey saying that a Castro agent, Hernandez, was behind the assassination and set up Oswald as a patsy?
> Shimon: Oh, no doubt. He was completely satisfied on that front, I think. Between you and me, Harvey probably caught the ear of somebody on the Committee. . . .
>
> You couldn't afford to put Oswald on the stand, or let any public statement be revealed to the American people concerning that assassination to where it concerns the Cubans. . . . There would have been a hell of a mess in the country. That's what LBJ was afraid of.

Shimon skips to the details of Oswald's shooting by Jack Ruby.

"All they had to do was contact somebody who had control over Ruby. . . . Ruby had the access to the [Dallas] police department. His control was Trafficante. . . . You know [Ruby] was a friend of Trafficante. They were both from Chicago originally. When Trafficante was in jail in Cuba, Ruby was over there visiting him. . . .
Summers: Did Harvey say what you just said about Ruby?
Shimon: We discussed that part of it because of the Chicago angle. . . .
Summers: The main thing that Harvey told you was that Castro's people set Oswald up?
Shimon: Harvey was satisfied that this had to be a Castro hit. . . . I'm talking about after Harvey retired from the CIA, and we used to talk about this at The Madison [Hotel, in Washington] with Johnny. . . . We discussed it back and forth, all the angles, and it all led back to Trafficante. . . . He was a double agent.
Summers: What was Harvey's basis for saying that Castro's agents had [killed JFK]?
Shimon: I don't know. He had a hell of a lot of information, and he couldn't tell me where he got it. The fact that he developed the connection between Trafficante and Castro, that Trafficante was the guy who was the double agent . . . that had to come from a pretty good source of information. . . .
[Shimon and Summers talk about a story that appeared "in a New York newspaper . . . about Trafficante being a double agent."]
Summers: Who leaked it?
Shimon: Between you and me, Harvey leaked it. . . . He wanted to show this, to the world, what this was all about. He knows he couldn't talk about the case. That was the rule with the CIA, and Harvey was well respected by the boys in the press. . . . He had a lot of friends in the press.
Summer: Harvey . . . actually named an agent . . . Hernandez?
Shimon: . . . That's what comes to me now. I don't know if it's correct. I remember a Number One guy directing all the activities for a hundred-some-odd Cuban agents working through Florida, and you know that Florida was infiltrated with all of Castro's guys."[36]

The Summers papers suggest that Jack Anderson submitted a secret report to president-elect George Bush in 1988, alleging that he had more information from Rosselli and Harvey than he had printed two decades earlier. "William Harvey was convinced that Oswald operated as Castro's agent. He communicated this to his CIA superiors, who had already confirmed this suspicion from 'independent sources.'"[37]

I am inclined to agree with Anderson and also Ed Becker, "if Rosselli knew, Harvey knew."[38] Note that Anderson and Becker come at the riddle of the assassination with widely different knowledge. But then again, the burden of Gus Russo's evidence weighs heavily against Mafia plotting or involvement.

TENTATIVE CONCLUSION

The question of Harvey's potential culpability in the assassination is not mentioned in any of the CIA or FBI documents that have been released for public scrutiny. If the CIA suspected him, the assumption must be that the Agency is still covering up whatever it knows. It may, indeed, have learned its lesson well and destroyed any lingering paper.

Soon after the assassination, the CIA came under real as well as imagined pressure. The Agency simply could not afford to have a huge scandal erupt. The Mafia connection was dicey; the DRE connection even more explosive.

The circle of those who knew about the DRE's bluster, in 1962, would have included Harvey, but that does not make him guilty of conspiracy.

I find it very hard to believe that sworn officers of the CIA plotted the death of the president of the United States. I think the Agency's top echelon knew more than it has admitted and was embarrassed that it had not yielded its knowledge instantly.

The Rosselli contact is another matter. CIA's top echelon was extremely suspicious of Harvey beginning in 1967, solely, as far as I can determine, because he refused to cut his ties to Johnny. What, Helms and his immediate subordinates wondered, what the hell was Harvey doing, continuing to pal around with a hoodlum like Rosselli? No doubt J. Edgar Hoover made acerbic back-channel comments to Helms on the same subject. But Bill repeatedly made it clear that he would not end his friendship with Rosselli to suit the tastes of the Agency leadership.

If we accept the Mafia theory, how could Rosselli be sure Harvey would not tell the CIA, during the planning stage, or thereafter? Was it because Rosselli had turned the tables and achieved the kind of hold over Harvey that a CIA case officer is trained to have over an agent? What was that control factor? Something Bill had done while drinking?

The Agency apparently still, four decades after the fact, prefers obfuscation to revelation on matters pertaining to the death of JFK. Without the CIA's cooperation, the case against Harvey as an active or passive conspirator in the assassination of John F. Kennedy must remain moot.

There's another possibility, albeit a backhanded one. When the CIA, in the person of Jim Angleton, suspected that Peter Karlow might be a KGB mole in the Agency, based on, at best, a shaky analysis anchored in a suspect defector's misleading tip, the U.S. government acted ruthlessly. The FBI interrogated Karlow mercilessly, and Peter suffered much—the least of which was humiliation and financial loss (much later, apologetically compensated). If the CIA's upper echelons had knowledge, or even suspected, that Harvey had information on the JFK assassination, would it not have detained Bill and questioned him exhaustively? (The Agency might not have called in the Bureau on Harvey, for reasons of face if nothing else.)

No evidence suggests that Bill was even interviewed on the subject. Thus, it may be surmised that Harvey had suspicions and reported them to Helms, meaning that such knowledge, if ever committed to paper, may still be locked away in Agency files. Or, the CIA simply did not feel there was cause to haul Harvey over the coals.

REBUTTAL: SAM HALPERN

Sam Halpern, that font of information on the Agency's dealings with Cuba during the early 1960s, doubts that Bill was in any way involved in the Kennedy assassination. I also asked Halpern about Santo Trafficante. "None of us ever talked about Trafficante. . . . Everyone knew we weren't involved with him."

Halpern says that Harvey probably did have contact with Dave Phillips. Halpern knew Phillips well, but "Dave Phillips never talked of any contact between Phillips and Harvey." Phillips does not even mention Harvey by name in his memoir.[39] And, as before, other FI officers are quick to praise and defend this particular PP cousin; this praise is in itself remarkable.

Halpern:

> And you'll never find any written records because there weren't any. There's simply nothing there. For instance, there was not much cable traffic between JMWAVE and Task Force W. . . . We handled most of it on the phone, double talking our meaning. . . .
>
> Bill was a very, very senior guy who didn't encourage inquiries. I doubt even Helms knew where Bill went when he traveled. He didn't write memoranda for the record. He carried it all in his head.

> It was a very difficult period. Bill was only head of Task Force W for eleven months. . . .
>
> I think the suspicions are made up out of whole cloth. . . . Harvey was never involved in anything [like the JFK Assassination]. If anyone would have known, it would have been Shackley. Maybe he would talk about it. Maybe.
>
> It was a very strange period.[40]

Ted Shackley died without shedding any further light on the matter. During my last conversation with Ted, he had this to say, with tight lips: "My relationship with Bill in the latter years was such that he would have said something about it. . . . I never had the impression that he knew anything about the JFK assassination. I guess it's possible, but any specific answer has to be a value judgment. . . . The speculation that the Mob went after JFK was not substantiated."[41] The phrasing is awkward, stiff, formal, but that's the way Shackley talked.

SAM PAPICH SUMMARIZES

Sam Papich, the long-serving liaison officer from the Bureau to the Agency, summarizes his feelings thus:

> Very early I did make it clear [to CIA] that I couldn't understand why the Agency ever considered getting involved with Johnny and his tribe. . . . Bear in mind that Harvey had little or no experience working in the organized crime field while in the Bureau. What he may have learned [was] from research, but . . . I can say he was entering a completely new atmosphere with Johnny. . . . In fact I doubt if any of the organizers in the Agency had any background in the organized crime field.
>
> Don't forget the Bureau did not participate in any of the [Castro] planning where Johnny and associates were involved. We were never briefed on any part of the planning. I realize it was so handled because of the tight security.
>
> One could say that because he was green in the OC field, Harvey would have been completely dominated by Johnny. However I do not exclude that H, in his own way, established a relationship which benefited the objectives of the Agency. After all, Johnny did not have any background in the Intelligence field. Also I do not know [how] Johnny, despite a long criminal background, looked at the matter of service to his country.

> What you need is access to H's reporting. . . . Did they actually develop a friendship or was it all business-business? I suppose it is unavailable but you would be cooking if you ever get access to Johnny's appraisal of his association with Harvey.[42]

Papich and Halpern both put their fingers on the missing link—operational files, especially those extending from, say, 1960 to Harvey's retirement in 1967, and the equally fascinating-but-distinct operational files on Rosselli. But, Harvey did not keep files, and the CIA is not about to oblige, even if any files do exist. Since Helms was even more aware of the pain and misery caused the CIA by public investigation, and since his inner circle was totally devoted to him, it is not beyond belief that key documents bearing on the CIA and the assassination of John F. Kennedy no longer exist. And who's to say there ever were such incriminating papers?

Finally, Dick Helms spoke some haunting words, when he was still DCI, in April 1971. They sound eerily apt once again, in the first decade of the twenty-first century. "The nation must to a degree take it on faith that we, too, are honorable men, devoted to her service."

As Sam Halpern said, it was, indeed, a very strange period.

11

ROME: DECLINE AND FALL

Beginning in late October 1962, when he was summarily relieved of duty as boss of Task Force W and ZRRIFLE, Bill Harvey found himself on a slippery slope—not yet careening, but on his way down. After that demeaning spell in the Langley basement purgatory, he was brought upstairs to the Italian Desk, then Harvey's road led him to Rome. It was there that Bill's plunge into the abyss snowballed. Tom Polgar, who had known Bill since the late 1940s, observed, somewhat acerbically, "Helms threw him what many would have considered a life-saving ring by getting him to Rome, but Rome required quiet finesse, tact, and sophistication in dealing with proud foreigners. And in Rome Harvey did not have the kind of branch chiefs who made him look as good as his subordinates made him look in Berlin."[1]

As we shall see, some interesting people lived in and around Rome.

WASHINGTON FAREWELL

Sometime in mid-1963, some of the Langley basement crowd and a crew of former Berliners memorialized the shafting they all felt Harvey had taken at the hands of their masters. It was a bittersweet farewell party for the enigmatic chief, an occasion to emphasize their enduring loyalty to him and their scorn for the political leaders whom he had dared to defy. Jim Angleton told David Martin years later, Harvey had "lost his self-confidence for the first time in his life!" Angleton, who as a hobby made fishing flies and lures, also "tried to cheer him up by handcrafting a small leather holster for Harvey's .38 Detective Special."[2]

It was a BOB kind of party—boozy sadness that he was leaving, admiration for what he had accomplished, gallows humor laced with the bravado people of a secret elite share, tall stories, gruff, stifled emotions, overly raucous laughter. There were short, embarrassed speeches of praise and devotion in among the tears of farewell. Their leader had been cut down when he should have been praised for forming and running Task Force W's global intelligence network under incredible oversight conditions.

Harvey had done what he was assigned to do, probably better than anyone could have expected. In a few months, his network penetrated Castro's Cuba and provided the required meat-and-potatoes intelligence. His people's efforts had produced high-profile stuff, too: reports of the transportation of the intermediate-range ballistic missiles through Havana, precise descriptions of their launching sites, solid material from diplomatic and shipping sources, and Warren Franks's contacts with Fidel's sister. But all that was not enough. Harvey had not fully carried out the first family's impossible, personal mandate, and he had made his disgruntlement profanely obvious.

Now Harvey was down in flames. At the farewell party, people reached out, in their gruff, boisterous way, trying to drown the depth of their feelings for their leader. No one could rescue him. There were sardonic mementoes: "A stuffed mongoose [in fact, a ferret, since Washington taxidermists apparently did not carry mongooses] and a roll of toilet paper with every sheet stamped 'PSM.' . . . And there were speeches—a satire on Shakespeare's *Julius Caesar* in which Harvey was Caesar."[3]

The cashiering of Bill Harvey, even if it was for cause, was sharp confirmation that henceforth, politics was boss. In 1963 the politicization of the Agency was still something new, and something ugly, to the professionals. They knew they were, symbolically, celebrating the last hurrah of the free-wheeling, buccaneering CIA. That Harvey could be humiliated and cashiered because he had—albeit too blatantly—failed to carry out the personal dictates of the nation's political leadership was a lesson those at the farewell also well understood. The CIA had lost what independence it still held. It had become and would remain a subservient branch of the executive. The lesson was even more blatantly reinforced some years later when Richard Nixon sought to bend the CIA to his own devices.

Before he left for Rome, though, Harvey did something that was typical of the man and what he stood for. Recall that Peter Karlow probably introduced Bill to CG that Christmastime of 1952. Years later, Karlow was the senior CIA officer hounded by Angleton as the possible KGB mole in the CIA.

Karlow recalls, "Bill was a lovely person, but he didn't take any shit from anyone. . . . When I was having the trouble with Angleton, in 1963 [and later] . . . and many of the CIA guys were trying to freeze me out, in order to protect the defector, Golitsyn . . . Bill Harvey went over to the FBI and talked to some of his old friends, then he came back and said to me, 'They've cleared you over there!'" The act was, in itself, one of considerable courage on Bill's part because it came at a time when CIA officers, even friends of long standing, backed away from each other in suspicion and fear. Harvey stuck by his friends.[4]

REASSIGNMENT

A painful period followed, after Bill "lost his usefulness." He could not be fired for many reasons, so the CIA had to find something for him to do. Meanwhile, he sat ignominiously twiddling his thumbs for several months in the Langley basement. David Martin notes it was not an easy reassignment. Harvey suggested Laos, but Helms vetoed that one; no more high-profile assignments for Bill. Rome was open and it was a slot that needed someone of Harvey's rank, but even before Bill left, people wondered audibly about the fit. '"They couldn't have picked a bigger bull for a better china shop,' one CIA officer snorted. . . .The irony cannot have escaped Harvey that it was he, not Rosselli, . . . who was being deported to Italy."[5]

Rome was an incongruous assignment for Harvey in so many ways. Even if he refused to show openly how deeply humiliated he felt, there was only a certain degree to which "professionalism" could conceal his remorse, even anger, that he had been removed from cutting-edge operations. On top of that, it would have been hard to put together a worse-matched pair than Harvey and an officer named Mark Wyatt. To this day, while bending over backward to be fair, Wyatt has abundant reason to splutter when he talks of his former boss.

Wyatt had a long career in intelligence and had the right social credentials. In late 1947, after World War II service in the U.S. Navy, he joined the CIA, having been introduced to the Agency by Senator William Knowland of California.[6] He "got to know Bill Colby very well."[7] Mark was now head of the Italian Desk.

In the winter of 1963 Harvey lurched onto Wyatt's scene. Even decades later Mark's resentment is plain. "McCone, the director at the time, had wanted to fire Harvey a couple of times. . . . McCone was embarrassed. . . .

"Harvey played McCone terribly well . . . cleverly . . . by backing McCone against McNamara on the Castro assassination thing. . . . Even if he had three martinis, he was no fool. Harvey was an icon in the intelligence community."

Wyatt continues, "So Helms called me in and said, 'Isn't it great! You're going to ROME!' I protested, 'But, Dick . . . Paris?'" Wyatt had been angling for a senior job in France; he asked point-blank if Rome was a "directed assignment," and Helms replied that it was. "It was flattering. Helms said, 'It was your great friend James Jesus Angleton who suggested it.' So I said, 'If Jim feels it's important, OK.' Next thing I knew, Angleton said, 'You're coming to dinner with Harvey!'"

Wyatt paused for recall. "Bill was fighting his way back" when he moved into Wyatt's Langley office for a short time, so he could read in on Italian cases.

Mark continues, "Bill was always excited. He said, 'Certain things have to finish after Mongoose.'. . . Bill thought he handled the Mafia guys terribly well.

"He would come back after lunch and talk, but then he would say, 'But that's all behind me.' . . . Rosselli was so close to Bill. . . .

"So, Bill went out to Rome in 1963. He was wonderful. Couldn't have been nicer. Italy was a good stock then."[8]

Harvey even helped the Wyatts find housing—"the most beautiful villa on the Appian Way . . . really sublime!" and a suitable place for official entertaining. "Des FitzGerald came there once and said, 'What a palazzo!' But we couldn't get help to manage the house."

Harvey "took over the chief's house in the American Academy and spent a lot of money redecorating it . . . in poor taste," Wyatt thought.

"He could have been successful. Instead, I was actually running the office most of the time, while he was off in Elba or some place, drying out.

"David Martin called me years later, but I wouldn't talk with him." Wyatt adds that Martin told him, "'You'll regret it.' And I did!" Wyatt exhibited two memos for the record, dated October 10 and 12, 1977, reporting that Martin had exerted "threats and pressure" on him. He was unhappy that Martin, in *Wilderness of Mirrors*, referred to him as "one of Harvey's subordinates." Wyatt: "I wasn't some little geek, as [Martin] portrayed me in that book!"[9]

Tom Polgar comments, "When I heard of Bill's assignment to Italy, I felt sorry for him. . . . He was not the *bella figura* the Italians liked to see. The Rome office was well known for its internal feuds and its ongoing battles with James Angleton, who had kept his hands in Italian operations since 1944.

As Polgar noted, they were not easy fits in the various Rome social circles. The Harvey residence was a handsome museum—not exactly CG

Harvey's down-home style. A sympathetic friend suggests, "Maybe her energy needed an outlet as she saw Bill spiraling down."

POINT, COUNTERPOINT

Years later CG spoke frankly to her Indianapolis church group about the Harveys' time in Rome. "I spent the three worst years of my life in Italy. Trying to operate on a day-to-day basis. Going to the market every day to buy supplies. I got tired of being cheated."

Sally Harvey interrupts her mother's videotaped monologue. When the family's furniture arrived from the United States, "it came in the front door, and they were loading it onto another truck out the back!" The Harvey's cook stole from them and had to be fired. Two or three others came and went. Finally the first chef was rehired and stayed because CG had his number.

Life was colorful.

> One time, they shut our water off. We were being asked to pay 2,000 lire [a little over $3.00] a day for water! Next day I sent to Sears for a pump and some water pipe and a lot of hose. I plugged into the [Roman] aqueduct, and we got our water. So, OK, we had to boil it five times to get rid of the amoeba, but we did it! . . . We didn't get caught, and we ran the local water merchant out of business! . . .
>
> There was a Communist compound close to our residence. They kept rats in cages, and would throw them over our walls, labeled 'LBJ.' We had rats climbing the dining room table. Bill was in Washington. He left me to deal with the rats and the Communists.
>
> Some of their people came over and said they wanted to talk. I ran and got Bill's elephant gun out of its case. You should have seen them scatter!!
>
> Driving to the [American military] commissary, we used a road that was two thousand years old. On the way back one day, a bunch of gypsies came down to steal and to grab Sally as a hostage. Jim was sixteen at the time. He was beating on some guy and hanging onto Sally at the same time. Just then a busload of priests came up behind us, and away the gypsies went. Sally was scared.

Watching the tape, Sally added that CG drove the family's big, white American Ford station wagon in Rome's narrow streets and always needed help to extricate herself, until she was finally assigned a chauffeur.[10]

OTHER VIEWS

It's understandable that Bill felt isolated in Rome. He organized the assignment of a friendly face, that of Henry Woodburn, who had been the key BOB inside case officer on the Tunnel. Henry came to Rome to serve as Harvey's operations officer.

"Bill was restless. He got along well enough professionally with the Italians, who respected him for his accomplishments. But he never learned any Italian. He would say, 'If you guys'd learn German, we could talk!' Which, of course, was more than partly a jest because Harvey's German never improved, even to conversational level."

Woodburn adds that in addition to his other problems in Rome "Harvey [predictably] did not get along with the ambassador, who was old-school Foreign Service. . . . Wives wore gloves and hats; cards were dropped on visiting days, with corners turned down, etc. Bill didn't bother to conceal his contempt.

"Rome was not a happy assignment for Bill. . . . He could be very impressive when he wanted to be, but Italy was a different world for him. . . . relaxed, whereas Bill was intense. Rome had only light operational responsibility. He should have geared down, but wasn't really capable of doing so.

"He was an ops man."[11]

Bill did have a few vest-pocket ops into Africa, which, according to Woodburn, did not pose a conflict of interest with the division to which he was nominally assigned, Western Europe. It's likely the cases had to do with Division D matters. Mark Wyatt comments, "Bill had an agent in deepest, darkest Africa. He saw this black man. . . . He talked about needing some place very secure to meet him. . . . A man who could be terribly important in Africa."

As I was digging, I heard a rumor that Woodburn had become so upset at Bill's decline that he wrote an eyes-only letter to the top brass urging that Harvey be withdrawn from Rome, for his own, as well as the service's, good. When I asked Woodburn point-blank, he emphatically said he had not written nor sent any such dispatch.

HARVEY, STAY-BEHIND OPS, AND SICILY

Harvey's tour in Rome took place during one of the chilliest periods of the Cold War. Beginning in the early 1950s, when the United States was preparing for Communist takeover or, indeed, a Soviet invasion of Western Europe, one of the important aspects of planning was the establishment of stay-behind teams to conduct clandestine operations against the occupiers. Mark Wyatt was the officer responsible for these teams.

Wyatt: "Overall, the stay-behind operation was a terrific success . . . a delight. . . . We did the training in Sardinia. Bill came over a few times, and drank a great deal."

But Italian officialdom did not hold sway in all areas. It is entirely plausible that the CIA and the Mafia found common interest in preparing guerrilla resistance, should the country fall to the Communists. It would have been renewal of a partnership that went back to World War II.

Wyatt: "I have reason to believe that Bill traveled to Sicily. . . .

"Once, when he had to come back [from Sicily at great speed] the Mafia gave him a carved wooden symbol to put on the front of the car, which guaranteed him free and quick passage. He definitely did not want to be tailed on that trip."[12] Wyatt seemed to be describing the figure also mentioned by CG, which was even recognized by Sicilian traffic policemen.

FIRING WYATT

Harvey abhorred the celebrities who hung around Hollywood on the Tiber. Wyatt again: "Orson Welles, Gina Lollobrigida, Sophia Loren, Ingrid Bergman. The consul general shoved them all on to me." Nor did Bill fare well with the diplomats in the embassy. Wyatt: "Ambassador Rinehart didn't like Bill, and he suggested that I come to the staff meetings."

"Bill kept a bottle of Campari and a bottle of gin in his desk. . .His secretary, Cleo, was very concerned.

"When he went down the Via Veneto for lunch, the waiters, who knew him, would say, '*vienne el Shariffo*!'" Italian officials also commented on Bill's drinking.

Then, "Rolfe Kingsley, the chief of WE [the Western Europe Division], came over to visit" on a routine tour of stations under his command. One day Wyatt stopped Kingsley in the hall to discuss a great fitness report Harvey had given him. The discussion made Kingsley late for an appointment with Bill.

"Kingsley was scared to death of Harvey. . . . I mean, he actually turned white when he saw him. . . .

"Harvey erupted. 'I'll not tolerate this kind of thing behind my back!'

"Later, Harvey said to me, 'I understand you want to leave.'

"'Yes, sir!'

"'Goddamit, you're staying. You can't leave after just two years!'" Harvey then quickly reversed himself: "OK, if you really want to leave, I'm giving you thirty days to pack up." The family had three children in school. Such a rapid transfer would cause major problems.

Why did Harvey flare up that day? "Because I went behind his back!"

Wyatt took care to tell Desmond FitzGerald, who was deputy director of plans (DDP) at the time, his side of the affair. "I want it clear in the record that there's no stigma attached to my leaving within thirty days!"

Jack Whitten, alias John Scelso, in testimony to the House Select Committee on Assassinations:

> A: Harvey cracked up in Rome.
>
> Q: In what way?
>
> A: He became practically paranoid, turned on his officers, threatened to have them ruined. One of his very best officers came home and was going to join my staff and told me the whole story. I do not remember the man's name. An outstanding operations officer. . . . He could not stand Harvey any more and asked for a transfer. . . . Harvey refused, [and] said he was going to give him a bad fitness report and have him fired and so on.
>
> Later on, Desmond FitzGerald came out on TDY and heard some of these stories and relieved Harvey. Harvey went [portion illegible] completely—which happens in the Agency. The strain is tremendous.[13]

ROMAN NADIR

Sam Halpern saw Bill only once after Task Force W, when he was on a National War College trip to Europe, in 1966. Sam slipped the tour and stayed over in Rome. He, Woodburn, and Bill had a lunch at Bill's favorite Italian restaurant. "He was drinking heavily.

"Then Des FitzGerald went over and yanked him."[14]

George Bailey, an ex-Berlin CIA man and a distinguished writer, saw Bill in Rome and privately told friends that Harvey was out of control.

Dave Murphy, by that time chief of the Eastern Europe Division, saw Harvey from time to time, too. "He would arrive in Frankfurt for division chiefs' meetings totally blasted. . . .

"When I saw him in Rome, what got me was, I'd talk with Bill like we did in the old days. [Dave still considered Bill his mentor.] I'd ask, 'How should we run this case?' And where before, he'd discuss it in detail, in Rome, he had no ideas. He only wanted to talk about the old days . . . the tunnel."[15]

When he could, Harvey also went to Munich because his son was at the Army-sponsored branch of a stateside university there. Bill undoubtedly welcomed the trips because they gave him a chance to get back into the familiar, orderly German ambience.

He once called one of his former Berlin subordinates, now stationed in the Bavarian capital, to ask if he could stay with the ex-BOB family. "Much as I loved Bill, it was awful. He nearly fell out of the lift on the way up to the base office. He walked around with a tear in his suit pants, and his knee showing bloody, without even noticing it. . . . He was twirling his revolver in public."[16]

In a Munich beerhall, one of those buxom, bucolic waitresses noticed something on the floor, leaned down, and came up with a revolver, which she offered to Harvey, with the Bavarian equivalent of, "Yours, I presume?"

Joe Wildmuth, a fellow Hoosier who had been in Berlin, recalls sadly, "The last time I saw Harvey was in Munich, which he visited on his way home from that disastrous tour in Rome, where his Indiana attitude met Renaissance Italy. Bill was pale, a bit shrunken and, it seemed to me, totally defeated."[17]

Dave Murphy: "If he had been able to curb his drinking in Rome, CG would have been happy. . . . Harvey suffered a heart attack. Two Agency doctors were sent to minister to him. . . . They warned him that he would have to stop drinking and smoking and keep regular hours."[18]

"The word was out. Junior people back in Washington were talking. It had gone beyond self-immolation."[19]

Harvey's recall from Rome in 1966 was probably organized by Dr. Arthur Tietjen, the Agency's director of medical services, who was studying the effects of stress on CIA officers with Dr. Jack Hall. Jim Critchfield called Tietjen, "a really fine person, whose recommendations were respected by all of us." Tietjen would have received the reports of the two doctors who examined Bill after his Rome heart attack. He also knew that Bill was suffering from blood clots in his legs, which were aggravated by his drinking. Perhaps, indeed, Tietjen persuaded FitzGerald to go to Rome, size up the situation, and recall Bill for medical treatment. The return from Italy may, in fact, have saved Bill's life.

"CG was heartily in favor of leaving Rome and getting Bill back to the States."[20]

Sam Halpern: "When [Harvey] came back, Helms gave him 'special assignments' at which he could work at his own pace and didn't have to show face in public."[21]

Bill was spiraling down.

12

THE DOLDRUMS

Bill Harvey was never an open book, but during the first twenty years of his career, he left a fairly well-blazed trail. Where records were missing or unavailable, there were, early in the twenty-first century, still people who vividly remembered him. After Rome, the trail becomes sketchy, and this is the way Bill wanted it. He intensely disliked the possibility that his history could be documented, even before he got into trouble, unless he controlled it. Others in the bureaucracy were not so chary of the written word.

In 1966–67 Harvey moldered in disgrace, his rare talents unused and largely unwanted; he was an object of sympathy, not adulation, when he showed up at the office. Sam Halpern's is the only evidence that Harvey was active at all. "He worked on 'the Moscow Signal' . . . where the Russians were bombarding the U.S. embassy in Moscow with sound waves. . . . I understand his report for the National Foreign Intelligence Board was excellent."[1] Other than that, nothing remains to indicate how Bill occupied his time.

Tom Parrott had an office just down the corridor from Harvey in 1966, the year Harvey returned from Rome. "I felt very sorry for him. There he was, sitting in the office, with nothing to do at all. It was pathetic.

"Once he came back from lunch and he was pretty worried, maybe even ashamed. He asked another guy if it was OK that he had had a third martini for lunch. It was very sad." The Harvey who had presided over the Martini Ritual, almost as a test of manhood, now appeared to cringe in despair or remorse over his inability to stop drinking and seemed afraid his lack of control would be noted.[2]

Bill's other problem, apart from hard liquor, was his continuing contact with Johnny Rosselli, by whom the CIA felt threatened. The Bureau badly wanted to nail Rosselli because he was an irritant, a challenge to Hoover's precise, neat worldview, and even worse, a chum of the excommunicated Harvey. But Rosselli was everything Harvey responded to: he knew how to keep a secret, he was used to guns, he drank without fear. Rosselli was an underdog who had made it to the top in a rough world and with whom Bill had shared some of the glory moments of the crusade against Castro, whose accident of birth was not what Georgetown deemed appropriate. He was a guy after Harvey's own heart.

When the CIA's quarterdeck learned that Harvey was once again in touch with Rosselli, after Bill's return from Rome, its attitude toward Bill shifted from compassion to dismay to increasing suspicion. Harvey was warned to break the connection, but he flatly refused to dump his beleaguered friend. The CIA, from Helms, the director, down, was sorry because it respected what Bill had been. But Harvey's stubbornness made the Agency, officially, begin to wonder where his loyalties truly lay.

INTO PURGATORY

As Harvey faced his second purgatory, he was almost a husk of a man, but I have come across no sign of repentance. He struggled to get off booze, probably at the insistence of Dr. Tietjen, but was only partially successful. At a lunch with one of the Agency seniors in late 1967, he indicated he was not enamored of the counseling he had been forced to accept; somehow, too, I find it difficult to imagine Bill Harvey being very forthcoming in an AA meeting.

He was still smoking, perhaps as many as three packs a day. He was still vastly overweight. He had problems with high blood pressure and with the clots in his legs. He almost undoubtedly had some intimations of his own mortality. And he was not going down commanding a clandestine battalion surging into secret battle, but succumbing to the consequences of his own tastes.

Harvey's fall from icon to object of suspicion is not a pretty story. Few of his old comrades knew, or wanted to know, his circumstances, nor did they want to hear the drumbeat of disapproval that Bill had to endure.

In the mid-1960s CIA officers went home and looked after their kids and watched TV; there weren't as many parties as there had been in the old days. A few of Bill's old friends stuck with him—came out to suburban Maryland for a meal or a chat when they could—but the Berlin Brotherhood, which might have offered him moral succor, was dispersed around the globe, and those in Washington were involved in the broad aspects of Indochina and the Cold War. Sally Harvey remembered that Cicely

Angleton came over to the Harveys' Chevy Chase house to spend time with CG after she and Bill had returned from Rome, despite the fact that the two women came from vastly different social milieus.

CIA foreign intelligence (FI) people were rattled. The Agency had suffered severe shocks in the past few years. There was the shameful case of Jim Angleton's mole hunt and Peter Karlow. Philip Agee went loudly public with revelations that blew the cover, and endangered the lives, of a number of officers. Drew Pearson was listening to Rosselli talk about the Kennedys' plans to assassinate Fidel Castro. In 1967 Lyndon Johnson demanded that Dick Helms provide proof that radical American protesters were being funded from abroad. To get answers, the CIA operated for the first time inside the United States on American targets. The country was lurching into upheaval over Vietnam. It was a very difficult time at Langley.

ON THE SKIDS

By early 1967 Harvey's situation vis-à-vis the U.S. government was anything but pleasant. He had been ordered to use up his accumulated sick leave. Hoover had never forgiven Harvey for not being a team player. The Bureau thought he was meddling in its righteous case against Rosselli, whose life they were determined to make miserable. Bill would be listened to if he wanted to report something to Sam Papich, who was still the FBI's CIA liaison officer, or one of the other seniors in the FBI, but he would be cut no slack.

Harvey became aware that Helms no longer trusted him and that he was being handled by Agency administrators—not his former operational colleagues—with asbestos gloves. The cast that ruled on Bill's fate was Helms's innermost cabinet: Howard J. Osborn, who had succeeded Col. Sheffield Edwards as CIA's director of security; Lawrence K. "Red" White, the executive director of the CIA; Jack Earman, the inspector general (IG); and Lawrence Houston, the CIA's general counsel. These very senior officers warily compiled a formidable file of very touchy memoranda on every aspect of Harvey's contact with the CIA's uppermost level in the months following his return from Rome. The Agency's quarterdeck was covering its collective ass; in so doing, they gave us insight into the final decline of the Tunneler. If Harvey made any notes on his waning days with the Agency, they were summarily destroyed by CG immediately after his death, or later.

On numerous occasions the CIA tried to get Bill to sever contact with Rosselli, but he would not. In March 1967 the situation became acute.

Word leaked that Drew Pearson had the Bobby Kennedy–Castro assassination story. The Agency IG team raced to investigate. Howard Osborn wrote a memorandum for the record on March 29, 1967.

> 1. Jack Earman, Inspector General, has been trying to locate Bill Harvey. . . . He told me that the Director had instructed him to investigate any and all aspects of the "Johnny" case . . . pointed out that before they expanded the circle of interviewees, they should have available to them all of the documentation held by me, plus the cooperation of the one individual now with the Agency that knows more about this case than anyone else, i.e. [name blacked out, but most probably Jim O'Connell].
> 2. . . . It seems that the White House, Congress and Drew Pearson are digging into the allegation . . . and [Helms] wants to be in a position to say that his Inspector General has investigated the matter thoroughly.[3]

Next, on May 3, 1967, Earman warily recorded that he and Papich had compared notes, probably because he knew there would be unrelenting Bureau surveillance of developments. Harvey had phoned both the Bureau and the Agency to ensure that they knew of Rosselli's impending arrival in Washington. Earman: "I told Sam that our official position was that there should be no contact between Harvey and Rosselli, but we are not in a position to dictate to Harvey on this. . . . I told Sam that Harvey is no longer an employee of this Agency. He has, in effect, retired, although he is presently being carried on sick leave."

Papich, who had known Bill since both were young FBI officers in the 1940s, told Earman,

> Rosselli . . . almost certainly will be kept under surveillance.
>
> CIA is in an extremely vulnerable position. Rosselli and . . . Sam Giancana continue to be in a position to publicly embarrass CIA . . . [and] have CIA over a barrel because of "that operation." He [Papich] said that the Bureau would like to get its hands on Rosselli and get him to talk, but he doubts that they will be able to do anything about either Rosselli or Giancana, because of "their previous activities with your people. . . ."
>
> Sam says that it would be nice if Harvey would agree to recording the meeting, but he doubted that Harvey would consent. . . . He was not much concerned if Harvey were sober during the

> meeting, but that he was worried about what Harvey might say if he got drunk.

Earman added an interesting note: "I told Papich to the best of my knowledge, Harvey had not met with Rosselli since their meeting in Washington in June 1963, just before Harvey left for Rome"; in other words, the CIA apparently had no record of telephone or cable contact between the pair while Bill was in Italy.

TROUBLED TIMES

Sam Papich had a "pleasant" lunch with Bill on Friday, May 5, 1967, and reported it to Osborn on May 8. "Harvey had had only one double Martini and, in response to a query by the waitress, refused a second one." Bill said he had not seen Rosselli since 1963 but had had several "general chitchat" phone conversations with him, dates and circumstances unspecified.

Harvey explained to Sam that his relationship with Rosselli was a personal one, stemming from his earlier use of Rosselli in an operational capacity. He told Sam that if one left the criminal aspect of Rosselli's activities out of the picture, the mafioso was a charming and personable man who could talk on a variety of subjects articulately and knowledgeably. This was not exactly what Papich wanted to hear. He warned Harvey against "continuing contact with an individual of Rosselli's ilk. He told him that the Bureau would be in no position to 'bail him out' if this association came to light." Harvey offered to report to Papich on his meeting with Johnny; Papich said, icily, that that was up to Bill. "He wanted to make it very clear that The Bureau was not requesting his cooperation."

After the Papich lunch, Harvey understood in no uncertain terms that he was on his own and that he had to bear the consequences for whatever he might do or not do with Rosselli. Osborn summed up: "Sam . . . got the impression that Harvey was bitter about the manner in which he had been 'forced out' of The Agency and seemed to focus his attention on The Director as the point of his resentment. Sam did not mention [Dick Helms's] name in this context and indicated that this part of our conversation was 'off the record'"—and then promptly put the details on paper.

"[Sam] did not intend to pass along the information to anyone else in The Agency and I have made no copies of this memorandum. I . . . request only that you not compromise my relationship with Mr. Papich by indicating that I have made it available to you."

Bill also bent over backward to keep the Agency informed. On May

11 he told Earman that Rosselli had arrived in Washington. Helms told the IG to tell Bill that the director "had no 'special instructions' for him." Also on May 11 Bill suggested lunch to Howard Osborn and Sheffield Edwards. Both put him off until the following week. When informed of the lunch invitation, Helms told his subordinates to "merely sit and listen to what Harvey has to say and not try to trade points with him."

Harvey told Papich that the meeting with Rosselli was to be at his house, i.e., not at the familiar rendezvous, the Madison Hotel, which was easier to cover. Papich told the CIA that the FBI did not "intend to try to cover it."

On May 18 Osborn noted for the record that he had made an effort to give Helms plausible deniability on the ramifications of the Rosselli case but that Helms had said he was fully aware of the affair. He told Osborn to "work closely with The Bureau on this matter. . . . He further directed that I handle this personally and not involve any other Agency personnel unless it became absolutely necessary.

"I also informed Mr. Helms of the actions of Mr. William K. Harvey in writing letters from [ ] to 'Johnny' suggesting that 'Johnny' assist him in some unspecified manner. Further I informed him that I had strongly suggested to Mr. Harvey that he have nothing further to do with Johnny." Whether Harvey wrote the letters to Rosselli from Rome remains an open question; what kind of help Harvey wanted from Rosselli remains a matter for speculation, as does the matter of how the letters got into the CIA's hands.

PUTTING ON THE HEAT

On July 21, 1967, Papich told Osborn "in the strictest confidence" that, according to a telephone intercept, Rosselli was coming to Washington on about September 20, 1967. "Apparently Rosselli has some sort of a problem." Papich added that the FBI was "really putting the heat on Rosselli. Several new things have come up, nature unspecified." Papich asked that the information be passed only to Helms and that the Agency inform the Bureau if Rosselli tried to get help from Harvey or "any of Rosselli's other CIA contacts. Papich specifically asked that Harvey not be told of The Bureau's intensified interest in Rosselli. . . . There was no doubt in [Osborn's] mind that Rosselli would call on The Agency to bail him out." The news of the trip so concerned Dick Helms that he called Papich in for a personal briefing.

The same day Harvey tried to reach both the IG and the head of security. That afternoon he dropped by Earman's office to report on the impending Rosselli visit and said that Johnny

> sounded more agitated than he had ever heard him before. . . . He was being harassed by the FBI. . . . The case The Bureau and the Justice Department has against Rosselli is hotter now than ever before . . . primarily on the probability that Rosselli is in the country under an assumed name. . . . In short, said Bill, "is Johnny Rosselli the Johnny Rosselli that was born in Chicago in 1907, or is he somebody else who was born in Italy in 1907?" Harvey added, "his concern was that Rosselli might turn to someone else and tell him the whole story [of the CIA's attempts to assassinate Castro]. . . .
>
> Bill said he thinks it is obvious that the Bureau is trying to get Sam Giancana and others of the Mob through Rosselli. Bill said he was quite sure that Rosselli would not rat on Giancana. The Mob just doesn't do things like that, and Rosselli knows better than to try it. . . . Bill mentioned that he knew of the possibility that Rosselli was in the country illegally.

Then the record is blank until Harvey checked back with Earman on September 26 to say that Johnny had been told by his Los Angeles lawyer that it might be a good idea "not to leave the jurisdiction, hence he had decided not to come to Washington. "Rosselli seemed much calmer than he had when he called earlier. . . . Harvey remains convinced that Rosselli will never be pushed to the point where he will try to use us to pull him out of a hole."

The next episode was a lunch Harvey and Osborn had on October 4, 1967, after Osborn had received approval from Helms and the IG "to evaluate [Harvey's] current physical and mental state of being." Osborn was careful to notify the FBI that he would be meeting Bill. Harvey obviously trusted Osborn, who, Bill said, was one of his few remaining friends in the CIA.

Osborn: "I met with Harvey who was about a half hour late and who entered the restaurant in dark glasses. I ordered a Martini and he ordered a beer, and we spent the first fifteen minutes or so in an exchange of information relating to our families, the tragic and untimely death of Desmond FitzGerald, the *burglary of his household*, and the current status of his application for admission to the District Bar." (Emphasis added.)

Bill then began to probe Osborn's knowledge of the Rosselli case. "He said he was a little annoyed with Helms, in that he had spread knowledge of the case so widely throughout The Agency, since he had had a very explicit understanding with [Helms] that it was to be extremely closely held. I pointed out that [the Pearson columns] had obviously made him decide that it was necessary to solicit the assistance and support of his Inspector General."

By now, Bill had had his second beer and was relaxed. Osborn:

> I asked him point-blank what was the nature of his relationship with Johnny. He . . . said that he didn't give a damn; that he would not turn his back on his friends, and that Johnny was his friend. I replied that while this was an admirable quality, I felt he was taking all sorts of risks in this regard. . . .
>
> . . . It was his opinion that it would be the worst thing he could do for himself or The Agency to turn his back on Johnny at this time. He said that he had told Johnny at the outset of their association that if anything happened to blow the operation, Johnny could not look to anyone other than Harvey for assistance, and that even Harvey would probably not be able to help him. He seemed to want to establish clearly with me the fact that it will be his neck if our use of Johnny comes out into the open, since he believes The Agency could not or would not admit involvement.
>
> Harvey then said he felt very uncomfortable about the entire situation, and fully realized the implications to The Agency if it ever surfaced publicly. . . . He felt sure that Johnny would never "pull the string" on us unless he was absolutely desperate, but that his concern was that Senator Robert Kennedy knew all about the operation.

This is about as clear a statement of Harvey's relationship with Rosselli as exists. Bill then reflected on the difficulty of his post-Agency life.

> He said (and I believe with provocative intent) that when he told Johnny about his intention to enter legal practice, Johnny suggested he send him an announcement and that he, Johnny, would be in a position to throw a lot of business his way. [Bill] said that he was sure he could clear $100,000 a year as an attorney for Johnny, but that he had no intention of getting involved in the type of legal activity this would entail.

In fact, Rosselli called Bill twice, on October 22 and 27, more than two weeks after the Osborn lunch, and asked Harvey to represent him legally. In both cases, Harvey refused, "saying he couldn't afford to be put in such a position." Rosselli wondered audibly why the CIA would not give him the same type of support it had given Robert Maheu, whom it had recently extricated from a pickle over the Las Vegas wire-tapping incident.

Osborn continues:

> In closing, I inquired as to his status with The Agency, and he stated that he had a couple of months to go with the 'stupid head-shrinker' that [ ] had forced on him.
>
> I asked him if he had located a law firm who would be willing to give him a hand, and he said he had several in mind, but had not yet decided on one. Since I am of the personal opinion that [ ] is one of these, I offered to make an informal check of the firm he selected if it would be helpful. He was most appreciative of this. . . .
>
> He closed by saying that he had more or less sealed off a lot of his relationships with the Agency, but that I was one friend with whom he wanted to maintain contact.
>
> Harvey was articulate, clear-eyed and presentable. I did not receive the impression that he had had too much to drink and he consumed only two beers in my presence.

Bill had applied for admission to the District of Columbia bar on June 5, 1967, while he was still officially on sick leave from the Agency. He retained a shred of dignity in his application. "From September 19, 1947 to date I have been employed by the Central Intelligence Agency in Washington DC and in various locations abroad in the positions of Staff Chief, Division Chief and . . . grades GS-13 through GS-18 ($25,890). I am now in the process of retiring voluntarily from the CIA to resume the private practice of law.

"Among my immediate supervisors during this period have been Mr. Richard Helms, Mr. Lawrence K. White and Mr. Desmond FitzGerald, as well as several previous Directors, Assistant Directors and Deputy Directors of CIA."

Harvey, rather grandiosely, gave J. Edgar Hoover as a character reference. The FBI file copy of Hoover's reply was hardly a positive endorsement. "In 1950, we learned he was unfriendly and hostile toward the Bureau. On 9-10-52, he was reported to be proselyting FBI personnel for CIA [ ] and on 5-6-67, we learned he had applied for retirement from CIA.

No comment is being made concerning the quality of his services and character in view of the above, although while with the Bureau in 1940–1947, his work had been satisfactory."

Bill got his law license. In 1968 George Bailey, one of the Berlin Brotherhood, wanted to throw some legal business in Bill's direction. The two had lunch in Washington. Bailey says that he "had no reason to assume Bill was on the wagon. He had a couple of martinis, but not three or four. Not the way he used to drink. He was still very fat. Not as fat as he had been in Rome, but still overweight."

The meeting was not a good one. "Bill asked me to list all the assets of the Ullstein family," the powerful Austro-German publishing empire into which George had married many years earlier. Bailey was offended by the question. The pair finished lunch and parted, and Bailey never saw Harvey again.[4]

A contrasting, much more favorable view of Bill in the post-Agency years comes from Richard W. Montague, who was a junior case officer and admirer of Harvey at BOB in the mid-1950s. "He 'found a seat' within a Washington, D.C., law firm in which several former FBI agents were active. . . . He handled a couple of personal legal matters for me with great skill in 1967–68, and I will always be thankful to him for his interventions on my behalf.

"I can recall his telling me how difficult he had found it to 'cut the cord' (his exact phrase) from The Agency and go it alone on his own as a lawyer, but also how rewarding he had found it to do pro bono legal work for the poor and for the disadvantaged in Washington. I think he took great pleasure in trying to 'right' matters."[5]

"DEFINITELY QUESTIONABLE"

After his October 4 lunch with Harvey, Howard Osborn dictated a further memorandum for the IG, which must have raised even more warning flags among the CIA hierarchy.

> The one thing I did not include in my Memorandum for the Record . . . was his extreme bitterness toward The Agency and The Director. He did not go so far as to condemn them for his "involuntary retirement," but he did castigate The Director very severely for his selection of [ ] replacement. I have the very uncomfortable feeling, albeit purely a visceral one, that Harvey would not hesitate to use his knowledge of the Johnny operation as a handle on the Director or The Agency if he thought he could benefit from it.

Harvey saw Dick Helms on October 30, 1967. It must have been an extraordinarily painful, tense meeting for both men, although undoubtedly it was conducted in the stiff, formal, phony-cordial, self-protective patois of senior government officialdom. Thereafter, both the CIA and the FBI considered Harvey a potential time bomb.

> DJ Brennan Jr. to WC Sullivan:
>
> On 10/31/67 . . . Helms advised SA Papich on 10/31/67 that he mistrusts Harvey; that he is not going to permit himself or CIA to be blackmailed by anybody; and he has no fear of threats which may emanate from subject.
>
> As far as he is concerned, The Bureau can treat Harvey as it sees fit.
>
> Rosselli is in a position to blackmail CIA. . . . Harvey periodically volunteers information to Special Agent Papich. . . . Harvey's role in this situation definitely questionable.
>
> Osborn advised in strict confidence that he and Helms had very serious doubts that Harvey was divulging all information he possesses concerning subject. Osborn is confident that Harvey is holding out and possibly has become involved in some financial proposition with subject.
>
> OBSERVATIONS:
>
> . . . He very clearly knows that Rosselli is a top hoodlum and subject of a Bureau investigation. Harvey has indicated that he has no intention of becoming involved in any illegal or criminal activities, and that he wants to cooperate fully with The Bureau. . . . Whether or not he has reported adequately is a matter of conjecture. It should be noted that instead of withdrawing from a relationship with Rosselli, he seems to be getting in deeper. His role in this situation is definitely questionable. . . .
>
> Harvey . . . maintains that he has not been able to sever contacts with subject for fear that Rosselli might become antagonized and consequently become a problem. . . .
>
> Harvey has been full apprised of the dangers stemming from any association he may maintain with subject. . . .
>
> SA Papich has been adhering to a line of accepting any information Harvey volunteers. No information is given to Harvey. . . .
>
> [Handwritten comment, author unknown:] We must be very careful in any meeting with Harvey.

[Handwritten comment by J. Edgar Hoover:] Right & vigorously press case against Rosselli.

Harvey met Papich on November 6 and bluntly asked him what the strength of the FBI/Department of Justice case against Rosselli was. Osborn recorded that, "Sam refused point-blank to discuss this, and warned Harvey that he was getting himself in an extremely dangerous position . . . might even be subpoena'ed as a witness at the trial. . . . The Bureau might even be covering their luncheon.

"Harvey described his recent conversations with Rosselli. Rosselli asked Harvey to act as his legal counsel, and Harvey claims he turned him down. . . . He inquired if Agent [Papich] could make any observations regarding the [immigration] case." Papich warned Harvey that he was, in effect, acting as Rosselli's lawyer and that no FBI man could leak information to an opposing attorney. Papich "reiterated that Harvey could not expect anything from him now or in the future. . . . Harvey stated that he knew where he stood. . . .

"At this point Harvey became quite incensed and said that if he broke off his relationship with Johnny, he was convinced that the Agency could get itself in serious trouble. . . . Johnny had no idea that Harvey had been keeping the Bureau informed of this relationship."

When Bill simmered down, he told Papich of "his proposed plans to enter law practice in conjunction with some established legal firm and queried Sam as to his knowledge of any reputable private investigators that might be willing to use Harvey's services to establish contacts and investigative coverage on the Continent. Mr. Papich suggested Wackenhut Corporation or the Fidelifax Company as having a good reputation in the trade."

Hoover's handwritten comment: "Press vigorously."

This and subsequent feelers that Harvey put out to the FBI and CIA have two possible interpretations: (1) he was playing a reasonably sophisticated double-agent game, seeming to keep both agencies informed about the activities of someone who was of extreme interest to both, but in reality, privately, siding with Rosselli, whom he felt was being persecuted, even as Bill himself was being persecuted by the CIA; or (2) he was operating as a conscientious former senior officer of the U.S. government, keeping the appropriate agencies informed of the doings of someone of interest to them and well aware that Rosselli was under physical as well as telephone surveillance by the FBI.

The final memo in the file is a non sequitur written by Hoover to the FBI Liaison Office. In part it reads, "Although it is realized that you will not have occasion to deal with Harvey, you nevertheless should be certain that you be most circumspect in any contact which you may have with him at any time in the future."

JOHNNY GOES TO WASHINGTON

The next step in the complex ballet of Harvey's decline was his notification to the CIA and the FBI that Rosselli would be in Washington in late November 1967. Bill told Osborn on the phone that "Rosselli will stay with Harvey, as he has in the past." Bill added that he was going hunting on the Eastern Shore of Maryland on November 21 and 22, indicating that his health was good enough for that kind of exposure. He also asked Osborn to check out a California law firm that Rosselli had brought into his court case. Osborn noted in his memorandum to Helms, "I do not trust Harvey and will not ask [General Counsel Lawrence] Houston to make any inquiries. However, irrespective of our distrust of Harvey, I believe it is important to keep him as long as possible as window into Rosselli's plans and intentions. . . .

"I recorded both his conversations for our protection. I plan to follow this practice whenever I talk to him, unless you do not consider it desirable." In other words, the CIA's top brass had almost completely swung around to view Bill Harvey, still, technically, a colleague, as an untrustworthy loose cannon, so much so that any conversations with Harvey were now being recorded, in the event that such records were later needed, for whatever purpose.

Bill and Johnny met in Washington from November 26 to November 28. Harvey reported to Papich and Osborn, successively on December 8 and 9, excusing the delay by saying that he had been on a hunting trip.

Johnny chose to stay at the Madison Hotel, not at the Harveys'. The pair met for three hours at the hotel on Monday, November 27, and for eleven or more hours on Tuesday, November 28, partially at the Bethesda Country Club, of which Bill was a board member. Officially, Rosselli was in town to talk with Ed Morgan, the former FBI agent and Jack Anderson source, about buying a radio station in San Jose, California. He appeared to be "well-heeled" and discussed his current love, a twenty-one-year-old California girl. He showed Harvey a copy of his indictment on the immigration charge and a letter of resignation from the Friars Club, where he was accused of skimming a rigged $400,000 card game. Johnny seemed wistful that Harvey continued to refuse to be his attorney.

Harvey told both the FBI and the CIA that Rosselli "continued to deny that he has any other identity or that he is engaged in any nefarious deals. He claims not to have seen Sam Giancana since 1965." Osborn noted, "Harvey says that unlike his past meetings with Johnny, these most recent ones were characterized by some friction, and a sense of resentment on Johnny's part. Harvey feels this is [because] Johnny feels Harvey is working with the U.S. Government and telling them everything Johnny tells him." Rosselli then added that he had other channels into CIA, that he had had lunch with Sheffield Edwards in California, as well as another brief meeting involving the CIA and Robert Maheu, also in California.

Osborn continued, "Harvey is quite resentful of the fact that The Agency did not 'level' with him and did not inform him of those meetings when we first discussed the case with him. I did not respond to this. . . . It is clear that Harvey wants to create the impression at least that he is working for us in this case and must be kept fully informed."

Bill felt that if Rosselli were threatened with deportation he "would immediately subpoena Messrs. Bissell, Karamessenes, Edwards, Osborn, O'Connell and Harvey. Harvey, I believe, slipped at one point when he indicated that Johnny said, 'Just because I was once convicted under the name of Philippo Sacco, doesn't mean I am an alien. I changed names to cover up the conviction.' This, to my knowledge, is the first time Johnny has admitted to using another name."

Then, "I asked Harvey if he was sure that his involvement with Johnny wasn't more than just to protect The Agency's interest. He became highly indignant at this and said that Johnny has no hold on him in the past or in the future. He further volunteered that he had only the highest regard for the Agency and the way we handled his problem. He said he would cooperate fully with us and The Bureau. He added, however, that he would never do anything to hurt Johnny." Read in cold type, it's hard to get the feel of what appears to have been an extremely see-saw meeting, involving a gamut of tactics by a skilled operator who, despite his calm appearance, was probably worried about the fix he had gotten himself into and who was on the verge of being pushed well beyond the pale legally, as well as in fact, when his resignation became final, in a matter of days.

Osborn's summing-up was the culmination of the queasy feelings the top brass had about Bill. "It is difficult to assess Harvey's role in this affair. . . . I cannot help but feel that there is something in his relationship with Johnny that he is concealing, and that his insistence on learning more about how good a case Justice has against Johnny is not entirely in The Agency's interests."

On December 19, 1967, only a couple of weeks before his retirement became official, Harvey's patience appears to have worn out. He called Osborn to ask if the Agency had been able to determine the strength of the Department of Justice case against Johnny and was brushed off. Helms had been "extremely busy . . . and was trying to get away over the Holiday Season." Osborn added that he doubted the CIA would query Justice on the Rosselli case, but would prefer to "sit tight." Harvey suggested that Helms and Hoover might have an "ears-only" conversation. Osborn: "I have the strong feeling that [Harvey's interest in the case] is a self-serving one . . .

"I would be inclined to say that he has already made some kind of deal with Ed Morgan who, as is known, already has Johnny as a client. . . . It is a possibility that Harvey intends to associate himself with Morgan's law firm in the future. I should emphasize that this is my own personal opinion, based on nothing more than speculation." With this statement, the Agency's director of security effectively labeled Harvey hostile to the CIA.

THE END OF A CAREER

In the months following his return from Rome, Harvey had been shunted aside—kept on the payroll but placed on long-drawn-out sick leave, consigned to rehab. The final job of demanding Bill's retirement had fallen many months earlier to Lawrence K. "Red" White. His account of the episode, extracted from an oral history interview, was printed in the CIA's unclassified *CSI Intelligencer*.[6] Perhaps significantly, as late as 1999, the CIA still felt it had to publicly blacken Harvey's reputation.

A Delicate Matter

> One day, I was summoned to a meeting in Dick Helms's office. I go in, and there's FitzGerald, Jim Angleton and, I think, Tom Karamessenes, and I don't know who else, and the subject was: what are we going to do with Bill Harvey? I thought, "What am I doing here?" Jim Angleton spoke up, and he said, "Dick, there's only one man in The Agency that can handle Bill Harvey today." And Helms said, "Who's that?" [Angleton] said, "Red."
>
> I said, "Wait a cotton-picking minute. . . . I've always known Bill Harvey, known he was a good operator and all that, but don't talk to me about taking over this thing now."
>
> Helms said, "You would if I asked you, wouldn't you?" I said, "I guess I wouldn't have much choice, if you ask me." He said, "I'm asking you."
>
> So I took charge of Bill Harvey, and I talked to him immediately.

> I said, "Bill, you've got a wonderful reputation, and you've got a drinking problem. You and I have never had any supervisory relationship, but starting right now, we have a clean slate."
>
> It wouldn't be long before Bill would show up at some meeting just crocked. [I'd send] for him. He'd come in the door, apologizing every time. After about the third or fourth time, he said, "If I ever embarrass you or this Agency again, I'll retire." It wasn't a month until he did; and he came in and said, "I made a promise to you, and I'm here to live up to it."
>
> I said, "Bill, I hate to see your career end this way, but I guess that's the way it has to be." I said, "You've got some sick leave coming, why don't you take that?" So he did, and he hung around town for about six months before he actually retired, but that was the kind of thing, once in a while, as Executive Director, you got into.

Howard J. Osborn recorded the final steps in Harvey's retirement in early 1968. "I met with Bill Harvey on Friday, January 5, 1968 in the Headquarters Building to debrief him of his clearances and pick up his badge. We parted amicably after he had grumbled and groused about the debriefing statements I had made him sign. He said that he plans next month to open offices with a small law firm in the Investment Building, but did not volunteer the name of the firm."

Harvey took the opportunity, however, to say that he didn't think Helms should intercede with the Department of Justice; "[Harvey] does not believe that Rosselli will turn on The Agency or on the Government unless actually convicted and facing deportation."

A CIA memorandum dated June 4, 1968, written by Jim O'Connell, now back in the Office of Security, records that "the FBI recently advised that Johnny Rosselli had been convicted on six counts involving illegal entry into the United States. . . . There may be cautious optimism that he will not divulge his relationship with the Agency for personal gain."

The writer then hangs tough, even cynical.

> One individual holds many of the answers to our quest. This individual is Bill Harvey who took over the role of Case Officer from me in April, 1962. With the exception of a brief social luncheon that I had with Johnny in January, 1966 in Los Angeles, and a one-time meeting Rosselli had with Col. Edwards in Washington DC, all contacts since that time have been made by Harvey. . . .
>
> We must assume that Harvey harbors a deep resentment for

> being terminated by the organization. This suggests the possibility that he may be encouraging Johnny to put pressure on The Agency. . . .
>
> I'm inclined to believe, as a result of my own dealings with Rosselli, that he would not involve The Agency, regardless of the outcome of his personal situation. He gave me his assurance to this effect and fortified this by pointing out that he had spent several years in prison, rather than be a stool pigeon in past activities. However, with Mr. Harvey in the picture, and to a lesser degree, Mr. [Ed] Morgan, it is difficult to say what course of action Johnny may be counseled to take.

Six weeks later, on July 26, 1968, O'Connell filed a further memorandum for the record, about a late night phone call he had from Rosselli. Johnny again asserted he would not ask for Agency testimony in his trials. But then he asked specifically for the date O'Connell had turned him over to Harvey in April 1962.

"At this point, I asked if [Johnny] had seen Bill lately, and he stated that he had, on several occasions, and volunteered that he had been in the Washington area four or five times in the last few months, but did not feel it prudent to contact me. I observed that Bill was in private law practice, having recently received an announcement to this effect. Johnny hesitated, and then said he had been keeping Bill occupied on some legal work in Europe. I asked him if Bill was doing well, and he laughed, but did not comment."

O'Connell met Johnny at the Gaslight Club for lunch on December 11, 1968. "He mentioned that he had seen Bill Harvey the previous day, and I gather he was at Bill's home, as he made reference to Harvey's wife and the fact that they invited him to stay with them, which he declined in favor of the Madison Hotel." Johnny told O'Connell that he didn't need the CIA's help in his legal problems. "He has many other people who are obligated to him that can help him. He implied that some are well-placed in the new [Nixon] administration. He seemed a little emotional when he told me that what he did for us was for himself and his country, and was in an entirely different category [from] things he has done during his lifetime."

Anthony Summers's 1994 interview with the ever-loquacious ex-detective, Joe Shimon, gives some feel of Harvey and Rosselli in the late 1960s. Recall, however, that Shimon liked to place himself at the center of all the action. "When Bill Harvey retired, he opened up a law office here in the Southern Building. . . . Every time Johnny came to town, he stayed at the Madison [*sic*—Johnny may also have at times stayed at the Harveys'.]

"Of course, that was our watering hole. It was only a couple of blocks from the Southern Building, and Harvey would come. And Harvey was a heavy drinker. . . . He could consume twelve martinis, and you'd never know he had one, and that was almost a daily thing.

"While Johnny was there, we'd sit and talk. Of course, that thing [the JFK murder] was over, so it was safe to talk about everything that took place very freely. . . . And any questions I asked, they answered."

Unfortunately, just at that point the tape ends.[7]

WASHINGTON MERRY-GO-ROUND

Rosselli appeared before a federal grand jury, and in 1970, when prison really loomed, he threatened the CIA with further exposure of its role in the Castro assassination plots. He went into detail in a meeting with a Pearson/Anderson representative, in the company of lawyers, on January 11, 1971, and went to prison on January 25.

A CIA memorandum on Rosselli was prompted by a call from Jack Anderson of the *Merry-Go-Round* column and is dated January 14, 1971. The signature is blanked out but is probably that of Jim O'Connell.

During his phone call, Anderson said that O'Connell "undoubtedly knew about Rosselli's present predicament and many people feel he is being given a 'bum rap.' [Anderson's] sources feel that as a result of Johnny's participation in certain government projects, he should be given a hero's medal rather than be deported. He went on to say that he understood that Bill Harvey and myself had directed Rosselli in a CIA venture in Miami which had to do with the Bay of Pigs. He asked if I knew Harvey and I said I did." Anderson tried to bait O'Connell with an allegation that Harvey had been the boss. He "asked if I was in Miami with Harvey and Rosselli at any time. I told him I did not want to discuss the matter any further. He could not be discouraged." Anderson tried to plead on Johnny's behalf, but the CIA officer "abruptly concluded the dialogue."

Anderson next had his assistant, Les Whitten, track down Harvey, who was by now living in Indianapolis. The memo continues, "Whitten tried to get substantiation . . . by calling Harvey, who was then retired from the CIA. 'I'd like to help, but I can't,' Harvey said." Whitten's version of the contacts came in a sworn affidavit to the U.S. District Court, Central District of California, dated February 17, 1971, in support of a plea to reduce Rosselli's prison sentence.

> I twice called William K. Harvey, a retired Central Intelligence Agency official, now of Indianapolis.
>
> On my first call, in January, I asked Harvey if it were not true that he had personally intervened with the Justice Department in order to mitigate the government's prosecution of Rosselli on the basis that Rosselli had done a formidable service for his country. Harvey said, "this is a long story. . . . I don't think it ought to be printed." I asked him whether it was not true that he had a high regard for Rosselli. "I still do," he earnestly replied.
>
> . . . I called Harvey again in Indianapolis, this date [February 17, 1971] and asked him whether he could comment on our story about Rosselli which by now has been published widely in the United States. He declined to comment. But he twice reaffirmed his "high regard" for Rosselli. . . . He expressed concern for Rosselli and said he would "follow up" on Rosselli's behalf from his end.

Six weeks later, on March 1, 1971, the CIA decided it had to intervene to protect its interests. Lawrence Houston and Edwards or Osborn called upon Immigration and Naturalization (INS) commissioner Raymond Farrell. "Houston got to the point by stating that we were concerned that Rosselli, in attempting to fight off deportation, may subpoena Bill Harvey and [O'Connell] to show that he worked for the Government, and use us as a plea for clemency."

The INS commissioner launched into a complicated explanation. Deportation would take a couple of years, and the Italian embassy would have to produce a document acknowledging that Johnny was Italian. It was INS's experience "that the Italians are reluctant to issue such a paper on an individual of Rosselli's ilk as they feel that he is a product of our environment and would prefer not to accept him back."

In a subsequent memo, the INS commissioner is quoted as having "assured us that they had no intention of returning Rosselli to Italy."

DISGRACE AND DRIFTING

Tom Polgar recalls that sometime in 1966–67, Sally Harvey and the Polgars' daughter exchanged overnights. "Bill was on the Board of Directors, Bethesda Country Club, and sponsored us for entry there.

"He was not like the man I knew in the late '40s and '50s. . . . [CG and Bill] were still spitting venom about Rome station personnel and about John and Robert Kennedy. CG seemed to do most of the talking. Bill seemed rather withdrawn and quiet."[8]

A resumé Bill put together, probably around 1971, said he was "6 feet tall, 200 lbs., Health Excellent. Married, two children, 24 and 13."

He summarized his work experience from BOB to JMWAVE thus: "I directed units of 30 to 500 employees. These employees ranged from clerk typists to GS-18 level executives, including military personnel, scientists and specialists . . . also included assignment, career development and evaluation with supervision of personnel records and procedures.

"I have an intimate knowledge of western Europe and the Middle East (12 yrs residence there). I have an excellent knowledge of German, usable Italian, fair French and some Russian." The last assertions would have considerably amused even his close friends.

That was the surface Harvey, out on the streets, looking for work. I asked Ted Shackley if Bill had been despondent after his retirement. Ted's answer was laconic. "It was another phase of his life. He had to adjust to it. He was not visibly bitter.

"Physically, he was beginning to have heart problems. He kept losing weight, then gaining it back. He stopped drinking for a while.

"After he retired, he did some investigative work for corporations here in D.C. But he didn't feel he had to work at it."[9]

JOHN BARRON ON THE OBSCURE YEARS

The final memorandum in Bill's FBI personnel file, dated June 12, 1969, notes that Harvey called Cartha DeLoach, a very senior Bureau officer, to make a matter of record that he had been approached by John Barron of *Reader's Digest* for cooperation on Barron's monumental book on the KGB. Harvey wanted to record that "he would probably talk with Barron."

Barron is one of the doughtiest supporters of Harvey, whom he first met when Barron was a Navy officer in Berlin in the early 1950s. The friendship waned until both were in Washington at the same time in the late 1960s.

"When I learned he was in law practice, I invited him to the very elegant *Reader's Digest* office on Rhode Island Avenue. . . . We had a drink, and he gave me the benefit of his judgment on the KGB. Then and later, he helped me a lot on the KGB book . . . gave me guidance and insights.

"He was practicing law then, but a lot of people don't know that he did a lot of pro bono work for his friends. . . .

"We developed the habit of meeting around five in the afternoon, having a few Scotches, talking till seven or eight, then going out to dinner, where we might have a glass of champagne and a bottle of wine.

"When RD first considered attempting the book, we did what amounted to a feasibility study." Bill helped Barron evaluate the confusing Soviet defectors. "Harvey gave me profound advice. . . . He told me how to appeal to the various foreign services. If you read the book, you'll notice stuff from the Middle East . . . from Syria and Lebanon. Significant stuff. That's because Bill told me [to cast a wide net].

"He facilitated meetings with distinguished CIA officers, Win Scott, for instance, in 1969–1970, when he was still in Washington. It got to be, I was taking more and more of his time. He began to review draft chapters.

"The *Reader's Digest* never paid anyone for an interview, but I thought it was unfair. . . . I didn't want to take too much advantage of him, so we offered to pay for his expertise. Bill answered, and I'll never forget it, 'What we are discussing is not for sale or barter!' Thereafter, and because of that remark, it never occurred to me later to suggest we collaborate on a book."[10]

HARVEY AS A ROMANTIC

Was Bill upset about leaving the Agency? Sally says, "He would never have let us know something like that, but it must have been a hell of a wrench for him."

There is a whiff of a story that his Chevy Chase house was burglarized in about September or October 1967, but we have no details. Sally Harvey recalls, "Dad said he was a marked man. There were bugs in our house in Washington. The Agency sent people out to debug it.

"We never felt the pressure, ever. I can't put emotions like 'sad' or 'depressed' on him. I simply didn't see them."

Despite all the ups and the many downs of his last years around Washington, it may be well-nigh impossible to picture Harvey as a romantic. But he had his moments.

Sally recalls that at some point, while they were still in Chevy Chase, Bill went to London on business and returned triumphantly with a beautiful one carat diamond, complete with authenticity certificate, which he presented to CG, to whom he never had given a ring. It was during a period when the family's finances were iffy, and CG was upset about the expenditure. She never wore the ring, which, prudently, went into the family's safe deposit box.

Harvey more than once showed this streak of impulsiveness. Once, when they were broke, he bought Sally a seventy-five-dollar christening dress, which provoked CG to ask, "Jesus, Bill, what are you doing?"

Then there was the time that he "went out and sold Mom's white

Ford station wagon—the one she had in Rome—just went right out and sold it, and bought a Dodge RV. One of those with a pop-top. He was so proud of it! It could sleep six. The back seat folded down to make a bed, and there were cots for us kids."

CG screamed, "What the hell have you done?"

Bill explained, "We're going to go camping for two months. . . . We'll go out the southern route and come back the northern way. We'll see the U.S. Hell, I know Europe better than I do my own country. . . . I even got a vehicle that has a toilet in it, just for you!"

CG did not come on the trip. Bill and his two kids drove off across America. "Bill had been an Eagle Scout, remember. He cooked over a campfire all the time. We had to stop at every saloon, too, to see the history." Sally says Bill was not drinking on the trip. "But Jim finally said, 'I'm not getting out of this car any more!'

"We did Kentucky and Tennessee, Wyoming—we saw Old Faithful and the bears, and Colorado, and North and South Dakota, Canada. We came back to Washington through Indianapolis."

When they got back, they beheld CG's revenge. She had put an addition onto the house in their absence. When Bill went back to work, he left the van with CG "to go shopping in." She soon "bought something more suitable."

"Was he happy? Yes, I guess so. But I really can't remember. If Bill talked to anyone, he talked to Mom, but he shielded us.

"I had a happy time in D.C."

Bill worked, probably in criminal law, for an outfit called Bishop Services, and he tried to practice on his own for about a year. "One dinnertime, Mom was on edge. Dad had to go out to meet a client, in a very bad section of Washington, at a very late hour. Even Dad was skeptical about the meeting, but he went.

"Then one day, he came home and said, very suddenly, 'We're moving.' I really didn't want to move out to Indianapolis."[11]

At some point, the Harveys must have assessed their situation and decided Washington 1969 was not Berlin 1956. Bill, for all his bravado, undoubtedly felt cut off from the brotherhood that had once crystallized around him. Maybe he felt bitter that the brothers so rarely looked him up or, when they did, that they acted awkwardly and could talk so little shop.

The possibility of making a respectable living in the capital must have seemed increasingly illusory. He managed to find odd legal jobs here and there, including some work for Rosselli, but the contacts he had—people like Ed Morgan—just didn't want to know. Bill's copybook was too stained.

Maybe Bill just felt life would be safer and more comfortable back in the Midwest. By 1970 the years of battering his physical self had taken their toll. The house next to his mother in Indianapolis's northern suburbs was available. Maybe that was the decisive factor: Why not retreat to midwestern tranquility?

TED AND BILL

One of Harvey's closest friends over the years was Ted Shackley, who died in December 2003. His widow, Hazel, who met Ted while working at Berlin Operations Base, reflected on that friendship some months after Shackley's death. "We were really good friends, all four of us. He used to stay with us when he came down to Miami; CG came and stayed with us in Bethesda after Bill died.

"It was a friendship based on mutual respect. But it took a while to develop. Neither of them gave their trust easily. Like a couple of boxers feeling each other out, at first. Then they became close, really close."[12] Harvey probably let Shackley as close as he'd let any man, save Rosselli. Yet Harvey and Shackley's friendship was one that yielded little to inquirers or to history.

13

BACK HOME IN INDIANA

CG Harvey undoubtedly campaigned strenuously to get out of metro Washington. Bill probably caved because he wasn't getting anywhere in the law business in the capital and many of his friends were otherwise occupied. Part of the decision may also have been based on the toll his life had taken on his health. Maybe he felt the need to come back to his roots and to succor his mother at the end of her life, and then, the house next door came onto the market.

Moving out of the seat of government was psychological resignation, a cop out; he was turning his back on what had been an absorbing way of life, even if, during the last few years, he hadn't really been part of it. Indianapolis was obscurity, but not an entirely welcome change. And in Bill's eyes, he was just as vulnerable in Indy as he had been in and around D.C.

Were there reasons other than the tug of the Heartland, mother, and the availability of accommodation? Did the move also have something to do with Johnny Rosselli? With the geographical location of Indy, not all that far from Chicago? In light of what follows, perhaps some other factors played into Harvey's decision to move.

As Bill and CG established their new life in Indiana, Sally Harvey grew into her teenage years. Today she recalls, "Bill found the job editing law decisions for Bobbs-Merrill drudgery! He needed stimulation—a challenge. And he didn't have that in Indianapolis. . . . There was no one here for him to connect with."[1] Bill scrawled little notes from humorous cases on scraps of paper so that the whole family could enjoy them around the dinner table. There were the horses and bridge and the church. Sally still called Rosselli "Uncle Johnny."

Bill did not let his guard down in Indiana, but seemed, rather, even to increase his readiness for trouble. His protectiveness of young Sally seemed almost to verge on paranoia. Did he have a premonition? Was his caution just the continuation of habits ingrained over years? Sally mentions that her father continued to make "trips" overseas. Why did he go abroad? At whose behest?

To the minister of his church, Rev. David P. Kahlenberg, Harvey once said, "There's a price on my head."

"From whom?" Kahlenberg asked.

"The KGB."

"He was always on his guard. He felt he was being watched," Sally says. After he left the CIA, Bill was "mostly sober, but CG was constantly after him to cut back or even stop his drinking."

THE GATEKEEPER

In Indianapolis, Harvey had few people with whom he could discuss common interests, but CG, the gregarious heartlander, felt right at home.

Maybe twice a year, the Harveys went down to Shelbyville, on the road to Cincinnati, for a weekend with Art and Sudsy Thurston. Art was one of Harvey's old pals from FBI days, one of the triumvirate with Dennis Flinn. The trips to visit him were a sheer pleasure. The two men sat on a riverbank, downing a few, reminiscing about days in the Bureau and the Agency, and firing a toy cannon across the river, laughing like delighted kids. Bill may have opened up to Thurston. Thurston, suffering from late-stage Alzheimer's disease, could not comment on the visits or the conversations, and Sudsy is long dead.

After he retired, Flinn made it a point to stop off in Indiana to see Art. But they never managed a reunion of all three. There was something about the atmosphere in Indianapolis. Flinn felt as if a visit to the Harveys' would not be welcome. He said, "CG was the gatekeeper."[2] "The gatekeeper" remark struck an odd, lingering note. It hurt Flinn that he had not been able to see his old pal.

Dennis had known Libby Harvey, and it's conceivable that, even decades later, CG wanted to keep the past sealed. Then, too, in Indianapolis, after he got sober, Bill was only a shadow of his former self. Perhaps CG wanted Harvey's oldest friend to remember him as the robust iconoclast he had been. Or maybe it was that CG feared Bill would confide to Flinn matters so sensitive they shouldn't be mentioned, even to one of the triumvirate, especially matters concerning Rosselli and the things that friendship had gotten him into.

It was Flinn who queried Harvey after his Church Committee appearances about the shortcomings of Bill's testimony. And it was to Flinn that Bill replied, memorably, if succinctly, "They didn't ask the right questions!"

A BUNCH OF RAGAMUFFINS

In young middle age, Sally is a petite blonde of sinewy build. She used to do laps in a swimming pool but had to give the exercise up because of the turmoil attendant on CG's death, which happened only a few months before we met. In a quiet moment, she hazards a querulous aside, as if the very thought was disloyal to the memory of Bill and CG. "Did you ever hear anything more about . . . Christa, my real mother? I think she married." Then Sally quickly changes the subject.

During her formative years, CG was the cop in the family. Bill, the softie, yielded, as do most fathers, to the blandishments of his daughter. "Dad always brought presents back from his trips. He never really disciplined me. Mom would ground me for the weekend, and then I'd tell Dad there was a party I just had to go to, he'd say, 'Well, how about if we ground you until Friday noon?'

"I really didn't get to know Dad until Indianapolis. It was the first time we really were a family! Out here, we were always together. He loved baseball, and he'd take us to games. We were a bunch of ragamuffins. Dad thoroughly enjoyed being back in a family situation. . . . CG was the glue that held us together."

CG took Sally and Jim to Berlin for Sally's tenth birthday. At one point, they were at Checkpoint Charlie, standing on one of the wooden viewing platforms that then looked over the wall into East Berlin. Nearby was a German, about thirty, talking guardedly to his wife, his mother, and his kids, all of whom were still in the East. Suddenly the East German sentry fired a single shot over their heads. The family scattered. The man broke into heaving, wrenching sobs. CG cried too and, through her tears, said to Sally, "See, that's Communism."

HOMELIFE

In Indianapolis, Bill used to sit in his favorite chair with his back to the front window, reading, always reading. He was fascinated by military history, and he took a reluctant Sally to Gettysburg more than once. "He knew where every damn bullet had been fired. I'd say, 'Aw, c'mon, Dad!' and he'd still continue, until he finished that particular story!"

And still, all those years after Indiana University, with all that had happened in between, he could still recite poetry and Shakespeare;

indeed he had poetry-quoting duels with his mother, recalling pieces he learned in school.

Sally continues, "He didn't exercise. He walked and groomed his mare, Bertha, but he didn't ride her. She had been abused by her previous owner, but she really settled down after they bred her, and she produced the filly, Lady Meyers. Then he bridle broke the filly. Mom taught him because she grew up around horses. . . .

"Bill had a way with animals. He always wanted a dog, but Mom wouldn't let him have one. She had Oriental rugs. . . .

"CG was the public face of the couple. She did the social life, but she was also tough as well as intelligent. CG was the only woman who was ever able to keep up with Dad intellectually."

Harvey and CG practiced and played bridge four or five times a week. CG really hoped to become a Life Master before she died.

They went to the Riviera Club, an emphatically dry country club with "a really huge pool" and "good, solid buffet food!" And, "Mom gave fantastic dinner parties, even though that was not a primary way of entertainment in Indiana."[3]

Herb Natzke, the last of the brotherhood to be chief of base, Berlin, visited Harvey in about 1973 on his way back to Washington from a vacation in Wisconsin. "Bill had stopped drinking. He was still overweight, but looking good." Bill showed Natzke Bertha, who nuzzled him.[4]

COVER BLOWN

Sally never told her school friends about her own or her family's background. But their anonymity exploded when the *Indianapolis Star* ran a wire story that Bill would have to testify before the Church Committee.

Sally says, "Dad was shocked!" She was a junior in high school at the time. "My government teacher made some half-assed comment about Dad. I just turned around and walked out.

"There were lots of media calls. Dad became the most nervous I had ever seen him. He said to all of us, 'You do not talk to anyone on the phone!' He had a strong concern about being recorded on the phone. We just hung up on all of them.

"Dad was always very cautious with me . . . checked on my plans. . . . Sometimes he came to pick me up, at the furniture store where I worked for a while, to escort me home in our two cars. . . . One day, there was a car in the parking lot" that followed Sally as she left in her own car. She pulled into a Steak & Shake and called Bill. "Dad came and got me. As soon as he got out of his car, they took off.

"Dad drilled into my head, 'You need to be aware of your surroundings, always!'"

Harvey "always sat with his back against the wall." Sally remembers circling an Indianapolis government building while Bill was inside, getting a gun permit. Suddenly she realized Bill might actually have to use his gun, and shortly thereafter the family had a discussion about what the jurisdictional problems might be if Harvey had to shoot someone.

It's possible, of course, that Bill's precautions came or were stepped up as the Church Committee swung into gear and as Harvey realized that he might become a publicized figure in the Washington hearings. But the general tone of Sally's remarks seems to indicate that Big Bill's sense of security did not diminish once he settled in Indiana, rather, to the contrary. The question remains: Why?

Oddly, says Sally, Bill had no safe in the house. "The feeling was that if there was a break-in, it would have been to kill Dad. We were always on hyper-alert status."

Was Bill paranoid at the time of the Church Committee hearings in 1975? Sally replies vigorously, "No! Not at all!"

Yet after Bill's death, the family discovered weapons stashed all over the house in sofa cushions, in air vents, crawl spaces, behind furniture. Jim, who was then living on the Pacific Coast, took two duffel bags full of guns to register them with the Los Angeles Police Department, "and the cops were flabbergasted." CG gave other guns to Art Thurston, down in Shelbyville, to dispose of.

PASTOR DAVID KAHLENBERG

Sally's birth mother made it a condition of her daughter's adoption that she be raised Lutheran. As a result of the stipulation, the Rev. David P. Kahlenberg, pastor of the Pleasant View Lutheran Church in a northern Indianapolis outskirt became the most influential man in the last stages of Bill Harvey's life.

When the family returned from Rome in 1966, Kahlenberg was pastor at St. Paul's Lutheran Church on Nebraska Avenue in Washington, D.C. Another minister had forewarned him that Harvey was not easy pickings. Sure enough, "almost at the outset, Bill said, 'Don't get any fancy ideas I'm going to join your church,'" just because he brought Sally into the church.

Shortly thereafter, Kahlenberg was called to Indianapolis where he became pastor to former U.S. Senator Homer Capehart and where he also comforted a former governor's wife when she was dying of cancer.[5]

The Harveys renewed their connection with Kahlenberg when they moved to Indianapolis. Sally: "Pastor Kahlenberg's sermons floated on an intellectual plane which appealed to Dad." They were "relevant to current events: America is a divine experiment in democracy. A light to the world." Bill at first mistrusted the concept of "a divine plan," which was Kahlenberg's theme on national holidays, but for the last years of Bill's life, and for CG's remaining quarter century, Kahlenberg was their source of strength.

One early spring morning in 2002, sitting in the wintergarden of Sally's house, Reverend Kahlenberg recalls, and it's almost as if Harvey's deep bass voice fills the room, "At first, Bill scared the heck out of me. That ring of authority! He had the strength of a Hannibal!" Kahlenberg is of an unassuming exterior, but his facade peels away gradually, as he allows his warmth and his love of humankind to show through.

"Bobbs-Merrill was a safe environment for him. He found something where he could use his talents. He wasn't always on his guard.

"Through Sally, I got to see Bill's soft side. She could do no wrong." Sally is slightly teary during this conversation, which takes place only months after her mother's death. "Then he began to show he cared for people . . . if he trusted you. . . .

"In time, he mentioned the pressures he had worked under."

Kahlenberg draws a deep breath. "One Sunday there was a small congregation at the 8:30 service, so I had the ushers rope off the last six rows. Bill came in, and he very abruptly pulled the ropes down, and proceeded to sit in the last row, with his back against the wall.

"After the service, he stormed in my direction and said, 'Don't you know the KGB has a price on my head, and I have to sit with my back to the wall, in any building?' Then he opened his coat, and revealed a gun in a shoulder holster, which he said he always had with him.

"He knew he had gotten through to me. . . . I assured him the ropes in the rear row would never happen again."

"HE NEEDED TO HAVE HIS FAITH VALIDATED."

Reverend Kahlenberg continues, "One day, Bill called me. 'I want you over here. Now!' It was a command performance!"

What followed was classic Harvey. The only thing missing was the .38 Police Special on the desk, pointing right at Kahlenberg.

"Bill had between twelve and fifteen places marked in his Bible, from beginning to end. He was troubled by some of what he had read, both intellectually and emotionally. He asked, 'How can a rational human being believe some of this stuff? Take Genesis. Do you really feel it's actual history? Do you really believe the world was created in six days?'

"I told him, being a geologist myself, from college, I did not and would not believe the Universe and the Planet Earth were created in six twenty-four-hour days."

Next Harvey asked, "Adam and Eve. Did a Creator start the human race with just two individuals?" Kahlenberg: "As concisely and honestly as I could, I told him that the word 'Adam' in Hebrew means 'mankind,' and the word 'Eve' means 'womanhood.' And, no, I didn't believe that the human race began with just two persons.

"Next, Bill went to the New Testament and asked several questions about Jesus, especially about His divinity and His miracles. I told him I had no problem believing Christ's miracles because I had come to the point of accepting that his twelve disciples would not have died for a lie.

"After many such questions, Bill closed the Bible, and, looking me squarely in the eye, said: 'When can you baptize me?'"

Kahlenberg says his reaction was, "You're kidding?!"

Harvey, says the minister, had by now recognized some questions could not be answered rationally. "I know spiritual transformation when I see it. We're all skeptics, but we learn and we take a great leap of faith."

The actual baptism was done discreetly, on a weekday evening, with only family present. CG was "ecstatic when Bill decided to be baptized," although she refused baptism for herself at the time. "In time, Bill became a member of the governing board of the congregation I served."

Some time later Pastor Kahlenberg, in the throes of an unwanted divorce, was ordered to resign by the local bishop. Sally: "Pastor was almost dead with what he had gone through. He was a toxic color."

Kahlenberg recalls, "Harvey read my typed resignation . . . and tore it into pieces. So, thanks to Bill Harvey, I stayed in the ministry and at Pleasant View Lutheran Church for a while." But the bishop insisted, and Kahlenberg had no option. He remained a minister but had to leave his parish.

Bill wrote the clergyman, "My heart goes out to you. We support you. Let me know what we can do. You are in my prayers."

Kahlenberg: "The one reason I'm still in the ministry is Bill Harvey."

"Then, not long after Bill's death, CG said she was ready to join. . . . She also became a member of the church council and served as a youth adviser for the teenagers as well."

HEALTH

Sally Harvey, who was in her teens in the 1970s, cannot recall that her father ever had any medical problems. She says that when Bill left the Agency, the admin people asked him what he wanted to do with all his accumulated sick leave, apparently still a positive balance, even despite the leave he had used up pending his retirement. Except for the enforced indolence in 1967, Bill had never taken a day off sick in his entire career. "And that's amazing when you consider the stress level at which he worked! And . . . and he smoked five packs of unfiltered Camels every day. Five packs!"

Yet Ted Shackley and a few others remember Harvey having heart and leg problems in the 1960s. And Clarence Berry, the Berlin Tunnel support officer, saw Bill in Suburban Hospital, Bethesda, in the spring of 1973. "I can visualize him shuffling down the hall. I believe he was in a green robe when we first met. We both said, 'What the hell are you doing here?' Bill said, 'I got a little problem,' and I said the same thing.

"We sat on a couch and discussed the old days, and he growled something about that SOB George Blake, among other things. There is absolutely no doubt in my mind about this. It must have been in early 1973."

Bill's state of health is important, in view of the suddenness of his death a couple of years later and the disbelief it caused among many people. It is, of course, impossible to get his medical records without the next-of-kin's consent, which was not forthcoming.

14

A MURKY PASSAGE: BILL HARVEY AND THE DEATH OF MICHAEL CHINIGO

So there was Bill in Indianapolis, in wavering health, performing a perfunctory job in which he tried to keep himself interested, a devoted family man, amateur horse trainer, baseball fan, bridge player, upstanding member of his church, and occasional traveler abroad.

Did his past come back to haunt him in Indy?

Despite the outward tranquility of his life, there was cogent, even pressing, reason for Bill's continued caution, which was certainly more than just the prudence of a longtime counterintelligence officer. Harvey was very, very wary of inimical forces, which he labeled, publicly, as KGB but which could hardly have been Soviet. By 1973, his knowledge of the CIA was dated and, as we have noted before, opposing intelligence services of any standing do not murder each other's people. It is more likely that Bill's vigilance was based in a domestic American concern and that he covered that concern with the more palatable explanation that the Soviets were out to get him. The question is, of which stripe were his true enemies? And were they so inimical that they would truly want to murder him?

Almost everyone who knew Harvey in the Cold War—those who bore him enmity excepted—wishes, devoutly, that his story would have had a mundane ending, involving him laying off the booze in a nice suburban house with family, friends, and community respect. Yet two questions hang over the memory of Bill Harvey, first being the question of foreknowledge of the JFK assassination. To delve into the second, we meet interesting new characters.

Apart from his testimony to the Church Committee, the biggest event in Harvey's latter years was the entrance into his life of Marajen Chinigo, whom he had certainly known of while he was in Rome a decade earlier. When Harvey and Chinigo connected in the United States in the 1970s,

Marajen was still married to her most recent husband, Michael Chinigo, though their marriage was teetering. Michael Chinigo was a journalist of sorts and also a former Office of Strategic Services (OSS) agent, an honorary papal count, and an owner of Sicilian property given him under peculiar circumstances. And there was more.

THE ALLEGATION

Joe Shimon was the only outsider on record who could be even partially authoritative on matters concerning dealings between Johnny Rosselli and Harvey. Richard D. Mahoney in his book, *Sons and Brothers*, writes that there was a "little problem Johnny took to Bill Harvey. One of Rosselli's old flames, the wife of a newspaper publisher, had called him in 1973 to say that her husband had put out a contract on her. Could Rosselli help? According to the story Rosselli told Shimon, he turned to Harvey, who did the job himself.

"The husband died of a massive (and induced, Rosselli says) heart attack. Whether the story is true or not, here was Rosselli ten years later claiming that he and Bill Harvey were still trafficking in murder."[1]

Mahoney cites a statement by Shimon to the FBI, dated September 8, 1976, i.e., shortly after Rosselli's death. Shimon had no axe to grind, except the fact that he loved being a source. It's possible that Shimon's tale was true, that Harvey did volunteer to take care of Michael Chinigo, a man he almost undoubtedly knew.

Sally Harvey says, "Around 1974, after he got out of prison, Uncle Johnny came to visit us, and then Dad drove Johnny to Chicago. . . . No! To Champaign. . . . And we came along. Johnny had a girlfriend there who owned the local paper. She was flamboyant, sort of exotic looking, wild, long hair. Sexy, but aging. Made a very big impression. Strange woman."[2]

MARAJEN STEVICK AND MICHAEL CHINIGO

It must be stipulated that, in what follows, a number of sources I talked with flatly refused to be identified for what seemed to me to be good cause: in one way or another, their livelihoods and their pensions depended on the goodwill of Marajen Chinigo and her estate.

That said, let's look at the dowager of Champaign, Illinois. Marajen Chinigo was born on September 12, 1912. She approached her ninetieth birthday determined to stave off death as long as she possibly could, but shortly after arriving at that milestone, she died.

Marajen is limned in the *Champaign News-Gazette*'s official corporate biography as being the very hands-on executive of the Champaign media miniempire created by her father in a 1919 merger. The official version of her life is all gracious smiles and good works. She was a beneficent philanthropist, a patron of the arts, and a painter in her own right. Mrs. Chinigo gave handsomely to causes she supported, among them Oral Roberts University in Oklahoma.[3]

The *News-Gazette*'s version excludes the spiteful streak she showed if she felt her interests were crossed. One who knew her well said she had "an exaggerated sense of paranoia." Someone else said, "She'll lie in a heartbeat. . . . She tells stories she comes to believe herself, but always with an eye to her own image."[4]

Marajen always believed she was the center of the universe. She lived to be adored. The family money was a tool to help her waltz her way into the circles of those with whom she sought to consort. She collected men who were achievers in fields of risk, even danger.

If she were done dirt, Marajen's revenge was vicious. With some cause, in 2000 she turned on her top executive, whom she had known since his teenage years, and effectively ruined his life. She had known of the man's shortcomings from 1991, yet proceedings against him were only instituted in 1999. Around 1998, she made discreet, not terribly idle, inquiries about a Mafia hit man whose name she knew, with the idea of disposing of the executive in mind.

Someone says of her early years, she "was one of those midwestern heiresses who went out to the Coast and had to be seen in the company of the movie crowd and the Mob." Another friend adds, "Her whole life was one big party." Others are less complimentary. A former employee says, "She was always an undisciplined child who had wealth coming out of her ears. If you wrapped Elmore Leonard, Harold Robbins, and John Grisham together, they still wouldn't do justice to Marajen Chinigo."

The man I refer to as Marajen Chinigo's conservator has a less cynical take on her life and habits. A distinguished gentleman, the conservator observed Marajen with wry humor and questioned her closely on my behalf.

THE MARRYING KIND

In its obituary, the *Chicago Tribune* detailed Marajen Stevick's six marriages. Two were with the same man, the brother of the old-time movie actor, Buddy Rogers. The most notable was with a Texan, Lt. Col. Edwin Dyess of the U.S. Army Air Force. They were married shortly before he sailed with his squadron for the Philippines in May 1941. Dyess was captured by the Japanese when American resistance collapsed; he survived the Bataan Death March, was imprisoned, eventually escaped, and was evacuated by an American submarine. Dyess was killed when he deliberately flew a crippled P-38 Lightning fighter plane into an unpopulated area near Los Angeles rather than crash it into a residential area. Marajen arranged to have his horrific POW camp experiences published in 1944.[5]

Even before she met Colonel Dyess, Marajen shimmered in Los Angeles with her mother. When the high rollers moved out to the desert, she and her mom headed for Palm Springs. Marajen was one of the pioneers, along with Alice Faye and Phil Harris and others, who made Palm Springs and Rancho Mirage bywords in the gossip magazines and later on television. There she met Frank Sinatra and at least one of his Mob friends, Johnny Rosselli. She once commented to a friend, with considerable surprise, "John is really an arsenal!"

Rosselli and Mrs. Chinigo had an on-again-off-again romance that flamed hot in the years before Rosselli was murdered. Immediately after the discovery of Johnny's mangled body in August 1976, the FBI, based on their surveillance and Johnny's chronic telephonitis, came calling, to talk with Marajen about Rosselli. It was evident that Marajen trusted Johnny and that he had considerable influence over her.

MICHAEL CHINIGO

Around the name of Michael Chinigo there hangs a heavy miasma of bad taste, double dealing, petty crime—a feeling that not everything was quite as it seemed to be or should have been.

Michael, son of Dimitri Chinigo, was born August 28, 1908, at Macchia Albanese, Cosenza, in Italy.[6] Of Albanian extraction, his brothers, Dimitri and Constantine, bore first names associated with the Greek Orthodox faith. In his later life, there are vague references to Michael's "Greek connections."

Michael's mother brought her children to the United States in 1915, four years after Rosselli arrived in Boston. The Chinigos settled in Norwich, Connecticut, and prospered sufficiently for Michael to attend Yale. He studied pre-med, started an internship at Bellevue Hospital in New York, then dropped out, allegedly to pursue his medical studies in Italy, but instead, before the outbreak of World War II, he appeared in Rome as a journalist.

A chronicler of OSS's activities in Italy during World War II notes that among the early recruits to the clandestine service was "Mike Chinigo, a reporter for International News Service (INS), who had returned to the States on one of the last ships from Italy, and who would go back under newspaper cover to participate in the Italian campaign."[7] Michael's most legendary exploit is retold in various versions, of which this is one:

> Michael Chinigo . . . accompanied the landing [on the south coast of Sicily] of the Seventh U.S. Army. . . . As he walked along the beach he heard a phone ringing in a house near the shore. Since no one was around Michael decided to answer it. A gruff voice said, "Ah it's you. It is all well, I presume? I have a report here that the Americans have landed in your sector." Chinigo answered, "Oh no, no. All is quiet here. No landing anywhere." "No wonder," the voice said, "In weather like this." Then hung up. The gruff voice belonged to Italian General Achile de Havet commandant of the 206th Coastal Division who was totally deceived by a reporter who happened to speak perfect Italian.[8]

Of course, Chinigo was an OSS agent, not a reporter. The ruse was no accident. Indeed, Chinigo may have placed the call. Later, "the first person to enter [Messina, as the Axis forces retreated] was 'Sorel,' . . . operating under media cover."[9] Sorel was an operational name for Chinigo.

Michael continued to serve throughout the war in Italy and probably knew Lester Houck, Harvey's predecessor in Berlin, and Jim Angleton, who then was a young OSS officer. After World War II, Angleton for a while headed OSS/SSU operations in Italy.

Out of uniform, Chinigo returned to Rome as a Hearst correspondent. It is highly possible that Angleton continued Chinigo as an ongoing contact, principal agent, or even deep-cover case officer in the late 1940s. Angleton was involved at that time in CIA operations against Albania—operations that were quickly and disastrously rolled up because of injudicious, boozy comments made by Angleton to Kim Philby.

It is logical that Angleton would have used Michael Chinigo in the Albanian ops. Not only did Angleton know Chinigo, but Chinigo's family was of Albanian origin, and even spoke a particular dialect, which was used in Albanian pockets, even in Sicily.

The *Chicago American*, one of the old Hearst chain of newspapers, ran a front-page story on Sunday, August 29, 1954—fifteen months after Michael married Marajen—headlined, "**Lowdown on Mafia Revealed** . . . Despite warnings that he would endanger his life, Michael Chinigo, INS

Chief Correspondent in Italy, visited Sicilian strongholds of the dreaded Mafia. . . . He tells herewith what he could and could not find out about the international ramifications of this organization, believed by many to have links in the US."

> I had met the late Don Calogere Vizzini [until his death in July 1954, reportedly the chief of the Mafia] at Villalba while US troops occupied Sicily. . . .
>
> In the meeting with Vizzini I had tried to establish a link between his cooperation with American troops and Lucky Luciano, the American gangster . . . [portion illegible] . . . the U.S. forces during the invasion of Italy. Vizzini had simply smiled and said: "Salvatore Luciana—Luciano as you call him—is an honorable man." . . . I got no further on the Luciano topic.

Chinigo added that Luciano was born in Lercara Friddi, which was in the Mafia "province" run by Vizzini.

The Hearst reporter visited Luciano. "Lucky won't even admit he is an 'honorable man' . . . which is in keeping with the unwritten rule of secrecy, mostly about yourself, if you are a Mafioso. Luciano told me, simply: 'I donna know nuttin.' Then shut up like a clam." Despite Lucky's reticence, the *Chicago American* ran a large photo of Chinigo and Luciano in what might have been cordial conversation.

The story contained intimations that the Sicilian Mafia from time to time sent ambassadors to the United States to help iron out difficult problems among its rambunctious American nephews.[10]

While Harvey was in Rome, a decade after the article on Chinigo was published, the CIA likely maintained some form of covert liaison with the Sicilian Mafia and with the Camorra in southern Italy. Harvey would not have wanted to jeopardize his official cover by visiting the Mafia, unless absolutely necessary. He might go to Sicily to pay a formal call or to negotiate important matters, but he would have left routine dealings to a trusted senior agent. And who was more trusted than Michael Chinigo, an American citizen with perfect cover and mobility and praiseworthy status from his service in the war?

The CIA studiously ignored my Freedom of Information Act requests for OSS and CIA files on Chinigo for more than two years. Finally, the Agency replied that it had searched high and low and could find no mention of Michael Chinigo. This is possible if the CIA cleanses its files periodically. Otherwise, a man like Chinigo, with his rich foreign background and his OSS past would undoubtedly have appeared in Agency files numerous times.

MICHAEL AND MARAJEN

The circumstances under which Michael Chinigo and Marajen Stevick Dyess met are unknown, although it's likely that Marajen and her mother were on a grand tour, absorbing culture and sieving the Continent in search of a European husband with class—all the better if he knew something about the news business. Michael fit the bill almost precisely. Even though he was not even minor nobility, he probably represented what the Champaign ladies thought of as Continental glamour. Similarly he wouldn't have minded marrying into money. Though Michael's divorce from his previous wife, a Romanian, was not yet effective, he married Marajen in Rome on May 7, 1953.

Michael told his bride that he would take her to "one place, an absolute must, for their honeymoon." He said he had spent his childhood there, which may have been a little white lie. For him the destination was more than just romantic, it was "a very spiritual place": a twelfth-century Italian monastery, Torre di Civita, at Ravello, overlooking the Amalfi drive.

The innocent American heiress was totally taken in. Her conservator notes, she "fell in love with the monastery. She bought the villa because Michael persuaded her to. . . . It was in ruins." The couple restored the monastery. "Michael even worked at it . . . laying cobblestones," which sounds unlikely but possible. Marajen Chinigo's conservator continues that Marajen had no understanding of art. "If Michael got it, it was OK with her." Among other things, Michael may have been involved in antiquities fraud. The conservator: "The marriage provided Michael with good cover, great mobility, a private expense account . . . and it also helped in his petty crimes." There is a symbiosis, well-known to customs inspectors and narcotics officers, between the trade in antiquities and drug smuggling.

Gore Vidal lived in Rome from 1962 to 1964, before he bought his own villa at Sorrento, near Marajen. Vidal calls Marajen "Margarine" and says she was "bad news." Vidal continues, "I thought Margarine was just your average good-time girl. Yes, she was a heavy drinker . . . an amiable drunk . . . a playgirl . . . a mother's girl. . . . [She] Always Did The Right Thing."

Michael Chinigo? "A most insignificant person. Plain. Very small. No charm. Boastful. I thought of him more as a crook. He knew shady types of people . . . thugs. . . . He worked for INS, which everyone knew was spook cover."[11]

BACK HOME IN CHAMPAIGN

Back in the United States, Marajen at some time in their marriage made Michael publisher of the *Champaign News-Gazette.* "Marajen treated Michael as the son she never had," said someone who knew the relationship.

Then, in the early 1970s, Michael's eye lit upon a young employee of the newspaper, who is variously described as a reporter or a cleaning woman, depending on who's talking. The glint developed into an affair. Toward the end of February 1974, Marajen had Michael's clothes and books tossed into the street.

One report says, "There was a restraining order on Chinigo. . . . Late in the evening of March 31, 1974, four private security men raced to the Chinigo residence in response to an emergency call about an intruder. Michael Chinigo emerged from the shadow of a low-hanging tree, and the team threw him to the ground. One held him down on the sidewalk at pistol point, "It was like, 'stay right there on the ground, motherfucker!'" Soon thereafter, Michael retreated to Rome.

Despite their differences, Marajen Chinigo asserted when questioned that she had never been afraid Michael would cause her bodily harm. "He never would have done that to me!" During this period, however, she had a goodly number of telephone conversations with Bill Harvey.

OTHER RECOLLECTIONS OF MICHAEL

Few of the recollections people have of Michael Chinigo are flattering. Indeed, there's an aura of sleaze in the memories heartlanders as well as expat Americans have of Marajen's last consort.

Doug Fleming was general manager of the *Rome Daily American* during the late 1960s and early '70s. His time in Rome did not overlap with Harvey's, but he did know Marajen and Michael Chinigo. "Michael had been a journalist, but he married money, so he didn't have to work too hard. Once, he tried to take the *Daily American* over and, when that didn't work, started a competitor, which didn't last." Physically, he was "not a gigolo type. A businessman, not a lady's man.

"You never really knew what he was doing. He was always away. I had no feeling that he was CIA. (Hell, everyone thought I was CIA!) I think maybe he bought the title of papal count. . . . He bought Marajen a ring with a crest."[12]

Michael Chinigo wrote an exposé series for King Features on the Sicilian Mafia in the months before he died. Marajen later told intimates that Michael "had gotten a note" as a result of the series, "saying he had better cool it."

Curtis G. (Bill) Pepper, also an alumnus of the *Rome Daily American* and a former *Newsweek* correspondent, recalls Michael Chinigo as "a son of a bitch . . . a chipmunk-face . . . sleazy . . . looked like the son of a pizza parlor owner." Michael got Pepper to ghost pieces on automobile racing, which went out on the Hearst service under Michael's byline.[13]

Other descriptions paint a man who lived on the law's borderline, not one of the standard expat crowd, nor part of Hollywood on the Tiber, nor one who hung around the storied Rome Press Club, but someone who also did not fit in Champaign. One anonymous observer comments, "Marajen didn't know shit from Shinola as far as Michael was concerned. He was a flim-flam man. Dapper. A conscious con artist . . . flamboyant. She just loved the glamour.

"He never stayed in the United States very much. Always moving back and forth to Italy. He only pretended to run the newspaper.

"When Michael died, we all thought he had been wasted because he was involved with the wrong people.

"She went to pieces. She was overcome with guilt, or whatever.

"But, she never mentioned Rosselli."

Years later Marajen Chinigo told the conservator, "I don't know. . . . Michael was involved in so many things . . . I never understood. . . . OSS? . . . I'm sure he was Mafia. . . . Michael made many trips to Sicily . . . and he always told me, 'It's better that you not know about it.' We were given property by the Mob in Sicily, but I never followed up on it. I didn't know where it was. I never knew."

Michael Chinigo may have been given land, maybe even buildings, deep in Mafia country in return for his role in the liberation of Sicily during World War II. He may also have tried to parlay the Mafia contacts he made during the war to his own advantage, at the very least in art smuggling, maybe also in drug trafficking. Apart from what appeared to be Mafia patronage, he had what must have seemed to be impenetrable cover, as a reporter and as an OSS/CIA asset. But then, maybe he got too greedy, or he thought he was bigger than the Sicilian organization because of his international contacts and he incurred the fatal displeasure of the Sicilians, or of the Camorra.

Finally, I picked up a further-unsubstantiated rumor from one of Marajen Chinigo's former employees. "You know Michael was [reputed] to have committed more than thirty murders, don't you?"

A HARVEY CONNECTION?

How did the life and activities of Michael Chinigo intersect with those of

Bill Harvey? Oddly, Marajen chose not to recall, when directly questioned on my behalf, that she had ever met Harvey while he was serving in Rome. On another occasion, when the subject was something else, she contradicted herself and remarked casually that Bill and CG Harvey had, as a matter of course, been her guests at the villa in Rome. These recollections, it must be said, came when she was aged and not far from death.

The Chinigos and the Harveys must have been, at the very least, nodding acquaintances on the 1960s Roman carousel, although, even if operational security had not been a concern, they would hardly have been close friends. But Marajen Chinigo knew Rosselli from the California desert oasis. Johnny, always the gallant, visited Marajen fairly often in Champaign, when she was free and he was not involved in CIA operations or in prison.

Sometime in the late 1960s or early 1970s, Johnny saw a chance to help his pal, Bill Harvey, who was not prospering as a lawyer and who had experience of Italy. Harvey had already done, and apparently continued to do, some legal work in Europe for Rosselli. From an uncertain date, perhaps not until early 1973, Bill started to advise Marajen on the telephone, and he may also on occasion have visited her in Champaign.

During March and April 1974, Marajen Chinigo, smarting from being tossed aside for a younger woman, increased her attention to Rosselli, now out of federal prison. She had a portrait painted of herself and sent it to Rosselli at his more-or-less permanent perch in California. Toward the end of April Johnny had a rough week with the Senate committee in Washington, and he discussed "a CIA meeting" with Marajen.

Marajen told Johnny she had thrown Michael out of the house because of his despicable behavior with that "cleaning woman" at the *News-Gazette*. She seems also to have told Rosselli she had learned, from sources unspecified, that Michael had put out a contract on her life. Johnny might well have agreed this kind of unseemly, adulterous behavior was to be deprecated. Be it noted that Marajen Chinigo was capable of dreaming up such dramatic allegations with little compunction, if they drew attention to her, or served her purposes.

It can be hypothesized that Rosselli turned the problem of Michael Chinigo over to Harvey, who had contacts in Europe and who, above all, knew the Roman scene. According to Mahoney quoting Joe Shimon, Harvey said he would handle the matter.

In April 1974 Harvey was getting by in the Bobbs-Merrill job in Indianapolis. Rosselli, newly released from prison, went to Washington and then came to Indianapolis. After a night, maybe two, as the Harveys' houseguest, the Harveys and Johnny bundled into the family car and drove to Champaign. On this occasion, when Sally was with them, the Harveys didn't stay long in Illinois, but on another occasion, Bill and CG were Marajen's guests for a lavish dinner at the Champaign Country Club. Whatever the nature of the professional relationship, there is no doubt that the Harveys joined the outer circle of the Marajen Chinigo court.

When drawn into discussion about Harvey in 2002, Marajen said, disarmingly and ingenuously, "He knew some interesting characters. . . . Bill was a very charming person. At a party or reception, he lit up the room. Of course he drank a lot, but he was always the same. Always had his sense of humor." Someone who was close to Marajen notes, "She really liked Bill Harvey. Of course he had problems with the bottle, but she never saw him out of control."

In May 1974 Marajen and Harvey had long talks, presumably about her legal affairs, and Marajen nearly went to Italy. Apparently, Michael had made a move to take control of the Sorrento villa and then reconsidered, perhaps under pressure. Marajen was relieved that she would not have to make forcible entry into what she considered to be her property.

Mrs. Chinigo's discussions with Harvey and Rosselli continued through June, during what appear to have been complicated negotiations with Michael, who had returned to the United States, and lawyers for both sides. Harvey does not seem to have taken part in the talks, yet it would be logical that the connection broadened, as Marajen came to know Bill better and to trust him more. The connection may, indeed, have led to Bill's "work in Europe," so elusively mentioned by Sally earlier.

Among the open questions are whether, how often, and why Harvey traveled to Europe during this period. We have Sally's recollection that he made trips. On whose behalf? Could he take time off from Bobbs-Merrill for freelance work? Was he acting as Rosselli's legal adviser? Had he, finally, accepted Johnny's offer of legal commissions abroad—the offer that Harvey had told the CIA he had initially rejected? Beginning in about 1973, did one of those legal commissions include work for Marajen Chinigo? Did any or all of it have to do with the Sicilian Mafia, with whom he had maintained official liaison when he was stationed in Rome a decade earlier?

MICHAEL AND BILL

It is almost a given that Michael Chinigo would have been, at the very least, a cleared contact of the CIA's Rome office. And it is conceivable that Harvey ran Michael Chinigo personally, perhaps as the Agency's primary conduit to the Sicilian Mafia. If this were the case, Harvey would have decreed that there be only passing social contact between the two as, for instance, at a diplomatic reception. CG Harvey might have been aware of this arrangement. Marajen almost certainly would not have been.

Then there are matters of timing. Michael Chinigo tried forcibly to reenter the marital house in Champaign on March 31, 1974. A Cook County investigator questioned Marajen about Sam Giancana on April 21, 1974. Giancana was murdered on June 19, 1974. Rosselli said, "Everyone knew the date." On the same day Michael Chinigo made a new will in the United States. He returned to Rome in mid-July. Bill and CG were in Champaign for the weekend of July 26, 1974. Shortly thereafter, Harvey talked with Marajen's Roman lawyer.

Rosselli went to Indianapolis to visit Bill and CG in mid-August. On August 14 or 15, 1974, a day or two after the attack on Michael Chinigo, described below, Rosselli and the Harveys drove to Champaign.

THE DEATH OF MICHAEL CHINIGO

Was Marajen Chinigo vindictive (or paranoid) enough to mention, apparently casually, to Rosselli that her about-to-be-ex-husband, Michael Chinigo, had put a contract on her life, even though she appeared to have no firm evidence of such a plot? Or, was there more to the death of Michael Chinigo than simply Marajen's revenge for philandering?

Would Rosselli, a man of considerable experience in matters of the street and of the heart, have taken the wistful plaint as a moral obligation to rid the world of Chinigo? Or would Rosselli have seized upon (perhaps even inspired) Marajen's contract to provide excellent cover for the disposal of an unwanted thorn in the Mafia's side?

Did any cell of the Mafia want revenge on Michael for some sin, for knowing too much, being too unreliable, being too flamboyant and/or too greedy?

If Chinigo was hit at the behest of organized crime, did Harvey play a role in arranging the murder? Would Rosselli have delegated Michael's termination to Harvey because he knew the scene in Rome and wasn't an obvious target of suspicion? Remember the words of Sam Papich: "Harvey had little or no experience working in the organized crime field while in the Bureau. What he may have learned [was] from research, but . . . I can say he was entering a completely new atmosphere with Johnny."[14]

Or are there other plausible explanations for the death of Michael Chinigo?

Why did the Rome police fudge the investigation in Chinigo's death and come to an implausible conclusion? Why did the U.S. State Department and the FBI legal attaché in Rome show no inclination to dig further into the matter? Why does the CIA adamantly contend that its files contain no information on Michael Chinigo?

After Michael Chinigo's death under mysterious circumstances, Marajen populated the bedrooms in her various residences with pictures of Michael in happier days. Why?

To answer these questions, I got in touch with a distinguished American lawyer who for decades had practiced in Rome. We corresponded cordially by e-mail, and he said he would contact a woman who had handled the Chinigo case and who knew far more than he did. I never heard from the lawyer again, despite several attempts. Why did he suddenly halt his helpful support without explanation?

THE ATTACK ON MICHAEL CHINIGO

Michael Chinigo was attacked on a Rome street at midnight on August 13, 1974. He was accompanied by a man named Giarizzo, who was allegedly left lying in the street in a coma, when an ambulance took Michael to the San Giovanni Hospital. A Rome police report identified the .38 pistol that shot Chinigo as Giarizzo's registered property. No further details have ever emerged about Michael's companion of that night.

According to the police report, Chinigo reached into his companion's pocket, grabbed a .38 pistol that happened to be there, shot himself in the left temple with the gun in his right hand, and survived. The Roman police ruled Chinigo's later death, somewhat incredibly, a suicide.

Michael spent two months in a Rome hospital. During that time he was alert and asked for a typewriter, but not once did he communicate to anyone any other version of the incident. On October 3, Michael had surgery to remove bone splinters from his brain. It was supposed to be an easy operation, not life threatening, but Michael died a few days later. No one seemed to think his death untoward.

Doug Fleming, of the *Rome Daily American*: Michael "was not the suicidal type. The guy who was with him was carrying a gun. Those were the days of the Red Brigades. Everyone was getting lots of threats.

"I went to the legal officer at the embassy, knowing he was FBI. [He was] a friend of mine. It was very friendly, casual. He simply said, 'Don't bother yourself. The Italian police are satisfied it was suicide.'"[15]

If the August attack was a Mob hit gone wrong, why didn't the Mafia send someone into the hospital to finish the job? Were they confident Michael was so incapacitated he would never again talk or write? Or did someone try to smother him in the hospital, as Marajen at one point contended?

Michael died on October 11. On October 20, 1974, Rosselli was at Torre di Civita. He or someone else made a final entry in the villa's guest book of that era, "New page, new life . . . affectionately John" and then printed across bottom of page "FINITO." Some pages were ripped from the book.

MARAJEN LEARNS

Marajen first learned of the attack in a phone call from a friend in Rome on August 14. Marajen's friend noted that Michael had lost thirty pounds over the previous three weeks; his friends suspected he had a massive tumor. The hospital doctors were not confident of his ability to survive the head wound, yet in a day or two, he was out of bed and receiving visitors.

On about August 15, Johnny Rosselli, Bill, CG, and Sally Harvey arrived in Champaign at midday from Indianapolis. Mrs. Chinigo professed to be mystified by what had transpired. For whatever reason, Rosselli decided not to tarry and flew on almost immediately to Los Angeles. The Harveys returned to Indianapolis.

As the news trickled in, a depressed and apprehensive Marajen worried that a recovered Michael might return to Champaign and harm her. Mrs. Chinigo inquired through a Champaign lawyer about the safety of her Rome premises and the villa. Mr. Bruno Bacci (further unidentified) "assured us everything had been arranged."

Eight days after the attack, by August 22, Michael was apparently well enough to sit up in bed, write letters, and make phone calls. He specifically wanted to talk to Marajen. As far as can be determined, he never leveled an accusation of attempted murder at his wife or anyone else. He did threaten to talk with the Internal Revenue Service about some jewelry Marajen had illegally imported, unless she came to visit him in Italy. He was apparently able to talk, or communicate in some way, when he chose to.

Doug Fleming went to see Michael in the hospital. "He was walking around. He smiled. But he didn't talk, he just touched the bandage wrapped around his head. Never said a word."

After Michael's death, Marajen cut her social contacts almost completely for a while. A six-man team provided round-the-clock security for her and her premises in Champaign. Despite all the obvious inconsistencies in the manner of Michael's death, no one apparently thought or wanted to ask any pointed questions.

THE HARVEY FACTOR

Had Harvey, at the behest of Rosselli, undertaken to arrange the killing of Michael Chinigo on a street in Rome during a night in August 1974? In November, not long after Chinigo's demise, Marajen had another meeting with Harvey.

Perhaps Marajen Chinigo's distaste for her husband's extramarital affair provided the American and Sicilian mafias with beautiful cover for what was actually a Mob hit. In that case, someone may have conveniently put the fix in with the Rome authorities so that they came up with an innocuous verdict on the affair. Italian organized crime knew the cops. And Harvey certainly knew some of the top brass, even eight years after his tour of duty in Rome ended abruptly. Still, it's hard to think that Harvey would have been complicit in a murder, even if it were an offshore contract.

Mrs. Chinigo remained singularly, vaguely forgetful on the key question: Did she hint to Rosselli that it would be nice if Michael were no longer a nuisance to her, sure that Rosselli would make the necessary arrangements?

Marajen later proved, in the ruination of her top executive, that bygones were not bygones. She at least thought about having that executive hit by a Mafia assassin.

In the case of Michael Chinigo, Marajen may have benefited from the doctrine of plausible deniability. Or maybe she was, indeed, used as cover for a more nefarious plot.

QUESTIONING THE CONTESSA

Confronted with blatant evidence of Michael's infidelity, Marajen must have been mortified. In a "theatrical panic" Marajen called Rosselli, who said, "We'll take care of it." The source for this interpretation of the hit is Joe Shimon, in conversation with Richard Mahoney.

Marajen's conservator muses, "I can't imagine that she would have said outright, 'I want him killed!' I think she'd be too naïve. She would have had dark pangs of conscience!"

Would Rosselli, Marajen's gallant, have passed what amounted to a contract on Michael Chinigo to Harvey? Would Bill have agreed to handle the matter as a heartlander who didn't like the idea of a slick Mediterranean wastrel, even one who had been OSS and a CIA contract agent, cheating on an upstanding American woman? Or because Rosselli now had Harvey under some form of control?

The conservator, brought up some key questions in a number of gentle interrogations of Marajen at Sorrento, back in Champaign in the fall of

2001, and finally, at Palm Springs, again, in December of the same year: Did Marajen recall ever mentioning to Rosselli that she believed Michael Chinigo wanted to kill her? Did Harvey arrange the killing of Michael Chinigo, whose death she has always insisted was not a suicide?

"'Oh, I just can't remember that!'

"Marajen turns blank. There are no signals from her eyes, or anything." The conservator continues, "The idea that Harvey did the job . . . that was a first-time thought for [Marajen]."

But, "Marajen sometimes says, 'They'll never make me believe he shot himself!'"

On another occasion, the same man asked Marajen bluntly, "Could Bill Harvey have killed Michael?" Her first reaction was a grimace of distaste. Then, "Oh, I wouldn't think so. They wouldn't have known each other." Which was false, although perhaps not intentionally so. "Rosselli knew Michael, but Harvey and Michael never met."

The conservator: "She doesn't mind talking about Chinigo, but she brushes aside any talk of the possibility of Rosselli being responsible for, or involved in, Michael's death. She covers it by saying, 'I can't imagine Johnny doing anything. He was always such a gentleman. So well dressed!'"

Why had Marajen not gone to Rome from Champaign when she heard the news of the attack on Michael? Well, it was after she had thrown him and his belongings, physically, out of the Champaign house, and he had subsequently gone to live with "that woman." Plus, she heard that that woman had gone to Rome to visit him in the hospital.

When the conservator reported that Marajen Chinigo was slipping away, both mentally and physically, I told him my suspicion that Michael was the CIA contract agent/liaison to the Mafia in Sicily had hardened. He replied, "I'd bet on it. There were so many little things that didn't add up with him."

SUMMARY

To summarize, the death of Michael Chinigo may have been:

a) a suicide;

b) the result of a contract passed from Rosselli to Harvey, ostensibly on behalf of Marajen Chinigo, and then from Harvey on to one or more parties unknown but probably from the European underworld;

c) because of Sicilian Mafia or Camorra dissatisfaction with Chinigo; or

d) because of American Mafia dissatisfaction with Chinigo.

It is possible that the murderer(s) had enough clout to ensure that the Rome police would not inquire too energetically into the circumstances of the attack, which could have been plotted by a Frederick Forsyth or a Ludlum.

A couple of significant snippets of information came my way from an anonymous source who was friendly with Marajen late in the weaving of the story. The woman says that Mrs. Chinigo "went to see a fortune-teller in Peoria the day before Michael was attacked" and that "Marajen was very agitated during the whole trip!" The fortune-teller told Marajen that something very bad was going to happen to someone very close to her very soon, and "the next night Marajen received a call from Miami that Michael had been shot and died instantly."

In general, the idea of Marajen racing to a soothsayer does not seem surprising, but why the about-to-be widow would want supernatural guidance the day before her formerly beloved was to be wasted is intriguing, if only because it sheds some light on Mrs. Chinigo's state of mind at the time.

More specific is the report that she was informed of the hit on Michael in a phone call from Miami, which almost certainly would have come from Rosselli. This phone call, if it happened, indicates that Johnny knew about the hit. That in turn somewhat increases the likelihood that Harvey may have been involved, perhaps only as a knowledgeable bystander, perhaps as something more.

It's hard not to be suspicious, but there simply isn't hard evidence to prove that Harvey was involved in the killing of Michael Chinigo. In the final stages of his life, Harvey didn't have booze to corrupt his judgment. And committing murder would have been totally at odds with his newfound religious convictions, as well as with his lawyerly respect for the law.

But something very, very strange did happen on that Roman street on the night of August 13–14, 1974.

Gore Vidal: "Chinigo? It was a typical Camorra killing."[16]

15

THE CONSCIENCE

The U.S. Senate's Church Committee looked into the entire matter of the government's assassination programs in 1974 and 1975. When Bill Harvey was called to Washington to testify, he told the truth as he saw it, but he did not answer any questions that were not specifically posed to him. When he got his copy of the draft committee report, he made many at-times-biting marginal notes in it. And, in what was probably the final letter of his life, Harvey expressed the rage and frustration of a senior, career intelligence officer at the damage done by a group of politicians reacting to public naiveté and dismay and the lengths to which the president's brother drove civil servants, trying to wreak vengeance on the man the family hated.

Bill's notes in the committee report are the bald comments of a man whose life was devoted to the covert service of his country, as sublime an intelligence-gathering officer as the United States has produced. The notes reflect disappointment, even disgust, with the charades that took place at the Church hearings, as sometimes-worthy intelligence officers, heretofore men of honor, writhed in their suits, feigned loss of memory, sought to protect reputations, or hustled to be seen as protecting secrets vital to the national interest.

CG Harvey gave Bill's annotated copy of the Church Committee report to Gus Russo, who used an excerpt as an illustration in *Live by the Sword.* That CG passed the copy to a non-CIA person seems to indicate that she thought Bill wanted his views published. Russo, in turn, passed the copy of the report along to me.

HARVEY TESTIFIES

The Church Committee hearings and other inquiries into the JFK assassination were analogous to the multiple post-9/11 hearings on and around Capitol Hill in the early twenty-first century.

Harvey's testimony to the Church Committee was the truth as he saw it. He made an indelible impression on the senators, all of whom showed up on the first day of his testimony to scrutinize the man they considered "America's James Bond." Right at the start, Bill put an object on the table in the hearing room and announced it was his recording device. Only after the senators gasped collectively did he chuckle and reveal it was his Zippo lighter. He had established his persona, and he had their attention.

A prominent member of the committee, Senator Gary Hart, knew the tale of Bill shucking his guns just before entering the Oval Office to meet President Kennedy. "Harvey seemed delighted with the story. Given his appearance, demeanor and especially that distinctive voice and the yellow shooter's glasses, he seemed everything but 007.

"We were all struck by the friendship he developed with Rosselli. Highly improbable. But then, everything about our investigation, especially involving Cuba, turned out to be highly improbable."[1]

Sally Harvey says, "He wouldn't lie under oath . . . but by then, Bill, physically, was a shell."

Sam Halpern: "He answered the questions that were put to him but gave only minimal information. . . . But he wouldn't lie under oath."

F. A. O. "Fritz" Schwarz Jr., chief counsel to the Church Committee, met Bill outside the hearings to prepare him for testimony. "We didn't subpoena him. Bill appeared voluntarily.

"I was surprised when I first saw him. He wasn't at all what I expected. No James Bond. . . . He was, well, pear shaped."

Schwarz and Harvey got on an easy, first-name basis. "Harvey told me the White House story with relish. Said he only gave up two of his guns, but that he habitually carried a third, too!

"He was enjoyable to talk to. . . . A real human being. . . .

"Harvey was not a cold person. . . . He was reaching out. . . . He was very straightforward with us. . . . He had a sense of humor.

"Our private sessions helped refresh his memory. . . . He was candid. . . . He never seemed to evade questions. . . .

"He showed no hostility towards the committee."

I said I thought Harvey had kicked the booze for good by the time of the Church Committee. Schwarz countered, "Are you absolutely sure he wasn't drinking? I'm not."

When our conversation moved on to the substance of the committee's investigation, Fritz Schwarz had an interesting, lawyerly take on his witness. "I got the impression that the Castro operation was never something Bill found at the center of his passion. He was openly contemptuous of those he did not agree with. . . . I definitely got the flavor . . . he thought very little of his bosses . . . especially the political bosses. . . .

"Bill felt he'd been given a job."

Schwarz reflected the layman's discomfort with the secret world's doctrine of plausible deniability. "If I ever would be critical of Bill, it would be that he and Helms both had weird views of whom they should and should not tell about the Castro assassination operations. They saw no reason to tell McCone because they had Dulles's approval, and they thought McCone wouldn't want to hear about their plans. . . .

"Everyone was very, very careful not to dump on a person one level above them."

And then, an interesting comment from a quintessential New York lawyer. In contrast to Harvey, "people like Bissell, who were my [social] type . . . were incredibly amoral." Senator Frank Church of Idaho also commented to Schwarz, "Bissell's so very Ivy League!"[2]

ELUSIVE BILL

During the hearings Harvey went to some lengths to avoid the scrutiny of the Washington press corps and especially to avoid photographers. Sally Harvey recalls, "He had seen what happened to Johnny Rosselli, whose picture was all over the place, especially on the front page of the *Washington Post*. The committee guaranteed Bill's security, but he didn't believe them. He said he would take his own chances."

When he had finished his appearance, Schwarz got Bill out through a side door. Then, with typical ingenuity and a Harvey flourish, he mingled with the swarm of baying reporters and photographers, joining in the cry, "Hey, where's Harvey. . . . Where's Bill?" He surged along with the media frenzy, echoing their cries of frustration, until he slipped away, slid into the taxi CG had waiting for him, and rode off, probably chuckling merrily.

While testifying, Bill stayed with Anita and Will Potocki, two old Berlin hands, because in their home he could escape media attention. One evening, after a day of being grilled, he was sitting in the living room, watching the evening news. Word came that George Blake, the KGB penetration of MI-6 who had been privy to the Berlin Tunnel, had escaped from the British Wormwood Scrubs Prison. Anita comments, "There may still be a grease spot on the ceiling where he hit it. He just exploded at the news."[3]

Ted Shackley: "When Bill came to Washington to testify for the Church Committee, he didn't want me to know . . . didn't want to get anyone else involved."[4]

Sam Halpern: "I didn't see him. . . . We didn't coordinate our testimony in any way. . . . I think he meant to teach those guys on the Hill what life is really like."[5]

Bill and CG were in Washington for a week. Sally was under strict orders not to go out of the Indianapolis house. "I mean, I was sixteen. You don't think I totally obeyed, do you?"[6]

Bill had, by now, ample reason for caution, even if he was not in the direct line of fire. On June 19, 1975, a week before he was due to testify to the Church Committee, Sam Giancana was murdered in the fortified basement of his Chicago apartment. The committee quickly scheduled Johnny Rosselli to testify on June 21. With all the skill of his Hollywood and Las Vegas years, Johnny regaled the enthralled senators with remarks such as "We don't take notes [in my business]." Johnny was called a second time on September 22 and made a third appearance on April 23, 1976.

Harvey died June 9, 1976. On July 16 Johnny, his sister, and her husband had dinner with Santo Trafficante. On July 27 Rosselli was warned by a Mob-connected lawyer in a phone call from Los Angeles to get out of Miami immediately. On July 28 Rosselli disappeared en route to a golf game. Ten days later his dismembered body was found floating in the oil drum in Dumfoundling Bay.

THE CIA'S CHURCH COMMITTEE PERFORMANCE

Bill's sense of disgust at the events surrounding the Church inquiry was echoed in the letter Jim Angleton wrote Harvey and then repeated to CG Harvey, years after Bill's death. Angleton and Harvey felt that their years of dedication to the service and to their country; their contributions toward building a tough, resourceful, alert, and nimble intelligence service as part of America's superpower role in the world had been destroyed, most specifically in the airings of the Church Committee and, especially, in the testimony and revelations of Bill Colby.

Dick Helms, whose prosecution for misleading Congress was enabled by Colby, and many others whose names did not become as widely known, believed in the practice of intelligence as a necessary bulwark for a nation with international responsibilities. They, and most other professional intelligence officers, felt the Church Committee report revealed far too much about the inner workings of the U.S. government. The final coup de grace came after Harvey's death, in the gutting of the Agency conducted by the next director of central intelligence (DCI), Adm. Stansfield Turner, who preferred machines to human intelligence gatherers.

BILL HARVEY'S NOTES ON THE CHURCH COMMITTEE REPORT

Harvey's margin notes underline the fact that the CIA had never gained the trust and status once enjoyed by the British Secret Intelligence Service (MI-6), which allowed it for many decades to be totally professional and wholly apolitical.

Harvey sat in the wings in Indianapolis during most of the Church Committee's inquiry. He watched what he could see, read what was available, and waited. His opportunity to amplify his views about the high drama in the CIA in the early 1960s came when he got an advance copy of the committee's interim report at Thanksgiving 1975.

Harvey's often-scathing comments reflect practically every aspect of his personality and his view of the CIA's hierarchy. They are Bill's paper trail.

And he found much to be scathing about. Even in 1975 he was probably still convinced he would have made a better DCI or, at the very least, deputy director of operations, than many, if not all, of the men who occupied or aspired to that chair during his time. But Harvey never would have made DCI, and by about 1960 he knew it. He was too impulsive and too confrontational in the eyes of the silky senior bureaucracy to be a reliable player in the intricate power game that crunches around Washington's pinnacle. He had shown his recklessness, and his contempt for the structure, during his years in the FBI, again in unmasking Philby, yet again in Berlin—when he recommended the military show of force on June 17, 1953, suggested BOB as the Agency's worldwide anti-KGB center, and recommended force again in October 1956, at the time of the Hungarian uprising—and finally, in his stewardship of Task Force W. Although Bill was a superb operator, for as long as he was capable, those who played at the top-stakes tables did not respect nor condone his habit of rocking the boat.

Perhaps Harvey thought of writing a book, although its publication would have been a dire contrast to his decades of covert service. I suspect that Big Bill, who, despite legends and appearance and bellicosity, was actually as close to egoless as any senior person I have ever encountered, wanted his side to be available to someone, somewhere, sometime.

The penultimate word on Harvey and the committee is Sally Harvey's. "Bill was not the same after his testimony to the Church Committee. He did what he felt he had to do, although it hurt him terribly to talk. His testimony was blunt, honest, brazen."

HARVEYS COMMENTS: "DISNEYLAND EAST"

Here's a sampling of the flavor of Bill's abrasive marginal comments on the Church Committee report:

On Allen Dulles's meeting calendar: "Signified nothing. Fearless Fosdick's calendar was maybe 30% accurate. . . . Obviously Shef would shield AWD, and properly so."

On the question of briefing McCone on ZRRIFLE: "Where was Jake the Fake?"

About the discussion of Castro's assassination in the Special Group Augmented in August 1962: "A loose, insecure assemblage. . . . This was said to McNamara and smilingly related to me by Mac the Knife [McCone] as part of his recounting his protest call to Mc the evening before."

About McCone's personal opposition to assassination as a tool: "I very much doubt this as it here reads. . . . Pat Carter would not have dared tell McCone. . . . Also note McCone's very close relationship with Little Brother."

On CIA Security Office figures recontacting Mafia figures: "O'Connell and Edwards should not have been discussing this in 1965."

On Helms's testimony about Mafia involvement in ZRRIFLE: "Re this and other portions of the report, there is a gratifying absence of offloading by the Boy Diplomat."

And so the notes go for more than three hundred pages of the committee report.

16

INDIANAPOLIS AND DEATH

Home was the heartland, where it had all begun, for both Bill and CG. Sally Harvey says their house, next door to Bill's mother, "isn't a farmhouse, but, oh, the land we have around us! It's like we have our own private forest with deer, fox, squirrels, hedgehogs, and we're within the city limits!"[1]

It's hard to imagine Bill in those surroundings in semiretirement, difficult to imagine him kicking the booze, strange to envision him kneeling in church. But he softened late in life, and when he learned to love, his love for CG, for Sally, and for the horses was all encompassing. Still, the only known photograph of Bill, taken a few years before his death, is a telling slice of an instant in time. Instead of the robust, hood-eyed, super-grade intelligence officer, brusque and bustling with self-confidence, the photo is a mug shot of a nearly broken man with the face of a wizened fellow who has been through a private hell. Behind tinted glasses lurk the eyes of someone who knew, though never admitted, ignominy.

Reverend Kahlenberg: "He unhesitatingly and unashamedly prayed in public . . . and even in those prayers there was not only eloquence, which was one of Bill's trademarks, but there was deep sincerity . . . a deeply devout and devoted Christian, once he came to the conclusion that what we say about God is true."

And, "Bill was a brilliant, clear-thinking, quick, decisive, determined, detail-oriented person who could size up a situation in a flash and know what to do or how to handle a given circumstance." This was the Harvey who had come through the disintegration of alcoholism, yet still, in public had that "razor-sharp tongue when needed. He had a commanding appearance and a deep, authoritative voice to go along with it."[2]

When Herb Natzke visited Harvey in 1974, however, he found him "lonely." "He was very curious about the Agency. Wistful. Nostalgic. Lonely. . . . Subdued . . . but still way overweight."[3]

But Harvey being Harvey couldn't leave this mortal coil like just anyone. He had to do it the hard and dramatic way. Whether by divine design or by accident, he created a mystery that lingered long after his death.

THE END

Sally Harvey says, "He had absolutely no premonition of death. He had to be down on the floor writhing before he would admit he was sick. He died the same week Sara's will came out of probate. He was working on his own will, but he hadn't finished it yet. That's how little he thought of dying."

CG Harvey recalled, "He loved John Wayne movies." But then, "he recited poetry to me. The way he delivered it was hypnotizing." At the time, "Bill had been feeling very tired, so he had his physical exam moved up a month. The doctor gave him a clean bill of health and said he found nothing unusual.

"That night, we had watched the baseball game on TV. The Reds hit seven home runs but still lost the game. Bill was a great Reds fan. He had enjoyed the evening. We planned to play in the duplicate bridge game at the club the following day, so he went up to bed.

"At 5:00 AM, he awakened me and said, 'CG, call the doctor. I'm very sick!'

"Bill never admitted to being sick, so I knew it was serious and called the ambulance. They had him in the emergency room in twenty minutes. The doctors said it was a serious heart attack. If they could keep him alive for forty-eight hours, he might survive."[4]

JACK HALL, MD

Because there had been so much suspicion, so many hints that Harvey's death was not a natural one, Sally put me in touch with Dr. Jack Hall, the heart specialist who cared for Harvey and later for CG as well. Hall is a product of Harvard Medical School, via Indiana University, a nationally known cardiologist, yet still a hometown physician who has resisted calls to more prominence, while pioneering techniques that have today become almost ordinary—angioplasty, for instance.

Sally: "At the end of twenty-four hours, Dr. Hall told Bill he wasn't going to make it. He asked the doctors if there wasn't something they could try. Dr. Hall said there was, but that it only worked once in five times, and he could not be moved to surgery or given an anesthetic."

Jack Hall: "Bill was in control of himself throughout. He didn't want to give up; he wanted to know the odds. I told him, 'With the surgery, maybe one in ten. Without it, two percent.'

"He said, 'I've beaten worse odds than that. . . . So what are you waiting on?' Go ahead!'"[5]

Sally: "Dr. Hall worked on him in his hospital room. There wasn't time to get him to surgery."

Dr. Hall continues, "His pump was so poor, his heart couldn't squeeze enough to circulate blood throughout his body. . . . He was not responding. I wanted to try a new technique, what in those days was called 'an artificial heart'. . . inserting a balloon from the groin to above the heart. We had had the procedure at the hospital for just one week!

"The odds with the pump were better than without. After, if the surgery had been successful, he would have had a fifty-fifty chance of survival.

"I didn't use anesthesia, except local. I wanted to be able to talk with him. After a few hours, it gets pretty uncomfortable, even painful. You can't put someone to sleep doing this. And he was there for nine hours!"

CG: "With no anesthetic and excruciating pain. . . . When they got there, that side of his heart was closed by scar tissue. . . . In Rome he had had a massive heart attack which closed off half his heart. It had been misdiagnosed as a potassium shortage in his blood and had never been treated.

"The discovery was a horrible blow, but Bill asked them to try the other side. Six hours later—after a total of thirteen hours of surgery—they got into the other side of his heart, but there were not enough cells in the heart still alive to function with the machine, and they told Bill he was going to die."

Reverend Kahlenberg: "The doctors came to get me . . . to have a last prayer with Bill. He was in pretty bad shape."

Sally: "Pastor Kahlenberg came out and got Mom and me. That was the end. His last words were, 'I'll always love you.'"

CG: "Twenty minutes later, he was dead. June 9, 1976."[6]

Bill died at about one in the afternoon. Sally: "Both surgeons cried, as did most of the people in the room. They said they had never encountered such a brave man in all their practice.

"They asked CG if they could do an autopsy, and she agreed." The autopsy showed it had been Bill's third serious heart attack.

Dr. Hall: "He never mentioned to me that he had been in the CIA. Just said, 'I've had a full life!'"

Hall was the recipient of many inquisitive phone calls in the years after Harvey died. "After Bill died, I got night and day calls, asking 'Is he really dead?' I figured it was the Agency just wanting to confirm his death." He never asked the callers to identify themselves. Hall doesn't go any further in his speculation.

Reverend Kahlenberg: "When Bill died, a little bit of me died, too." Kahlenberg echoed the words of St. Timothy. "I have fought the good fight. I have finished the race. I have kept the faith."

Bill is buried in Danville, Indiana, where it all began. Few attended the burial. Dave Murphy came up from Florida, and Alex MacMillan came from California. Many simply didn't hear about Bill's death until later.

Kahlenberg, too, got calls, seeking to confirm Bill's death. "Many people hoped it was a hoax. . . . They thought it might not really have happened."

On June 22, 1976, not quite two weeks after Harvey's death, his old friend and former FBI colleague, Art Thurston, who was himself a gun connoisseur and collector, made an inventory of Harvey's collection. Bill owned thirteen handguns and ten long guns. The total valuation of the collection at the time of Bill's death was $5,025.

A STRANGE INCIDENT: THE BREAK-IN

In September or October 1976, about three months after Bill's death and one month after Johnny Rosselli's brutal demise, the Harveys' Indianapolis house was broken into. CG had been outside, in front. When she entered the house, she heard noises in the basement, which opens onto a gently sloping rear lawn. She went down to investigate and interrupted what appeared to have been a burglary in progress, thieves going through the papers that remained in Bill's office files.

Is it possible that the Agency organized the burglary to see what documents Harvey had taken with him that should have remained secret? Was the break-in performed by latter-day Second-Story Men?

WILDERNESS OF MIRRORS

After Harvey's death, two books appeared that raised considerable ire among Harvey loyalists. The first was David Martin's *Wilderness of Mir-*

rors, which, in turn, at least partially inspired Norman Mailer's *Harlot's Ghost*.

Martin had been tracking Harvey and Jim Angleton, as a reporter for the *Washington Post*, since the 1970s. Indeed, his lengthy postmortem on Bill inspired a nearly half-page charcoal drawing by David Suter of Harvey's backside as Bill got ready to meet Jack Kennedy in the Oval Office. *Wilderness* came out in 1980. After I read the book I got in touch with CG about a riposte. When I picked up the traces years later, CG had just died.

CG waxed nearly profane about *Wilderness* in her letter to me. "I did not cooperate with Martin, nor did anyone who had worked successfully with Bill. When I heard from my friends, who called and told me the tenor of Martin's questions and asked me if I wanted them to talk to him, I said, 'No!'[7]

"Bill had been contacted by Martin while he was still alive and didn't want anything to do with him, so I knew I was following Bill's desires."

CG was so incensed after *Wilderness of Mirrors* appeared, she cancelled plans to go to Australia, bought a Buick Riviera, and set out across the country. "She was gone four months, collecting memories of Dad." Sally pointed to CG's huge Rolodex. "She never spent one night in a hotel!" During the trip CG taped statements from people who had worked with Bill, which cast a completely different light on him from that in *Wilderness*. CG destroyed this material after the CIA told her that she could not publish anything and that Bill's files would not be available until 2063.

CG's letter to me continues, "My exceptions [to the Martin book] make a book! You say I am in no position to comment on the rivalry between Bill and Jim Angleton, [but] I am! . . . I received a letter from Jim on 22 Apr 1980, after he saw [*Wilderness*].

"[Jim] was so upset, he pulled out of his file and returned to me a letter which he received from Bill, written on 3 June 1976. . . . Bill died on 9 June.

"Here, after four years, to open a letter in Bill's handwriting gave me quite a shock."

The handwriting is a bit more sprawling than of old, though not noticeably wobblier. The expression of thought, especially the bitter condemnation of those he (and Angleton) felt had betrayed the Agency is pure, unadulterated Harvey, even to the mock German phrase at the end.

> Dear Jim,
>
> I was pleased to receive your letter. . . . As I think you know, I

> agree, basically, with your views as expressed. Personally, and I have so stated with little tact and much bluntness, among friends, I cannot view the posture and actions of [DCI Bill] Colby specifically and the [Ford] Administration [in caving in to the Church Committee] generally as other than an evil compound of arrant cowardice, crass abdication of responsibility and almost incredible stupidity.
>
> The actions of the concerned elements of The Congress, in my opinion, at least, fall four-square within the Cromwellian if not the Constitutional definition of treason.
>
> The utter disarray and the revolting sanctimonious holier-than-thou breast-beating of the past 18 months I find not only personally disgusting. But also gravely concerning, as a signet of national infantilism.
>
> Forgive the Hyde Park soap box approach. No reason I should carry coals to Newcastle by off-loading it on you, of all people.
>
> I just got back from the stable after working two horses for a couple of hours, which is a damned sight more satisfying than agonizing over the current state of the Republic.
>
> Please give my best to Cicely. CG sends her regards to you both.
>
> Keep in touch, *als immer*,
>
> WKH[8]

In her 1983 handwritten memoir to me, CG said, "Jim's covering letter said, 'I cut out one page of Bill's letter which had to do with a sensitive case.' . . . We were all good friends right up to Bill's death, and even though in 1980, Jim tried to counter the [Martin] lie, nothing he did or said was ever acknowledged.

"It has become a very discouraging picture to me. But this letter six days before [Bill's] death certainly proves the lie of the rivalry. They talked on the phone and discussed cases and visited back and forth, and each had tremendous respect for the other."[9] In the end, the two cold warriors had more than made peace.

Angleton renewed contact with CG slightly less than two years after Bill's death, on March 7, 1978. In a letter Angleton expresses deep thanks for a Victorian era Christmas card CG had sent, which so touched the mole hunter, he thought it worth framing. Then he reflects the deep anger and bitterness that he and others felt about congressional investigations.

> There is no need to describe the decompression of the past three-plus years. The agony of the Church Committee which destroyed

some 30 years during which we all dedicated our lives to the country, never believing that we would have Director or president who could sell us out not as individuals, but the service and its traditions.

. . . Many an evening—alone—I relive the days of the past when we were a well-knit group who knew where we were going and who was the enemy.

I think of Bill often . . . and many others when I am alone late at night . . . and then I remember vividly the meetings we had, and my spirits are revived, knowing that if they were here, they would be in battle as it once was.

These reveries have given me strength and renewed conviction in what our mission and contribution meant to the country. In the end it will come out—perhaps when it is too late, and the Churches and Mondales will be held accountable—along with Admiral Turner—[for] firing the old guard—what's left of it.

. . . We are losing badly in the world, as a country—and the service is in a shambles with indifferent esprit-de-corps which is a sad indication of the Administration's lack of basic understanding of the enemy, and what to do about it . . . Italy, France, Angola, Ethiopia and so it goes.

Enough of that! What can I do to help on Bill's papers, or anything of concern to you? I am ready to give this time if you wish. I am always ready to preserve the true traditions which we all shared.

Kindest personal regards to you, CG.

Jim

(Please write)

The letter could almost have been written in 2006 from one recently retired CIA man to a colleague.

CG had, almost voluntarily, gone into a retirement home in 1995. It was not an easy adjustment; she didn't socialize with the others. By October 2000 she was obviously declining in health. The home's administrator threatened to kick her out because, he said, his place was for the living, not the dying. Sally: "She was failing physically. She wanted to die so bad. It was very hard." In late September she fell down twice in one week and was taken to the emergency room. "When she got to the hospital the last time, she argued with Dr. Hall about her meds, and Hall replied, 'Clara, I'm the doctor!'

"She knew she was going; Jack Hall made it easy for her and told her it was OK." Sally said, "Mom, let go!" But, "she wouldn't die in front of the boys." Sally's son and Jim left the room.

Dick Cady, a reporter for the *Indianapolis Star* who had come to know CG well, delivered the eulogy at her funeral on October 7, 2000. "She was the whole package, and then some. . . . She would be well-pleased to be memorialized with the Greatest Generation."[10] CG was cremated and placed in the family plot in Danville.

To persuade Sally to talk with me, I sent her a copy of CG's 1983 letter. Sally replied, "I didn't have to check any farther. . . . She gave you everything . . . Everything." When we met, Sally added that she had had a sense of guidance from CG when she started looking for material for me. "CG told me where to look."

This, in part, is what CG said in that letter, dated April 10, 1983:

> The reason I cried was because I had tried to do exactly what you suggested to set the record straight and I failed to get permission from CIA after Bill's death—naturally the cowards did nothing while he was alive.
>
> I visited at least a hundred people who had worked for Bill, like you. Their testimonials were filled with praise and respect. I took tape recordings, got groups together, and worked out specific operations which were very successful, then went to Washington to get permission to publish it. They rolled out the red carpet, treated me like a VIP, said they would let me know.
>
> Six months later, they sent the head of the Freedom of Information Section out here to Indianapolis to tell me positively NO!
>
> I was crushed but seem to have no recourse since my pension comes from CIA.
>
> I worked for them for 25 years and have signed the secrecy agreement.
>
> They told me that they do not officially acknowledge that Bill ever worked for CIA. All his operations have been classified for 50 years, and they said the best I could do was write into my will that his grandchildren can have the material.[11]

None of this satisfactorily answers the question, why Bill Harvey went to extraordinary lengths—including preparations to ward off an invasion of his house—to protect his family in Indianapolis. Were all those guns merely the hangover of a decades-long habit? Or were they stashed because Bill was seriously concerned about a specific danger, and if so, what was that danger?

17

AFTERLIFE

Despite Dr. Jack Hall's protestations and because rumors persist to this day, it's worthwhile looking briefly at the people who might have wanted Harvey prematurely dead—even years after he had left the CIA and months after he had completed his testimony in Washington.

Heading the list of potential slayers is Santo Trafficante, the Miami Mafia chief and suspected double agent for Castro. Trafficante stood most to gain when and if Castro reopened Cuba for tourism and rackets as usual. He tops the list of potential organizers of the JFK assassination. He very probably issued the contract for Johnny Rosselli's demise. What could Bill have known that might have been so dangerous to the Mob nearly thirteen years after November 22, 1963?

Could a Mafia hit on Harvey have been designed to serve as a dire lesson to Rosselli about talking with senators? Could it serve any other exemplary or covert purpose? The speculation must remain just that—speculation—and fairly wild, at that.

Could feral Miami Cubans have wanted to liquidate Harvey, for real or imagined cause, such as his "failure" to kill Castro, or even, conceivably, because of his run-in with Bobby Kennedy? Terminating a former CIA officer, in the heartland, fifteen-or-so years after his very indirect role in their lives? The logic is barely credible, even for the anti-Castro-ites.

It is likewise inconceivable that Castro and/or his security services would have troubled themselves to defy obvious risks in order to liquidate Bill, as an act of revenge, or for any other reason.

WHO ELSE?

Who else could have wanted Harvey out of the way when he was, truly, a burnt-out case? The European underworld, specifically the Sicilian Mafia,

Camorra, Union Corse, and/or the Marseilles drug underground? The only plausible explanation I can come up with for the murder of Harvey by foreign criminals on American soil is revenge for the murder of Michael Chinigo, who may have been one of theirs. But that reasoning is pretty far-fetched.

Any suggestion that the CIA's latter-day incarnation of assassins grouped under ZRRIFLE, whatever it may have been called in 1976, would have rubbed Harvey out is equally inconceivable, despite what many would like to believe. By the mid-1970s Harvey was far out of the loop; his operational knowledge was dated and useless. The threat he once posed to the CIA was no longer effective.

The KGB? The Soviets might have fantasized about kidnapping Harvey in, say, 1956, or 1964, even in 1967, when they might have thought they could squeeze some useful operational information out of him. But kidnapping has never been used by one service against another's staff personnel. Even intelligence agencies operate under certain unwritten rules.

WHO THEN?

There remains the puzzling question of Harvey's wariness during his waning Indianapolis days. He covered it with the useful-but-misleading remark to Pastor Kahlenberg that he was on the KGB hit list.

Of course Bill was careful. He carried guns, continuing the habits of a lifetime in the shadow world, and he stashed that armory all over the house. He was superprotective of Sally. Did he think something threatened him? Ghosts from the Kennedy era?

I requestioned F. A. O. Schwarz, the Church Committee's counsel who interviewed Bill prior to his appearances, only months before Bill died. "No. I can't remember that he showed any fear or apprehension. And we didn't only talk business. Our conversations were relatively natural, given the circumstance."[1]

Yet Harvey took those extraordinary precautions to ensure that the swarm of cameras did not snap him when he came out of the Church Committee sessions, and he stayed in Washington only with the most trusted and obscure of his subordinates from Berlin days. Sam Halpern and Ted Shackley, for instance, did not see him. They would have been easier for the media to trace.

What else could have made him so secretive? Habits of a lifetime? Did he simply know too much? About what? Who tried to burgle the Harveys' house in Chevy Chase, and years later who was in Bill's study in the Indianapolis house shortly after his death and why? Why, too, did the CIA quickly send security experts to install special equipment in the house and then remove most of it before the house was sold? Why did the CIA tell CG that papers relating to Bill would not be declassified until 2063, an interesting date in itself?

CG once told Sally and others a story about CIA officers having "unexpected heart attacks on tennis courts." At the time, Sally guessed her mother might have been ruminating on the stressful lives they had led. But was that all that was in her mind?

What was the "sensitive" case on which Bill commented to Jim Angleton in the last letter he wrote?

Though these questions loom, Dr. Jack Hall is courteously adamant that Bill died a natural death—natural, that is, for one who had led the life Harvey had—and that he had not been the victim of any murderous attack.

ANOTHER DEATH

Jack Anderson, by now partnered by Les Whitten, went into some gruesome details about Johnny Rosselli's death in a column dated August 27, 1976. "The autopsy indicated [Rosselli's killer] may have shot him and then dug out the bullet with a knife. Then they brutally hacked off his legs. It is possible that he was still alive when they stuffed his body into a 55-gallon oil drum.

"They wrapped chains around the drum to weight it down and tossed it into Biscayne Bay. The autopsy suggests that he may have died of asphyxiation inside the drum before it hit the water. The gases from the decomposing body floated the heavy container to the surface."

The columnists then review their history with Rosselli.

> We first encountered Johnny Rosselli more than five years ago when we were investigating his role in the Central Intelligence Agency's plot to assassinate Cuban Premier Fidel Castro.
>
> The CIA case officer, William Harvey, told us that Rosselli had been the hero of the abortive venture. Harvey broke his oath of secrecy because he thought it might help Rosselli who was in trouble with the law. The CIA agent had nothing but praise for Rosselli's daring.
>
> In the strictest of confidence, Rosselli himself confirmed that he had directed six assassination attempts against Castro. We protected his confidence, so he came to trust us.

> So when he vanished last month, his associates came to us for help. . . .
>
> We have learned that Rosselli was not the amiable, retired old duffer he pretended to be. . . . He became a specialist in white-collar crimes. It's a profession, apparently, he never gave up. . . . Competent sources say . . . Rosselli was involved in stolen securities and financial swindles. . . . He handled millions in illegal gambling money, which he forwarded to the Chicago underworld. . . .
>
> He dressed in the latest styles, dined at the best restaurants and dated beautiful women. The thought of going back to prison horrified him. . . .
>
> He began to talk to the government as early as 1970. He gave information . . . which resulted in grand jury confrontation for Tony Accardo . . . [who] grumbled to associates that he would pay back Rosselli some time. . . .
>
> Perhaps the last straw was Rosselli's testimony in the Castro case. He identified two mobsters, Sam Giancana and Santo Trafficante, as being involved in the assassination attempts. It's no secret in the underworld that Trafficante detests publicity.

BILL AND BOOZE

Booze led to the unraveling of Harvey's career. His drinking got worse after his withdrawal from the White House firing line, in the face of Kennedy ire, but the roots of his problem lie in his early days. My interpretation is that Bill was, from day one, a misfit. He felt, even before Pearl Harbor, that the good and true fight was in the trenches or on the beaches. Remember that CG said he had wanted to be a Marine Corps general. His teenage marriage to Libby was a rebellion against his mother. He tried politics and failed. Small-town law didn't interest him. The FBI gave him a springboard, and he quickly discerned enemies against whom he could joust, first the Germans, then the Soviets.

He had found his purpose, but he writhed at the toils of bureaucracy and at the superciliousness of routine- and rote-driven people, and he kicked at J. Edgar Hoover's traces, an early indication of the rebelliousness that marked his later career. Harvey's dream had been to be out there, countering the country's enemies, not inside, among bureaucrats whose behavior disillusioned and dismayed him.

Part of the cause of his alcoholism was undoubtedly, too, the feeling of inadequacy or not meeting a recognizable standard brought on by his lack of public recognition, in the form of military and, especially, of combat service. Some of his sense of inferiority was his ungainly appearance, and part of it, the unease he felt in the early CIA years, when he was surrounded by Ivy Leaguers. He emphasized that differentness by demonstrating openly his passion for guns, by cultivating the reputation as a ladies' man, and by drinking at his wellborn antagonists. It tickled him to portray himself as a superstud.

Harvey broke the mold of the CIA's Ivy League leadership. He turned his apparent drawbacks into assets in Berlin, where he was out from under the incessant, incestuous scrutiny of CIA headquarters and where he was the unchallenged leader of a formidable band of iconoclasts.

In Berlin, too, Harvey came to term as the preeminent American espionage operations expert. He had learned the ways of the KGB in the atomic spy cases, back in his Bureau days. In Berlin, with Dave Murphy's and Ted Shackley's probes into the East and the tunnel operation, Bill absorbed much more about the enemy, and he, perhaps partially unconsciously, adapted some of the KGB's modus operandi for himself: long-term approach, dedication, deviousness, tight security, a degree of fanaticism, and subtlety, not flag-waving, on the barricades.

Berlin was Harvey's power base and his springboard. It was his front-line glory moment. But after a while, Bill began to realize he couldn't save the world.

By the end of his tour of duty in Berlin, Harvey had become overconfident; he felt he had become invaluable, irreplaceable. He was sure that he was on the fast track to a very senior slot in the Agency. Task Force W could have been a way station on his ascent of Everest; he had always been a sort of Edmund Hillary, a John Wayne, or a William Walker. The two Cuba assignments, Task Force W and ZRRIFLE, hurtled him from the upward slopes of the pinnacle to his dungeon.

When Bobby Kennedy entered the game plan, Bill, at age forty-six, threw his life's work and his future away, in uncontrollable, irrevocable disgust. The idealist, the canny street fighter, the brilliant, innovative operator, the patriot just couldn't stomach the perversion of the true cause by his political masters. Until then he had been able to handle the booze; then, it then began to handle him. The deciding factor was his, as opposed to Bobby's, view of the national interest. Inevitably the Kennedy muscle won. Bill's was a lose-lose situation. He may have objected to assassination, but he went along with the president and the attorney general, then he overplayed his role, and as a true alcoholic, he drank at his antagonists and thought he could get away with it.

How could Harvey, who was so intelligent, so canny, not have realized he was sabotaging himself in the eyes of others—even the Berliners of the brotherhood—with his addiction to the bottle? Why didn't he realize he was giving his detractors all they needed to denigrate, even destroy, him?

Bill had been comfortable in his own skin, at least as long as he was in charge of his world, and that world was clear-cut, black and white. Rome was gaudy, not his scene. There, he was surrounded by people who were not of the Bogart mold, so he escaped to the Via Veneto and drank at them, then continued in his office and at home, drowning in martinis or whatever happened to be handy.

Perhaps Bill had what today would be called an identity crisis. In Rome, he was no longer a cutting-edge operator; rather he was forced to play at diplomatic niceties, several steps removed from whatever espionage action Italy may have offered. He sought occasional, at-times-embarrassing refuge in the country he far better understood, Germany. He could find no middle ground that offered him stability.

Then, back in America, it all caught up with him. But he had a buddy with whom he could drink and commiserate, whenever they got together. Johnny Rosselli played skillfully and compassionately to Bill's needs.

And finally, Harvey felt he had reason to be deeply concerned about his and his family's safety in Indianapolis. What was it that made the flawed patriot supercautious in his last years? We will probably never know. Harvey died an enigma, and that probably pleased him enormously.

"A SPECIAL CODE OF HONOR"

The CIA showed on two occasions that it will not, either gracefully or grudgingly, give Harvey his deserved place in the history of American intelligence. First, it denied him mention in the 1992 colloquium on the Cuban Missile Crisis, and second, it omitted him, despite his nomination, from the list of fifty "trailblazers" published to commemorate the Agency's fifty years of existence. Yet Harvey lives on, long after his death, in the memories of those who served with him—almost all men, a few women—who openly said they owed their professional careers to Bill.

Sally Harvey opened the file of more than three hundred letters of condolence sent to CG as people, in some cases very belatedly, heard that Bill had gone. These are a few.

"I know what a blow this is to you. Life has not been easy for the two of you these last years. . . . My hand of friendship reaches out to you in this most difficult time." Richard M. Helms, U.S. ambassador, Tehran.

"He was a good friend, both personally and professionally and contributed enormously to the relationship between our two services. I worked with him off and on from 1949, but, of course, particularly whilst I was at the Embassy in 1960–64. It is a great and sad loss." Sir Maurice Oldfield, former chief of the British Secret Intelligence Service (MI-6).

"In his time in Germany, your husband became a very esteemed friend of all of us, and I may assure you that all my former co-workers who heard of his death were very touched by this bad news. I liked him very much, not only as a really reliable friend, but also as an experienced professional in his field." Retired Gen. Reinhard Gehlen, first director of the Federal German Intelligence Service.

"The years [my wife and I] spent in Berlin were among the most pleasant and rewarding we have enjoyed and one of the greatest factors in this was having you and Bill as friends and, for me, having Bill as my most important colleague. I loved his absolutely straight view of life, his loyalty to friends and causes, regardless of consequences, and his dry and ever-ready humour. And your house was a glowing hearth of kindness and companionship." Robert, a former head of the British SIS station in Berlin.

"I remember how Bill, many times, late at night, got a message from his office and disappeared, only to come back a beaten man. Again, one of his Berlin volunteers had not come back from his mission to the other side. Bill, as you know, had a great admiration for the Berliners, for their dedication to our common cause. . . . We all, his foreign brothers-in-arms, felt his intellectual and technical superiority." A Dutch intelligence officer.

"It is difficult to believe that one so rich in human qualities is gone. . . . In the years ahead, you will have happy memories and feelings of just pride." Gordon Stewart, former chief of mission, Germany, and chief of personnel, CIA.

"I worked long enough with Bill to learn of many of his significant contributions to the security of our country. Because of their very nature, he could never receive full recognition for them. But that was the way he wanted it. He was a dedicated patriot, and I am proud that he chose me as a friend." Frank B. Rowlett.

"I don't have to tell you how much Bill meant to me during our relationship, the depth of our friendship or the fact that I know of no one in my lifetime for whom I had greater personal admiration or professional respect. . . . He made a great contribution to our country and its security. . . . He will always be a legend in the annals of the country he served so well.

This is, of course, true also of the Agency. The number of people he has taught, inspired and directed is legion. None of us will ever forget him or the lessons he taught us. He was a unique combination of toughness, kindness and sympathetic human understanding." Howard J. Osborn, former director of security, CIA.

"Bill and I had a special relationship . . . a deep friendship . . . dating back to the Spring of 1941, when he joined me on the German and Minorities Desk at the FBI. We probably worked across the desk from each other 70–80 hours a week for more than two years. We ended up the best of friends, which says something personal besides the working relationship. . . . Bill had a special code of honor, of integrity, of comradeship and decency that endeared him to many. Add to this a certain flair of showmanship and a brusqueness in tolerating stupidity, and excellent intellect and a great capacity for work, and you have the man we all loved and respected." Dennis Flinn, former FBI special agent.

WATERSHED

Harvey's removal from Task Force W at Bobby Kennedy's behest was a watershed event for the CIA, even though it may not have been recognized as such at the time.

From October 1962 on—after Helms and McCone replaced Harvey with Desmond FitzGerald, who was far more acceptable to the Kennedys as a person—the CIA was vulnerable to political manipulation. This became evident again in 1967, when Helms hastily called for the inspector general's report, in anticipation of fallout from Drew Pearson's revelations, and then again from 1971 on.

Helms himself became a victim to Richard Nixon's political whims. George H. W. Bush, Bill Colby, Adm. Stansfield Turner, Bill Casey, Jim Woolsey, Bill Gates, George Tenet, and most recently, Porter Goss—all have been political figures and players. The 1950s were the heyday of the CIA. Since then, one way and another, the Agency has gone downhill, even to today's realignment of the entire U.S. intelligence structure.

Harvey's story sounds incongruous when stacked against the political figures who are identified with the latter-day CIA and also incongruous when America's enemies today are elusive members of cultures far different from the northern Europeans we faced in Bill's day. But even back then, Harvey was not the kind of guy who was easily limned by a stereopticon. He was always a nonconformist to the max, and he paid for his nonconformity, but not until he had taught a lot of people a lot of things, some of which, it is alleged, are still being taught in obscure places.

The causes for the CIA's decline in popular and political esteem go back, really, to the Bay of Pigs in 1961, which opened the Agency to the prolonged and recurring scrutiny under which it withered. Harvey, the flawed patriot, unfortunately was one of the senior officers who aroused media and political curiosity and thereby rendered the CIA vulnerable. In 2005 and 2006 the decline that started in 1962 became an avalanche, as the CIA was picked over for political purpose, lost its preeminence in American intelligence, and became just another agency in the bureaucratic web.

Some professional intelligence officers wish we had a few irreverent Harveys in the clandestine establishment today, even while facing enemies of totally different stripe.

As Dave Murphy said, after he had read a proof copy of this book, "Sad. Sad. It was so sad." But the saddest comment of all was, "You know, there were only two of us from the Agency at Bill's funeral—Alex MacMillan and me! Just two!"

APPENDIX

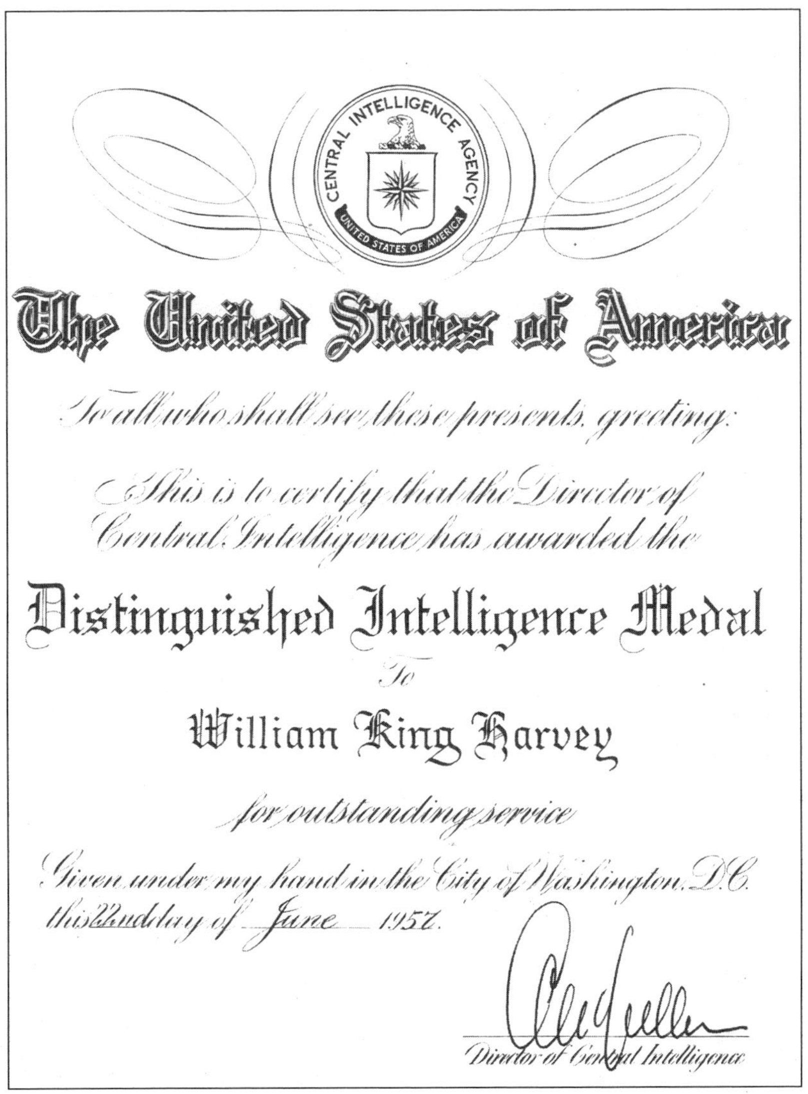

CENTRAL INTELLIGENCE AGENCY

UNITED STATES OF AMERICA

The United States of America

To all who shall see these presents, greeting:

This is to certify that the Director of Central Intelligence has awarded the

Distinguished Intelligence Medal

To

William King Harvey

for outstanding service

Given under my hand in the City of Washington, D.C. this 22nd day of June 1957.

Director of Central Intelligence

1. Bill Harvey's Distinguished Intelligence Medal certificate. Bill fought with CIA security to allow him to take the medal and certificate home. *Sally Harvey, Harvey Family Papers*

MORI DocID: 31155

5/5 - 070

January 28, 1966

Mr. William Harvey

Dear Bill:

I am sorry to have missed you during your recent visit here in Washington. Unfortunately, when you were here I had to go to New York for several days, and by the time I got back I found you had left for [redacted] I hope I will have better luck on your next trip.

All best wishes.

Faithfully yours,

Allen W. Dulles

Approved for Release
Date OCT 1992

002704

2. A delicate letter from retired CIA director Allen Dulles, avoiding Harvey, about the same time Harvey was recalled from Rome. *Sally Harvey, Harvey Family Papers*

CENTRAL INTELLIGENCE AGENCY
WASHINGTON, D. C.

OFFICE OF THE DIRECTOR

13 February 1968

Mr. William King Harvey
28 West Irving Street
Chevy Chase, Maryland 20015

Dear Bill:

I am sorry that due to a busy schedule and my absence for several days during the Christmas holidays I didn't have an opportunity to see you prior to your retirement at the end of the year.

Red White has told me of his visit with you, and I ~~am par~~ticularly appreciative of your expression of continued loyalty to the Agency and your offer to be of assistance should an appropriate occasion arise.

I extend to you, personally and officially, my sincere appreciation for the important work you have done and my warmest hopes that you will find full enjoyment in the years ahead.

Sincerely,

Dick

Richard Helms
Director

3. A letter from "the Boy Diplomat," Richard Helms. Helms had defended Bill against his critics for many years, but Bill's downward spiral shook Helms's confidence. This letter suggests that Helms avoided seeing him before Bill's retirement, and Helms began to regard Bill with deep suspicion because of his continued friendship with mob figure Johnny Rosselli. *Sally Harvey, Harvey Family Papers*

NOMINATION FORM *(for Retirees)*
CIA 50th Anniversary
1947-1997

I. I nominate William K. Harvey as a "**CIA Trailblazer**" on the occasion of the Agency's 50th anniversary.

II. **Nomination Statement** *(must be typewritten)*: After reviewing the nomination criteria, please provide a written statement, giving as much narrative comment as necessary to explain why the person you nominated should be considered for a "Trailblazer" award. Use additional page(s) as needed.

Highlights of Mr. Harvey's career with CIA: Transferred to CIA from the FBI in 1947; long tenure as Chief of Staff D; Chief of Base, Be for 8 years during the 1950's; head of Task Force W during the earl 1960's, leading up to the Cuban missile crisis; Chief of Station, R

I believe Mr. Harvey was one of the most effective intelligence officers in CIA's 50-year history. It is indeed fortunate that we had a few leaders of his calibre in the Agency at this particular t of the Cold War. He was shrewd, innovative and daring, always displaying a fearless, uncompromising attitude for taking on tough ass ments and seeing them through. A good example of this was the fact he masterminded the Berlin tunnel project which gave us a sorely-needed victory over the Soviets. He was a true patriot and should b so honored. ~~His wife~~, C.G. Harvey, should be invited to accept hon

Signed ______ Date: March 30, 1997

Printed name: ______

Mail nomination statement* to:

D/AIS
Re: Trailblazers
Central Intelligence Agency
Washington, D. C. 20505

***Must be received by April 15, 1997.**
Mail postmarked April 15, 1997

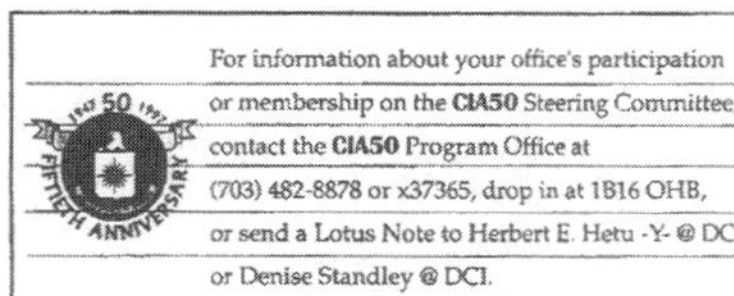

For information about your office's participation or membership on the **CIA50** Steering Committee, contact the **CIA50** Program Office at (703) 482-8878 or x37365, drop in at 1B16 OHB, or send a Lotus Note to Herbert E. Hetu -Y- @ DCI or Denise Standley @ DCI.

4. The 1997 nomination of Bill to be one of fifty CIA trailblazers. The nomination was rejected. *Clarence Berry*

NOTES

NOTE: The wealth of original material I accumulated for the book is available to qualified researchers in the special collections section of the Davidson Library at the University of California, Santa Barbara.

Some references to original source materials in the book appear without attribution. I had kept the originals in e-mail folders that were destroyed when my computer hard drive was consumed by a worm.

CHAPTER 1: GROWING UP MIDWESTERN

1. CG Harvey, in conversation with David E. Murphy, November 15–16, 1993.
2. Photocopy from Harvey family papers.
3. Anita Potocki, in conversation with the author, March 19, 2001.
4. Sally Harvey provided a wealth of family information and some documentation in a series of e-mails to me in January 2001 and during a visit I made to Indianapolis in March 9–12, 2001.
5. B. F. Small, letter to Bill Harvey, June 29, 1933.

CHAPTER 2: THE SECRET WORLD

1. Unless otherwise sourced, quotations in this chapter are taken from the three-hundred-page FBI personnel file on William K. Harvey, which the Bureau provided under the Freedom of Information Act (FOIA). That file was not only redacted, but some very significant matters were deliberately omitted from it, apparently at the behest of J. Edgar Hoover, who wanted nothing creditable to be associated with Bill's name.
2. *The House on 92nd Street,* directed by Henry Hathaway (Los Angeles, CA: Twentieth Century Fox, 1945). The film is a paean to the FBI and, of course, to J. Edgar Hoover, who gave the worshipful makers, Darryl Zanuck, Louis De Rochement, and Henry Hathaway, lavish support.
3. Ernest Volkman, *Espionage: The Greatest Spy Operations of the Twentieth Century* (New York: John Wiley & Sons, 1995), 48.

4. CG Harvey, in conversation with David E. Murphy, November 15–16,1993. The operation was a tragicomedy from the start, as noted in some detail by Al Kamen in the *Washington Post* on March 29, 2004.
5. Dennis Flinn, phone conversation with the author, March 13, 2002. Dennis died in 2004. When Bob Woodward first acknowledged that Mark Felt was Deep Throat in the *Washington Post* on June 2, 2005, he wrote: "In Felt's earliest days in the FBI, during World War II, he had been assigned to work on the general desk of the Espionage Section. Felt learned a great deal about German spying in the job, and after the war he spent time keeping suspected Soviet agents under surveillance." Felt probably learned some tradecraft from Harvey. Felt was two years younger than Bill.
6. Sadly, Thurston was unable to contribute to this memoir because, in the latter stages of life, he was a victim of Alzheimer's disease.
7. CG Harvey, conversation, November 15–16,1993.
8. G-Men, for "government men," was a popular term for FBI special agents back when the Gangbusters caught big-name criminals like Al Capone and John Derringer. In the CIA, the equivalent of an FBI special agent is called a "case officer" or, today, an "operations officer."
9. Here and throughout the book, I use KGB to stand for the Soviet foreign intelligence apparatus and its efforts. There is a direct line of succession from the Imperial Russian Cheka through the OGPU, NKVD, MVD, MGB to the KGB and today's SVR.
10. To this day, there is still confusion, even controversy, about who handled the initial stages of the Bentley case, the cornerstone of the massive FBI investigation and conviction of a string of post–World War II Soviet espionage agents. The most authoritative source is Linda Williams, who is a walking compendium on the Bureau's activities in the 1940s. Faced with the conflicting claims, Ms. Williams says, "Look, Harvey was in charge of Division Five, which was charged with investigating communism. He was the first one to take Bentley's statement. He had three or four interviews with Bentley on which he wrote reports, before he got into the hassle with Hoover." Linda Williams, phone conversations with the author, June, July, and October 7, 2002. Clarence Berry adds, in an e-mail to the author, July 13, 2002: "I really have a strong feeling that Bill handled Bentley pretty much exclusively. Perhaps she does not appear in the [personnel file] due to the sensitive nature of the case. . . . My guess is that he kept a lot close to the vest . . . and that may have been the reason they found the files so screwed up when he resigned, that he took a lot of important details away in his head. If so, one can understand why Hoover was so POed at him." This is the first of many communications from Clarence (a pseudonym, at his request) that helped enormously in throwing light, on many matters, but especially on the background to the Berlin Tunnel.

The Bentley case is inextricably entwined with the Venona intercepts, an intelligence legend. Briefly, a very select group of people in Washington began to read KGB cable traffic late in World War II and thus to learn of Soviet perfidy. A comprehensive summary is in a CIA document, *Venona: Soviet Espionage and the American Response, 1939–1957*, which is available at http://www.cia.gov/csi/books/venona/venona.htm. There is no mention of Bill Harvey in the study. See also, John Early Haynes and Harvey Klehr, *Venona: Decoding Soviet Espionage in America* (New Haven, CT: Yale University Press, 1999). Bob Lamphere, who became the case officer on Venona material, also discusses it in his book, Robert J. Lamphere and Tom Shachtman, *The FBI-KGB War: A Special Agent's Story* (New York: Random House, 1986).

11. Linda Williams (FBI FOIA Section), phone conversation with the author, October 7, 2002.
12. See also Curt Gentry, *J. Edgar Hoover: The Man and the Secrets* (New York: W.W. Norton, 1991), 342ff. There is a fairly full account of the Eisler case in Lamphere and Shachtman, *FBI-KGB War*, 42ff.
13. Peter M. F. Sichel, in conversation with the author, March 11, 2002.
14. Ibid.
15. Ronald Alexander MacMillan, in conversation with the author, February 10, 2001. Alex died not long thereafter.
16. Clarence Berry, e-mail to the author, 2002.
17. On the general subject of FBI transfers to the young CIA, Tom Polgar commented in e-mails to the author dated July 12 and 13, 2002: "When I got transferred to WH [Western Hemisphere] (later LA [Latin America]) Division I picked up folklore about Col. J. C. King and his merry band from the FBI. Until August 1947, when CIA emerged, FBI was responsible for clandestine HUMINT in Latin America. In 1947 CIA took over, but had no personnel. The easiest solution was to leave FBI people in place and some remained through the 1960s. Thus CIA's new WH Division relied heavily on former FBI personnel. Bill Broe, ex-FBI was chief of WH Division later, during my days there, and often recalled his wartime experiences with the Bureau. Broe was later inspector general of CIA.

"Another group came to OSS/CIA via the military. Some FBI agents decided to go into the armed forces in World War II and during the Korean War and then came to intelligence from the service. Harvey was exception to above.

"When Des FitzGerald came into WH Division . . . he made a determined effort to move out leftover FBI types. The latter, in Fitzgerald's opinion, were too much at home with disreputable liaison types and American business.

"In general, prominent ex-FBI included, but were certainly not limited to, Win Scott, ex-FBI, ex-Navy captain, later chief in London and Mexico

City, the latter until about 1968. Ned H., chief in Uruguay; John Flinn, deputy chief, Western Hemisphere Division for Cuba Operations; Bill Broe, chief, Japan, who later succeeded Des Fitzgerald as chief of WH Division; Justin O'Donnell, CI [Counterintelligence] Staff, later chief, Netherlands and Thailand. We had two officers named Bill D.; one was ex-FBI and was chief in Mexico City before Win Scott. A former FBI man was chief, Yugoslavia, in the 1950s, when Belgrade was considered a very important post. "I worked closely with FBI in Washington, Buenos Aires, and Mexico City. I found no problems and got good cooperation. I think problems reflected in the media, perhaps falsely, were and are caused by sheer weight of paper that has to be disseminated, analyzed, and digested, rather than an unwillingness to work together."

18. Sichel, conversation, March 11, 2002.

CHAPTER 3: THE HEARTLANDER

1. Adam Horton, letter to the author, May 26, 2001.
2. Tom Polgar, e-mails to the author, July 12 and 13, 2002.
3. William Hood, phone conversation with the author, February 19, 2001.
4. Paul Haffner, interview by David E. Murphy, undated (c. 1991).
5. Ronald Alexander MacMillan, in conversation with the author, February 10, 2001.
6. Richard M. Helms, phone conversation with the author, January 2001; and Richard M. Helms, *A Look Over My Shoulder: A Life in the Central Intelligence Agency*, with William Hood (New York: Random House, 2003), 152.
7. Hood, phone conversation, February 19, 2001.
8. Clarence Berry, e-mail to the author, July 13, 2002.
9. MacMillan, conversation, February 10, 2001.
10. There is a considerable bibliography on Kim Philby. See the KGB's officially sanctioned "autobiography": Kim Philby, *My Silent War* (London: MacGibbon and Kee Ltd., 1968; reprint, New York, Ballantine Books, 1983). Then there are Peter Wright's *Spy Catcher: The Candid Autobiography of a Senior Intelligence Officer* (New York: Viking Penguin, 1987); Andrew Boyle's *The Climate of Treason* (London: Hutchinson & Co., 1979), as well as fairly similar versions of the notorious dinner party at Philby's Nebraska Avenue house in David Martin's *Wilderness of Mirrors* (New York: Harper & Row, 1980), Burton Hersh's *The Old Boys: The American Elite and the Origins of the CIA* (New York: Scribners, 1992), Seymour M. Hersh's *The Dark Side of Camelot* (Boston: Little, Brown, 1997), and Evan Thomas's *The Very Best Men: Four Who Dared: The Early Years of the CIA* (New York: Simon & Schuster, 1995). The story of the party made its public debut in *Wilderness of Mirrors*, but all versions are substantially the same, even the one in Norman Mailer's *Harlot's Ghost* (New York: Random House, 1991).
11. Lamphere and Shachtman, *The FBI-KGB War*, 229.

12. Ibid.
13. John Barron, phone conversation with the author, July 13, 2003. Barron died in 2004.
14. As full an account of the Philby-Harvey-Angleton relationship as is publicly available is in Martin's *Wilderness of Mirrors*, 36. The rivalry is well covered in Tom Mangold's subsequent biography of Angleton, *Cold Warrior: James Jesus Angleton: The CIA's Master Spy Hunter* (New York: Simon & Schuster, 1991). There is also a wealth of fascinating material, including recollections and biographical notes, plus discussion of Angleton by Robin Winks, Bill Hood, Sam Halpern, and others in a special edition of www.thefinalphase.com, brought to my attention by Peter M. F. Sichel.
15. Barron, phone conversation, July 13, 2003.
16. Philby, *My Silent War*. Originally published in Britain by MacGibbon and Kee in 1968. The American paperback edition quoted here, published by Ballantine Books in 1983, does not include even a pseudonym. See pages 158 and 189.
17. See Peter Karlow's remarkably even-tempered autobiographical book, *Targeted by the CIA: An Intelligence Professional Speaks Out on the Scandal That Turned the CIA Upside Down* (Paducah, KY: Turner Publishing Company, 2002). Karlow died in 2005.
18. Horton, letter, May 26, 2001.
19. Dennis Flinn, phone conversation with the author, February 16, 2003.
20. Sam Papich, phone conversation with the author, February 14, 2003. Sam Papich died in 2004.

CHAPTER 4: BAPTISM IN BERLIN

1. Tom Polgar, e-mail to the author, July 10, 2003.
2. Peter M. F. Sichel, e-mails to the author, April 28, 2001 and May 8, 2001.
3. Polgar, e-mail, July 10, 2003.
4. David Chavchavadze, interview with David E. Murphy, undated (c. 1994). This interview is among miscellaneous papers most kindly provided to me by Murphy.
5. Ibid.
6. From Peter Grose, *Gentleman Spy: The Life of Allen Dulles* (New York: Houghton Mifflin, 1994), 356.
7. Herb Natzke, interview with the author, February 11, 2001.
8. Bob Kilroy points out that "Horton was not exaggerating here. We met with agents at night mostly and usually got rid of them sometime before midnight. But then we either went back to the office or to our homes and sat down and made copious notes on the operational info and take they had presented us with. . . . I can still remember my wife muttering sleepily when I finally staggered into bed, 'he must have talked an awful lot tonight!'" Bob Kilroy, e-mail to the author, August 9, 2001. Kilroy is a pseud-

onym for a late, close friend. He sent me many e-mails and letters that contributed enormously to the BOB and Berlin Tunnel chapters of this book. Bob Kilroy died after a lengthy joust with cancer in 2003.

9. Peter M. F. Sichel, e-mail to the author, February 18, 2001.
10. Adam Horton, letters to the author, June 20 and August 16, 2001.
11. See Clarence Ashley, *CIA Spymaster* (Gretna, LA: Pelican Publishing Company, 2004). Bill Hood also wrote a fascinating, detailed account of the case. See William Hood, *Mole: The True Story of the First Russian Intelligence Officer Recruited by the CIA* (New York: W. W. Norton, 1982). Also, Tom Mangold, *Cold Warrior: James Jesus Angleton: The CIA's Master Spy Hunter* (New York: Simon & Schuster, 1991).
12. John Barron, phone conversation with the author, July 13, 2003.
13. CG Harvey, in conversation with David E. Murphy, November 15–16, 1993.
14. In his biography of Allen Dulles, Peter Grose quotes a report by two ultimate, patrician insiders, Robert Lovett and David Bruce, who looked into the CIA's 1950s "covert action" ops. "We felt some alarm. . . . The idea of these young, enthusiastic fellows, possessed of great funds, being sent out in some country, getting themselves involved in local politics, and then backing some local man and from that, starting an operation, scared the hell out of us." Grose, *Gentleman Spy*, 446, quoting a letter by Lovett dated May 11, 1961, in the Robert F. Kennedy Papers.
15. Tom Parrott, phone conversations with the author, December 20 and 23, 2005.
16. Stan Gaines, in conversation with the author, March 15, 2001. Stan died in 2004.
17. Barron, phone conversation, July 13, 2003.
18. Capt. John Corris, USN, in conversation with David E. Murphy, January 22, 1994.
19. Donald R. Morris, newsletter, August 15, 2001. This item was passed to me by a friend.
20. Corris, conversation, January 22, 1994.
21. M. Neill Prew, in conversation with the author, March 17, 2001. Neill Prew died in April 2006.
22. Corris, conversation, January 22, 1994.
23. Stan Gaines, e-mail to the author, February 6, 2003.
24. Clarence Berry, e-mail to the author, February 7, 2003.
25. David E. and Star Murphy, e-mail to the author, February 6, 2003.
26. Gaines, e-mail, February 6, 2003. There was the matter of Harvey's gun collection. When Bill and CG packed their Berlin household to ship back to Washington in 1959, Bill included his private arsenal. Someone who didn't feel charitable toward the chief of base thought the shipment was, at the very least, unusual, perhaps illegal, and wrote an anonymous denunciation of Harvey to the Agency's inspector general. Harvey composed an exculpatory secret/eyes-only memorandum dated August 15, 1960, which

remained in the Harvey family papers years after Bill's death. The memo details the steps Harvey took to ensure that the shipment did not run afoul of any regulations or embarrass CIA and ends, "Although the allegations of the anonymous letter are subject to fairly nasty interpretation, I believe the above account of this shipment demonstrates there was no real impropriety involved. I hope this will serve as a satisfactory answer to your request."

27. David E. Murphy, "How I Got to Berlin," (personal Memorandum for the record, May 25, 1994).
28. Ibid.
29. Ted Shackley, in conversation with the author, May 18, 2001. Despite a fatal illness, Shackley's answers to my questions came like machine-gun bullets, interspersed with tracers. He died in 2003.
30. Natzke, conversation, February 11, 2001.
31. Shackley, conversation.
32. Barron, phone conversation, July 13, 2003.
33. Henry Woodburn, in conversation with the author, May 20, 2001. Woodburn is an alias requested by the officer.
34. Gaines, e-mail, February 6, 2003.
35. Polgar, e-mail, July 10, 2001.
36. CG Harvey, in conversation with David E. Murphy, 1989.
37. Polgar, e-mail, July 10, 2001.
38. While I cannot guarantee the letter's authenticity, I am convinced it is genuine for a number of reasons from style to format to content.
39. Natzke, interview, February 11, 2001.
40. CG Harvey, conversation, 1989.
41. Tom Polgar, e-mail to the author, May 4, 2003.
42. CG Harvey, conversation, 1989.
43. Considering that at its peak BOB had over two hundred employees, living under tension in the boisterous city, the base's disciplinary record under Harvey was surprisingly good—a tribute to morale under Bill. During the nearly ten years I knew much about BOB, one officer resigned from the Agency under a cloud. Another, whose dereliction had been misuse of safe houses, was merely reprimanded. A third case officer, caught driving under the influence by Danish police while on vacation, spent a considerable time bicycling around Berlin after his return.
44. A far more formal and heavily documented history of BOB is contained in the landmark work by David E. Murphy, Sergei Kondrashev, and George Bailey, *Battleground Berlin: CIA vs. KGB in the Cold War* (New Haven, CT: Yale University Press, 1997), which deals in some detail with base operations during the 1950s. Murphy was Bill Harvey's deputy, ran the Soviet operations section of BOB, and succeeded Bill as Chief, BOB. He also most generously provided considerable information from his files for this book.

CHAPTER 5: HARVEY'S HOLE

1. See Robert J. Lamphere and Tom Shachtman, *The FBI-KGB War: A Special Agent's Story* (New York: Random House, 1986).
2. Siegfried Hoxter, a prewar German refugee, an ardent Socialist, a former leader of the Socialist Youth in Germany, and a double PhD in chemistry and mathematics, was one of the most notable OSS/CIA officers and one of the least known. He died in 1957.
3. Quotes from Donald P. Steury, ed., "The Berlin Tunnel," in *On the Front Lines of the Cold War: Documents on the Intelligence War in Berlin, 1946 to 1961* (Washington, DC: CIA, 1999), http://www.cia.gov/csi/books/17240/art-7.html.
4. Bob Kilroy, letters, e-mails, and phone conversations with the author, March 2001ff. All quotations in this chapter, unless otherwise sourced, are from this series of communication with Kilroy.
5. Richard M. Helms, *A Look Over My Shoulder: A Life in the Central Intelligence Agency*, with William Hood (New York: Random House, 2003), 134–135.
6. David Stafford's *Spies Beneath Berlin* (London: John Murray, 2002; reprint, Woodstock, NY: Overlook Press, 2003) adds considerable information, primarily from the British side, about the Vienna Tunnel operation and about London's vital contribution to Harvey's Hole. Stafford also has a wealth of interesting detail on Peter Lunn, Harvey's British opposite number in Berlin—for instance, Lunn was involved in SILVER in Vienna. (See also below on Lunn.) Actual technical details on location, etc., are abundantly available in David E. Murphy, Sergei Kondrashev, and George Bailey, *Battleground Berlin: CIA vs. KGB in the Cold War* (New Haven, CT: Yale University Press, 1997).
7. A word of explanation about CIA cryptonyms and pseudonyms. Inside the Agency, cryptonyms were written AMLASH, JMWAVE, not AM/LASH or JM/WAVE. Area desks in the CIA had different two letter prefixes, many of which remain classified, but for instance, RE denoted a Soviet operation; KU was an activity within CIA, which was itself KUBARK; ZR was a Staff/Division D operational slug; the polygraph was LCFLUTTER. We often wondered if someone somewhere spent his or her entire time dreaming up the names.

   Then there is the matter of pseudonyms. Everyone in the Clandestine Services was issued a name that was used exclusively in correspondence; mine was Ralph S. Hanlon; Bill Harvey at first was Henry M. Rogall, later Frederick B. Presland. To complicate matters even further, all operational people in Berlin had phony names and phony identity documents. One of the minor problems many officers had was trying to remember which name one had used, even in making restaurant reservations.
8. James Bamford, *Body of Secrets: Anatomy of the Ultra-Secret National Security Agency* (New York: Anchor Books, 2002), 2. By 1945 Rowlett was a

lieutenant colonel and was in charge of American efforts to read the dispatches of other nations' delegates to the San Francisco Peace Conference. "The feeling in the Branch is that the success of the Conference may owe a great deal to its contribution." (Bamford, pp. 22–23.) See also Karen Kovach, "Frank B. Rowlett: The Man Who Made 'Magic,'" *Inscom Journal* 21:4 (December 14, 1998).

9. Clarence Berry, various e-mails to the author, June–July 2001. Without the frequent help, advice, and steering of Clarence and Bob Kilroy, this chapter would have been skimpy indeed.
10. Peter M. F. Sichel, e-mails to the author, July 27, 2001 and October 6, 2002; and Peter M. F. Sichel, in conversation with David E. Murphy, undated (c. 1994).
11. Tom Polgar, e-mail to the author, July 10, 2001.
12. Berry, e-mails, June–July 2001.
13. Clarence Berry added, in an e-mail of July 31, 2002, "Fleetwood left Frankfurt for Washington in early 1956. . . . Let's face it: no one could replace Fleetwood."
14. See Murphy et al., *Battleground Berlin*, appendix 9
15. M. Neill Prew, memorandum to David E. Murphy, undated (c. 1994).
16. Berry, e-mails, June–July 2001.
17. The 9539 TSU designation might have covered all the military at the tunnel site.
18. Steury, "The Berlin Tunnel"; and "Clandestine Services History: The Berlin Tunnel Operation, 1952–1956," prepared August 25, 1967, published (in two original copies) June 24, 1968 (Washington, DC: CIA, 1968).
19. M. Neill Prew, in conversation with the author, March 17, 2001.
20. Ernie Leichliter, phone conversation with the author, May 29, 2002.
21. Berry, e-mails, June–July 2001; Ted Shackley, in conversation with the author, May 21, 2001; and David E. Murphy, e-mail to the author, January 4, 2001.
22. Steury, "The Berlin Tunnel"; and "Clandestine Services History."
23. George Blake, *No Other Choice: An Autobiography* (New York: Simon & Schuster, 1990). This is Blake's KGB-approved version of his career and his escape from British prison. Page 24 gives Blake's version of how he alerted the KGB in London. Pages 172ff deal with his meetings with KGB in Berlin. At age seventy-nine, Blake suddenly surfaced as a lecturer at the Russian Federal Security Service's headquarters in Voronezh. "Georgii Ivanovich" boasted he had betrayed four hundred British agents, but his relative importance to the KGB is indicated by the fact that he was only made a colonel, whereas Kim Philby was given the rank of major general. *Radio Free Europe Security and Terrorism Watch* 3:14 (April 23, 2002).
24. Blake, *No Other Choice.*
25. David E. Murphy, in conversation with the author, January 19, 2001, and April 2001.

26. George Bailey, letter to and phone conversations with the author, January, March, and April 2001. George was a much-honored correspondent for and editor of Max Ascoli's *Reporter* magazine, and he also worked for ABC. He was head of Radio Liberation in Munich for a while, and thereafter he concentrated on books. He was a notable linguist, a distinguished writer, and a gentleman. He died in Munich on September 11, 2001.
27. David E. Murphy, "How I Got to Berlin: Personal Memorandum for the Record," May 25, 1994.
28. Henry Woodburn, in conversations with the author, May 20–21, 2001.
29. Clarence Berry, e-mail to the author, May 28, 2001.
30. Woodburn, conversations, May 20–21, 2001. Another version has a GI manning the machine gun, and Bill ordering him to slam the bolt. Henry Woodburn, letter to the author, August 4, 2001.
31. Murphy, "How I Got to Berlin."
32. Clarence Berry, e-mail, May 17, 2002.
33. Woodburn, conversations, May 20–21, 2001.
34. Murphy, "How I Got to Berlin."
35. Clarence Berry, e-mail to the author, July 13, 2001.
36. Clarence Berry, e-mail to the author, July 29, 2001.
37. Helms, *A Look Over My Shoulder*, 137.
38. Clarence Berry, letter to the author, August 21, 2002.
39. Ibid. Berry explains, "Demuxing: a process of isolating and printing out on teletype (or reading voice) each 'channel' of information which is transmitted on a single 'circuit.' Each 'circuit' consists of one pair of wires or one radio signal. Generally, there are many channels on a single circuit. In the case of the tunnel, there were three landline 'cables' consisting of over 170 circuits, with multichannels on each circuit. [*Wilderness* claims there were at least 18 channels on each 'circuit,' and I have no reason to doubt this.] In other words, taps were made on each pair of the 170-odd pairs of wires [a circuit], and this circuit was tape-recorded back at the site at 15 inches per second.

    However, each circuit contained a potential 18 signals which made it sound like a jungle of noises and mish mash. Each channel had to be isolated and printed out in some fashion to make it intelligible. This is where the demuxing came in. One channel might consist of clear text teletype or voice, another on the same circuit might consist of cipher text, another, possibly facsimile. I have the impression that the teletype signals were normally on one circuit, while voice was more likely on other circuits. I don't know this for certain however. I know that teletype signals were the big problem, and this was done back in Washington in T-32; the voice signal traffic went to London."
40. Ibid.
41. Peter Grose, *Gentleman Spy: The Life of Allen Dulles* (New York: Houghton Mifflin, 1994), 397ff.

42. Clarence Berry, e-mail to the author, July 16, 2001.
43. James Critchfield, e-mail to the author, August 12, 2001.
44. Clarence Berry, e-mail to the author, June 5, 2001.
45. Grose, *Gentleman Spy*, 498.
46. Clarence Berry, e-mail to the author, July 29, 2001.
47. Richard W. Montague, letter and email to the author, March 29, 2004.
48. Tom Polgar, letter to the author, August 10, 2001.
49. Peter Lunn, telephone conversation with and letter to the author, February 22, 2001.

CHAPTER 6: HARVEY'S SUPPORT SYSTEM

NOTE: Many of the documents referred to in this chapter are in the Harvey family papers, which are held by Sally Harvey, who gave me completely free access to them in March 2001. More documents and artifacts are in the possession of Bill's son by his first marriage, Jim Harvey, who declined to cooperate on this book.

1. Rita Chappiwicki Merthan left the CIA and became Mrs. Jimmy Carter's private secretary at the White House. She died of a heart attack in 1982.
2. Sally Harvey, in conversations with the author, March 9–12, 2001; and Sally Harvey, e-mails to the author, January and June 2001. Unless otherwise sourced, all quotes by Sally Harvey in this chapter come from these communications.
3. Henry Woodburn, letter to the author, April 17, 2002.
4. Sally Harvey, in conversation with David E. Murphy, 1993.
5. CG Harvey, in conversation with David E. Murphy, November 15–16, 1993.
6. Peter Karlow, phone conversation with the author, March 14, 2002.
7. CG Harvey, conversation, November 15–16, 1993.
8. Star Murphy, e-mail to the author, October 18, 2002; and Star and David E. Murphy, conversations with the author, January 26–27, 2001.
9. Herb Natzke, phone conversation with the author, May 15, 2002.
10. Tom Polgar adds, "CG did not fly to United States with scientists. CG was a good friend of mine, but I have problems with most of stuff [quoted from the Murphy conversation] attributed to her." Polgar, e-mail to the author, May 4, 2003, after reading draft of this chapter.
11. Unless otherwise sourced, all quoted material in this section comes from Sara King Harvey, handwritten note headed, "Further Comment . . .with much love," January 18, 1959. The letter was in CG's papers.
12. West Berlin Police incident report, translated into English, undated.

CHAPTER 7: INTO THE CAULDRON

1. James Critchfield, e-mail to the author, April 18, 2002.
2. Arthur Schlesinger Jr. quoted in *Boston Globe*, April 17, 2001.

3. Critchfield, e-mail, April 18, 2002.
4. Evan Thomas, *The Very Best Men: Four Who Dared: The Early Years of the CIA* (New York: Simon & Schuster, 1995), 205. Jim Critchfield's recollection of who attended the meeting is slightly different from the list given in Thomas's book.
5. James Critchfield, e-mail to the author, June 5, 2002.
6. This interesting document was in the trove of material supplied to the author by the British writer, Anthony Summers.
7. The material and quotes in this section are woven together from Peter Wright, *Spy Catcher: The Candid Autobiography of a Senior Intelligence Officer* (New York: Viking Penguin, 1987), 146–162.
8. For most of the story of Task Force W in the Langley Building, I am deeply indebted to Sam Halpern, who was a key player throughout the period and who delved deep into his memory bank for details in the course of a long conversation on May 23, 2001, and telephone conversations on June 3, 2001, and in March 2002. Halpern's quotes throughout this chapter are from these three conversations.
9. Cecil B. Currey, *Edward Lansdale: The Unquiet American* (Boston: Houghton Mifflin, 1988), 244ff.
10. The "fascinated listener" was F. A. O. Schwarz Jr. Schwarz, phone conversation with the author, April 11, 2001.
11. CG Harvey, in conversation with David E. Murphy, November 15–16 1993; and CG Harvey, videotaped monologue, given at the Indianapolis Lutheran Church, February 22, 1998.
12. The following is an excerpt from a lengthy biographical sketch by a famous American correspondent of the late nineteenth century, Richard Harding Davis:

> At thirty-seven . . .Walker beheld greater conquests, more power, a new South controlling a Nicaragua canal, a network of busy railroads, great squadrons of merchant vessels, himself emperor of Central America. On the gunboat the gold-braided youth had but to raise his hand. . . but the gold-braided one would (pardon Walker) only on the condition that Walker would appeal to him as an American. . . .
>
> "The President of Nicaragua," he said, "is a citizen of Nicaragua."
>
> They led him out at sunrise to a level piece of sand along the beach, and as the priest held the crucifix in front of him he spoke to his executioners in Spanish, simply and gravely: "I accept my punishment with resignation. I would like to think my death will be for the good of society."
>
> From a distance of twenty feet three soldiers fired at him, but, although each shot took effect, Walker was not dead. So, a sergeant stooped, and with a pistol killed the man. . . .
>
> Had Walker lived four years longer to exhibit upon the great board of

> the Civil War his ability as a general, he would, I believe, to-day be ranked as one of America's greatest fighting men.
>
> And because the people of his own day destroyed him is no reason that we should withhold from this American, the greatest of all filibusters, the recognition of his genius."

I wonder whether Bill chose to name his task force in honor of Walker because he was in some way related to the freebooter. Note that the Cleveland birth certificate cited in chapter 1 mentions "Drenan R. Walker of Danville," then age twenty-seven, a lawyer, as father of the baby born to Sara J. King, also of Danville.

13. Star Murphy, e-mail to the author, July 28, 2001.
14. M. Neill Prew, in conversation with the author, March 17, 2001.
15. Ted Shackley, in conversation with the author, May 21, 2001, and follow-up phone conversations, February–March 2002. Shackley's posthumous biography, *Spymaster: My Life in the CIA*, with Richard A. Finney (Washington, DC: Potomac Books, 2005), 50ff, adds some detail to FI operations into Cuba, especially at the time of the missile crisis. See also David Corn, *Blond Ghost: Ted Shackley and the CIA's Crusades* (New York: Simon & Schuster, 1994), 74–75.
16. Shackley, conversation, May 21, 2001; and Shackley, phone conversations, February–March 2002.
17. Ibid.
18. Herb Natzke, in conversation with the author, February 11, 2001.
19. Warren Frank, in conversation with the author, March 15, 2001. Warren joined the CIA in 1950 and worked Eastern European/Soviet bloc matters in Germany, where he stayed until 1958. After a tour of duty at Langley, "I was selected by Ted Shackley and Bill Harvey in 1962 to be chief of the FI Branch at JMWAVE, where I remained until 1965. Once a Berliner, always a Berliner." Warren returned to Berlin as deputy chief of base. He spent years in German and Eastern European operations, then switched to Indonesia and East Asia. He retired in 1985.
20. Ibid.
21. Ibid.
22. David C. Martin, *Wilderness of Mirrors* (New York: Harper & Row, 1980), 132–136, 137–138.
23. Ibid.
24. Ibid.
25. Currey, *Edward Lansdale*.
26. Thomas A. Parrott, "Memorandum of Mongoose Meeting in the JCS Operations Room, October 26 1962, at 2.30PM."
27. Tom Parrott, phone conversations with the author, December 20 and 23, 2005.

28. Richard M. Helms, *A Look Over My Shoulder: A Life in the Central Intelligence Agency*, with William Hood (New York: Random House, 2003), 196.

CHAPTER 8: PLOTTING ASSASSINATION

1. Richard M. Helms, *A Look Over My Shoulder: A Life in the Central Intelligence Agency*, with William Hood (New York: Random House, 2003),182.
2. Sam Halpern, in conversation with the author, May 23, 2001; and Halpern, phone conversation with the author, June 3, 2001.
3. See James Bamford, *Body of Secrets: Anatomy of the Ultra-Secret National Security Agency* (New York: Anchor Books, 2002).
4. Evan Thomas, *The Very Best Men* (New York: Simon & Schuster, 1995), 223, 288ff; Halpern, conversation, May 23, 2001, and phone conversation, June 3, 2001.
5. Clarence Berry, e-mails to the author, June 2001. O'Donnell background: Douglas Valentine, e-mail to the author, March 24, 2001. O'Donnell served in Bolivia, the Netherlands, Thailand, and Turkey, an interesting group of countries.
6. Halpern, conversation, May 23, 2001, and phone conversation, June 3, 2001.
7. Helms, *A Look Over My Shoulder*, 182.
8. Senate Select Committee to Study Government Operations with Respect to Intelligence Activities, *Alleged Assassination Plots Involving Foreign Leaders*, 94th Cong., 1st sess., 1975, 83.
9. Central Intelligence Agency, *Report of the Inspector General*, U.S. Government: Documents on the Cold War in Berlin, 1946–196? (Washington, DC: CIA Center for the Study of Intelligence, March–May 1967).
10. David C. Martin, *Wilderness of Mirrors* (New York: Harper & Row, 1980), 137.
11. Halpern, conversation, May 23, 2001.
12. Lansdale's account of the Castro assassination planning is in Cecil Currey, *Edward Lansdale: The Unquiet American* (Boston: Houghton Mifflin 1988), 240–250.
13. Harvey's notes are without doubt genuine. They came into my hands in a sheaf of material provided by the kindness of Anthony Summers, who had obtained the sheaf from CIA under the FOIA. Other inquirers have also seen and pored over them.
14. These documents were also provided to me by Anthony Summers.
15. Both versions of the memo were provided to me by Anthony Summers.
16. This memo was also provided to me by Anthony Summers.
17. QJWIN was run in the late 1950s, at the behest of the then–Bureau of Narcotics, out of the Luxembourg station by Arnold S., the Division D/Second-Story Group case officer. Where QJWIN materialized from is unknown. The drug enforcement people gave him an "excellent" performance rating.
18. Berry, e-mails, June 2001.
19. Stephen J. Rivele, *The National Spectator*, date unknown (c. 1976, although

maybe considerably later), 6. Also, untitled essay by Rivele in Eric Hamburg, ed., *Nixon: An Oliver Stone Film* (News York: Hyperion, 1995); and Rivele, phone conversation with the author, October 13, 2002.

CHAPTER 9: BILL AND JOHNNY

1. Much of the biographical material on Johnny Rosselli in this chapter is digested from Charles Rappleye and Ed Becker, *All American Mafioso: The Johnny Rosselli Story* (New York: Doubleday, 1991).
2. Central Intelligence Agency, *Report of the Inspector General*, U.S. Government: Documents on the Cold War in Berlin, 1946–196? (Washington, DC: CIA Center for the Study of Intelligence, March–May 1967).
3. Sally Harvey, quoting CG, in conversation with the author, March 12, 2001.
4. Rappleye and Becker, *All American Mafioso*,187 and 211. See also Ted Shackley, *Spymaster: My Life in the CIA*, with Richard A. Finney (Washington, DC: Potomac Books, 2005), 51–53ff.
5. Robert Maheu, phone conversations with the author, April 2 and 4, 2001.
6. Rappleye and Becker, *All American Mafioso*, 187.
7. CIA, *Report of the Inspector General*, 81.
8. Ibid.
9. Ibid.
10. David C. Martin, *Wilderness of Mirrors* (New York: Harper & Row, 1980).
11. Ibid.
12. Cecil B. Currey, *Edward Lansdale: The Unquiet American* (Boston: Houghton Mifflin, 1988).
13. The official version of the Rosselli handover, was covered in a memorandum from the CIA to Bobby Kennedy dated May 22, 1962.

> SUBJECT: THE JOHNNY ROSSELLI MATTER:
>
> 1. In August 1960 Mr. Richard Bissell approached the then Director of Security, Colonel Sheffield Edwards, to determine if the Office of Security had any assets that may assist in a sensitive mission requiring gangster-type action. The mission target was Fidel Castro.
>
> 2. . . . Maheu was asked to approach Rosselli. . . . Maheu was to tell Rosselli that he had recently been retained by a client who represented several international business firms which were suffering heavy financial losses in Cuba as a result of Castro's action. . . . It was to be made clear to Rosselli that the United States Government was not and should not become aware of this operation. . . .
>
> In May 1962 Mr. William Harvey took over as Rosselli's case officer and it was not known if he was used officially from that point on.

After a heated discussion between CIA topsiders and RFK, the Agency general counsel wrote, "If you have seen Mr. Kennedy's eyes get steely and his jaw set and his voice get low and precise, you get a definite feeling of unhappiness." Still in May 1962 the two top brass assured Kennedy that the plot to kill Castro had been terminated, a statement that one of them knew to be a lie. Sheffield Edwards returned to the CIA from that meeting and wrote a memo for the record stating that "Mr. Harvey called me and indicated he was dropping any plans for the use of Subject [Rosselli] for the future." The memo "was not true," Harvey later commented, "and Colonel Edwards knew it was not true." But then, as General Carter, the Agency's deputy director once said, "Memorandums for the record have very little validity in fact." David C. Martin, *Wilderness of Mirrors* (New York: Harper & Row, 1980), 138.

14. Joe Shimon, interview by Anthony Summers, May 7, 1994; and Anthony Summers, phone conversation with the author, January 4, 2002.
15. Toni Shimon, phone conversation with the author, May 2, 2004.
16. CIA, *Report of the Inspector General, 1967*.
17. Rappleye and Becker, *All American Mafioso*, 223.
18. Ted Shackley, in conversation with the author, May 21, 2001.
19. David E. and Star Murphy, e-mail to the author, June 8, 2002. Warren Frank, meeting with the author, March 14, 2001.
20. Richard D. Mahoney, *Sons and Brothers* (New York: Arcade Publishing, 1999), 166–170. Mahoney quotes in part Bradley Earl Ayers, *The War That Never Was: An Insider's Account of CIA Covert Operations Against Cuba* (Indianapolis: Bobbs-Merrill, 1976). Ayers's book is impossible to find these days. An interesting coincidence is that it was published by Bobbs-Merrill, for whom Harvey worked in Indianapolis until shortly before his death. I have heard one claim that Harvey actually edited the book, but I cannot confirm the story.
21. Ibid., 170.
22. Ibid., 167.
23. U.S. Senate, *Alleged Assassination Plots*, 85.
24. Ibid.
25. Ibid.
26. CIA, *Report of the Inspector General, 1967*.
27. Rappleye and Becker, *All American Mafioso*, 293.
28. I asked some former CIA people whether Ken Greer and Scott Breckinridge were old FI hands who had been handed an unenviable job. Dave Murphy responded: "Scott Breckinridge was in the Agency from 1953 to 1979. . . . He was a very likable chap, very straightforward. He wrote a book, *The CIA and the Cold War*, about his career."
29. CIA, *Report of the Inspector General, 1967*.
30. See Tom Mangold, *Cold Warrior: James Jesus Angleton: The CIA's Master Spy Hunter* (New York: Simon & Schuster, 1991), for detailed discussion of the Golytsin and Nosenko cases.

CHAPTER 10: BILL HARVEY AND THE ASSASSINATION OF PRESIDENT KENNEDY

1. Jim Lesar, director of the Assassination Archives and Research Center, the private group that took over when the publicly funded JFK Assassination Records Review Board (ARRB) went out of business in 2000, in conversation with the author, 2002.
2. Gus Russo, author of *Live by the Sword* and *The Outfit*, e-mails to the author, December 2005–January 2006. Russo has spent more than thirty years looking into the JFK assassination. In his discussion of that affair, he included the comments I reprint herewith, based upon his investigations into the Chicago Mob, which led to *The Outfit*. At the end of the quoted segment, Gus writes, "There is much more I could write about the Frank Ragano contentions about Marcello's alleged involvement, but for starters, see Posner, p. 462–463." I did not follow that lead, although I knew of Posner's work, because it did not appear to bear directly on Harvey.

   Russo has collaborated with noted German filmmaker Wilfried Huismann to write a documentary on JFK's assassination, *Rendezvous With Death*, which premiered on German television in early January 2006.
3. Charles Rappleye and Ed Becker, *All American Mafioso: The Johnny Rosselli Story* (New York: Doubleday, 1991), 244–248. Also, Ed Becker, phone conversations with the author, 2002 and January 25, 2004.
4. Rappleye and Becker, *All American Mafioso.*
5. Ibid.
6. Russo, e-mails, December 2005–January 2006.
7. G. Robert Blakey and Richard N. Billings, *The Plot to Kill the President* (New York: Times Books, 1981), 245.
8. *The Outfit*, exerpted from Russo, e-mail, December 31, 2005. Fratianno's quotes are from Ovid DeMaris, *The Last Mafioso*.
9. Harvey's copy of Senate Select Committee to Study Government Operations with Respect to Intelligence Activities, *Alleged Assassination Plots Involving Foreign Leaders*, 94th Cong., 1st sess., 1975, 295.
10. Ibid.
11. Stephen J. Rivele, Untitled Essay, in Eric Hamburg, ed., *Nixon: An Oliver Stone Film* (News York: Hyperion, 1995); and Rivele, phone conversation with the author, October 13, 2002.
12. Gus Russo, *Live by the Sword: The Secret War Against Castro and the Death of JFK* (Baltimore: Bancroft Press, 1998), 304.
13. Mark Wyatt provided me with the information that Harvey flew back to Rome in an official Italian plane, but he omitted the details about Bill's boozy state at the time of the assassination. The "deputy" cited in the Russo quotation is almost undoubtedly Wyatt, who bore Harvey no goodwill for a series of real and imagined slights. Harvey did terminate Wyatt's tour of duty in Rome abruptly and earned Wyatt's undying enmity, but

not because Wyatt was telling stories about Bill's condition at the time of the Kennedy assassination. Mark Wyatt, in conversation with the author, March 13, 2001. Wyatt died in June 2006.

14. CG Harvey, in conversation with David E. Murphy, November 15–16, 1993.
15. House Select Committee on Assassinations, Testimony of John Scelso, May 16, 1978, 144ff. This also appears in his testimony: "Helms never forgot my work as a polygraph operator from 1948 on for a few years. . . . And I was immediately given all your really nutsy cases to go over, and I cracked one of them after another. Helms never forgot this."
16. Michael Goldsmith, former staff counsel to the HRSCA, Select Committee on Assassinations, phone interview by the author, March 3, 2002.
17. HRSCA, Scelso testimony.
18. Ibid.
19. Ibid.
20. Anonymous, e-mail to the author, February 4, 2003.
21. Blakey and Billings, *Plot to Kill the President,* 179ff.
22. G. Robert Blakey, e-mail to the author, March 13, 2002.
23. David Corn, *Blond Ghost: Ted Shackley and the CIA's Crusades* (New York: Simon & Schuster, 1994), 107.
24. Dan Hardway, phone conversations with the author, March 19 and 23, 2002.
25. Jeff Morley, "Revelation 1963," *Miami New Times*, April 12, 2001. Exerpts are used here with the explicit permission of the author. The lead was, "After nearly four decades, the CIA has been forced to disclose the identity of a Miami agent who may have known too much too early about Lee Harvey Oswald."
26. Untitled draft article provided by Jefferson Morley.
27. Virtually all the information in this section came from Jeff Morley's draft and published articles, all of which he provided most graciously over a period of about a year. After the *Miami New Times* publication in 2001, interest in the subject languished, but Morley persisted with his research. At the time of the fortieth anniversary of the Kennedy assassination, it began to pay off, first in an article in the *Washington Monthly* for December 2003, next in a piece in *Salon.com*, December 17, 2003. The *Salon.com* piece announced a lawsuit aimed at forcing the Agency to open its files and followed up on a call on the CIA by a group of well-knowns, including Blakey, Norman Mailer, Don DeLillo, and the retired judge who presided over the records review board, to come clean. That petition first appeared in an open letter in the *New York Review of Books* for December 18, 2003. The CIA's Tom Crispell's response was also quoted in that article.

    As this is written, Morley continues to investigate. See also "The Lie That Linked CIA to the Kennedy Assassination," *Studies in Intelligence*,

Fall–Winter 2001, http://www.cia.gov/csi/studies/fall_winter_2001/article 02.html.

28. Warren Frank, e-mails to the author, May 9, June 4, and October 9, 2002, including his discussions about George Joannides with Ted Shackley and another former JMWAVE officer who preferred to remain anonymous.
29. Warren Frank, e-mail to the author, date unknown (c. February or March 2003).
30. Frank, e-mails, May 9, June 4, and October 9, 2002.
31. Bayard Stockton, e-mail to Jeff Morley, October 30, 2002.
32. Hardway, phone conversations, March 19 and 23, 2002.
33. Ibid.
34. Blakey and Billings, *Plot to Kill the President*, 386ff.
35. Toni Shimon, phone conversation with the author, March 18, 2002.
36. Joe Shimon, interview by Anthony Summers, May 7, 1994, transcript provided by Anthony Summers; and Anthony Summers, phone conversation with the author, January 4, 2002.
37. Russo, *Live by the Sword* 445–446.
38. Jack Anderson, phone conversation with the author, February 6, 2002; and Ed Becker, phone conversation with the author, January 25, 2004.
39. David Atlee Phillips, *The Night Watch: 25 Years of Peculiar Service* (New York: Atheneum, 1977). Phillips not only fails to mention Harvey in his memoir, he also does not mention any operations involving New Orleans. He does write of his time in Mexico City and makes slightly more than passing reference to Lee Harvey Oswald's appearance there.
40. Sam Halpern, in conversastion with the author, May 23, 2001.
41. Ted Shackley, in conversation with the author, May 21, 2001.
42. Sam Papich, e-mail to the author, July 23, 2002.

CHAPTER 11: ROME

1. Tom Polgar, e-mail to the author, July 13, 2002.
2. David Martin, *Wilderness of Mirrors* (New York: Harper & Row, 1980), 147.
3. Ibid.
4. Peter Karlow, e-mail to the author, March 13, 2002.
5. Martin, *Wilderness of Mirrors*, 146.
6. "Cold Warriors' Tales," Special Report, *U.S. News & World Report*, October 18, 1999. Wyatt confirmed in a conversation with the author, March 2001, that he had acted as a courier for British intelligence in prewar Germany. Wyatt intimated in the *U.S. News* report that he had set up the CIA's stay-behind program in Italy.
7. Mark Wyatt, in conversation with the author, March 2001. After Rome, Wyatt was content with the peace of being number two at the Agency's training establishment, the Farm. Then he was transferred to Saigon. "I was ordered to go with Shackley."

8. Ibid.
9. Ibid.
10. CG Harvey, videotaped monologue, given at the Indianapolis Lutheran Church, February 22, 1998. Sally's comments were made during my visit to Indianapolis, March 2001.
11. Henry Woodburn, in conversation with the author, May 20, 2001.
12. Wyatt, conversation, March 2001.
13. House Select Committee on Assassinations, Testimony of John Scelso, May 16, 1978.
14. Sam Halpern, conversation with the author, June 3, 2001.
15. David E. Murphy, e-mail to the author, June 8, 2002.
16. Anonymous, e-mail to the author, July 2002.
17. Joe Wildmuth, comment to an anonymous friend, undated.
18. Murphy, e-mail, June 8, 2002.
19. Anonymous, e-mail, July 2002.
20. Murphy, e-mail, June 8, 2002.
21. Halpern, conversation, June 3, 2001.

CHAPTER 12: THE DOLDRUMS

1. Sam Halpern, in conversation with the author, June 3, 2001.
2. Tom Parrott, phone conversation with the author, December 20, 2005.
3. This and a number of other official documents used in this chapter, bearing on Harvey's relations with the CIA and the FBI during the late 1960s, before he moved to Indianapolis, were graciously provided me by Anthony Summers, from his voluminous files. He in turn got them using FOIA. Each document is identified and dated in the chapter text.
4. George Bailey, phone conversation with the author, April 11, 2001.
5. Richard W. Montague, letter to the author, March 2, 2004.
6. James Hanrahan, "Soldier, Manager, Leader: An Interview With Former CIA Executive Director Lawrence K. 'Red' White," *CSI Intelligencer*, Winter 1999–2000, 29–30, http://www.cia.gov/csi/studies/winter99-00/art3.html. Red White was a West Pointer, and a career Army officer until he was invalided out of the service in 1945. Thereafter, he became a career CIA administrative officer; he was executive director–comptroller of the CIA from 1965 until his retirement in 1972.
7. Joe Shimon, interview by Anthony Summers, transcript provided by Summers, May 7, 1994.
8. Tom Polgar, e-mail to the author, July 13, 2002.
9. Ted Shackley, in conversation with the author, May 21, 2001.
10. John Barron is the celebrated author of several books on the KGB, including the standard reference work of the 1970s, *KGB: The Secret Work of Soviet Secret Agents* (New York: Readers Digest Association, 1974), which

he wrote while working for *Readers' Digest*. John Barron, phone conversations with the author, July 7 and 13, 2003. Harvey's contribution to *Secret Work* is acknowledged on p. 436.

11. Sally Harvey, in conversation with the author, March 9–March 12, 2001.
12. Hazel Shackley, phone conversation with the author, June 18, 2003. Ted Shackley had been working on his book for some time, despite his advancing prostate cancer. Warren Frank, Ted's deputy and close friend, read an early version of the chapter on Cuba, in which Ted tells at some length how Bill Harvey selected him for the Miami job. "Respectful tone, but as I recall, no real details of his opinion of Bill. Ted tended to be rather short and cryptic in his opinions of people. But Ted and Bill obviously were close. I recall that, after Bill died, CG often was guest of Ted and Hazel in Bethesda." In an email of February 4, 2003, Warren reported on Ted Shackley's funeral: "Ambassador Jim Lilley gave very fine eulogy at Ted's funeral. He mentioned only three of Ted's associates in the agency, Bill Harvey, Gordon Stewart, and myself. Jim said, Ted, two days before he died, had specifically instructed him to mention only these three names. I feel quite honored to have been included. . . . Don't recall old Berlin hands at funeral. There are not very many left."

CHAPTER 13: BACK HOME IN INDIANA

1. Sally Harvey's recollections, which appear throughout the chapter, are condensed from our conversations from March 9 to March 12, 2001, in Indianapolis.
2. Dennis Flinn, phone conversation with the author, March 13, 2002.
3. David Martin writes a version of Harvey's last years in Indianapolis and his appearance in front of the Church Committee in *Wilderness of Mirrors* (New York: Harper & Row, 1980), 218–222. Martin's take on Bill's performance at Bobbs-Merrill and his struggles with alcohol are probably more accurate, though tinged with skepticism-verging-on-malice, than those given by CG Harvey, who was, of course, a fierce defender of her husband.
4. Herb Natzke, in conversation with the author, February 11, 2001.
5. The account of Harvey's conversion, baptism, and relations with the minister is a combination of a letter to me from Pastor Kahlenberg, dated February 2, 2001, and a lengthy conversation I had with Kahlenberg on March 11, 2001, at Sally Harvey's house in Indianapolis.

CHAPTER 14: A MURKY PASSAGE

Note: Elsewhere, I have tried to indicate in full where information has come from. In this case, because of the nature of the material and the personalities involved, I have protected a number of sources who presented cogent reasons for concealing their identities.

1. Richard D. Mahoney, *Sons and Brothers: The Days of Jack and Bobby Kennedy*

(New York: Arcade Publishing, 1999), 269. I made repeated attempts to talk with Mr. Mahoney, but he did not reply to my messages.

2. Sally Harvey, in conversation with the author, March 9–12, 2002.
3. I met Marajen Chinigo only once, very briefly, at her villa in Palm Springs. The dowager died December 22, 2002, having survived to see her ninetieth birthday. The *Chicago Tribune*'s obituary contained a quote from "former singer and game show host Peter Marshall, who was a neighbor of Mrs. Chinigo in the Palm Springs, Calif., area, and who became a good friend. 'Her [Palm Springs] circle included a lot of stars, especially Loretta Young, who was one of her closest friends. She was so wonderful. Really, she was from a different era. You don't find that gentility much any more.'"
4. The quotes and the substance of this section are from a series of interviews, conducted during 2002, with former employees of the Chinigo complex of interests. They were fleshed out in many, frequent conversations I had from 2001 to 2004 with the man I identify as Marajen Chinigo's conservator. During those conversations, he reported his chats with Marajen; he relayed questions from me and supplied answers she had given him. Our conversations are simply too numerous to note individually. I have extracted, edited, and consolidated the substance.
5. William E. Dyess, *The Dyess Story* (New York: G. P. Putnam Sons, 1944), 38.
6. A Google search of Macchia Albanese yields this information, which includes some tantalizing gems: "This dialect of Albanian is spoken in several 'village pockets' in Calabria, Avellino, Molise, Puglia, and Sicily in Southern Italy. There are about 80,000 to 100,000 speakers out of an ethnic population of 260,000. Anyway, speakers are diminishing and the language is very endangered. . . . The Arberesh are descendants from migrants of the 15th century."
7. Max Corvo, *The OSS in Italy, 1942–1955: A Personal Memoir* (New York: Praeger, 1990), 35.
8. Ibid.
9. Ibid., 94.
10. Michael Chinigo, "Lowdown on Mafia Revealed," *Chicago American*, August 29, 1954. I queried John Foreman about the "nine sensational stories" I had heard were buried in the *News-Gazette* morgue and requested a clearer photo of Chinigo and Luciano than the smudgy photocopy reproduction he had sent me, along with the *Chicago American* story. Foreman had earlier told me that further information conceivably linking Chinigo to the Mob, with specific undertones of threat to his life, did exist in the deep files of the *Champaign News-Gazette*. Then, Foreman replied brusquely that he didn't have time to search further and that this was all he knew. John Foreman, e-mails to the author, June 10 and 23, 2003.
11. Gore Vidal, phone conversations with the author, January 8 and 11, and September 24, 2002.

12. Douglas Fleming, phone interview by the author, January 14, 2002.
13. Curtis G. Pepper, phone interview by the author, January 18, 2002.
14. Sam Papich, e-mail to the author, July 23, 2002.
15. Fleming, phone interview, January 14, 2002.
16. Vidal, phone conversation, January 11, 2002.

CHAPTER 15: THE CONSCIENCE

1. Senator Gary Hart, letter to the author, April 16, 2001.
2. F. A. O. Schwarz Jr., phone conversation with the author, April 11, 2001.
3. Anita Potocki, phone conversation with the author, January 13, 2001.
4. Ted Shackley, in conversation with the author, May 21, 2001.
5. Sam Halpern, in conversation with the author, May 23, 2001.
6. Sally Harvey, in conversation with the author, March 9–12, 2002.

CHAPTER 16: INDIANAPOLIS AND DEATH

1. This and other quotes by Sally Harvey are from our conversations, March 9–12, 2002.
2. Rev. David P. Kahlenberg, sermon at Bill's funeral, June 12, 1976; and David P. Kahlenberg, letter to the author, January 2001.
3. Herb Natzke, in conversation with the author, February 11, 2001.
4. CG Harvey, letter to the author, April 10, 1983; and CG Harvey, videotaped monologue, given at the Indianapolis Lutheran Church, February 22, 1998.
5. Jack Hall, in conversation with the author, March 10, 2001. When Jack Hall was studying and teaching in Boston, he came to know the Kennedys. "Part of their campaign strategy was tea parties in various neighborhoods. I used to go with Rory Childers who was the son of the Irish prime minister. After a while, I started treating Jack, at the Baptist Hospital in Boston, for Addisons Disease. . . .

   "Jack Kennedy was well-meant but superficial. Impetuous. Bobby Kennedy was focused. He would do whatever it took.

   "I'm not surprised there was trouble between Bobby and Bill Harvey. The Kennedy's didn't track. They were all show—touch football and Marilyn Monroe. They learned that way of life from Joe Kennedy."

   On Cuba: "They had an inability to make decisions. They liked a lot of show.

   "Clara [CG] had great distaste for Bobby. She used to say, 'He warped information . . . shut off information he didn't want to hear.'"

   Hall was careful not to make a connection, but in another part of our conversation, he seemed to go off on a tangent. "I knew a man, an ex-student of mine, who was the CIA doctor. He was doing appraisals of the health of CIA people." The man was, of course, Dr. Arthur Tietjen, and he and Hall published the work *Probability Risk Research, or Health Hazard Appraisal Prospective Medicine*. "We were trying to identify the useful life expectancy of people in their mid-sixties."

Dr. Hall says that he hoped to persuade one of his very wealthy clients "to build a museum here in Indianapolis for outstanding women, and Clara would certainly be among the first to be in it." Jack Hall is the only person I've ever met who referred to CG by her true first name. No one else would have dared.

6. David C. Martin, *Wilderness of Mirrors* (New York: Harper & Row, 1980), 222. "He died holding his wife's hand, at ten minutes past two in the afternoon of June 8.

   "'Bill was 60, too young to go,' his wife wrote in a letter to his colleagues at Bobbs-Merrill. 'He had many plans ahead. He had lived a very full and satisfying life by his own estimation. He said few men were blessed with the opportunity he had to serve his country.' She had received more than three hundred letters of condolence from all over the world, she said. She had also received some unexpected callers—two attempted break-ins at the Harvey home. 'They're after his papers,' she said, 'but I burned everything.'"
7. CG Harvey, letter, April 10, 1983.
8. Bill Harvey, letter to Jim Angleton, June 3, 1976, photocopy returned by Angleton to CG, April 22, 1980. Angleton returned the letter specifically to undercut allegations in *Wilderness of Mirrors* that there was bitterness and rivalry between Harvey and himself.
9. CG Harvey, letter, April 10, 1983.
10. Dick Cady, a retired *Indianapolis Star* reporter, eulogy at the memorial service for CG Harvey, October 7, 2000.
11. CG Harvey, letter, April 10, 1983.

CHAPTER 17: AFTERLIFE

1. F. A. O. Schwarz, phone conversation with the author, April 11, 2001.

BIBLIOGRAPHY

Alsop, Stewart, and Thomas Braden. *Sub Rosa: The OSS and American Espionage*. Cornwall, NY: Cornwall Press, 1948.

Anderson, Jack. *Peace, War, and Politics: An Eyewitness Account*. New York: Tom Doherty Associates/Forge, 1999.

Ashley, Clarence. *CIA Spymaster*. Gretna, LA: Pelican Publishing Company, 2004.

Bailey, George T. *Verbindungsmann: Ein Leben Zwischen Ost und West*. Munich: Ullstein Verlag, 2002. The original English-language unpublished manuscript, tentatively entitled *Epilogue*, is held at Boston University Library Special Collections and at the University of California Santa Barbara Davidson Library, Cold War Center/Special Collections.

Bamford, James. *Body of Secrets: Anatomy of the Ultra-Secret National Security Agency*. New York: Anchor Books, 2002.

Barron, John. *KGB: The Secret Work of Soviet Secret Agents*. New York: Reader's Digest Association, 1974.

———. *KGB Today: The Hidden Hand*. New York: Reader's Digest Press, 1983.

———. *Operation Solo: The FBI's Man in the Kremlin*. Washington, DC: Regnery Publishing,1996.

Blake, George. *No Other Choice: An Autobiography*. New York: Simon & Schuster, 1990.

Blakey, G. Robert, and Richard N. Billings. *The Plot to Kill the President*. New York: Times Books, 1981.

Bohning, Don. *The Castro Obsession: U.S. Covert Operations Against Cuba, 1959–1965*. Washington, DC: Potomac Books, 2005.

Boyle, Andrew. *The Climate of Treason*. London: Hutchinson & Co., 1979.

Branch, Taylor, and George Crile III. "The Kennedy Vendetta," *Harpers Magazine*, August 1975.

Breckinridge, Scott D. *The CIA and the Cold War: A Memoir*. Westport, CT: Praeger, 1993.

BIBLIOGRAPHY

Burke, Michael. *Outrageous Good Fortune.* Boston: Little, Brown, 1984.

Central Intelligence Agency. *Report of the Inspector General, 1967.* U.S. Government: Documents on the Cold War in Berlin, 1946–196?. Washington, DC: CIA Center for the Study of Intelligence, March–May 1967.

Chavchavadze, David. *Crowns and Trenchcoats: A Russian Prince in the CIA.* New York: Atlantic International, 1990.

Colby, William, and Peter Forbath. *Honorable Men: My Life in the CIA.* New York: Simon & Schuster, 1978.

Copeland, Miles. *The Game of Nations*. London: Weidenfeld and Nicholson, 1969.

Corn, David. *Blond Ghost: Ted Shackley and the CIA's Crusades.* New York: Simon & Schuster, 1994.

Corson, William R., Susan B. Trento, and Joseph J. Trento. *Widows: Four American Spies, the Wives They Left Behind, and the KGB's Crippling of American Intelligence.* New York: Crown Publishers, 1989.

Critchfield, James. *Partners at the Creation: The Men Behind Postwar Germany's Defense and Intelligence Establishments.* Annapolis, MD: Naval Institute Press, 2003.

Currey, Cecil B. *Edward Lansdale: The Unquiet American.* Boston: Houghton Mifflin, 1988.

De Silva, Peer. *Sub Rosa: The CIA and the Uses of Intelligence.* New York: Times Books, 1978.

Dobbs, Michael. "One Minute to Midnight: The Most Dangerous Day of the Cuban Missile Crisis." Unpublished manuscript, ca. 1990.

Earley, Pete. *Confessions of a Spy: The Real Story of Aldrich Ames.* New York: Berkley Books, 1997.

Felfe, Heinz. *Im Dienst der Gegner*. Hamburg: Rasch und Röhring Verlag, 1986.

Fonzi, Gaeton. *The Last Investigation*. New York: Thunder's Mouth Press, 1993.

The French Connection. Directed by William Friedkin. Los Angeles: Twentieth Century Fox, 1971.

Furiati, Claudia. *ZRRIFLE: The Plot to Kill Kennedy and Castro*. Translated by Maxine Shaw. Melbourne, Australia: Ocean Press, 1994. Distributed in the United States by the Talman Company.

Fursenko, Aleksandr, and Timothy Naftali. *One Hell of a Gamble: The Secret History of the Cuban Missile Crisis: Khrushchev, Castro and Kennedy, 1958–1964.* New York: W. W. Norton, 1997.

Garbler, Florence Fitzsimmons. *CIA Wife*. Santa Barbara, CA: Fithian Press, 1994.

Gentry, Curt. *J. Edgar Hoover: The Man and the Secrets.* New York: W. W. Norton, 1991.

Grose, Peter. *Gentleman Spy: The Life of Allen Dulles*. New York: Houghton Mifflin, 1994.

Hamburg, Eric, ed. *Nixon: An Oliver Stone Film*. New York: Hyperion, 1995.

Helms, Richard M. *A Look Over My Shoulder: A Life in the Central Intelligence Agency*. With William Hood. New York: Random House, 2003.

BIBLIOGRAPHY

Hersh, Burton. *The Old Boys: The American Elite and the Origins of the* CIA. New York: Scribners, 1992.

Hersh, Seymour M. *The Dark Side of Camelot.* Boston: Little, Brown, 1997.

Hood, William. *Mole: The True Story of the First Russian Intelligence Officer Recruited by the CIA.* New York: W. W. Norton, 1982.

The House on 92nd Street. Directed by Henry Hathaway. Los Angeles, CA: Twentieth Century Fox, 1945, 1977.

Kantor, Seth. *The Ruby Cover-Up.* New York: Zebra Books/Kensington Publishing Co., 1978.

Karlow, S. Peter. *Targeted by the CIA: An Intelligence Professional Speaks Out on the Scandal That Turned the CIA Upside Down.* Paducah, KY: Turner Publishing Company, 2002.

Lamphere, Robert J., and Tom Shachtman. *The FBI-KGB War: A Special Agent's Story.* New York: Random House, 1986.

Littell, Robert. *The Company: A Novel of the CIA.* New York: Overlook Press, 2002.

Mahle, Melissa Boyle. *Denial and Deception: An Insider's View of the CIA from Iran-Contra to 9/11.* New York: Nation Books, 2004.

Mahoney, Richard D. *Sons and Brothers: The Days of Jack and Bobby Kennedy.* New York: Arcade Publishing, 1999.

Mailer, Norman. *Harlot's Ghost.* New York: Random House, 1991.

Mangold, Tom. *Cold Warrior: James Jesus Angleton: The CIA's Master Spy Hunter.* New York: Simon & Schuster, 1991.

Martin, David C. *Wilderness of Mirrors.* New York: Harper & Row, 1980.

Masterman, J. C. *The Double-Cross System in the War of 1939 to 1945.* New Haven, CT: Yale University Press, 1972.

Moldea, Dan E. *Dark Victory: Ronald Reagan, MCA and the Mob.* New York: Viking, 1986.

Morley, Jefferson. Untitled. Unpublished biography of Winston MacKinlay Scott, 2004–2006.

Murphy, David E., Sergei Kondrashev, George Bailey. *Battleground Berlin: CIA vs. KGB in the Cold War.* New Haven, CT: Yale University Press, 1997.

O'Donnell, Patrick K. *OSS: Operatives, Spies and Saboteurs: The Unknown Story of the Men and Women of WWII's OSS.* New York: Free Press, 2004.

Philby, Kim. *My Silent War.* London: MacGibbon and Kee Ltd., 1968. Reprint, New York: Ballantine Books, 1983.

Phillips, David Atlee. *The Night Watch: 25 Years of Peculiar Service.* New York: Atheneum, 1977.

Powers, Thomas. *The Man Who Kept the Secrets: Richard Helms and the CIA.* New York: Alfred A. Knopf, 1979.

Ranelagh, John. *Agency: The Rise and Decline of the CIA.* News York: Simon & Schuster, 1987.

Rappleye, Charles, and Ed Becker. *All American Mafioso: The Johnny Rosselli Story.* New York: Doubleday, 1991.
Rififi. Directed by Jules Dassin. Paris: 1955.
Rodriguez, Feliz, and John Weisman. *Shadow Warrior.* New York: Pocket Books, 1989.
Rositzke, Harry. *CIA's Secret Operations: Espionage, Counter-Espionage and Covert Action.* New York: Reader's Digest Press, 1977.
Russo, Gus. *Live by the Sword: The Secret War Against Castro and the Death of JFK.* Baltimore: Bancroft Press, 1998.
———. *The Outfit: The Role of Chicago's Underworld in the Shaping of Modern America.* New York: Bloomsbury, 2002.
Scott, Peter Dale. *Deep Politics and the Death of JFK.* Berkeley: University of California Press, 1993.
Shackley, Ted. *Spymaster: My Life in the CIA.* With Richard A. Finney. Washington, DC: Potomac Books, 2005.
Stafford, David. *Spies Beneath Berlin.* London: John Murray, 2002. Reprint, Woodstock, NY: Overlook Press, 2003.
Summers, Anthony. *Not in Your Lifetime.* New York: Marlowe and Company, 1980.
Thomas, Evan. *The Very Best Men: Four Who Dared: The Early Years of the CIA.* New York: Simon & Schuster, 1995.
Twyman, Noel. *Bloody Treason: The Assassination of John F. Kennedy.* Rancho Santa Fe, CA: Laurel Publishing, 1997.
U.S. Congress. Senate. *Alleged Assassination Plots Involving Foreign Leaders: An Interim Report of the Select Committee to Study Governmental Operations with Respect to Intelligence Activities.* Washington, DC: U.S. Government Printing Office, 1975.
Volkman, Ernest. *Espionage: The Greatest Spy Operations of the Twentieth Century.* New York: John Wiley & Sons, 1995.
Weiner, Tim. *Blank Check: The Pentagon's Black Budget.* New York: Warner Books, 1990.
Winks, Robin W. *Cloak and Gown: Scholars in the Secret War, 1939–1961.* New York: Morrow, 1987.
Wise, David. *Molehunt: The Secret Search for Traitors That Shattered the CIA.* New York: Random House, 1992.
Wolf, Markus. *Memoirs of a Spymaster.* With Anne McElvoy. London: Pimlico, 1998.
Wright, Peter. *Spy Catcher: The Candid Autobiography of a Senior Intelligence Officer.* New York: Viking Penguin, 1987.
Wyden, Peter. *Bay of Pigs: The Untold Story.* New York: Simon & Schuster, 1979.

INDEX

INDEX

INDEX

INDEX

INDEX

INDEX

ABOUT THE AUTHOR

BAYARD STOCKTON (1930–2006) was recruited by the CIA while still an undergraduate at Williams College. He was posted to Berlin in 1951, where he served under Bill Harvey for two years. He stayed in touch with Harvey during his next assignment at Pullach, Germany. Stockton resigned from the CIA in 1957 and became *Newsweek*'s bureau chief in Bonn and later London. After *Newsweek*, he was a freelance foreign correspondent in Greece, the eastern Mediterranean, and other points of the globe before finally settling in Santa Barbara, California, where he continued to write, edit, and work in radio. Bayard Stockton died shortly after completing final revisions to *Flawed Patriot*.